D0604936

# DIGITAL COMMUNICATIONS:

## Microwave Applications

**KAMILO FEHER,** Ph. D., M. Sc. A., P. Eng.

*Professor, Electrical Engineering,*
*University of Ottawa, Ottawa, Canada*

*Adjunct Professor, Concordia University,*
*Montreal and Carleton University, Ottawa*

*Consultant, Spar Aerospace Limited;*
*Editor Radio Communications,*
*IEEE Transactions on Communications*

PRENTICE-HALL INC., Englewood Cliffs, N.J. 07632

*Library of Congress Cataloging in Publication Data*

Feher, Kamilo.
Digital communications.

Includes bibliographical references and index.
1. Digital communications. 2. Microwave communication systems. I. Title.
TK5103.7.F43 1981 621.38'0413 80-13904
ISBN 0-13-214080-2

Editorial/production supervision
and interior design by Lori Opre
Manufacturing buyer: Anthony Caruso

*Left-hand cover photo*: Tower and antenna system for multichannel digital radio transmission. (Courtesy of Raytheon Data Systems Company)

*Right-hand cover photo*: Measured eye diagram of Dr. Lender's correlative coded duobinary signal.



Printed in the United States of America

10 9 8 7 6 5 4 3 2 1

PRENTICE-HALL INTERNATIONAL, INC., *London*
PRENTICE-HALL OF AUSTRALIA PTY. LIMITED, *Sydney*
PRENTICE-HALL OF CANADA, LTD., *Toronto*
PRENTICE-HALL OF INDIA PRIVATE LIMITED, *New Delhi*
PRENTICE-HALL OF JAPAN, INC., *Tokyo*
PRENTICE-HALL OF SOUTHEAST ASIA PTE. LTD., *Singapore*
WHITEHALL BOOKS LIMITED, *Wellington, New Zealand*

*In loving memory*
*of my father* KAMILO FEHER, Sr.

# CONTENTS

# FOREWORD

It is with pleasure that I could introduce this comprehensive book on *Digital Communications: Microwave Applications*. To my knowledge, this is the first book published on this subject, a subject that will continue to be one of the most important subjects of modern telecommunications.

We are just on the edge of a new communication world and forthcoming era. This book will be widely used by telecommunication professionals in industry, in research, and in government organizations. It is a pragmatically written book and I highly recommend it to universities and other educational institutions for the teaching and training of their engineering students. We are short of communication microwave engineers and there is, and will be, a very high demand for these professionals. Students entering this field will be required to have a solid knowledge of the principles and the state-of-the-art techniques used in digital communication systems. This book is a good starting point.

For a number of years, my associates and I have been acquainted with Dr. Kamilo Feher's outstanding industrial and academic research, teaching, and consulting engineering achievements. His expert knowledge of digital communications and microwave transmission is reflected in this book. Frankly, we need such a book. I wish to congratulate both the author and the publisher, Prentice-Hall, for this successful project.

J. THOMAS MARKLEY

*Vice-President, Raytheon Company*
*President, Raytheon Data Systems*
*Norwood, Massachusetts*

# PREFACE

Digital microwave communications systems have been developed to provide high quality, reliable communications for digitized voice and video signals. Digital systems are particularly useful for interlinking computers and other digital sources over long- and short-haul transmission media. In this book, transmission concepts and techniques of digital systems are presented. Practical state-of-the-art implementation of digital communications systems by line-of-sight microwaves are also described. This is a subject that will continue to be one of the most important in communications for years to come.

At the present time, most major operational terrestrial line-of-sight and satellite microwave systems use *analog* FM modulation techniques. However, the trend in *new development* is such that the overwhelming majority of new microwave systems employs *digital* methods. This trend has been reinforced by the fact that a number of recent system additions in the United States and Canada (also many other countries), clearly indicates the predominance of the digital approach for new transmission facilities. Should the present trend continue, it is expected that by 1990, almost all new system additions will be digital. Consequently, engineering *students*, telecommunications professionals, and academics must become familiar with *principles*, *design*, *applications*, and *planning* of digital communications networks and systems. The transmission media utilized most by these new systems is microwave; thus, an understanding of this subject is also important.

This book is written for *engineers* and *managers* employed by the operators of communications networks, systems and equipment designers employed by manufacturers of telecommunications equipment, manufacturing engineers and managers, marketing managers, product planners, consulting engineers, engineers engaged in research on telecommunications, and also those of the managerial and technical staff of government agencies concerned with the regulation of telecommunications. This book is also intended to be suitable for use as a *text* at the first year *postgraduate* or advanced *undergraduate* level, as well as for reference purposes, in *universities* and other technical institutions. It is expected that the reader of this book has been exposed to the fundamentals of communications systems. A prior exposure to probability theory would be an asset.

Even though a large number of books have been written on communications systems, this is the *first book* on digital line-of-sight microwave (radio) communication engineering. Probably, the major reason is that with the *exception of a few universities*, this important subject has not been taught in most institutions. Since a large number of graduating engineers will be employed in the communications, and specifically in the digital transmission area, more and more educational institutions will be *required to offer courses covering the material in this book*. Truly, this is an area of electrical engineering where intense growth is taking place.

In Chapter 1, the description of transmission trends in the telecommunications industry is given, and followed by a presentation on telephony, data and video services, digital hieararchies, and digital microwave system configurations. The principle of operation of the most frequently used analog-to-digital conversion technique, known as PCM, is also described.

In Chapter 2, the essential statistical methods required for digital transmission systems analysis are presented. This chapter has been included to provide background material for the practicing engineer who requires a revision on the fundamentals of statistical communications. The practical applications and limitations of the stated theories are also highlighted. Hopefully, this chapter will also be of interest to the reader who has a thorough knowledge of statistical communication theory but desires a more pragmatic engineering view of the subject.

In Chapter 3, the fundamentals and performance characteristics of frequently employed digital modulation techniques are presented. The described modulation techniques have been used in *line-of-sight microwave*, *satellite*, *coaxial cable*, *wire* (*telephony*), and *optical fiber* systems. Here, the study of baseband processing and of modulation techniques is limited to the linear channel model. However, microwave amplifiers operate more efficiently in a non-linear mode at, or near, saturation.

In Chapter 4, the characteristics and current status of microwave amplifiers is described.

In Chapter 5, reliability objectives of typical digital microwave systems are presented, after which system gain requirements necessary to meet these objectives are specified. An in-depth discussion of microwave propagation effects of multipath fading and its impact on radio systems performance follows.

In Chapter 6, the principle of operation, performance characteristics, design guidelines, and typical performance of bandwidth-efficient $M$-ary PSK and QAM radio systems are presented.

Chapter 7 deals with the fundamental concepts and design of correlative (partial response) techniques, that have been discovered by Dr. A. Lender. Applications to microwave systems and other transmission media are also described.

The material presented in Chapters 8 and 9 includes, various single-channel dedicated digital and hybrid microwave systems, overall single-channel system design problems including jitter and error accumulation, service-channel transmission, and regulatory aspects of communications.

In Chapter 10, diversity and protection switching arrangements essential to meet the stringent performance quality and availability requirements of long-haul microwave systems are described.

Specialized measurement techniques required for the evaluation of digital transmission systems are presented in Chapter 11. Of particular interest here are the on-line (in-service) probability of error and jitter measurement methods that were first reported in the literature by the author.

Chapter 12 reports on research and development trends and unresolved problems related to digital microwave communications systems. This chapter is of particular interest to telecommunications professionals, research personnel, and professors and students who wish to have an insight into the challenging field of new digital microwave system development and research efforts.

Specifications of modern digital microwave systems are presented in a number of chapters. These are included to illustrate the specifications of typical-state-of-the-art systems. In addition to the illustrative *design examples* and solutions given in the text, carefully selected problems are given at the end of chapters where additional emphasis on problem solving is desirable. Classroom instructors may obtain a *complete solutions manual* from the publisher. I believe that the reader will find the design examples and the problems educative and interesting. After a careful reading of the first eight chapters, he will have no difficulty in solving the interesting and challenging problems. Problem 8.1 is reproduced here to wet the readers appetite.

**A challenging problem of the digital microwave systems engineer (Problem 8.1)**

Suppose you are a product-planning manager who is responsible for the development program of a new generation of 90 Mb/s radio equipment. You have just received a note from your boss that the company vice-president requires, within one hour, a brief, one-page comparative, technical performance summary of 8-PSK, 16-PSK, and 16-APK systems. Even though you feel that such short notice is ridiculous, you know that you have to report in time. Good luck: Go ahead and prepare your report, *within one hour*! ■

In a number of chapters *original research* material has been included. Even though this book is intended to be an *introductory text* to digital microwave communications fundamentals, design, and applications, I felt that it is worthwhile to introduce modern research concepts and ideas. To limit the size of this volume and to meet its original objective, to be a *practical digital communications book* that could be *understood* by readers who *do not* necessarily have the *mathematical* sophistication of research engineers, we omitted most derivations. The physical interpretation of final equations, the practical hardware, system constraints, and the microwave systems applications have been described in depth. The numerous up-to-date references provided at the end of each chapter should be helpful to those who wish to study the theoretical derivations and obtain a more in-depth knowledge of the material covered in that chapter.

Considering the evolution style and philosophy of this book, I feel it is appropriate to state how this book was conceived. Throughout my background, which included over 10 years of full-time industry research, design, and applications engineering, approximately 7 years of university teaching, research, and consulting, I realized that the vast majority of practicing telecommunications engineers seldomly used sophisticated mathematical tools. For their successful professional advancement they are required to have a solid knowledge of the principles of system and equipment operation and to apply this knowledge to the design of modern cost-effective systems. In 1977, my book, "*Digital Modulation Techniques in an Interference Environment*" was published by Don White Consultants, Inc. (DWCI). The material in the DWCI book was based on material covered in a number of short courses and seminars given in the U.S.A. and Canada. This material was supplemented by both regular graduate and undergraduate course material which I teach at the university. The positive feedback that I have been continuously receiving from telecommunications professionals, students, and professors who have been studying or teaching from the DWCI book, encouraged me to have the same pragmatic and progressive approach in *Digital Communications: Microwave Applications*.

K.F.

# ACKNOWLEDGMENTS

I wish to thank with appreciation: Dr. Adam *Lender* (GTE Lenkurt Incorporated) for his chapter on correlative transmission techniques and his valuable suggestions during the preparation of this manuscript, Dr. Wolfgang *Hoefer* (University of Ottawa) for his chapter on microwave amplifiers, and Messrs. R. *Lunnan* and R. *Cowper* (Farinon Canada) for their permission to present the material in Chapter 5 on system gain. This chapter is based on their report, which has been written to fulfill the requirements of a graduate course that I taught.

My graduate students at the University of Ottawa, Concordia University, and Carleton University had valuable comments during the preparation of the manuscript. Participants of numerous short courses in the USA and in Canada from various companies, government organizations, and educational institutions suggested improvements and encouraged me to follow a pragmatic approach. Dr. Ron *Brown* of GTE Sylvania and Mr. A.O. *Stretten* of Saskatchewan Telecommunications carefully edited the draft manuscript and had valuable suggestions.

As Radio Communications Editor for the *IEEE Transactions on Communications*, I received numerous suggestions from my reviewer colleagues. Prentice-Hall's editor, Mr. Bernard Goodwin, and his review board members, were most cooperative and had excellent suggestions that improved the manuscript.

Being a consultant of Spar Aerospace Limited (previously RCA Limited) for many years, I have had the opportunity to work on challenging assignments. The drive and enthusiastic approach of Mr. M. *Morris* (Spar Aerospace Limited) inspired me to complete this project in a relatively short time. At the request of the President of Raytheon Data Systems, Mr. T. *Markley*, I had the opportunity to evaluate their digital radio equipment in Hawaii. This challenging and pleasant assignment contributed to my enthusiasm towards digital transmission engineering by microwaves.

The dean of our faculty, Dr. P. *Morand*, the chairman of the Electrical Engineering Department, Dr. W. Hoefer, and my colleagues provided an excellent milieu to work on this book.

The substantial operating, strategic, and equipment grants received from the Natural Sciences and Engineering Research Council of Canada (NSERC), and industry and government contracts enabled us to establish at the University of Ottawa one of the most active Canadian digital communications laboratories. A number of original research results discovered by members of our research team and our graduate students are described in this text.

In my family circle I wish to thank: My *father* who prepared most of the drawings of the manuscript. Even though daddy's age is over 76 and sometimes has been weak, he had the drive and endurance to help and encourage me, whenever possible.

My *mother* fostered my ambition and love towards my engineering profession.

At home, *Elisabeth* and our little daughter *Catherine* were patient during weekends and long evening hours while I was writing this book, instead of being with them. Elisabeth encouraged me and gave good suggestions concerning the style and content of this book. Without her encouragement, this book would not have been completed.

*University of Ottawa, Canada* DR. KAMILO FEHER, P.Eng.

# 1

# TRANSMISSION SYSTEM ENVIRONMENT

Many developments in the communications field have contributed to the recent growth of digital microwave system applications. Some of the most important of these developments are an ever-increasing rate of growth in the amount of telephone traffic that can economically be handled entirely by digital methods; demands for new services such as facsimile, digitized television and high-speed data; demonstrated high radio-frequency (RF) spectrum efficiency for mixtures of data; digitized voice traffic; and the opening up of frequency bands above 10 GHz, which are more viable for digital than for analog transmission methods.

During the late 1970's the countries most active in the application of digital line-of-sight microwave systems (digital radio systems) were the United States, Canada, Japan, the United Kingdom, Italy, France, and Norway. Of these, Japan is probably the world leader in operating high-capacity digital radio systems. For example, by 1977 one Japanese manufacturer had over 1500 such transmit/receive terminals installed for operation [1.9]. In Europe, Italy probably leads in the field of digital radio by having over five hundred 13 GHz digital transmit/receive terminals in operation. Canada is committed to an 8 GHz all-digital high-capacity system, of about 6000 km in length, that will stretch from the Atlantic to the Pacific coasts. Initially, the major application in the United States has been to interconnect *pulse code modulation* (PCM) transmission links between switching centers. The Federal Communications Commission (FCC) in the United States has issued well-defined rules for digital microwave systems. These rules, summarized in FCC Document No. 19311 have contributed to the orderly development and applications of modern digital microwave systems.

In this chapter the evolution of digital microwave systems and a comparison with analog facilities is presented. This is followed by a description of the telephony, data, and video services provided by digital radio systems and the presentation of current digital multiplex hierarchies. Typical digital microwave system configurations are described in the final section of this chapter.

## 1.1 TRANSMISSION TRENDS

The overwhelming majority of new developments in the communications engineering field employ digital methods. Digital signal processing, digital multiplexing, digital switching and transmission techniques are already with us. These techniques will have continually increasing applications in modern communications systems. The trend in some of the recent transmission system additions in the United States and Canada, which has been paralleled in many other countries, clearly indicates the predominance of the digital approach for new digital transmission facilities. Figures 1.1 and 1.2 show the U.S. and Canadian telephone industrie's terrestrial microwave, satellite, cable, and fiber optics transmission system investment trend for medium-length distances [1.1]. A comparison of the new facilities projected for 1984 and 1990 indicates that in 1990 considerably more digital than analog transmission systems will be added to the existing U.S. network. This trend will continue, and it is expected that *by the end of this century almost all new system additions will be digital.* For systems longer than 2000 km, digital radio and digital

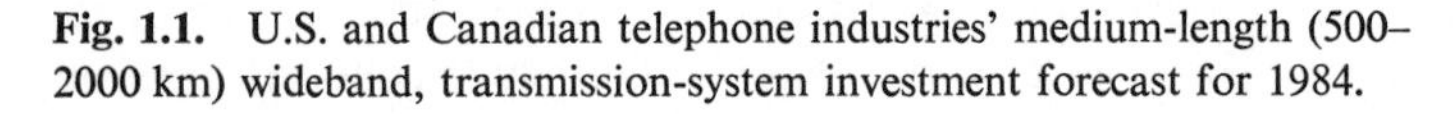

**Fig. 1.1.** U.S. and Canadian telephone industries' medium-length (500–2000 km) wideband, transmission-system investment forecast for 1984.

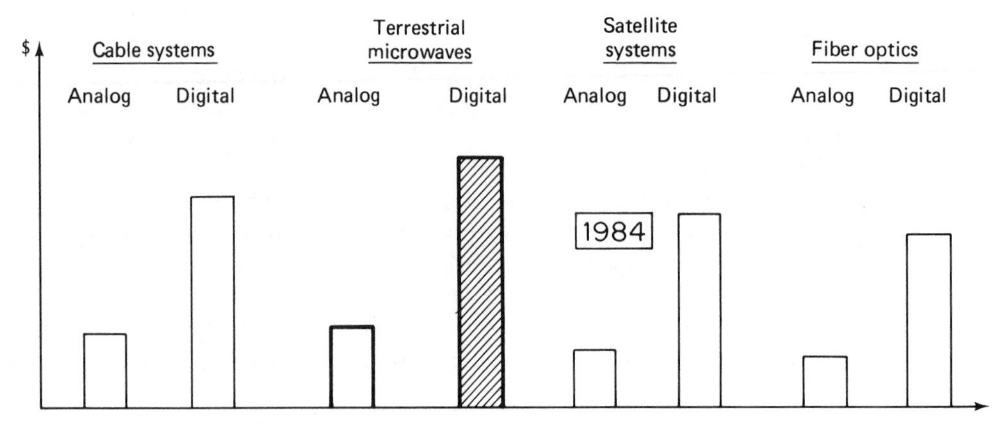

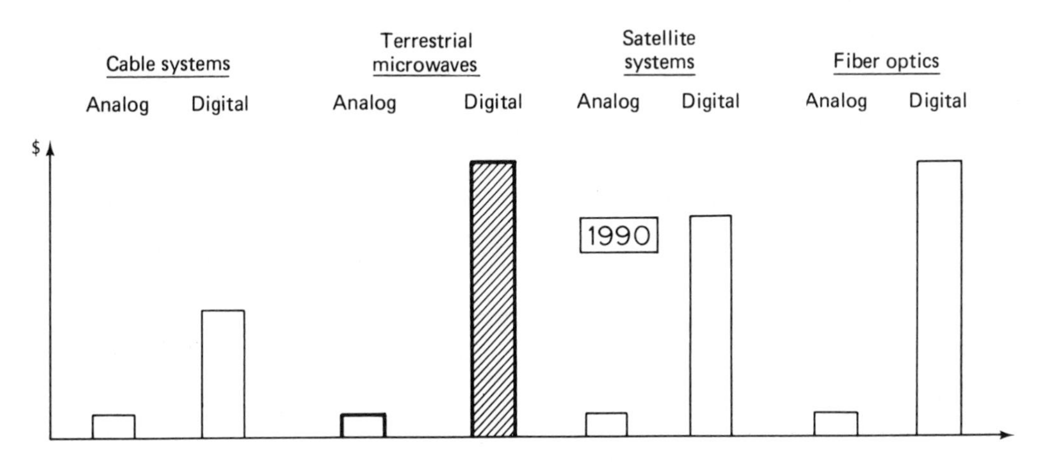


**Fig. 1.2.** U.S. and Canadian telephone industries' medium-length (500–2000 km) wideband, transmission-system investment forecast for 1990.

satellite transmission networks will predominate. The modulation concepts and techniques presented in this book are applicable to *cable*, *optical fiber*, and *satellite* systems as well as to *digital radio* systems.

In communications systems the most frequently employed analog-to-digital (A/D) and digital-to-analog (D/A) conversion technique is pulse code modulation (PCM). The principles of this technique were initially established about 50 years ago. Early microwave systems depended on PCM applications. However, for many years digital microwave systems were not employed because analog transmission facilities had a more efficient radio-frequency (RF) bandwidth utilization capability and were lower in cost. The revival of digital microwave systems began with the successful introduction of time-division multiplexed (TDM)-PCM short-haul cable carrier systems known as *T-1 carriers*. This carrier system, introduced in the U.S. by Bell Telephone Laboratories, has a capacity of 24 digitized voice channels. It has a transmission rate of 1.544 Mb/s and forms the fundamental building block of the North American digital hierarchy. This PCM system was introduced in the early 1960's; by the mid 1970's there were about two million channels in service. In Europe 30 voice channels are A/D converted and time-division multiplexed by means of PCM converters. The resulting 2.048 Mb/s bit rate forms the basic building block of the European digital hierarchy recommended by the CCITT [1.2 and 1.7]. Japanese operating companies standardized on multiples of the 1.544 Mb/s rate. Paralleling the large-scale resurgence of PCM terminals in the United States and Canada, a large number of PCM terminals and cable carriers have been installed throughout Europe, as well as in Japan, Egypt [1.16] and many other countries. With modern digital radio systems it is economical to provide short-haul and long-haul intercity linking of PCM or other digital traffic. Depending on the system configuration, capacity, and length, digital radio systems are frequently more *economical* than new digital cable optical fiber or satellite transmission facilities. A comparison of the most important characteristics of digital and analog line-of-sight microwave systems (radio systems) and the related interface equipment shows that digital systems will be predominant in the near future and used almost exclusively beyond 1990. The mass production of sophisticated, high-speed, *digital integrated circuits* has contributed to the significant price reduction of time-division multiplexed PCM channel banks. The price of these channel banks is about one-half of comparable analog frequency-division multiplexed (FDM) channel banks. Since there are many manufacturers of modern TDM equipment it is expected that the cost of PCM channel banks will be further reduced by continuing competition. A comparison of the annual program cost of new analog FDM and digital equipment, illustrated in Figure 1.3, shows that by the late 1980's almost all new multiplex equipment will use digital techniques [1.8]. Time-division switching (TDS) systems which have been designed to interface

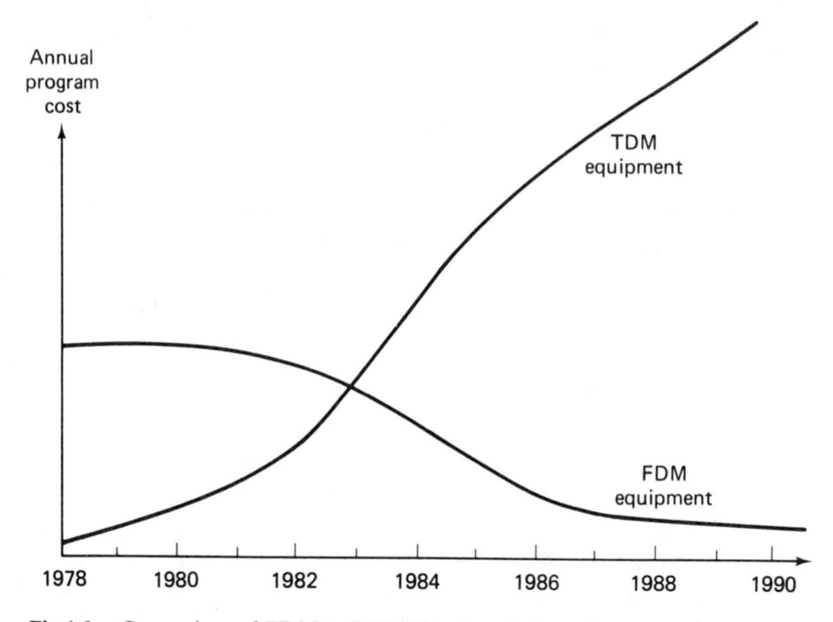


**Fig 1.3.** Comparison of FDM and TDM equipment growth.

directly with digital and analog trunks are presently operational [1.11]. The combination of time-division multiplex, time-division switching, and digital radio systems is more economical than the corresponding analog facilities. Some of the additional advantages of digital microwave radio systems include the following [1.3]: (1) The transmission performance is almost independent of the number of repeaters and with it the system length and topology. (2) Ease of interface of the digital radio, digital fiber optic, digital satellite, and cable systems with digital switching machines. (3) The possibility of efficient simultaneous transmission of digital source information, digitized voice, digitized television, and other analog sources which have been converted into the digital transmission format. (4) For long-haul microwave systems operating above 10 GHz, many repeaters are required. Digital modulation techniques having regenerative repeaters are more suitable than their analog counterparts.

Due to frequency congestion problems in the lower frequency bands, telephone operating companies are sometimes forced to use frequencies at 18 GHz or above for higher-capacity radio systems. For example, in the United States the Bell DR-18A system operates in the 17.7 to 19.7 GHz common-carrier band. This system transmits 4032 digitized PCM voice channels of 4 kHz in each of eight RF channels. The major limitation on the distance between repeaters is due to fading. This system has a repeater spacing between 2.9 km and 8.1 km, depending on the fading statistics of the particular location. In the 18 GHz frequency band the fading is predominantly caused by rainfall [1.4]. If this high-capacity system is employed for long distance transmission, about 800 repeaters might be required for a 4000 km system. Using digital regenerative repeaters the *noise does not accumulate*; thus, even with this large number of radio repeaters an excellent transmission performance can be achieved. In a similar analog radio system the accumulative noise increase due to the large number of repeaters would degrade the signal-to-noise ratio below acceptable levels. This means that, for long-haul radio systems operating in these high-frequency bands, there is *no choice* but to employ digital modulation techniques.

The aforementioned advantages of digital transmission systems have been fully recognized by the Nippon Telegraph and Telephone (NTT) Public Corporation of Japan. The NTT long-haul transmission line digitization program, shown in Table 1.1 [1.10], indicates that by 1993–1997 almost all (90%) long-haul circuits will be digital. It is expected that in the United States, Canada, Europe, and on all other continents the growth of digital systems will be as dramatic as that of the Japanese systems.

**TABLE 1.1 Japan's Long-Haul Transmission Line Digitization Program** *(By permission from the IEEE Ref. 1.10)*

| Planning Period | Analog Transmission Line | Digital Transmission Line | Digital-to-Analog Circuit Ratio (%) |
|---|---|---|---|
| 1978–'82 | Route duplication completion | Digitization commencement | 10 |
| 1983–'87 | Stabilized period | Growing period | 50 (Analog) |
| 1988–'92 | Decreasing period | Route duplication commencement | (Digital) 70 |
| 1993–'97 | Decaying period | Route duplication completion | 90 |

## 1.2 DIGITAL TELEPHONY, DATA AND VIDEO TECHNIQUES, SERVICES, AND HIERARCHIES

Among the most important specifications for a digital radio system is its transmission *capacity*, expressed in terms of transmitted bits per second. Some of the low-capacity microwave systems transmit at a rate of less than 1 million *bits/second* (abbreviated as 1 Mb/s), while high-capacity systems transmit at a rate of 300 million bits/second (300 Mb/s) or at even higher rates. A basic two-way digital microwave system is shown in Fig. 1.4. The digital source might include many

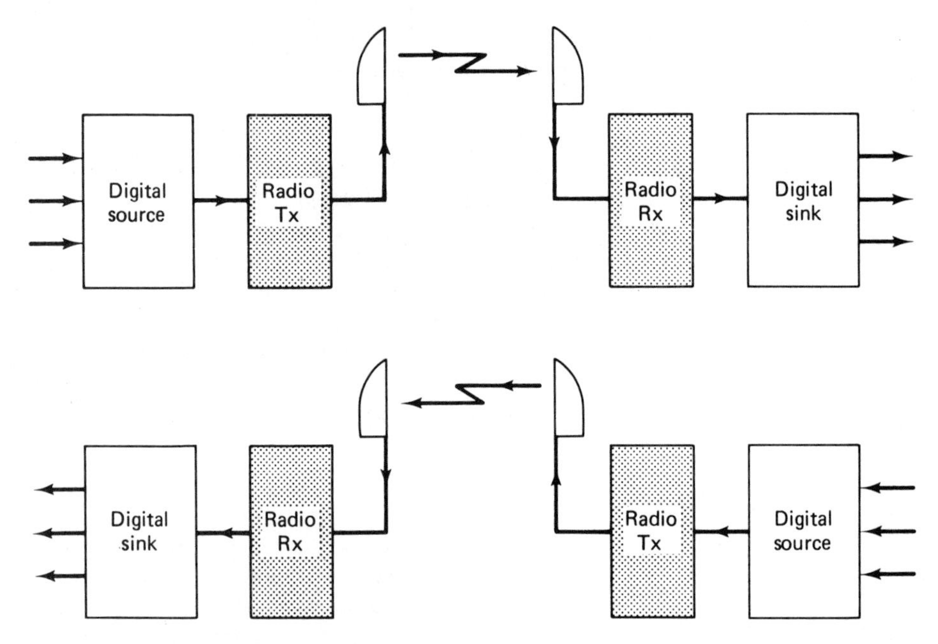


**Fig. 1.4.** Basic two-way digital microwave system.

digitized (PCM converted) voice channels, one or more A/D converted broadcast-quality television signals, and a large number of digital computer or other data channels. The microwave (radio) transmitter (Tx) unit accepts from the source the digital information in the form of one or more bit streams, having a specified bit rate, and converts it into a digitally modulated radio-frequency carrier. The radio receiver (Rx) demodulates the received RF carrier and provides the digital information to the digital sink. Figure 1.5 is a photograph of an 8 GHz digital microwave transmitter and receiver.

From the radio transmission viewpoint we do not require a knowledge of the original information; that is, we do not need to know whether the source bit stream is formed solely by PCM time-division multiplexed voice channels or is a mixture of data traffic and digitized video signals. It is sufficient to know the source bit rate and the code of the digital signal. Time-division multiplexed PCM channel banks are the most frequent sources of digital radio systems. For this

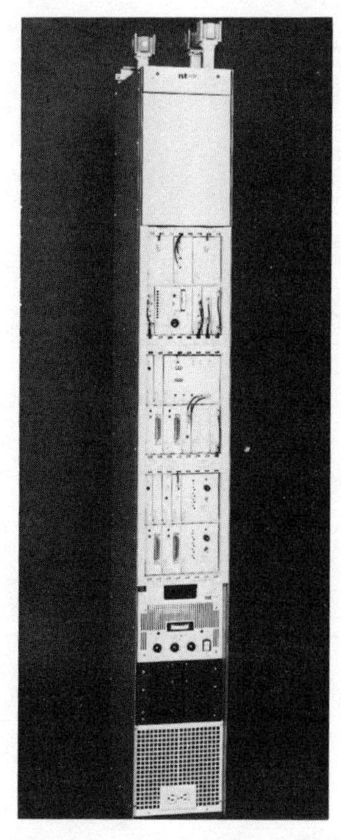

**Fig. 1.5.** An 8 GHz digital microwave transmitter and receiver. (Courtesy of Northern Telecom Canada Limited)

reason some authors refer to digital radio systems as *PCM radio systems*. However, in a number of system applications the A/D conversion process of the video signals is not performed by means of conventional PCM conversion methods, but by more sophisticated and efficient composite interframe coding techniques [1.5]. In other instances, the digital source information might be made up of time-division multiplexed A/D converted 4 kHz voice channels using the delta modulation (DM) method of A/D conversion [1.6]. Thus, it is more appropriate to use the terms "digital line-of-sight microwave," "digital microwave," or "digital radio" than "PCM radio."

In the same way that standardized hierarchies were established in analog FDM transmission systems, the successful development of digital transmission networks required that digital hierarchies be established. Hierarchies are essential to standardize the transmission bit rates, the through-connection and interface specifications, and signal coding formats. The important factors which influence the choice of the levels and bit rates for a TDM system hierarchy include the bit rates of the individual signal sources, the multiplexing efficiency and flexibility, the requirements of time-division switching, and the transmission capabilities of the available and planned radio cable and satellite systems. The two widely accepted hierarchies are shown in Figs. 1.6 and 1.7. Figure 1.8 is a photograph of TDM equipment installed in an exchange station in Ramsis, Egypt.

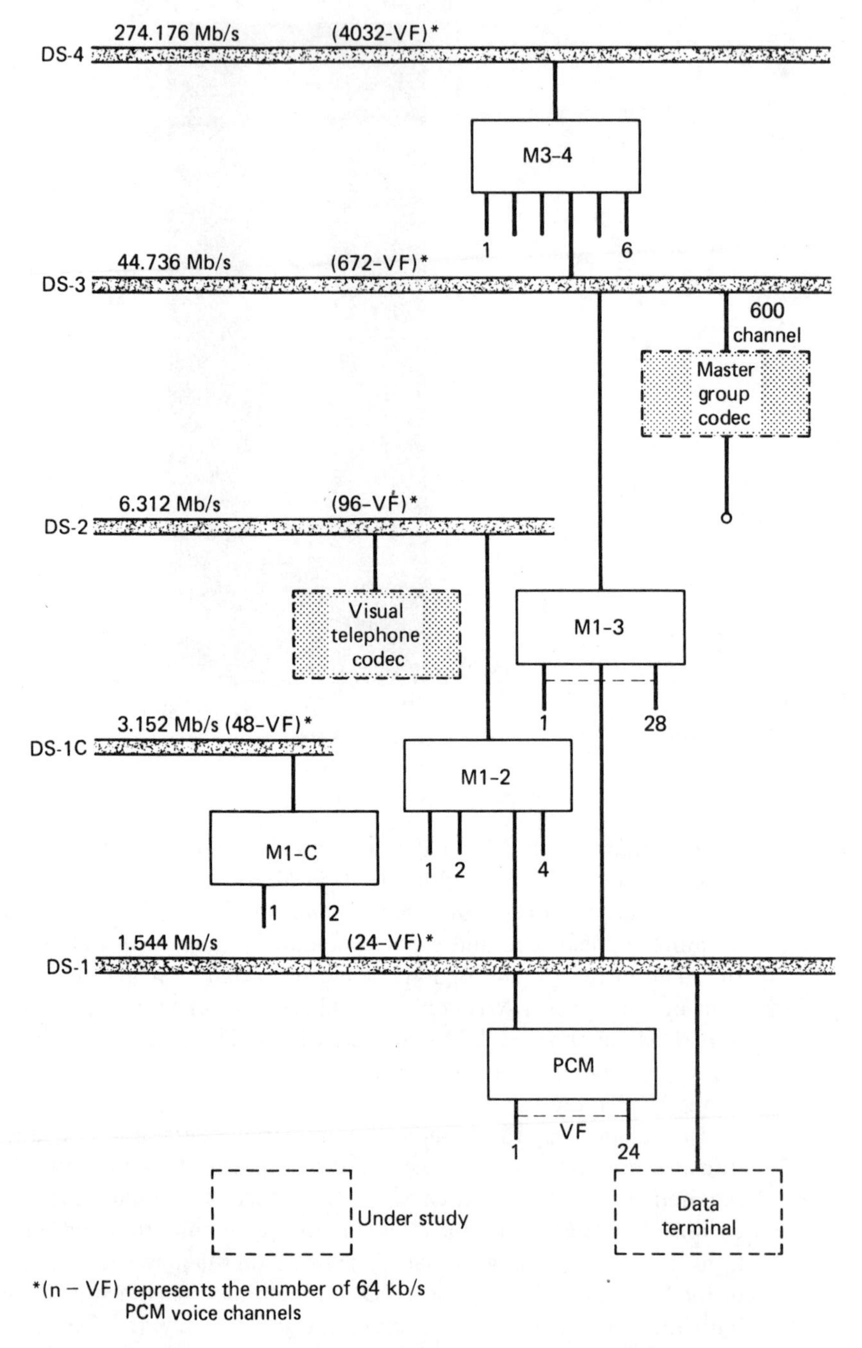


**Fig. 1.6.** North American hierarchy based on 1.544 Mb/s primary PCM multiplex equipment.

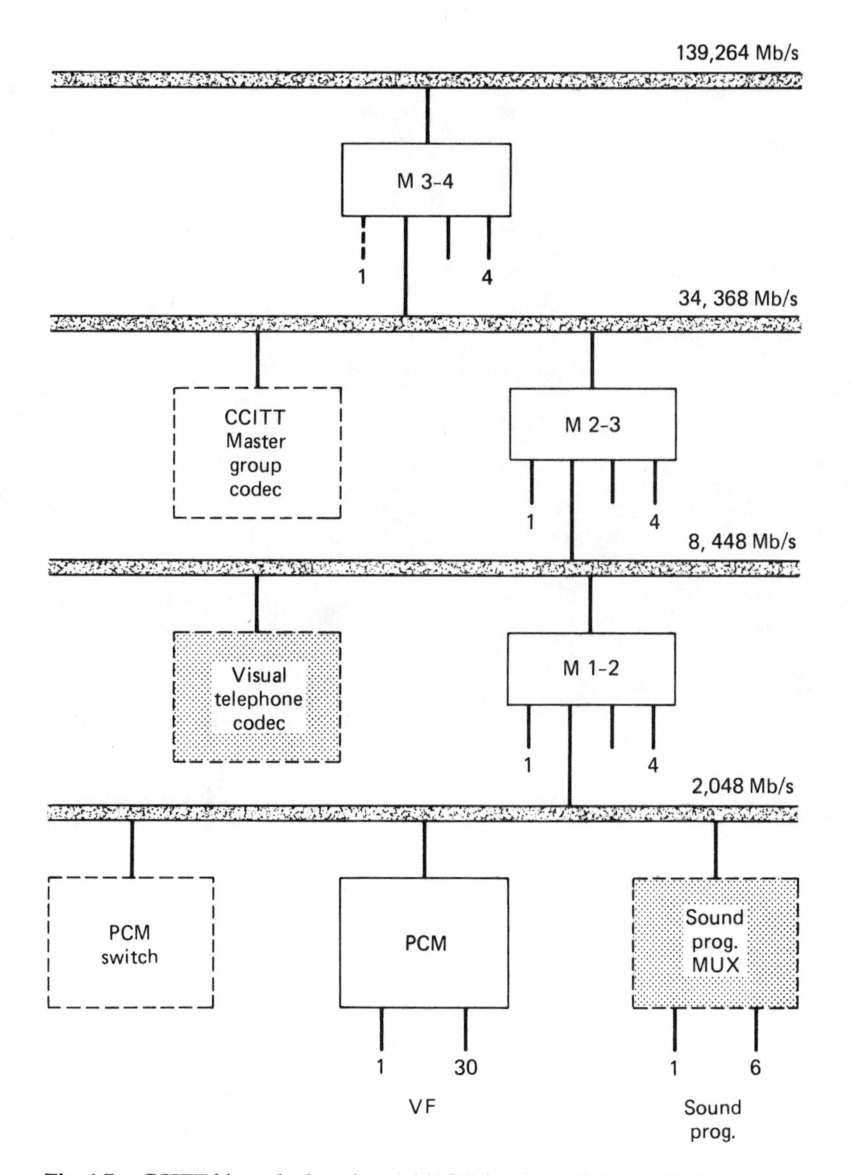


**Fig. 1.7.** CCITT hierarchy based on 2.048 Mb/s primary PCM multiplex equipment.

**Fig. 1.8.** Time-division multiplex (TDM) equipment. These mastergroup multiplex bays, installed in an exchange station in Ramsis, Egypt, time-division multiplex 28, 1.544 Mb/s digital signals. (Courtesy of Raytheon Data Systems Company, Norwood, Mass.)

The primary *PCM terminal* equipment used in North America time-division multiplexes 24 PCM encoded voice-frequency (VF) channels. Each VF channel is band-limited to the 300 Hz to 3400 Hz range and sampled at an 8 kHz sampling rate. Each sample is encoded into 8 bits. This PCM conversion process results in a 64 kb/s rate for each voice channel. Framing bits are time-division multiplexed with 24 digitized voice channels, and the final output provides a 1.544 Mb/s digital stream to the DS-1 through-connection level. This and other through-connection levels are, in many cases, accessible at *digital distribution frames*, where interconnections are achieved in a flexible manner.

To enhance your understanding of the operation of PCM terminals it is necessary to review the principles of sampling, quantizing, coding, and companding as follows.

The *sampling theorem* in a restricted form states that: If the highest frequency spectral component of a magnitude-time function $m(t)$ is $f_m$, then the instantaneous samples taken at a rate $f_s \geq 2f_m$ contain all the information of the original message. A proof of this theorem is provided in most textbooks on communications systems and can be found in references [1.6, 1.13, 1.14, 1.15]. Figure 1.9 illustrates a typical telephony application of this theorem, where the voice signal is band-limited to $f_m = 3.4$ kHz and is sampled at a rate of $f_s = 8$ k samples per second.

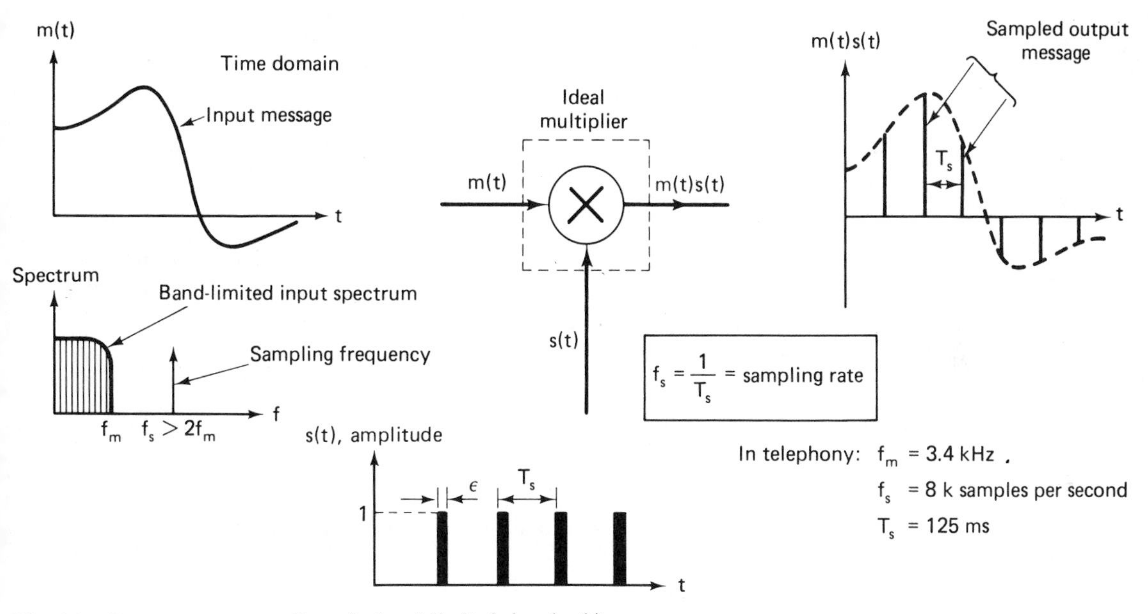


**Fig. 1.9.** Instantaneous sampling of a band-limited signal $m(t)$.

The sampled output signal $m(t) \cdot s(t)$ has an infinite number of non-zero amplitude states. To encode this signal it is required that the amplitude levels be quantized.

For simplicity, only eight *quantization levels* are shown in Fig. 1.10. The continuous signal $m(t)$ has the following sample values: 1.3, 3.6, 2.3, 0.7, . . . , −3.4 volts. The quantized signal takes on the value of the nearest quantization level to the sampled value. The eight quantized levels are represented by a 3 bit *code* number. (Note: With 3 bits, $2^3 = 8$ distinct levels can be identified.) The amplitude difference between the sampled value and the quantized level is called the *quantization error*. This error is proportional to the step size $s$, that is, the difference between consecutive quantization levels. With a higher number of quantization levels (smaller $s$) a lower quantization error is obtained. Experimentally, it has been found that, for an acceptable signal-to-noise ratio, $2^8$, or 256, quantization levels are required. This represents 8 bits of information per quantized sample.

In order to have the same signal-to-noise ratio for a small amplitude signal as for a large amplitude signal, a quantizer with a non-uniform step size is required. To achieve this non-uniform step-size quantization, given a uniform step-size quantizer such as shown in Fig. 1.10, it is necessary to precede it with a non-linear

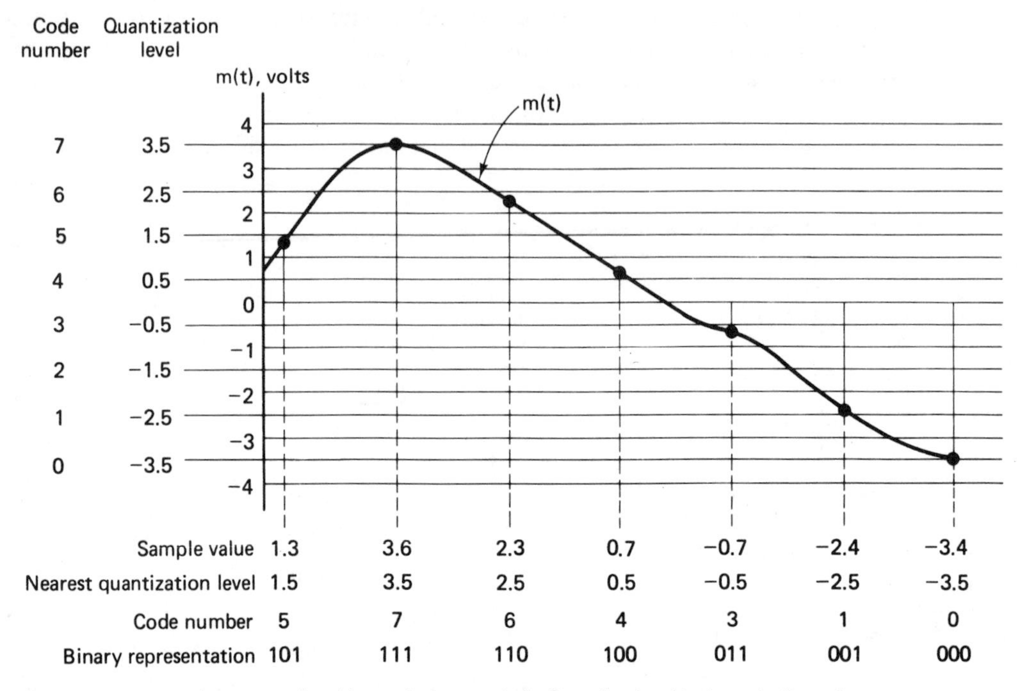


A message signal is regularly sampled. Quantization levels are indicated. For each sample the quantized value is given and its binary representation is indicated.

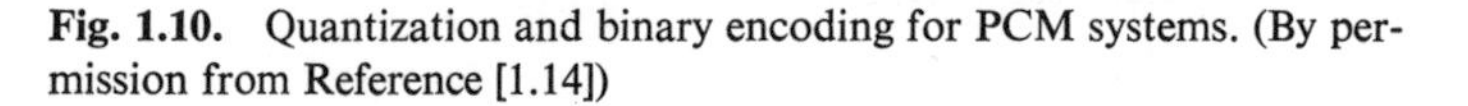

**Fig. 1.10.** Quantization and binary encoding for PCM systems. (By permission from Reference [1.14])

input-output device known as a *compressor*, or *companding*, *device*. The most frequently used compressor characteristics are shown in Fig. 1.11. The companding function is given by

$$\frac{v(x)}{V} = \frac{\log(1 + \mu x/V)}{\log(1 + \mu)} \qquad (0 \leq x < V)$$

where $v(x)$ is the output voltage, $x$ is the input voltage, $V$ is the peak voltage of the input signal, and $\mu$ is a parameter. At the receiving terminal the inverse signal processing to that performed at the transmitter has to be done in order to recover the transmitted signal [1.6 and 1.14].

To summarize, we may conclude that in telephony systems the signal is band-limited to $f_m = 3.4$ kHz. To convert this analog signal into a binary PCM data stream, a sampling rate of $f_s = 8$ k samples per second is used. Each sample is quantized into one of the 256 quantization levels. For this number of quantization levels, 8 information bits are required ($2^8 = 256$). Thus, one voice channel being sampled at a rate of 8 k samples per second and requiring 8 bits per sample will have a transmission rate of 64 k bits/second. In PCM terminals which meet the

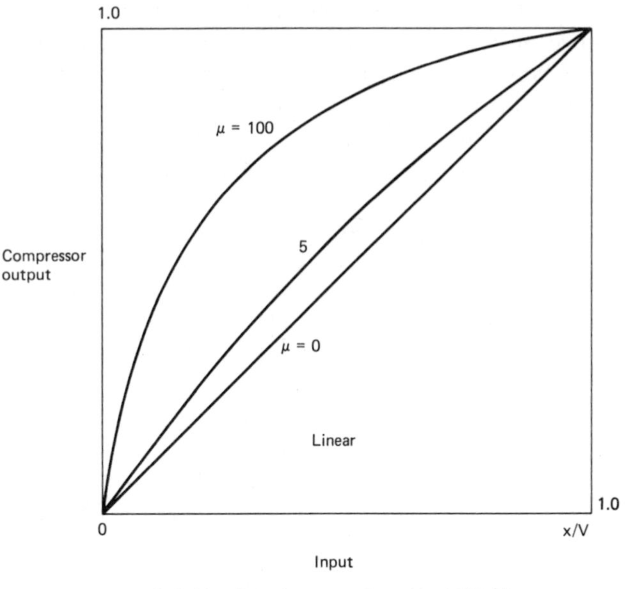


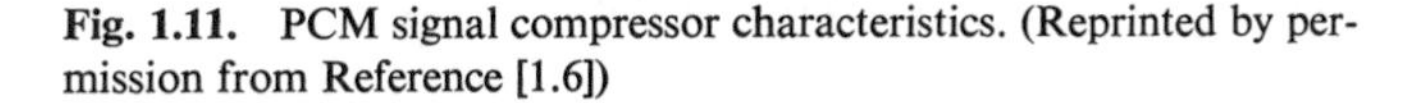


**Fig. 1.11.** PCM signal compressor characteristics. (Reprinted by permission from Reference [1.6])

North American standards, framing bits are also time-division multiplexed with 24 PCM encoded channels. The resultant baseband bit rate for this data terminal is, therefore, 1.544 Mb/s [1.4].

In addition to the standardized PCM voice terminals, data terminals for the multiplexing of a large number of relatively low data-rate digital sources are also employed [1.7]. A number of recently developed digital microwave systems have a nominally 90 Mb/s capacity. These systems are employed for the transmission of two time-division multiplexed DS-3 signals. The visual telephone codec having an input analog bandwidth of 1 MHz and a digitized output data rate of 6.312 Mb/s interfaces in the North American system at the DS-2 through-connection level.

Broadcast-quality color television signals have an analog baseband bandwidth of somewhat less than 5 MHz. For conventional PCM encoding of these video signals, a sampling rate of $f_s = 10$ M samples per second and a 9 bit per sample coding scheme is used. Thus, the resulting transmission rate is 90 Mb/s. Most television pictures have a large degree of correlation, which can be exploited to *reduce* the transmission rate. It is feasible to predict the color and brightness of any picture element (pel) based on values of adjacent pels that have already occurred. Digital broadcast-quality color television signals requiring only 20 to 45 Mb/s transmission rates, obtained by means of predictive techniques, have been reported [1.17, 1.18].

The CCITT hierarchy shown in Fig. 1.7 is based on the PCM terminal which time-division multiplexes 30 voice-frequency channels and has an output bit rate of 2.048 Mb/s. Higher cross-connect levels include the 8.448 Mb/s, (telephony and video codec) the 34.368 Mb/s, and the 139.264 Mb/s data rates. A summary of the various standardized transmission rates at 1.544 Mb/s and at higher rates is presented in Table 1.2 [1.9 and 1.10]. The exact transmission rate of level 5 signals

**TABLE 1.2 Standard Transmission Rates in the U.S./Canada, Japan, and Europe**

| Hierarchy Level No. | U.S./Canada (Mb/s) | Japan (Mb/s) | Europe (Mb/s) |
|---|---|---|---|
| 1 | 1.544 | 1.544 | 2.048 |
| 2 | 6.312 | 6.312 | 8.448 |
| 3 | 44.736 | 32.064 | 34.368 |
| 4 | 274.176 | 97.728 | 139.264 |
| 5 | — | 396.200 | 560–840 |

has not been standardized in Europe; in United States and Canada there are no firm plans to implement level 5. The corresponding 64 kb/s PCM voice-channel capacities are summarized in Table 1.3.

**TABLE 1.3 Standard PCM Voice-Channel Capacities in the U.S./Canada, Japan, and Europe**

| Hierarchy Level No. | No. of PCM Voice Channels (capacity) | | |
|---|---|---|---|
| | U.S./Canada | Japan | Europe |
| 1 | 24 | 24 | 30 |
| 2 | 96 | 96 | 120 |
| 3 | 672 | 480 | 480 |
| 4 | 4032 | 1440 | 1920 |
| 5 | — | 5760 | 7680–11520 |

## 1.3 DIGITAL MICROWAVE SYSTEM CONFIGURATIONS

A block diagram of a hypothetical one-way digital radio path is shown in Fig. 1.12. The concept of a hypothetical reference circuit having a length of 2500 km has been actively used for analog FM radio systems and is also used in digital radio systems engineering. The hypothetical digital radio path, defined by the CCIR, contains nine radio terminals connected through nine sets of higher-order digital multiplex equipment. It has a length of 2500 km and assumes a 64 kb/s data stream at each end of the system. The transmit section of the TDM equipment

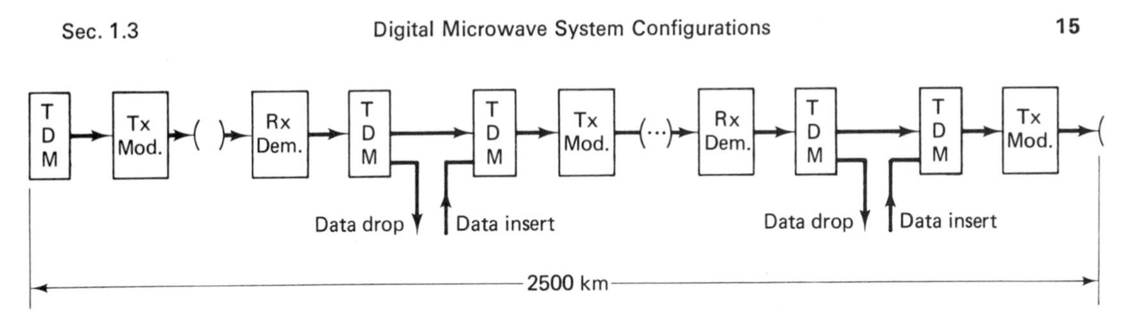


**Fig. 1.12.** Hypothetical digital radio path.

provides the digital input stream to the modulator (Mod) of the radio transmitter. The receiver demodulates (Dem) and regenerates the digitized information and feeds it to the receive section of the TDM equipment. At the regenerator output, the signal which has been impaired by band limitations and channel noise is reconstructed to its original digital format. At this point part or all of the data information can be dropped and new data inserted, or the complete multiplexed data stream might be cross-connected to the next modulator in the chain. In this latter case there is no need for TDM equipment at the cross-connect location. The carrier modulation and demodulation process in digital radio transmitters and receivers (transceivers) can be performed at an intermediate frequency (IF) in a heterodyne system or directly at the radio frequency of the microwave system. Two frequently employed transceiver block diagrams are shown in Figs. 1.13 and 1.14. In the transmitter (Tx) of the heterodyne transceiver the digital baseband modulates an IF oscillator (Oscil). This modulated IF wave is up-converted (U/C) by a "mixer" and RF local Oscillator (LO) to the desired radio frequency [1.3]. At the receive end the modulated radio wave is down-converted (D/C) to an IF frequency and in most systems is coherently demodulated. For coherent demodulation it is essential to obtain the exact carrier frequency and phase of the modulated signal. Finally, the demodulated signal is restored to its original format in the

**Fig. 1.13.** Heterodyne transceiver block diagram.

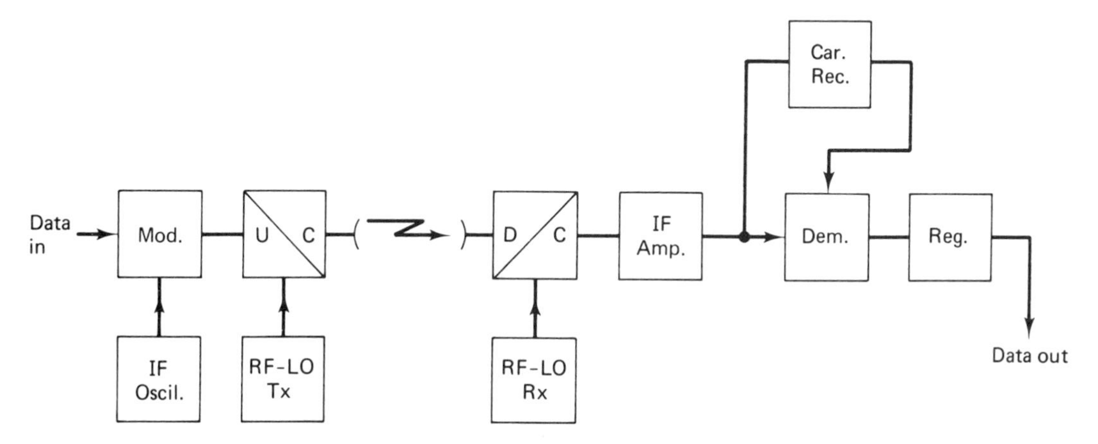

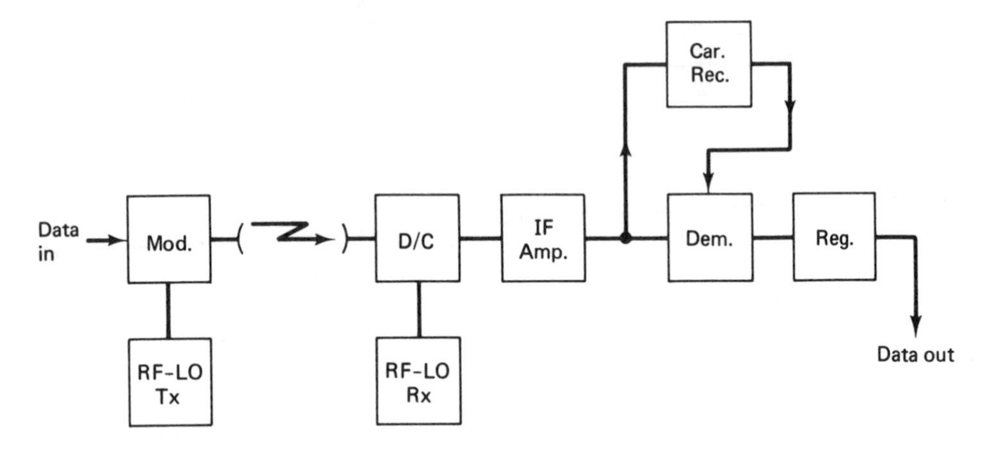


**Fig. 1.14.** Direct RF modulation transceiver block diagram.

regenerator (Reg). In the direct baseband to RF modulation process, shown in Fig. 1.14, the digital information directly modulates the RF signal, without the use of any IF stages.

To improve the reliability of digital microwave systems it is customary to use protection switching and diversity system configurations. A typical 1 + 1 terminal station having one main channel and one protection or diversity channel is illustrated in Fig. 1.15. The digital source signal is split into two twin paths by a highly reliable hybrid (H) unit. The split signals modulate separate carriers and are fed to the two RF transmitters. These RF signals are connected via RF circulators to cross polarization filters which provide the combined polarization diversity signal to the transmit antenna system. In the receiver the RF signals are down-converted to the IF frequency, demodulated, and regenerated. The switch circuits

**Fig. 1.15.** Typical 1 + 1 two-way digital terminal using polarization diversity.

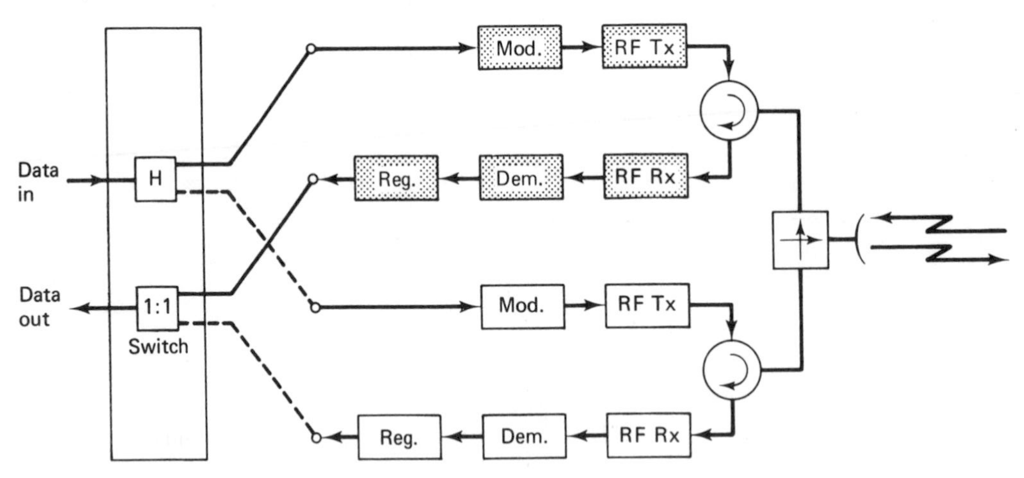

select the output signal that shows the *best performance*, which is defined in accordance with certain criteria presented in Chapter 10.

Most digital microwave systems use regenerative repeaters. A transceiver is considered to be a regenerative repeater if the signal goes through the complete modulation-demodulation-regeneration process. Regenerative repeaters are suitable for interfacing with TDM equipment and thus for data insert and drop-locations. Heterodyne equipment also can be used in non-regenerative IF repeater stations. These repeaters, illustrated in Fig. 1.16, are simpler and less expensive than regenerative repeaters but have the disadvantage that the noise and signal distortions accumulate from repeater to repeater. In *regenerative repeaters* the

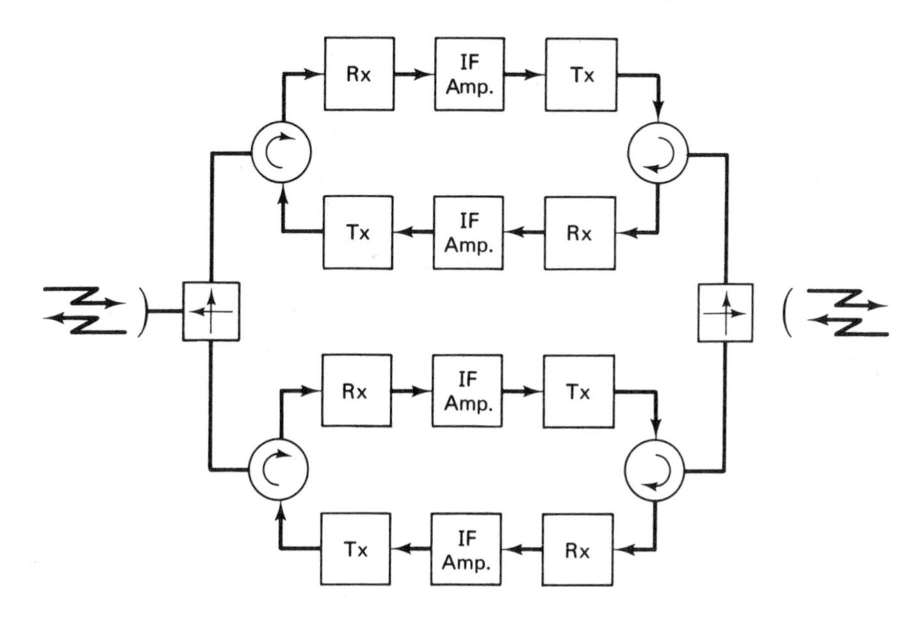


**Fig. 1.16.** Typical 1 + 1 two-way IF repeater (non-regenerative) repeater station.

noise and distortion is largely removed in the regeneration process, and thus there is *no noise accumulation*.

In addition to the two radio system configurations shown in Figs. 1.15 and 1.16, a number of other configurations are in use. These include 1 + 1 and $n + 1$ space and frequency diversity, the $n + 1$ diversity/protection mode being used when a large number of radio-frequency channels are in use over one transmission path.

Figure 1.17 shows the antenna system of a multichannel digital microwave system operating in a diversity/protection switching mode with 11 antennas installed. Two additional antennas are to be installed at a later time. These antennas provide 34 radio channels with a growth capability of over 60 channels. The use of high-directivity antennas and cross polarization is what permits such a large

**Fig. 1.17.** Tower and antenna system for multichannel digital radio transmission. (Courtesy of Raytheon Data Systems Company)

number of radio channels to be used. Each of these channels has a capacity of 672 PCM voice channels or one DS-3 master group. This microwave system was installed in Egypt by Raytheon Data Systems.

## REFERENCES

[1.1] Culbertson, A. F., "The Role of Digital Microwave Systems in World Telecommunications," Proc. World Telecommunications Forum, International Telecommunications Union, Geneva, October, 1975.

[1.2] Colavito, C., G. Paladin. "Transmission Media for a 34 Mb/s Hierarchical Level," Proc. World Telecommunications Forum, International Telecommunications Union, Geneva, October, 1975.

[1.3] Feher, K., *Digital Modulation Techniques in an Interference Environment*, *EMC Encyclopedia*, Vol. 9, Don White Consultants, Inc., Germantown, MD. 20767, 1977.

[1.4] Technical Staff, American Telephone and Telegraph Company, Bell Telephone Companies and Bell Telephone Laboratories, *Telecommunications Transmission*

*Engineering*, Vol. 2, Bell System for Technical Education, Winston-Salem, N.C., 1977.

[1.5] Linuma, K., Y. Lijima, T. Ishiguro, H. Kaneko, S. Shigaki, "Interframe Coding for 4 MHz Color Television Signals," IEEE Trans. Communications, December, 1975.

[1.6] Spilker, J. J., *Digital Communications by Satellite*, Prentice-Hall, Inc., Englewood Cliffs, N.J., 1977.

[1.7] International Telecommunications Union: "Transmission Systems," Economic and Technical Aspects of the Choice of Transmission Systems Gas 3 Manual, ISBN 92-61-00211-0, Vol. 1, Geneva, 1976.

[1.8] Whyte, J. S., The United Kingdom Telecommunications Strategy," Proc. International Telecommunications Exposition Intelcom-77, Atlanta, GA., October, 1977.

[1.9] Welch, H. E., "Applications of Digital Modulation Techniques to Microwave Radio Systems," Proc. IEEE International Conference on Communications, ICC-77, Chicago, June, 1977.

[1.10] Minami, T., T. Murakoni, T. Ichikawa, "An Overview of the Digital Transmission Network in Japan," Proc. IEEE International Conference on Communications, Vol. 1, ICC-78, Toronto, June, 1978.

[1.11] Freeny, S. L., "An Introduction to the Use of Digital Signal Processing for TDM/FDM Conversion," Proc. IEEE International Conference on Communications, Vol. 3, ICC-78, Toronto, June, 1978.

[1.12] Colavito, C., "Digital Transmission for Radio Systems," Telecommunication Journal, Geneva, July, 1978.

[1.13] Black, H. S., *Modulation Theory*, Van Nostrand Reinhold Company, New York, 1953.

[1.14] Taub, H., A. L. Schilling, *Principles of Communication Systems*, McGraw-Hill Book Company, New York, 1971.

[1.15] Haykin, S. S., *Communication Systems*, John Wiley & Sons, Inc., New York, 1978.

[1.16] Kiryelejzo, M. C., F. El. Ganagy, "Digital Radio for Cairo Telephones," Proc. International Telecommunication Exposition, Intelcom, Dallas, March, 1979.

[1.17] Bond, J., P. Lee, B. Neale, "Digitized TV Pictures Go Better, Cheaper," Telesis, Bell-Northern Research Ltd., Ottawa, Canada, February, 1979.

[1.18] Flanagan, J. L., et al., "Speech Coding," IEEE Trans. Communications, April, 1979.

# 2

# STATISTICAL METHODS IN DIGITAL TRANSMISSION SYSTEMS ANALYSIS

Digital and analog signal transmission are disturbed by the presence of undesired waves. These waves can be generated by the thermal motion of electrons in the front-end receiver of a microwave amplifier, by adjacent radio transmitters, or by any other means including deliberate jamming. By analogy with the familiar term used in acoustics, these disturbing waveforms are considered as *noise*, or *interference*. Noise is most certainly one of the system parameters over which the designer has only partial control and is usually hard to describe in exact mathematical terms. It is a nuisance factor in error-free system operation, but if a positive approach to the noise problem is taken then we can consider it as a providential gift to the telecommunications engineering profession. Without noise our professional life would be dull: There would be no challenging problems of long distance transmission; any data rate could be achieved in a noiseless channel. Through continuous combat with various noise problems, new and more efficient signal processing, coding, and modulation techniques have been discovered.

The receiver of a digital microwave system has at its input the desired radio signal, front-end noise, and undesired adjacent or co-channel interference waves.

This composite signal is random in nature. In order to evaluate the quality of this radio system, probabilistic solutions have to be sought. The final performance of a digital radio system, in addition to the conventional specifications of transmitter power, radiated spectrum, and receiver noise figure, is specified in terms of the *probability of error*, $P(e)$, and the availability time in which $P(e)$ is smaller than a predetermined number. These two quantities are calculated or measured by means of statistical measurement techniques and are "bread and butter" for the digital transmission engineer. The most important definitions and equations of statistical communications theory, required for the understanding of the performance of digital microwave systems, are summarized in this chapter. Wherever possible the physical significance of the mathematical equations is stressed. If you are mathematically inclined, the references listed at the end of this chapter provide additional reading material. For a fundamental mathematical treatment of the problem see references [2.4, 2.7, 2.8, 2.15, 2.18]; for advanced system studies, applications, and research, references [2.3, 2.9, 2.13] are suggested.

The classical concepts and techniques used in the frequency and time domains are not sufficient for the digital communications systems engineer. The probability domain, infrequently used in analog systems, is an essential domain of digital communications engineering. In this chapter we stress the fundamentals and applications of this domain. All random processes considered here are *ergodic*, and therefore the statistics of one sample function are representative of those of the whole random process considered.

## 2.1 PROBABILITY DENSITY FUNCTION (pdf) AND CUMULATIVE PROBABILITY DISTRIBUTION FUNCTION (CPDF)

One of the most important statistical properties of a random variable, e.g., random voltage (current or power), is the likelihood of that variable having a specified value or being within a specified range. The concept and definition of the *probability density function* (pdf) and of the *cumulative probability distribution function* (CPDF) is essential for the understanding of digital transmission systems. These functions are introduced by means of the following digital communication examples.

In Fig. 2.1(a) the output signal of a random binary data generator is illustrated. In the time domain this signal has two discrete states, $v(t) = +100$ mV and $v(t) = -100$ mV. These voltages represent the $L = 1$ and $L = 0$ logic states, respectively. In Fig. 2.1(b) the corresponding power spectral density is shown in the frequency domain. In synchronous random-data transmission systems the unit pulse (bit) duration is $T_b$ seconds; that is, a transition can only occur at integer multiples of $T_b$ seconds.

In most practical systems the source is random and equiprobable; thus, the probability of occurrence of a $+100$ mV signal state is the same as the probability

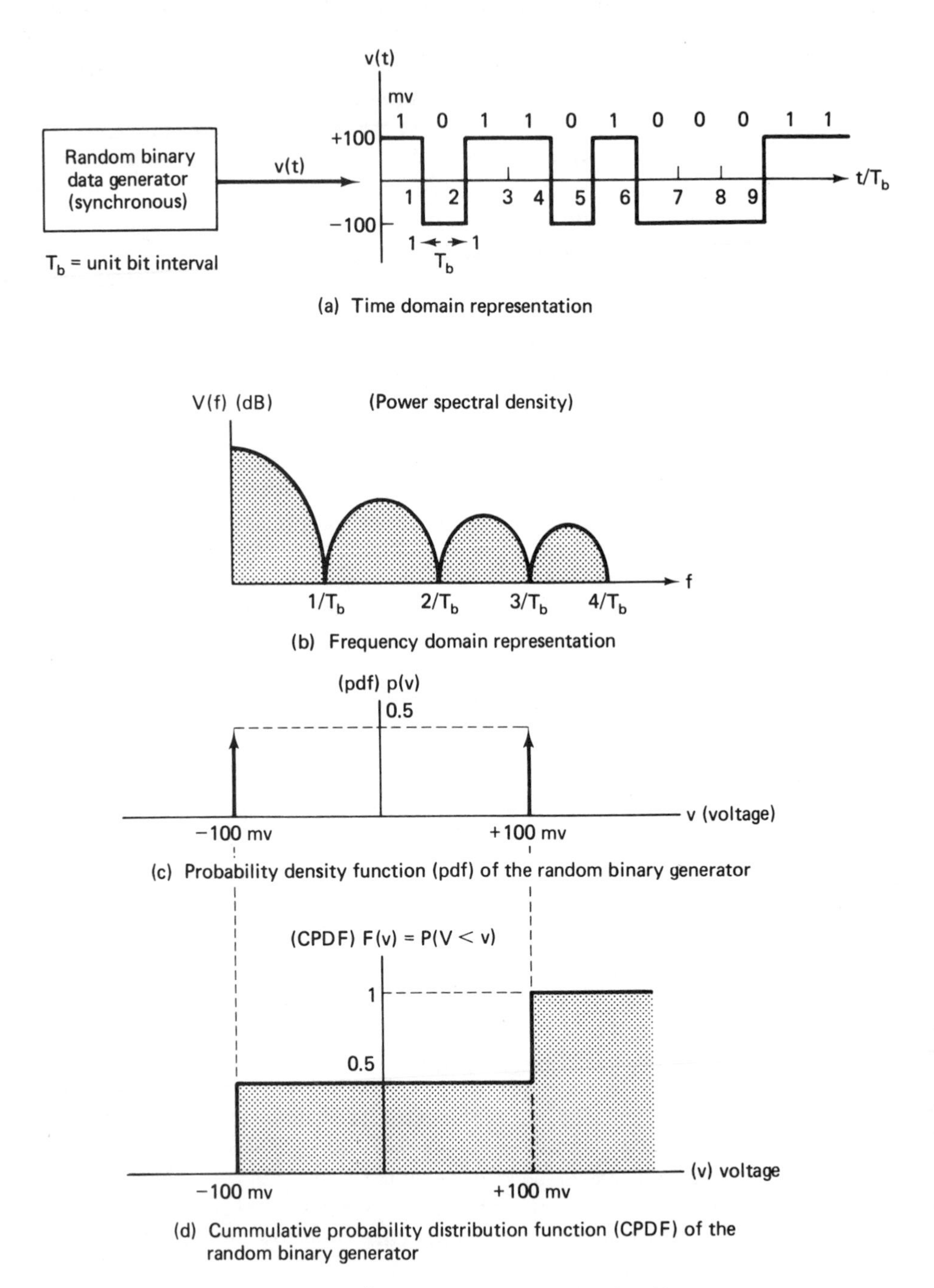


**Fig. 2.1.** Time, frequency, probability density and distribution functions of a binary synchronous random-data source.

($p$) of occurrence of a $-100$ mV signal state. Mathematically stated,

$$p[v(t) = -100\text{ mV}] = p[v(t) = +100\text{ mV}] = 0.5 \quad \text{or} \quad p(L = 0) = p(L = 1) = 0.5$$

The corresponding pdf is shown in Fig. 2.1(c). The magnitude of this pdf is zero for all values of the random variable $v$, with the exception of $v = \pm 100$ mV.

The area which is obtained by multiplication of the pdf by an infinitesimal width $dv$ represents the probability that the signal (or noise) has a value in an interval of infinitesimal width.

The probability that the value of a signal or noise sample is less than a predetermined numerical value is known as the *cumulative probability distribution function* (CPDF) and is illustrated in Fig. 2.1(d) for this example. This means that the CPDF represents the probability that the signal $v(t)$ has a value $V < x$, where $x$ has a specified value. In this example there are no levels below $-100$ mV. Thus, the value of the CPDF for $V < -100$ mV is zero; that is, $F(v) = P(V < v) = P(V < -100\text{ mV}) = 0$. The probability that the generator output voltage $v(t) < 100$ mV is 0.5, while the probability that $v(t) \leq 100$ mV is 1.

If you have an expert's knowledge of statistical communications theory I suggest that you skip the rest of this section. Otherwise, before any further reading of this section turn to the end of the chapter and try to **solve Problems 2.1, 2.2, and 2.3.** If you are reading this suggestion and do not solve or at least attempt to solve Problems 2.1, 2.2, and 2.3, then you are a "naughty" reader. I suggest again that you attempt to solve these problems prior to further reading.

The cumulative probability distribution function, $P(V \leq v)$,* also known in the literature as distribution function and the probability-density function, $p(v)$, are related (for a continuous random variable) by equations (2.1) and (2.2):

$$\text{CPDF:} \quad F(v) \triangleq P(V \leq v) = \int_{-\infty}^{v} P_V(v)\, dv \tag{2.1}$$

$$\text{pdf:} \quad p(v) = \frac{dP_V(v)}{dv} \tag{2.2}$$

The distribution function has the following properties:

$$0 \leq F(v) \leq 1 \tag{2.3}$$

$$P(V < -\infty) = F(-\infty) = 0, \qquad P(V < +\infty) = F(+\infty) = 1 \tag{2.4}$$

$$P(V \leq v_1) \leq P(V \leq v_2) \quad \text{if } v_1 < v_2 \tag{2.5}$$

A simple conceptual measurement set-up to measure the CPDF and the pdf is shown in Fig. 2.2. This set-up could be employed for the measurement of continuous noise sources and also for the measurement of random discrete signal sources or a combination of both. The output of the threshold comparator will

*The *term $P(V \leq v)$ represents the probability that the value of the random variable $V$ is smaller than or equal to a specified value $v$.* Discontinuous CPDF and pdf examples are illustrated in Fig. 2.1.

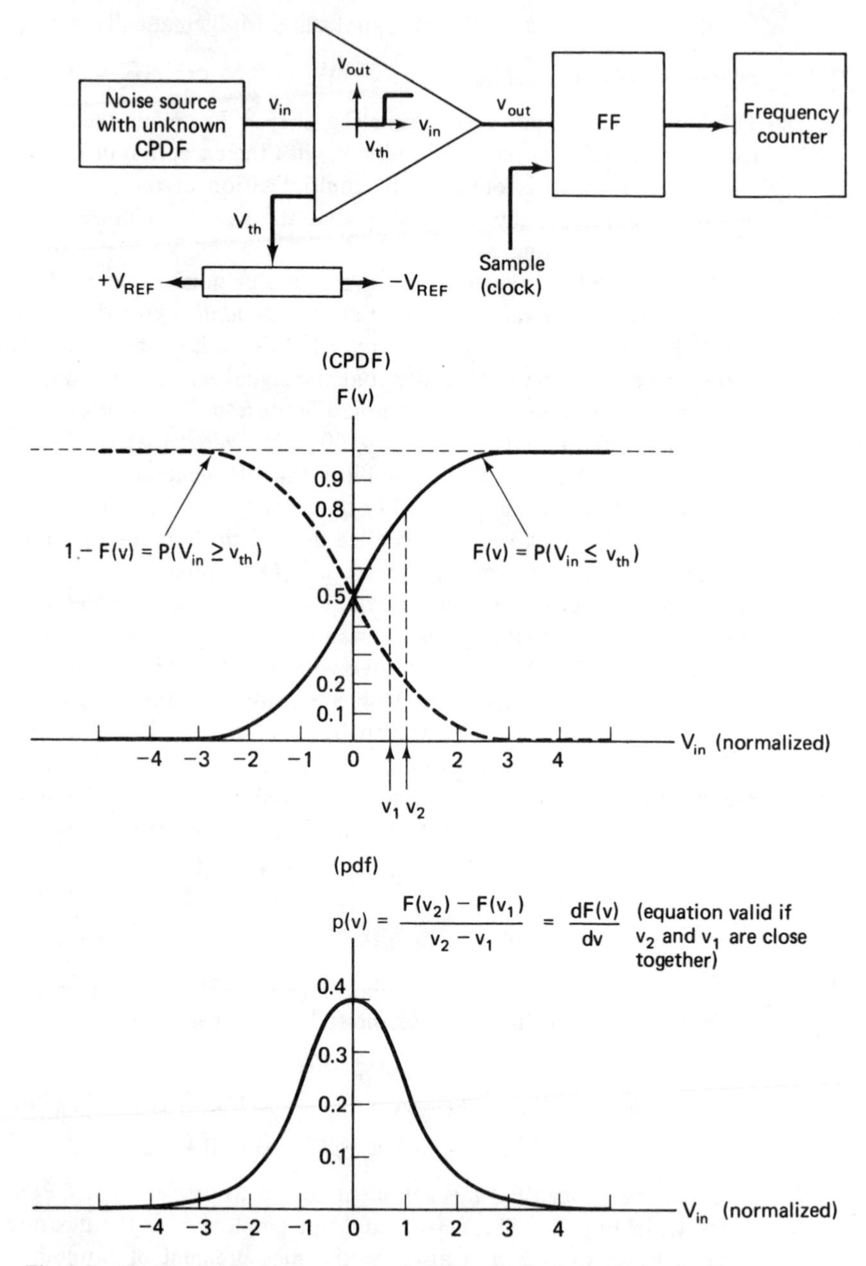


**Fig. 2.2.** Test set-up to measure the probability distribution and density of a noise source. The measured results show typical continuous $p(v)$ and $F(v)$ curves.

have a positive voltage (e.g., +3 V) whenever the input level is higher than the preset threshold level $v_{th}$; otherwise it provides a zero output to the flip-flop (FF) circuit, which performs the sample and hold function for the $v_{out}$ signal. If a large number of samples are taken, then the ratio of the number of positive samples to the total number of samples approaches the exact numerical value of the probability that $v_{in} > v_{th}$. This probability can be written as

$$P(V_{in} > v_{th}) = 1 - P(V_{in} < v_{th}) = 1 - F(v) \tag{2.6}$$

where

$$F(v) \equiv P(v_{in} < v_{th}) \tag{2.7}$$

With variable $v_{th}$ level settings a number of points of the $1 - F(v)$ curve are measured. A smoothed estimate of the $F(v)$ curve is traced. A point by point differentiation of the CPDF gives the pdf function. **(Solve Problem 2.4).**

It is important to note that the probability density and distribution functions do not provide any information about the signal or the noise bandwidth. For example, in Fig. 2.1 the same pdf and CPDF are obtained independent of whether the random binary data generator transmits at a speed of 1000 bits/second (1000 b/s corresponding to $T_b = 1$ ms) or at 300 M bits/second (300 Mb/s; $T_b = 3.33$ ns). Similar comments are valid for the continuous noise generator shown in Fig. 2.2. The probability functions present information about the likelihood of an *error event* but do not characterize the frequency of this event. In digital microwave systems the final system performance is frequently specified in terms of the average probability of error $P(e)$. This term is also known in various references as the average *bit error rate* (BER). The $P(e)$ performance specification is a measure of the *average* performance but does not give any insight into the frequency of the error occurrence. For example, a transmission system having an average $P(e)$ of $10^{-6}$ might have error-containing seconds in every hour or might have only error-free seconds throughout 24 hours, with the exception of a single large-error burst. However, when the $P(e)$ specification is combined with the error-free second requirement, then an insight into the frequency of error events is gained.

## 2.2 PRINCIPAL PARAMETERS OF PROBABILITY FUNCTIONS

The term *random variable* defines a relationship by which a number is assigned to each possible result of a test. Among the most important terms that define the characteristics of random variables are the *expected value* (*mean value*), the *median*, the *variance*, and the *standard deviation*.

Experimentally the *expected*, or *mean value*, of a discrete random variable $V$ is estimated by

$$E(V) = \bar{V} \approx \frac{\sum_{i=1}^{n} v_i}{n} \tag{2.8}$$

where $n$ is the total number of sampled values, and $v_i$ is the numerical value of the random variable $V$ for the $i$th experiment. The estimate of the mean value is more accurate if the number of sampled values is larger. The expected value can also be obtained from

$$E(V) = \bar{V} = \sum_{i=1}^{n} v_i P(V = v_i) \tag{2.9}$$

where $v_i$ are the discrete values which the random variable $V$ can assume.

For continuous random signals the *expected value* is defined by

$$m = E(V) = \bar{V} = \int_{-\infty}^{\infty} v p(v)\, dv \tag{2.10}$$

In this equation $E(V)$ is the mathematical expected value and $p(v)$ the pdf of the random variable $V$. If a very large number of samples are taken in a stationary (time invariant) system, then the limit approached by the measured mean is the expected value. The mean value is frequently measured with dc voltmeters. Physically, $[E(V^2)]$, that is, $\bar{V^2}$ represents the normalized power measured across a 1 ohm load.

The *expected value* of *any function* $g(V)$ is

$$E[g(V)] = \int_{-\infty}^{\infty} g(v)p(v)\, dv \tag{2.11}$$

The *median* of a random variable is defined as the point at which the cumulative probability distribution function $F(v) = 0.5$.

The *mean square* value is obtained from (2.11) if $g(v) = v^2$. It is given by

$$E(V^2) = \int_{-\infty}^{\infty} v^2 p(v)\, dv = \bar{V^2} \tag{2.12}$$

If $v$ is the noise (or random signal) voltage across a resistance of $R$ ohms, then the average power dissipated in this resistor equals $E(V^2)/R$. This power includes the ac and dc terms. In a number of applications if the load resistance is *normalized* to $R = 1$ ohm, then $E(V^2)$ represents the average power in this load.

The *variance* is defined by

$$\sigma^2 = \int_{-\infty}^{\infty} (v - \bar{V})^2 p(v)\, dv$$

$$= \int_{-\infty}^{\infty} v^2 p(v)\, dv - 2\bar{V} \int_{-\infty}^{\infty} v p(v)\, dv + \bar{V}^2$$

$\int_{-\infty}^{\infty} p(v)\, dv = 1$ since probability of entire sample space $= 1$

$$= \bar{V^2} - 2\bar{V}^2 + \bar{V}^2$$

$$\boxed{\sigma^2 = \bar{V^2} - \bar{V}^2} \tag{2.13}$$

The variance $\sigma^2$ represents the ac power dissipated in a 1 ohm normalized load. It equals the difference between the mean square value and the square of the mean voltage. The square root of the variance is the root-mean-square, or rms, value of the ac wave, given by

$$\sigma = \sqrt{\bar{V^2} - \bar{V}^2} \tag{2.14}$$

When measuring random noise or random signal sources, special attention must be given to the rms voltage measurement. In general pdf-s are not dependent on units. However, here the units of volts have been assumed since these frequently are measurable quantities. A number of commercially available voltmeters which have peak detectors might lead to large inaccuracies of several decibels in the measurement of the rms voltage. To avoid measurement errors only true power or true rms voltmeters should be used. **(Solve Problem 2.5.)**

## 2.3 FREQUENTLY USED pdf-s AND CPDF-S

### *2.3.1 The Gaussian (Normal) Distribution*

The *gaussian* pdf is the function most frequently used for the description of noise and random signal sources. This pdf represents with high accuracy the noise sources of a number of thermal noise generators as well as the front-end noise of radio receivers.

The gaussian pdf is given by

$$p(v) = \frac{1}{\sigma\sqrt{2\pi}} e^{-(v-m)^2/2\sigma^2} \tag{2.15}$$

where $v$ is a chosen value of the random variable, and the dc component $m$ and the rms value $\sigma$ were defined in equations (2.10) and (2.14), respectively. The corresponding CPDF is

$$F(v) \triangleq P(V \leq v) = \frac{1}{\sigma\sqrt{2\pi}} \int_{-\infty}^{v} e^{-(u-m)^2/2\sigma^2}\, du \tag{2.16}$$

If the average value (dc component) of the noise source is zero, then the pdf and the CPDF of the gaussian noise are given by

$$p(v) = \frac{1}{\sigma\sqrt{2\pi}} e^{-v^2/2\sigma^2} \tag{2.17}$$

$$F(v) = P(V \leq v) = \frac{1}{\sigma\sqrt{2\pi}} \int_{-\infty}^{v} e^{-u^2/2\sigma^2}\, du \tag{2.18}$$

The normalized gaussian pdf of a noise source is obtained if it is assumed that this source does not have a dc component ($m = 0$) and that it has a 1 V rms voltage ($\sigma = 1$ V rms). This normalized pdf is known as the *unit normal*, or *standardized gaussian density function* and is given by

$$p(v) = \frac{1}{\sqrt{2\pi}} e^{-v^2/2}, \qquad (m = 0, \sigma = 1) \tag{2.19}$$

The CPDF corresponding to the unit normal pdf is

$$F(v) = P(V \leq v) = \frac{1}{\sqrt{2\pi}} \int_{-\infty}^{v} e^{-u^2/2}\, du \tag{2.20}$$

where $u$ represents the dummy variable of integration. The unit normal density and cumulative distributions are shown in Fig. 2.3. The values of the pdf are computed directly from equation (2.19). **(Solve Problem 2.6.)**

The distribution function, equation (2.20), is not expressible in terms of elementary functions. It is customary to relate this function to the error function erf ($v$), which has been numerically computed and appears in most mathematical handbooks. It is defined by*

$$\text{erf}\,(v) \triangleq \frac{2}{\sqrt{\pi}} \int_{0}^{v} e^{-u^2}\, du \tag{2.21}$$

The complementary error function erfc ($v$) is defined by

$$\text{erfc}\,(v) \triangleq 1 - \text{erf}\,(v) = \frac{2}{\sqrt{\pi}} \int_{v}^{\infty} e^{-u^2}\, du \tag{2.22}$$

In Fig. 2.4 erfc ($v$) is plotted on a logarithmic scale for the $0 < v < 5$ range, and in Table 2.1 the corresponding exact values are listed. The cumulative distribution function $P(v)$ of equation (2.18) may be expressed in terms of the complementary error function [2.7] as

$$\begin{aligned} F(v) &= 1 - \frac{1}{2}\,\text{erfc}\left(\frac{v}{\sqrt{2}\,\sigma}\right) \quad \text{for } v \geq 0 \\ F(v) &= \frac{1}{2}\,\text{erfc}\left(\frac{|v|}{\sqrt{2}\,\sigma}\right) \quad \text{for } v \leq 0 \end{aligned} \tag{2.23}$$

The computed values of the $1 - F(v)$ function are shown on a logarithmic scale in Fig. 2.4. **(Solve Problem 2.7.)**

The gaussian noise has a continuous pdf. The maximum value of the normalized ($\sigma = 1$) function is 0.399 (see Fig. 2.3) and is obtained for $v = 0$ volts. If a dc component of $m$ volts is present, then the maximum is obtained for a value of $v = m$ volts.

The likelihood that a measured noise sample is within an infinitesimally small region $\pm\Delta/2$ centered around $2\sigma$ is $0.054\Delta$. The CPDF, Fig. 2.3, shows that the cumulative probability that a noise sample is less than $2\sigma$ is 0.977. From Fig. 2.4, the values for higher $\sigma$'s are obtained. For example, it is evident from this figure that the probability that a noise sample exceeds the value of $4\sigma$ is less than $10^{-4}$. In other words, the likelihood that a measured value exceeds four times its rms value is only 0.01%. Even though this likelihood is small, it is still finite and is

*One should note at this point that some authors, e.g., Papoulis [2.8] define erf ($v$) as erf ($v$) = $1/(\sqrt{2\pi}) \int_0^v e^{-u^2/2}\, du$. These two definitions coexist in the literature but should not cause any confusion.

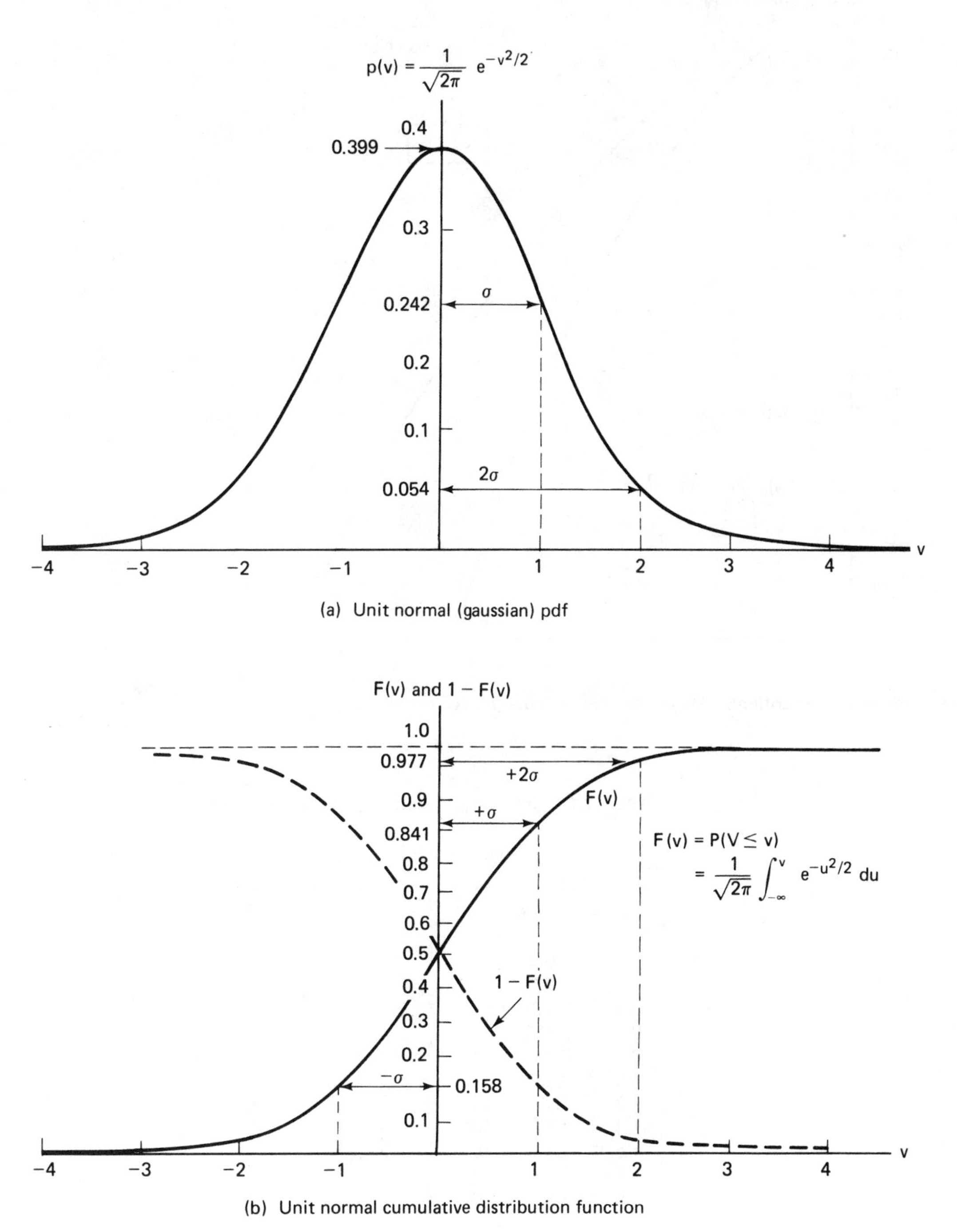


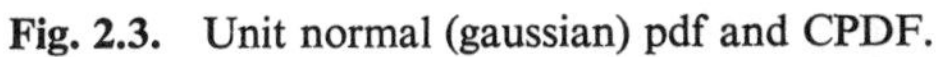

**Fig. 2.3.** Unit normal (gaussian) pdf and CPDF.

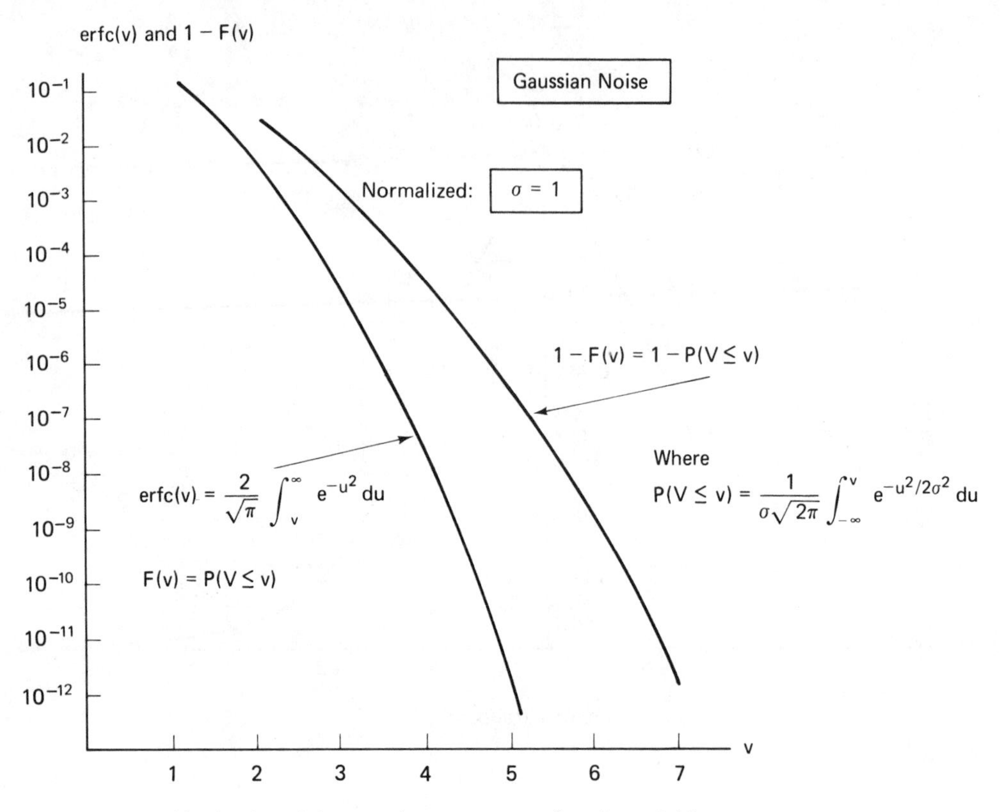


**Fig. 2.4.** Logarithmic plot of the complementary error function erfc($v$) and of the $1 - F(v)$ function.

**TABLE 2.1 The Complementary Error Function***

$$\text{erfc}\,(x) \equiv \frac{2}{\sqrt{\pi}} \int_{x}^{\infty} e^{-u^2}\,du$$

| $x$† | erfc ($x$) | $x$ | erfc ($x$) |
|---|---|---|---|
| 0.0 | 1.000 | 2.2 | $1.86 \times 10^{-3}$ |
| 0.2 | 0.777 | 2.4 | $6.9 \times 10^{-4}$ |
| 0.4 | 0.572 | 2.6 | $2.4 \times 10^{-4}$ |
| 0.6 | 0.396 | 2.8 | $7.9 \times 10^{-5}$ |
| 0.8 | 0.258 | 3.0 | $2.3 \times 10^{-5}$ |
| 1.0 | 0.157 | 3.3 | $3.2 \times 10^{-6}$ |
| 1.2 | $8.97 \times 10^{-2}$ | 3.7 | $1.7 \times 10^{-7}$ |
| 1.4 | $4.87 \times 10^{-2}$ | 4.0 | $1.5 \times 10^{-8}$ |
| 1.6 | $2.37 \times 10^{-2}$ | 5.0 | $1.5 \times 10^{-12}$ |
| 1.8 | $1.09 \times 10^{-2}$ | | |
| 2.0 | $7.21 \times 10^{-3}$ | | |

*By permission from Ref. [2.7].

†For large values of $x$, erfc $(x) \simeq e^{-x^2}/(x\sqrt{\pi})$.

the major contribution of the error-generating mechanism in digital transmission systems.

Theoretically, an ideal gaussian noise process has infinitely high peaks; that is, there is a finite likelihood that a peak as high as $7\sigma$ or even higher will occur. This theoretical probability that a peak of $7\sigma$ occurs is only $10^{-12}$ (Fig. 2.4). *Practical gaussian noise generators resemble the theoretical gaussian density and distribution functions closely, up to* $\pm 4\sigma$ *or* $\pm 5\sigma$ *values* (*within* 1%). Above these voltages most generators clip and thus do not follow the theoretical gaussian curve.

One of the most important characteristics of the gaussian noise is, that if it is passed through *any linear* network, the output process remains gaussian. For example, if a 200-kHz-wide gaussian generator is fed to a 20 kHz band-pass filter having a center frequency of 100 kHz, then the output of this filter will be a 20-kHz-wide band-limited gaussian process. However, if the network is not linear then a probability density transformation occurs [2.1, 2.3, 2.4, 2.5, 2.8, 2.11].

In Fig. 2.5 an experimental set-up and the measured results of relatively wide-band and of narrow-band band-pass filtered gaussian noise processes are shown. The approximately 200-kHz-wide bandwidth of the employed noise generator is much wider than the 20 kHz double-sided bandwidth of the band-pass filter (BPF). In practical terms, this noise generator has an infinite bandwidth and is known as a *white gaussian noise* (WGN) generator. The linear BPF significantly shapes the noise power spectral density and the time domain response of the generator. However, the shape of the pdf remains the same. In other words, the filtered output is a narrow-band gaussian noise process.

### *2.3.2 The Rayleigh Probability Density Function*

The *propagation* of radio signals through fading media can be described by the Rayleigh probability density function. If a radio carrier is incident on the medium and this medium produces scattered beams caused by multiple reflections or by atmospheric variations, then the transmitted constant amplitude signal is converted into one with randomly varying amplitude. This random amplitude term at the input of the receiver appears as multiplying the radio wave. For this reason, this random fluctuation is known as *multiplicative noise*, and its pdf is given by equation (2.24).

The front end of a radio receiver is considered to be narrow-band if the receiver bandwidth is small compared with the radio frequency. The gaussian noise generated in the front-end amplifier of a narrow-band receiver has the appearance of a sinusoidal carrier amplitude modulated by a low-frequency wave. This wave has a low-frequency envelope. The probability density function of this envelope is also described by the Rayleigh density and is defined by

$$p(v) = \begin{cases} \dfrac{v}{\alpha^2} e^{-(v^2/2\alpha^2)}, & (0 \leq v \leq \infty) \\ 0, & (v < 0) \end{cases} \tag{2.24}$$

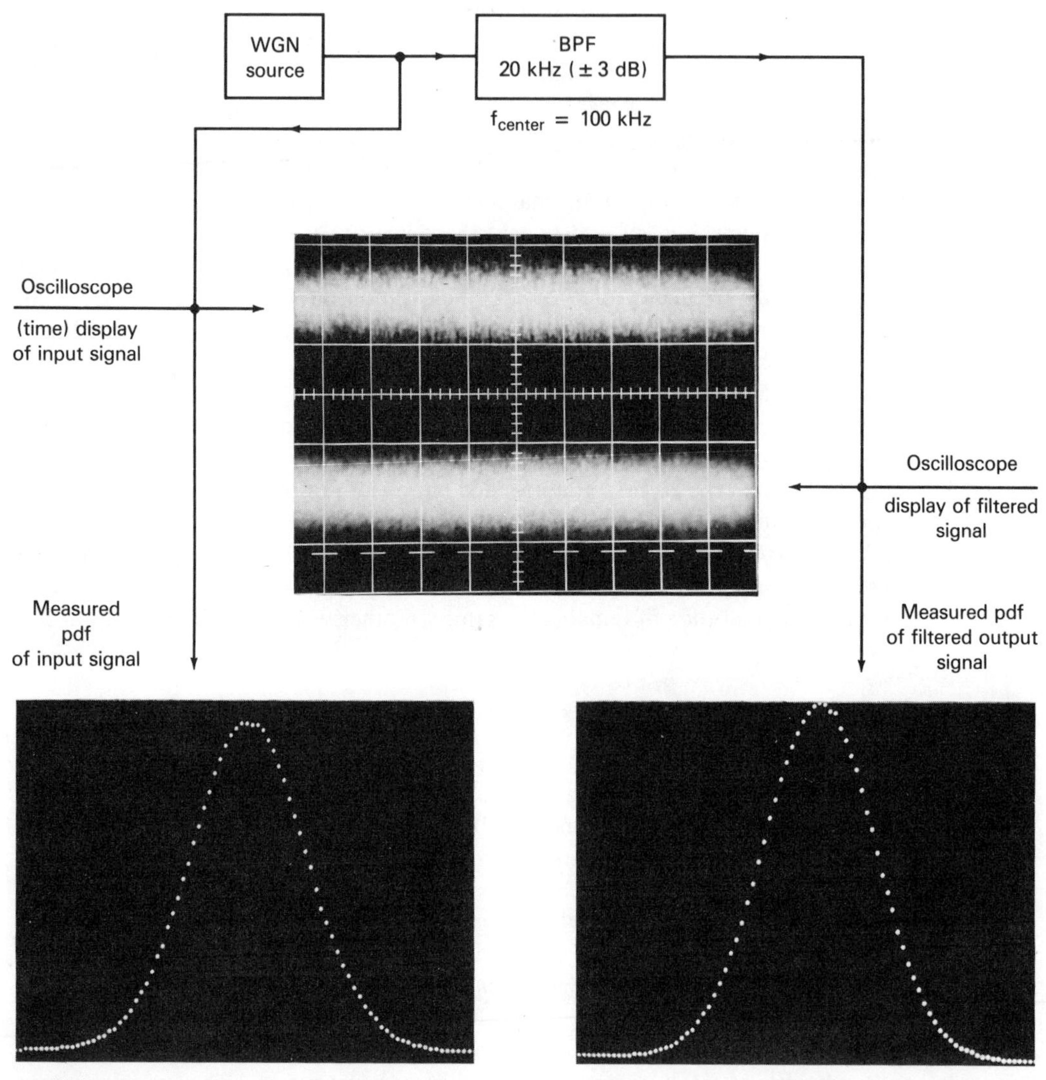

**Fig. 2.5.** Oscilloscope and probability density measurements of a wide-band and narrowband gaussian noise process. (Photos courtesy of P. Amlekar, University of Ottawa)

and the corresponding CPDF is

$$F(v) = P(V \leq v) = \begin{cases} 1 - e^{-v^2/2\alpha^2}, & (0 \leq v \leq \infty) \\ 0, & (v < 0) \end{cases} \tag{2.25}$$

Curves for these functions are shown on a linear scale in Fig. 2.6 and on a logarithmic (dB) scale in Fig. 2.7 [2.14].

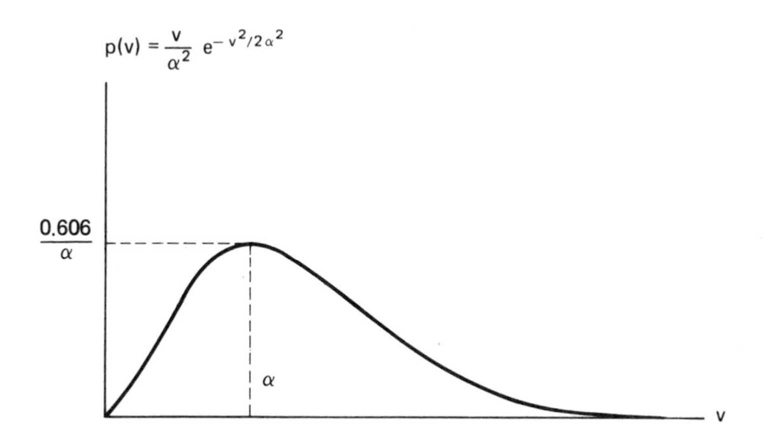

**Fig. 2.6.** Rayleigh probability density function.

The average (mean) value of the Rayleigh density function is given by

$$E(v) = \int_0^\infty \frac{v^2}{\alpha^2} e^{-v^2/2\alpha^2} \, dv = \sqrt{\frac{\pi}{2}} \alpha \tag{2.26}$$

The rms ac component is $0.655\alpha$. **(Solve Problem 2.8.)**

From the CPDF shown in Fig. 2.7 it is evident that the received radio signal has a smaller attenuation (less severe fade) than 18 dB from its median value during 99% of the time and a less severe fade than 28 dB during 99.9% of the time. The probability distribution is an order of magnitude higher for a received signal value that is 10 dB lower. Modified versions of the Rayleigh distribution and its applications to multipath radio propagation are discussed further in Chapter 5.

### *2.3.3 Uniform Continuous and Discrete Probability Density Functions*

The uniform pdf (rectangular pdf) and its corresponding CPDF are shown in Fig. 2.8. In this figure, it has been assumed that the random variable represents a continuous voltage which is limited to $\pm V_m/2$ volts. **(Solve Problem 2.9.)**

We will apply the uniform pdf's in the analysis of interference effects of unmodulated carrier waves in phase-shift keyed radio signals.

In a number of systems applications, the random variable is uniformly distributed in discrete steps. That is, only a number of discrete equiprobable states

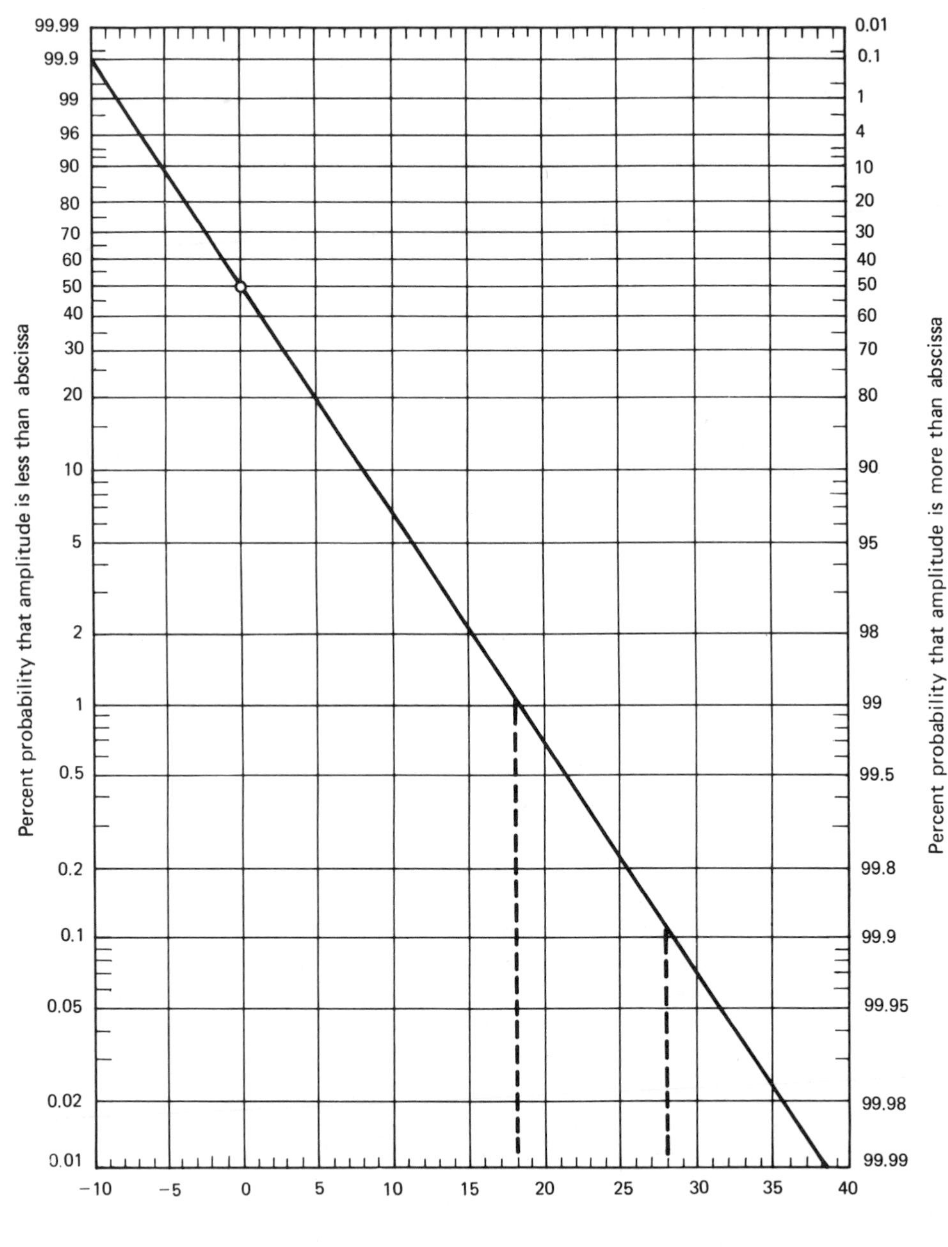

**Fig. 2.7.** Rayleigh probability distribution of rapid fluctuations in the envelope of a received carrier owing to multi-path propagation. (Reprinted by permission from Sunde, Reference [2.14])

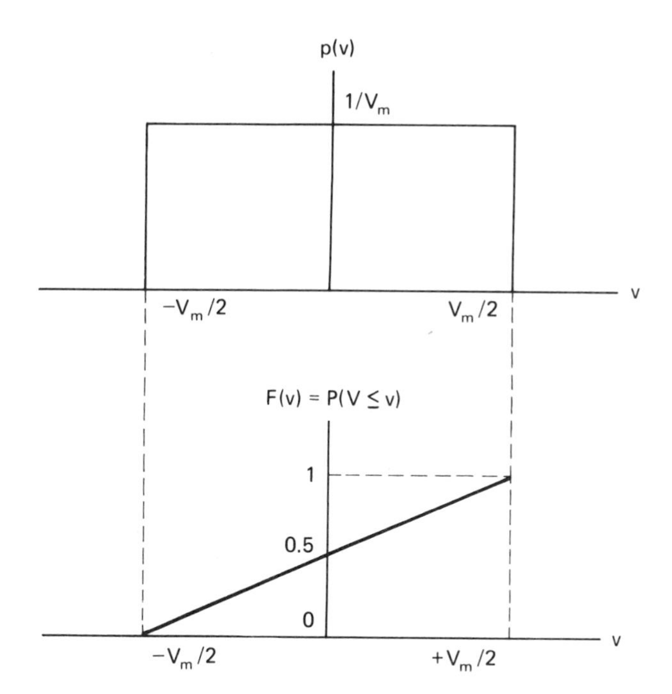


**Fig. 2.8.** Uniform (rectangular) pdf and CPDF.

are possible. The pdf and CPDF of such a process are shown in Fig. 2.9. Examples of these probability functions are 8-level PAM and 8-phase PSK systems, described in Chapters 3 and 6. In Fig. 2.9 the eight equiprobable phase states of an 8-phase PSK system and the corresponding signal-state space diagrams are shown.

## 2.4 ADDITION OF INDEPENDENT NOISE SOURCES; THE CENTRAL LIMIT THEOREM

In the analysis of digital communication systems, calculation of the pdf of the sum of two independent random quantities is frequently required: for example, computation of the pdf and CPDF of the additive interference and noise component.

Assume that $p_1(x)$ and $p_2(y)$ are the known pdf's of the independent random quantities $x$ and $y$. If the pdf of $z = y + x$ is represented by $p_{12}(z)$ then

$$p_{12}(z) = \int_{-\infty}^{\infty} p_1(x)p_2(z - x)\,dx \equiv p_1 * p_2 \tag{2.27}$$

Thus, the pdf of the sum of two, independent, random quantities is the *convolution* of the individual pdf's given by equation (2.27). An illustration of the application of the convolution integral and the resultant pdf is provided in Problem 2.10.

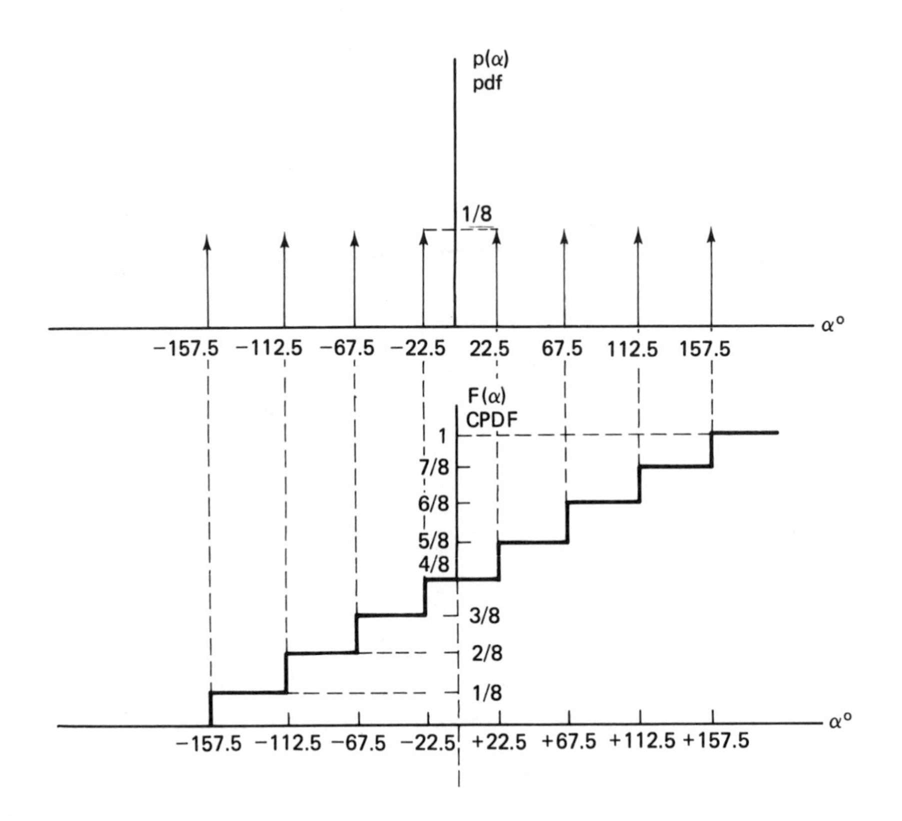


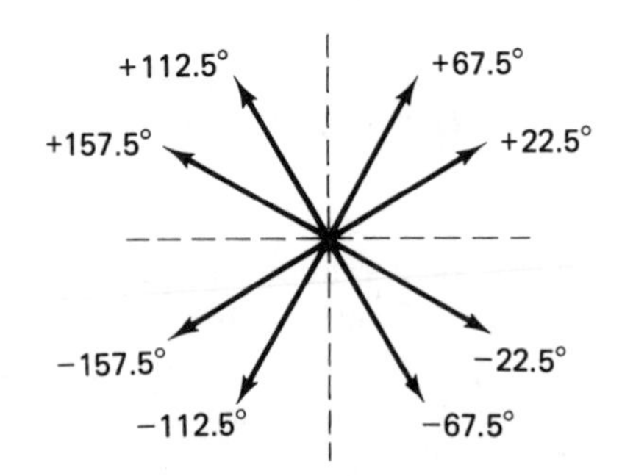


**Fig. 2.9.** Equiprobable discrete pdf and CPDF and their corresponding signal-state space diagram. This figure illustrates the equiprobable phase states of an 8-phase PSK system.

The *central limit theorem* is an extension of the convolution integral to a large number of random variables [2.8 and 2.15]. This theorem states that:

> *If N, a relatively large number of independent random sources, are added, then the resultant probability density function approaches the gaussian density function. The resultant density function has a mean and a variance equal to the sums of the means and the variances of the N random sources, respectively.*

An application of the central limit theorem is now described. For computer simulation of digital communications systems the gaussian noise, equation (2.15), can be represented by an alternate, useful mathematical model. In this model the gaussian noise, based on the central limit theorem, is approximated by the sum of a large number of sine waves of different frequencies. This alternate gaussian noise representation is given by

$$n(t) \equiv \sum_{k=1}^{k_n} N_k \cos(2\pi f_k t + \theta_k) \tag{2.28}$$

where $k_n$ = the number of sine waves used to generate an approximation to the gaussian noise signal $n(t)$

$N_k$ = the peak value of the amplitude of the $k$th sine wave

$f_k$ = the frequency of the $k$th sine wave

$\theta_k$ = the uniformly distributed random phase of the $k$th sine wave.

For most computer simulations it has been found that $k_n = 10$ sine waves closely approximate the gaussian density function. The amplitudes and the frequencies of the $k_n$ sine waves should be chosen in such a manner that they are good approximations of the gaussian noise in the frequency, time, and probability domains. The Monte-Carlo techniques present the methodology required to generate these tones [2.15, 2.16, 2.17, 2.18].

## 2.5 NOISE BANDWIDTH OF RADIO RECEIVERS

To compare various digital microwave systems it is essential to define the noise bandwidth of the radio receiver. Figure 2.10 is a simple model of a radio transmitter and receiver. Due to the noise figure of the front-end wideband receive amplifier, a noise power spectrum which is considerably larger than the receive band-pass filter (BPF) bandwidth is generated at point $A$. This wide-band noise power spectrum is known as a *white spectrum*. The pdf of this source is approximately gaussian. Hence, at point $A$ we have additive white gaussian noise (AWGN). The receiver BPF modifies the noise spectrum by a factor of $|H(f)|^2$, where $H(f)$ is the transfer function of this filter.

The *noise bandwidth* of a filter is defined as the width of an ideal brick-wall filter which delivers the same average power from a white noise source as the

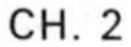

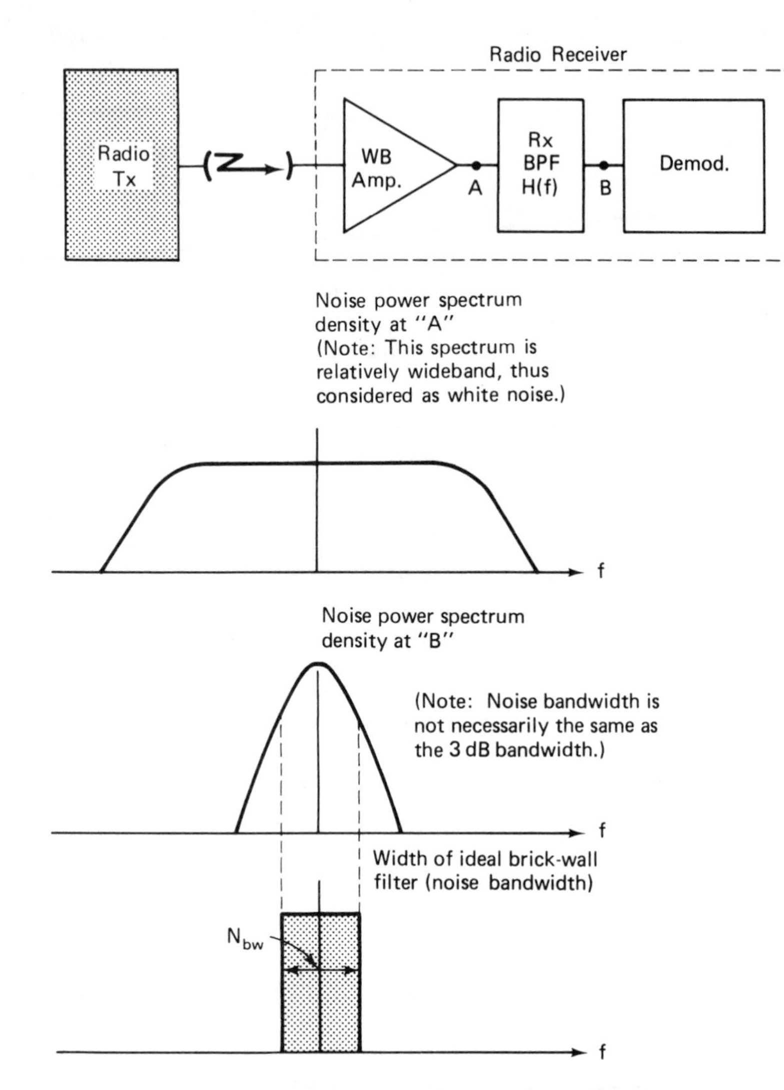


**Fig. 2.10.** Noise bandwidth of a radio receiver.

filter with the given transfer function $H(f)$. It is assumed in this definition that the transfer function is normalized to $|H(f)| = 1$ in the center of the band (at dc for low-pass filters). Thus, the noise bandwidth $N_{bw}$ is defined by

$$N_{bw} = \int_0^{\infty} |H(f)|^2 \, df, \quad \text{(Hz)} \tag{2.29}$$

**Solve Problem 2.11** and note from the solution that the noise bandwidth is not necessarily the same as the 3 dB bandwidth.

## 2.6 AUTOCORRELATION AND POWER SPECTRAL DENSITY FUNCTIONS

In this final section of our *review* of frequently used statistical methods, we define the joint cumulative probability distribution function, the autocorrelation function, the Wiener-Khinchine relation, and derive the power spectrum of random data. The Wiener-Khinchine relationship is of fundamental importance in analyzing random signals because it relates the time domain representation of a signal (autocorrelation function) to the frequency domain (spectral density).

If $X$ and $Y$ represent two random variables, then the joint cumulative probability distribution function is defined as

$$F(x, y) = P(X \leq x, Y \leq y) = \int_{-\infty}^{x} \int_{-\infty}^{y} p(u, v)\, dv\, du \tag{2.30}$$

where $p(u, v)$ is the joint probability density function [2.19].

The autocorrelation is defined to be

$$R_e(t_1, t_2) = E(X_1, X_2) = \int_{-\infty}^{\infty} \int_{-\infty}^{\infty} x_1 x_2 p(x_1, x_2)\, dx_1\, dx_2 \tag{2.31}$$

where $X(t)$ is a sample function from a random process, and $X_1 = X(t_1)$ and $X_2 = X(t_2)$ are defined as the random variables.

If a random process is ergodic, then the *time autocorrelation* function defined by

$$R(\tau) = \lim_{T \to \infty} \frac{1}{2T} \int_{-T}^{T} x(t)x(t + \tau)\, dt \tag{2.32}$$

is the same as its corresponding autocorrelation function defined by equation (2.31).

The *Wiener-Khinchine* relation has been derived in most classical textbooks on statistical communication [2.3, 2.4, 2.7, 2.11, 2.19]. This relation states that the power spectral density $S_x(\omega)$ of a random process is given by the Fourier transform of its autocorrelation function. That is,

$$\boxed{S(\omega) = \int_{-\infty}^{\infty} R(\tau) e^{-j\omega\tau}\, d\tau = \mathfrak{F}[R(\tau)]} \tag{2.33}$$

In the following illustrative example we use equations (2.32) and (2.33) to derive the power spectral density of a random data stream.

**EXAMPLE 2.1.** Derive the power spectral density of a random equiprobable binary data stream $x(t)$, of which a segment is illustrated in Fig. 2.11. This type of binary stream is known as a $1/T_b$ rate, *balanced, non-return-to-zero* (NRZ) signal. This signaling format has many applications in digital transmission systems.

***SOLUTION:*** Here we follow the derivation which was given by Le-Ngoc [2.20]. The $x(t)$ signal can be described by

$$x(t) = \lim_{n \to \infty} \sum_{k=-n}^{k=n} x_k g(t - kT_b) \tag{2.34}$$

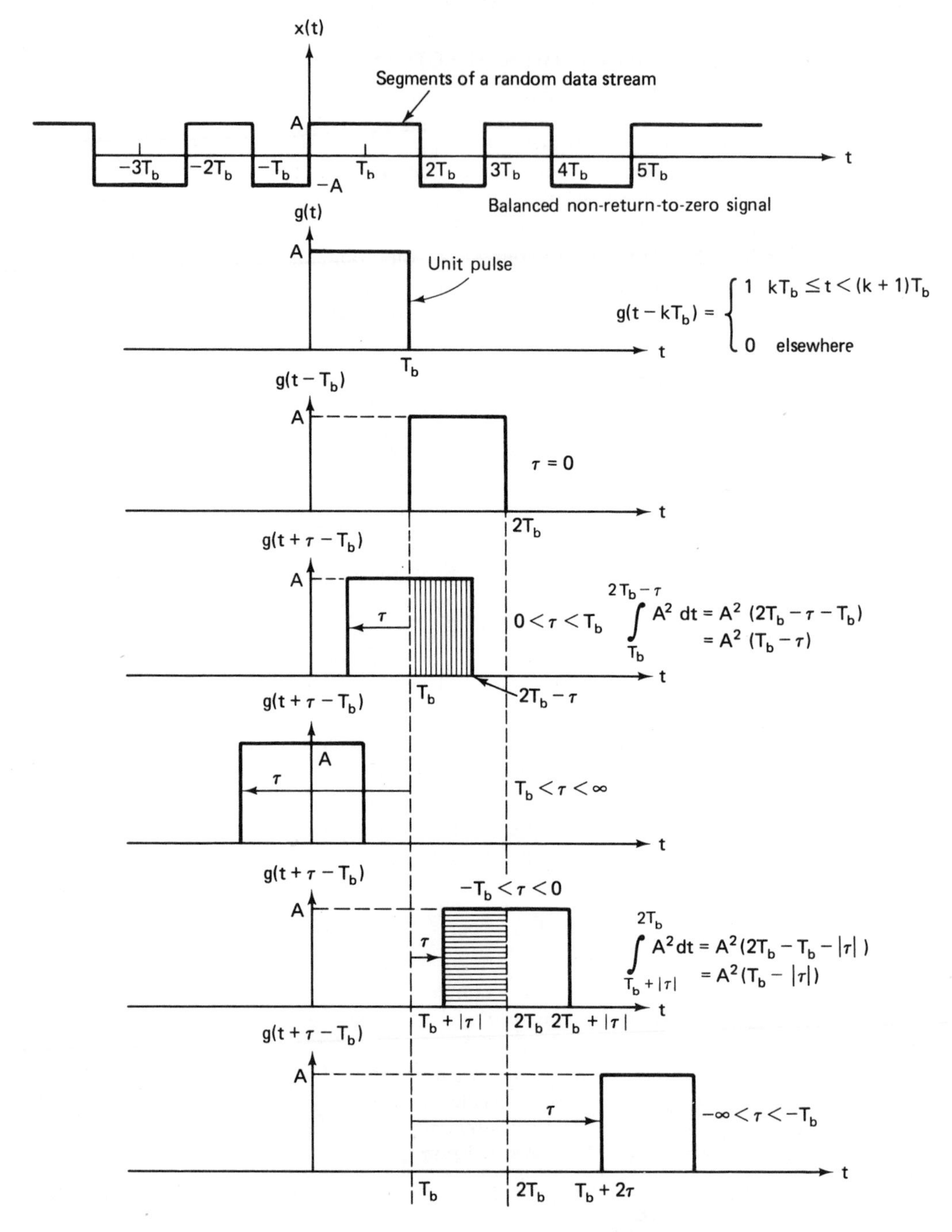


**Fig. 2.11.** Evaluation of the autocorrelation function of an equiprobable binary data stream.

where

$$g(t - kT_b) = \begin{cases} 1 & \text{for } kT_b \leq t \leq (k+1)T_b \\ 0 & \text{elsewhere} \end{cases} \tag{2.35}$$

and

$$x_k = \pm A \tag{2.36}$$

with

$$p(x_k = +A) = p(x_k = -A) = 0.5 \tag{2.37}$$

By substitution of (2.34) into (2.32), the autocorrelation of $x(t)$ is obtained. It is given by

$$\begin{aligned} R(\tau) &= \lim_{T\to\infty} \frac{1}{2T} \int_{-T}^{T} x(t)x(t+\tau)\,dt \\ &= \lim_{n\to\infty} \frac{1}{(2n+1)T_b} \int_{-nT_b}^{+nT_b} \left[\sum_{k=-n}^{+n} x_k g(t - kT_b)\right]\left[\sum_{l=-n}^{n} x_l g(t + \tau - lT_b)\right] dt \end{aligned} \tag{2.38}$$

In this expression there are $2n + 1$ terms of which the autocorrelation function has identical values. The autocorrelation function of one of these terms is given by

$$R_n(\tau) = \frac{1}{(2n+1)T_b} \int_{-nT_b}^{+nT_b} [x_1 g(t - T_b) x_1 g(t + \tau - T_b)]\,dt \tag{2.39}$$

The integration required to evaluate (2.39) has been performed graphically with the aid of Fig. 2.10. From the graphical integration we obtain

$$R_n(\tau) = \frac{1}{2nT_b} A^2(T_b - |\tau|) \tag{2.40}$$

Finally, the complete autocorrelation function is given by

$$R(\tau) = \lim_{n\to\infty} (2n+1)R_n(\tau) = \lim_{n\to\infty} \frac{2n+1}{2nT_b} A^2(T_b - |\tau|) \tag{2.41}$$

$$\boxed{R(\tau) = A^2\left(1 - \frac{|\tau|}{T_b}\right)} \tag{2.42}$$

The integral of equation (2.39) has a finite value for $|\tau| < T_b$ and is zero elsewhere, or, in other words, the autocorrelation function is zero for $|\tau| > T_b$. This can also be ascertained from the fact that, for $|\tau| > T_b$, the signal elements $g(t + \tau - nT_b)$ and $g(t - nT_b)$ cannot lie in the same symbol intervals, and consecutive symbol intervals are statistically independent. The autocorrelation function of the NRZ signal is shown in Fig. 2.12.

The power spectral density is obtained from

$$\begin{aligned} S_x(\omega) &= \mathfrak{F}[R(\tau)] = \int_{-\infty}^{\infty} R(\tau) e^{-j\omega\tau}\,d\tau \\ &= \int_{-\infty}^{\infty} A^2\left(1 - \frac{|\tau|}{T_b}\right) e^{-j\omega\tau}\,d\tau \end{aligned} \tag{2.43}$$

The evaluation of this integral gives the final result:

$$\boxed{S_x(f) = A^2 T_b \left(\frac{\sin \pi T_b f}{\pi T_b f}\right)^2} \tag{2.44}$$

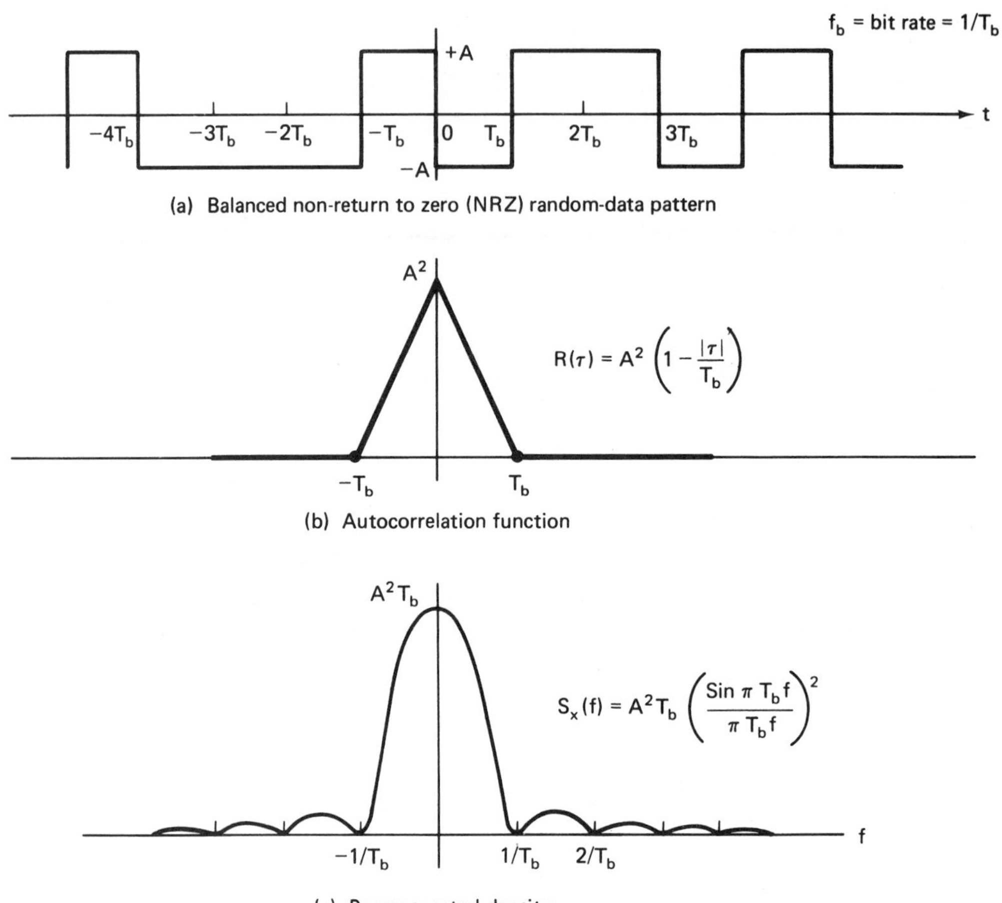


**Fig. 2.12.** NRZ data pattern, autocorrelation, and power spectral density functions.

Figure 2.12 shows the calculated autocorrelation and power spectral density functions plotted on a linear scale. In Chapter 3 we will see how the measured power spectral density of a random NRZ data stream illustrates the $\sin x/x$ shape of $S_x(f)$ displayed on a logarithmic (dB) scale. ■

## PROBLEMS

**2.1** Describe the probability density function (pdf) and the cumulative probability distribution function (CPDF) of a random synchronous binary generator having equiprobable 0 V and +5 V output levels.

**2.2** Sketch the pdf and the CPDF of a random synchronous binary generator which has a +3 V output 40% of the time and a 0 V output 60% of the time.

**2.3** Sketch the pdf and the CPDF of a "duobinary" 3-level random synchronous data generator. The output pulses of this generator equal $+A$ volts 25% of the time, equal $-A$ volts 25% of the time, and have a zero value 50% of the time.

**2.4** The rms output voltage of a noise source is 500 mV. If you wish to construct a CPDF measurement set-up, such as shown in Fig. 2.2, determine the range of the required threshold voltage settings $V_{th}$ and the reference voltages ($\pm V_{ref}$) to obtain a complete CPDF curve of the unknown noise source.

**2.5** Compute the mean value (dc component), the variance, and the ac voltage of the random equiprobable binary source of which an output segment is shown in Fig. P2.5. Assume that the load resistance has been normalized to 1 ohm.

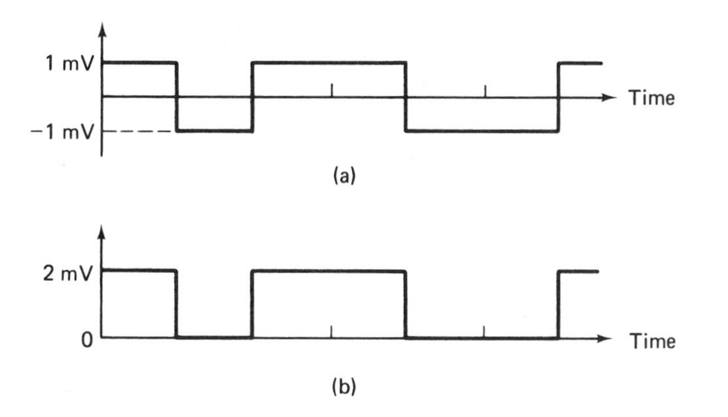


**Fig. P2.5.**

**2.6** The root-mean-square (rms) voltage of a gaussian noise generator is $\sigma = 1$ V. The noise bandwidth of this generator is 10 MHz. What is the value of the probability density function (pdf) at $-2$ V, $-0.5$ V, 0 V, and $+2$ V? Compare your computation results with the values presented in Fig. 2.3. Are previously computed values changed if the noise generator bandwidth is reduced to 1 MHz but the rms voltage is maintained at 1 V?

**2.7** Calculate the values of the CPDF for $v = 3$ and $v = 5$ if it is assumed that $\sigma = 1$ and the values of the complementary error function erfc ($v$) have been given in Table 2.1. Compare your results with the value shown on the plot of Fig. 2.4.

**2.8** Show that the mean value of the Rayleigh density function defined by

$$f(r) = \begin{cases} \dfrac{r}{100} e^{-r^2/200}, & (0 \leq r < \infty) \\ 0, & (r < 0) \end{cases}$$

is $\bar{R} = \sqrt{\pi/2} \cdot 10$. Also show that the variance is $\sigma^2 = (2 - \pi/2)\,100$.

**2.9** Assume that the interfering signal into a digital radio system is an unmodulated carrier wave. The phase relationship of this interfering signal and of the modulated digital radio system is random and has a uniform pdf. Due to circular symmetry of the desired signal and of the interfering wave the maximal value of this phase is $\pm 180°$. Calculate the probability that the phase of the interference is within $\pm 45°$ of the radio wave.

**2.10** The random variable $x(t)$ has a uniform probability density in the range of $-100 < x < +100$ mV. A second random noise voltage source $y(t)$ has a uniform probability density in the range $-200 < y < +200$ mV. Find the plot of the pdf of the sum of these two random variables. *Hint:* Use the convolution integral given in equation (2.27).

**2.11** Calculate the noise bandwidth of a first-order *RC* low-pass filter with a 3 dB frequency $f_c$. *Hint:* The transfer function of this filter is $H(f) = 1/(1 + jf/f_c)$, and note that $\int_{-\infty}^{\infty} dx/(1 + x^2) = \pi$.

## REFERENCES

[2.1] Bennett, W. R., *Introduction to Signal Transmission*, McGraw-Hill Book Company, 1970.

[2.2] Technical Staff, American Telephone and Telegraph Company, Bell Telephone Companies and Bell Telephone Laboratories, *Telecommunications Transmission Engineering*, Bell System for Technical Education, Winston-Salem, N.C., 1977.

[2.3] Wozencraft, J. M., I. M. Jacobs, *Principles of Communication Engineering*, John Wiley & Sons, Inc., New York, 1965.

[2.4] Schwartz, M., *Information Transmission, Modulation, and Noise*, McGraw-Hill Book Company, New York, 1970.

[2.5] Panter, P. F., *Modulation, Noise, and Spectral Analysis*, McGraw-Hill Book Company, New York, 1965.

[2.6] Spilker, J. J., *Digital Communication by Satellite*, Prentice-Hall, Inc., Englewood Cliffs, N.J. 1977.

[2.7] Taub, H., D. L. Schilling, *Principles of Communications Systems*, McGraw-Hill Book Company, New York, 1971.

[2.8] Papoulis, A., *Probability, Random Variables, and Stochastic Processes*, McGraw-Hill Book Company, New York, 1965.

[2.9] Franks, L., *Signal Theory*, Prentice-Hall, Inc., Englewood Cliffs, N.J., 1969.

[2.10] Raemer, H. R., *Statistical Communication Theory and Applications*, Prentice-Hall, Inc., Englewood Cliffs, N.J., 1969.

[2.11] Haykin, S., *Communication Systems*, John Wiley & Sons, Inc., 1978.

[2.12] Munford, W. W., E. H. Scheibe, *Noise Performance Factors in Communications Systems*, Artech House, Inc., Dedham, Mass., 1968.

[2.13] Van Trees, H. L., *Detection, Estimation, and Modulation Theory*, John Wiley & Sons, Inc., New York, 1968.

[2.14] Sunde, E. D., *Communication Systems Engineering Theory*, John Wiley & Sons, Inc., New York, 1969.

[2.15] Technical Staff, *Transmission Systems for Communications*, Revised Fourth Edition, Bell Telephone Laboratories, Winston-Salem, N.C., 1971.

[2.16] Medhurst, R. G., J. H. Roberts, "Evaluation of Distortion in FM Trunk Radio Systems by a Monte Carlo Method," Proc. IEEE, Vol. 113, April, 1966.

[2.17] Bennett, W. R., "Distribution of the Sum of Randomly Phased Components," Quarterly of Applied Mathematics, Vol. 5, January, 1948, pp. 385–393.

[2.18] Feher, K., "Digital/Analog Microwave Transmission Study," Ph.D. Thesis, Genié Electrique, Université de Sherbrooke, Sherbrooke, Canada, 1974.

[2.19] Cooper, G. R., C. D. McGillem, *Probabilistic Methods of Signal Analysis*, Holt, Rinehart and Winston, New York, 1971.

[2.20] Le-Ngoc, T., "Derivation of the Power Spectrum and of the P(e) for NRZ and PAM Systems," Private Correspondence, Ottawa, April, 1979.

# 3

# DIGITAL MODULATION METHODS

In this chapter we consider the principles and performance characteristics of digital modulation techniques that are frequently employed. Before dealing with bandwidth-efficient modulation techniques, we shall review the principles of the simplest baseband signal processing and modulation methods. This introductory material is the foundation for the understanding of more complex, higher-state $M$-ary systems.

The performance of pulse amplitude modulated (PAM) baseband and of coherent phase shift keyed (PSK) systems in an additive white gaussian noise (AWGN) environment is considered in depth here. In this chapter it is assumed that the channel does not contain any non-linearities such as those caused by traveling-wave tube (TWT) amplifiers or by power-efficient solid-state non-linear amplifiers. The non-linear effects of these microwave amplifiers on the performance of digitally modulated systems, such as AM to AM or AM to PM conversion, are presented in later chapters. A linear AWGN channel is a somewhat simplistic theoretical model for a microwave system. However, for deeply faded channels this model can represent real conditions if employed carefully. It is simple, mathematically tractable, and permits system comparison.

In addition to PAM baseband and PSK modulated systems, a number of other modulation techniques are in use in digital microwave systems. Correlative coding, also known as generalized duobinary or partial response, amplitude phase keying (APK), digital vestigial-sideband suppressed carrier (VSB-SC), quadrature digital AM (QAM), and pulse amplitude modulated FM are among these modulation techniques. Here the probability of error, $P(e)$, performance of these systems in an AWGN environment is presented even though the principles and the detailed description of these modulation techniques is given in later chapters. This is done to give the system designer a fast performance comparison of the various transmission methods.

## 3.1 PRINCIPLES OF PULSE-AMPLITUDE MODULATED (PAM) BASEBAND TRANSMISSION TECHNIQUES

We wish to transmit $f_b$ bits per second (b/s) in a baseband channel having a bandwidth of $B$ Hz. In most applications, the transmission system is considered to be more cost effective if, in a given bandwidth, more bits per second can be transmitted. If $f_b$, the transmission rate, is normalized to a bandwidth $B = 1$ Hz, then the system efficiency can be characterized in terms of transmitted *bits per second per hertz* (b/s/Hz). This is a convenient and frequently employed characterization of digital transmission systems.

In the *Nyquist theorems* on minimum bandwidth transmission systems it has been shown that it is possible to transmit $f_s$ independent symbols in a channel (low-pass filter) having a bandwidth of only $B = f_n = f_s/2$ Hz [3.3]. In binary transmission, one transmitted symbol contains only one information (source) bit; hence, the bit rate $f_b$ is the same as the symbol rate $f_s$; that is, $f_b = f_s$. In $M$-ary ($M$-level) transmission systems, each transmitted symbol contains $n$ information bits, where $n = \log_2 M$. The symbol rate $f_s$ is given by $f_s = f_b/n$. For example, if it is necessary to transmit the information content of an $f_b = 6$ Mb/s source then, theoretically, this could be accomplished by a binary transmission scheme in which the required baseband channel bandwidth equals $f_s/2 = f_b/2 = 3$ MHz. Alternatively, if an $M = 8$-level PAM technique is employed, then the minimum channel bandwidth is only $f_s/2 = f_b/6 = 1$ MHz. **(Solve Problem 3.1.)**

Symbols transmitted at a rate of $f_s$ symbols per second through a theoretical Nyquist channel, having a bandwidth of $f_s/2$ (hertz), attain their full value in the sampling instants [3.1 and 3.3]; thus, there is no performance degradation due to ideal Nyquist filtering. The required amplitude and phase characteristics of Nyquist channels having different $\alpha$ roll-off factors is shown in Figs. 3.1, 3.2, and 3.3. The amplitude response of the Nyquist channel $|H(f)|$ has different shapes for impulse and for pulse transmission. In theoretical system studies and computer

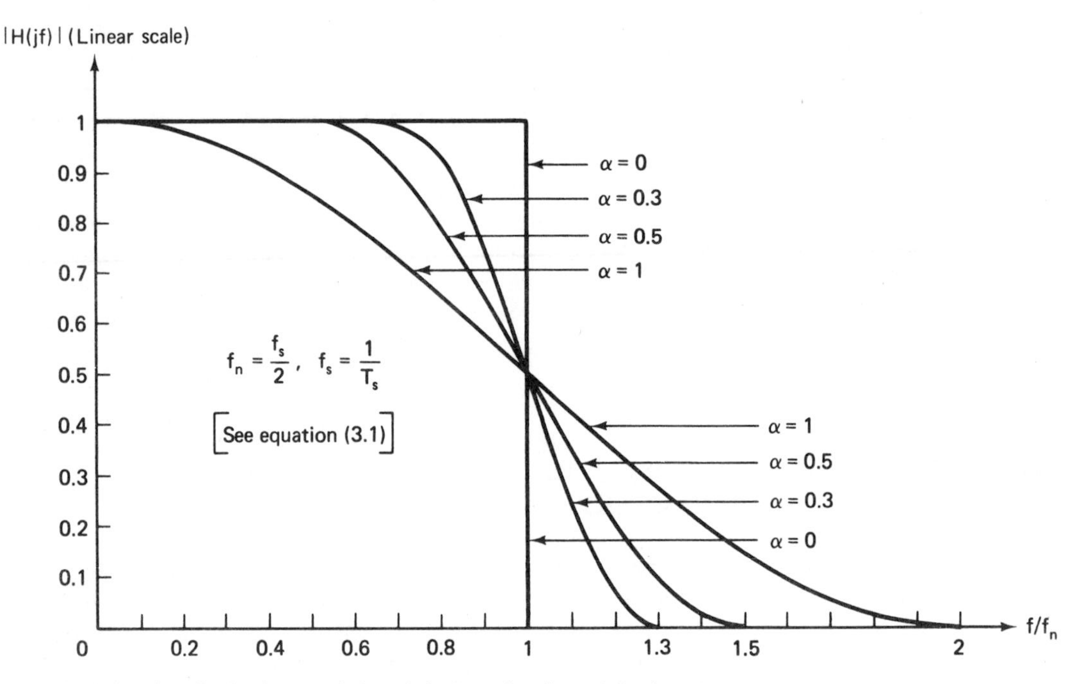


**Fig. 3.1.** Amplitude characteristics of the Nyquist channel for impulse transmission.

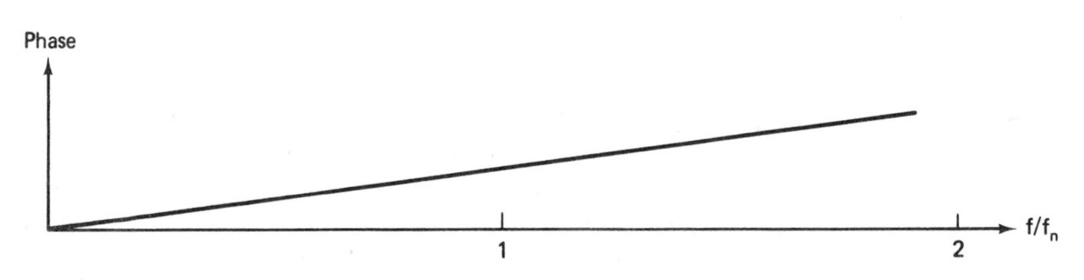


**Fig. 3.2.** Phase characteristics of an ideal Nyquist channel.

simulations, it is convenient to study the impulse response of the transmission channel. In most practical systems, rectangular pulses having unit symbol durations of $T_s = 1/f_s$ seconds are used instead of the theoretical, infinitesimally narrow impulses. For these pulses, the overall Nyquist channel shaping is shown in Fig. 3.3(a) on a linear amplitude scale and, in Fig. 3.3(b), in decibels on a logarithmic scale. **(Solve Problems 3.2 and 3.3.)**

As shown in Fig. 3.2 the phase of the theoretical Nyquist filter is linear, up to the frequency where $|H(f)| = 0\ (-\infty$ dB). However, for most practical applications it is sufficient to equalize the phase characteristics, up to the 10 to 15 dB attenuation point. By cascading the transmit filter, the channel attenuation, and the receive filter characteristics, the amplitude function of the complete Nyquist

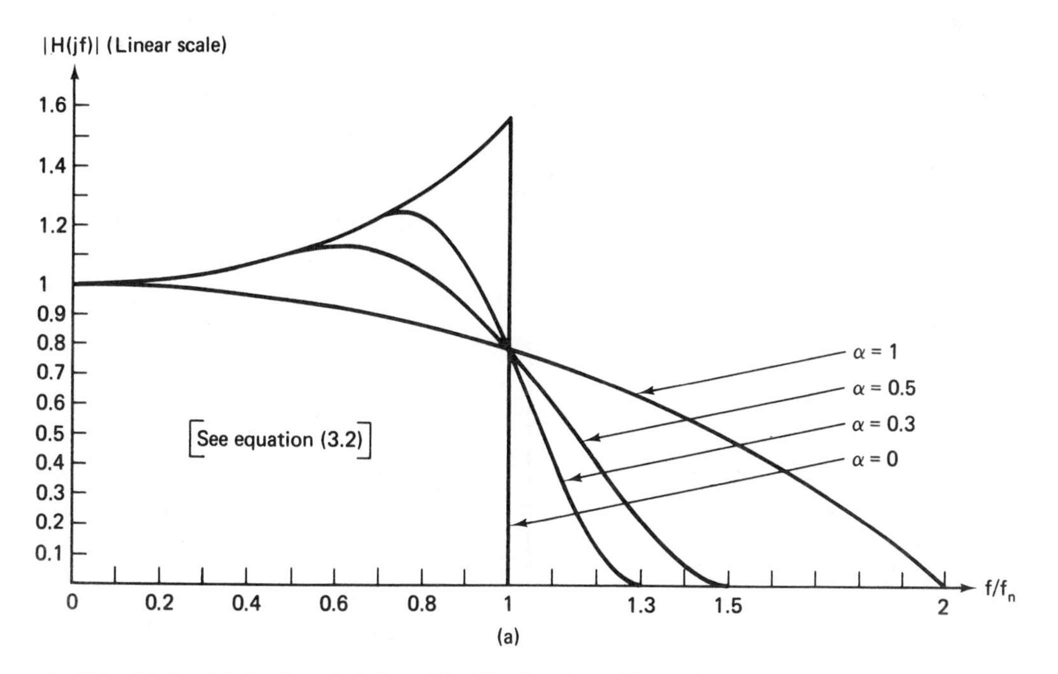


Fig. 3.3. (a) Amplitude characteristics of the Nyquist channel for pulse transmission.

channel is obtained. This theoretical channel (filter) model for infinitesimally narrow impulses is given by:

$$H(j\omega) = \begin{cases} 1, & \left[0 \leq \omega \leq \dfrac{\pi}{T_s}(1-\alpha)\right] \\ \cos^2\left\{\dfrac{T_s}{4\alpha}\left[\omega - \dfrac{\pi(1-\alpha)}{T_s}\right]\right\}, & \left[\dfrac{\pi}{T_s}(1-\alpha) \leq \omega \leq \dfrac{\pi}{T_s}(1+\alpha)\right. \\ 0, & \left[\omega \geq \dfrac{\pi}{T_s}(1+\alpha)\right. \end{cases} \quad (3.1)$$

where $\omega = 2\pi f$. For a practical rectangular random-data source having a rate of $f_s = 1/T_s$ symbols per second, the amplitude function of the Nyquist channel is given by

$$H(j\omega) = \begin{cases} \dfrac{(\omega T_s/2)}{\sin(\omega T_s/2)}, & \left[0 \leq \omega \leq \dfrac{\pi}{T_s}(1-\alpha)\right] \\ \dfrac{(\omega T_s/2)}{\sin(\omega T_s/2)}\cos^2\left\{\dfrac{T_s}{4\alpha}\left[\omega - \dfrac{\pi(1-\alpha)}{T_s}\right]\right\}, & \left[\dfrac{\pi}{T_s}(1-\alpha) \leq \omega \leq \dfrac{\pi}{T_s}(1+\alpha)\right] \\ 0, & \left[\omega > \dfrac{\pi}{T_s}(1+\alpha)\right] \end{cases} \quad (3.2)$$

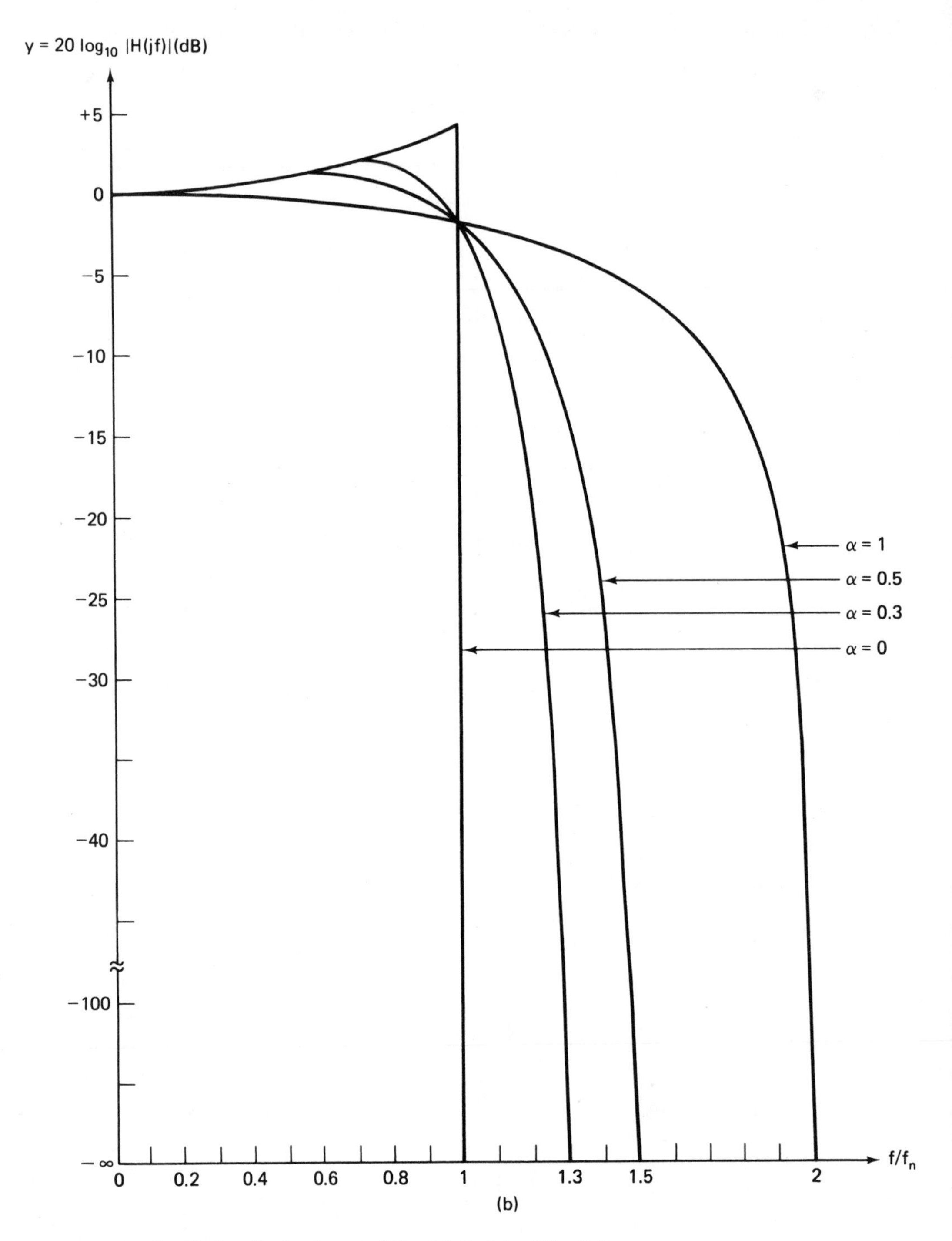


**Fig. 3.3. (cont.)** (b) Amplitude characteristics (plotted in dB) of the Nyquist channel for pulse transmission.

The design of a minimum bandwidth $\alpha = 0$ channel would require an infinite number of filter sections, thus making it impractical. The goal of hardware designers is to design channel filters which approximate, the *raised-cosine* characteristics of the Nyquist channel, equation (3.2), and have the smallest possible bandwidth. With present-day technology an approximation of the $\alpha = 0.3$ filters requiring only a 30% excess Nyquist bandwidth is feasible [3.1]. In a normalized channel ($B = 1$ Hz), having an $\alpha = 0$ roll-off factor, it is possible to transmit at a rate of 2 symbols per second; that is, for binary transmission systems this rate is equal to 2 bits/second/hertz. If the roll-off factor is $\alpha = 0.3$, then the transmission rate is $2: 1.3 \approx 1.54$ b/s/Hz. Let $v_i(t)$, the input signal to an ideal minimum bandwidth low-pass filter (LPF) be a balanced, random, binary non-return-to-zero (NRZ) sequence, as shown in Fig. 3.4. Then the output signal $v_0(t)$ will reach, in the sam-

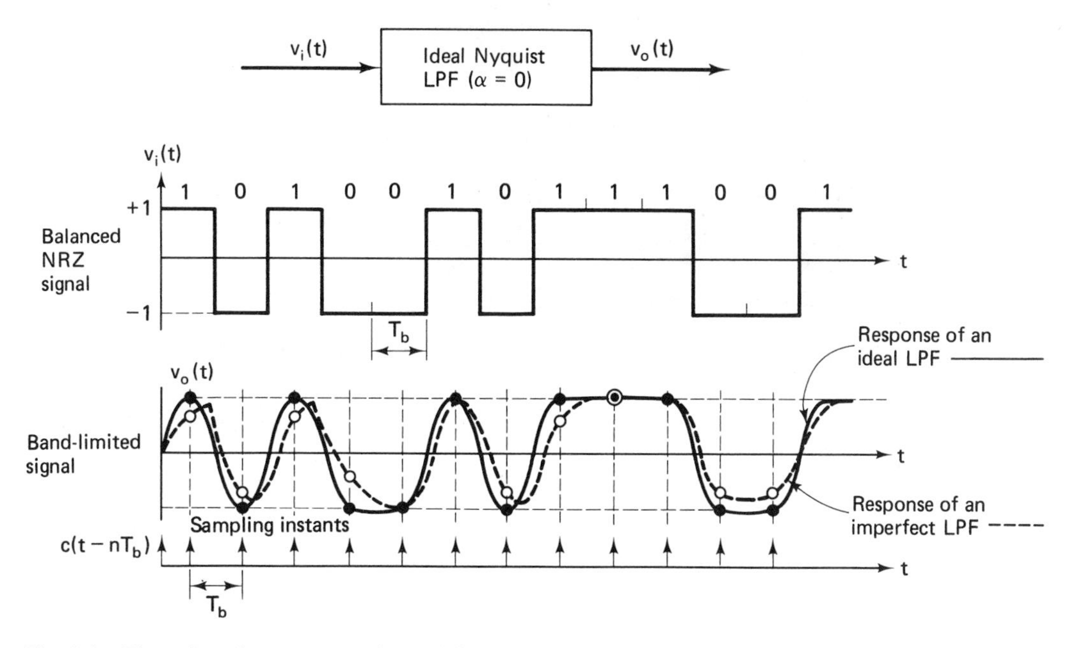


**Fig. 3.4.** Time domain response of a minimum bandwidth ($\alpha = 0$) Nyquist LPF.

pling instants $c(t - nT_b)$, its full value for each transmitted bit. Thus, this filter does not introduce intersymbol interference (ISI) at the sampling instants. However, if the LPF is imperfect, that is, if it does not have the theoretical phase and amplitude characteristics such as shown in Figs. 3.2 and 3.3, the output response might then be as shown by the dashed line in Fig. 3.4. At the sampling instants this signal does not always attain its maximum value. Whether this distorted output attains its maximum depends on the value of the previous bits. Thus, the imperfect filter introduces ISI.

A convenient way to evaluate the channel imperfections is by means of the *eye diagram*, or *eye pattern*. This pattern is obtained from an oscilloscope if a signal, such as $v_0(t)$ shown in Fig. 3.4, is fed to the vertical input of the oscilloscope. The sampling clock $c(t - nT_b)$ is fed to the external trigger of the oscilloscope, and the horizontal time base is set approximately equal to the symbol duration. The inherent persistence of the cathode-ray tube will display the superposed segments of the $v_0(t)$ signal. As an illustrative example, the measured eye diagram of an $f_b = 45$ Mb/s random NRZ signal transmitted through a seventh-order phase-equalized elliptic filter, which approximates the theoretical Nyquist LPF having a roll-off factor $\alpha = 0.3$, is shown in Fig. 3.5. The measured 3 dB cut-

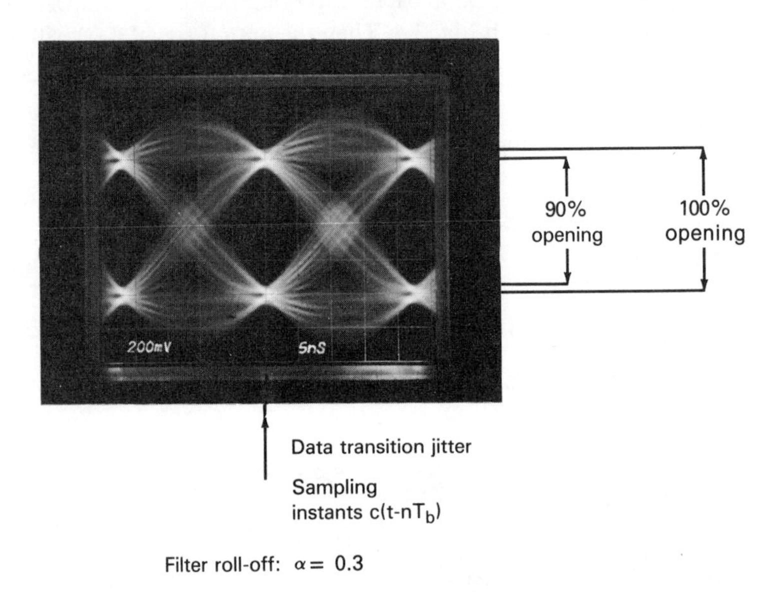


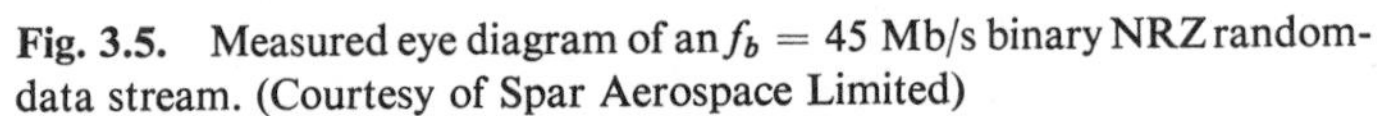

**Fig. 3.5.** Measured eye diagram of an $f_b = 45$ Mb/s binary NRZ random-data stream. (Courtesy of Spar Aerospace Limited)

off frequency of this filter is $f_n = 22.5$ MHz, whereas the out-of-band attenuation is more than 35 db for all frequencies above $1.3\,f_n$, that is, 29.25 MHz. From Fig. 3.5 it is seen that at the center of the eye (sampling instant) the opening is about 90%; thus, there is only a minor ISI degradation due to filter imperfections. The 90% eye opening corresponds to a $20 \log_{10} 90/100 = 0.9$ dB ISI degradation. The small degradation in the eye diagram is due to the non-ideal Nyquist amplitude and phase characteristics of the filter. This $\alpha = 0.3$ roll-off filter was designed by the engineers of Spar Aerospace Limited.

When systems engineers specify a new digital transmission system they have to predict the system degradations caused by ISI prior to the existence of the hardware. These degradations are most frequently predicted by computer simulations [3.1 and 3.9]. Figure 3.6 shows the computer-generated eye diagram for an

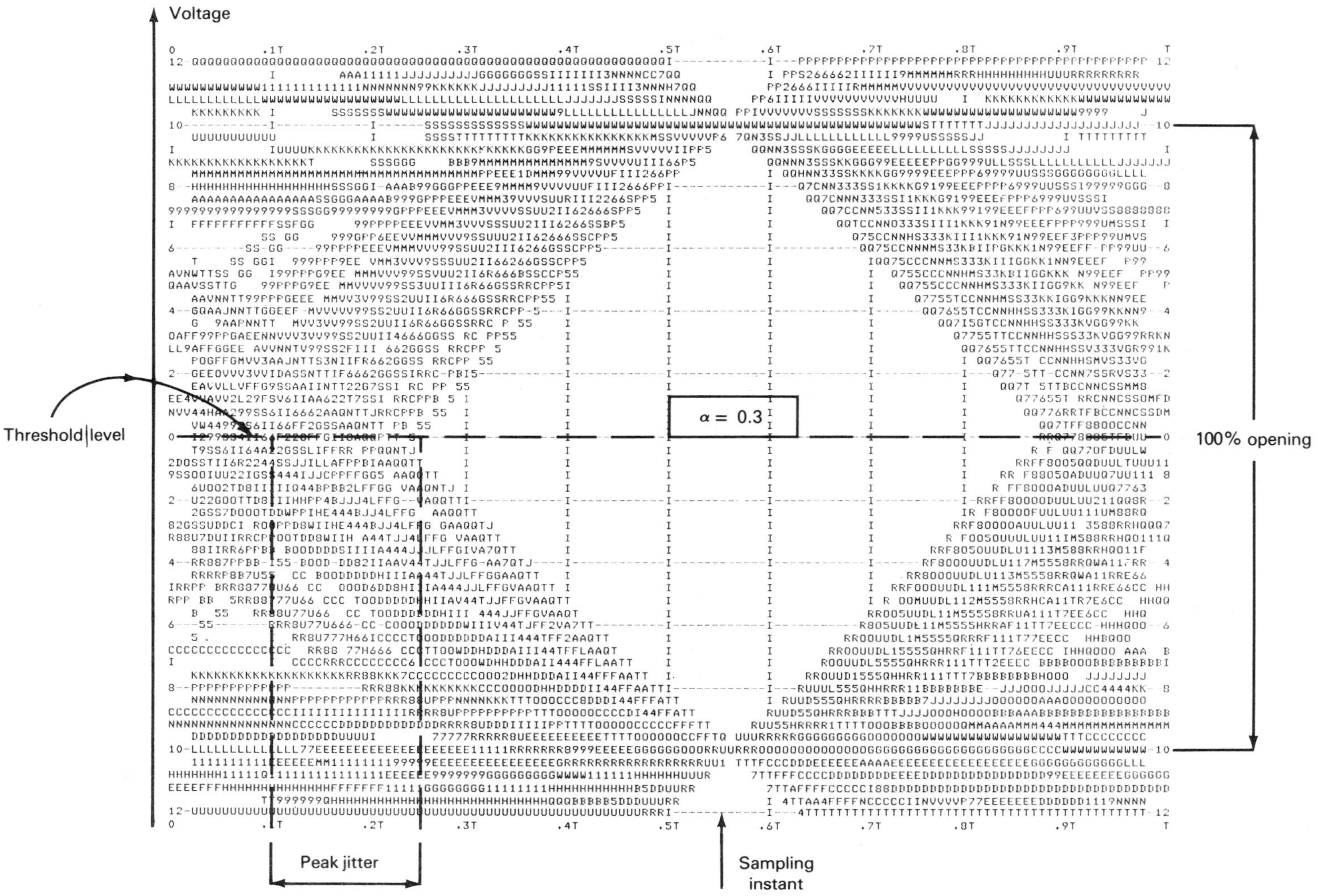

Voltage

Threshold level

$\alpha = 0.3$

100% opening

Peak jitter

Sampling instant

**Fig. 3.6.** Computer-generated eye diagram of the linear phase $\alpha = 0.3$ filter shown in Fig. 3.3.

*ideal* linear phase filter with $\alpha = 0.3$. The simulated filter has an $x/\sin x$ amplitude equalizer [Fig. 3.3(a) and equation (3.2)]; thus, it is the ideal Nyquist filter for pulse transmission. In this computer simulation the random sequence of $T_b$ duration pulses has been transmitted at a rate of $f_b = 1/T_b = 45$ Mb/s through a low-pass filter having an $f_n = 22.5$ MHz Nyquist frequency. The ISI caused by this filter is negligible, but the *timing jitter* is significant. The timing jitter shown in Fig. 3.6 is converted in the symbol-timing recovery circuit to sampling clock jitter [3.12]. The propagation of this timing jitter and its effect on multi-section microwave systems is studied in Chapter 9. The computer-generated eye diagram (Fig. 3.6) resembles the measured eye diagram shown in Fig. 3.5. Figure 3.7 shows the eye diagram of the wider roll-off $\alpha = 1$ Nyquist filter. In the sampling instant both the $\alpha = 0.3$ and the $\alpha = 1$ filters are 100% open. The $\alpha = 0.3$ filter has a maximal eye opening for only a small percentage of the bit duration time; the $\alpha = 1$ filter has a wider maximum. This means that the more bandwidth-efficient $\alpha = 0.3$ channel will be more sensitive to clock timing jitter and to a drift of the sampling instant. This drift may be caused by temperature variation or equipment misalignment.

It is rather difficult and costly to design bandwidth-efficient (e.g., $\alpha = 0.3$) Nyquist filters. If the filter designer is successful in designing the required amplitude and phase characteristics of a nearly ideal Nyquist channel, this channel will still have significant data transition jitter (see Figs. 3.5 and 3.6). In a search for simpler, cost-effective hardware designs, the non-linear switching filter was developed. With a family of these filters, known as *Feher's non-linear processor* (*filter*), *band-limited signals which do not contain ISI and are jitter-free* have been generated. The detailed design guidelines and applications of these simple but powerful filters are described in [3.14, 3.15, 3.16]. Figure 3.8 illustrates the principle of operation of one of these filters.

For a $-1$ to $+1$ transition of the unfiltered NRZ input signal, the rising segment of a sinusoid is switched on (connected to the transmission medium). For a $+1$ to $-1$ transition, the falling segment of a sinusoid is switched on. The 0° and the 180° reference sinusoidal generators, shown in Fig. 3.8(b), provide the required sinusoidal waves. For a continuous sequence of 1's or $-1$'s (more than one input bit without transition) a positive or negative segment is switched on. The decision logic provides the switch position control signals. Figure 3.9 shows the measured bandwidth-efficient, jitter- and ISI-free output eye diagram and spectrum.

The eye diagram of a filter with a non-linear phase response is shown in Fig. 3.10. The diagram shows an eye closure of 25% (eye opening 75%). The peak degradation due to ISI is approximately $20 \log \frac{75}{100} = -2.5$ dB. **(Solve Problems 3.4 and 3.5.)**

The normalized *power spectrum* density of equiprobable $p(0) = p(1) = 0.5$ binary NRZ random data is derived in Section 2.6. This spectrum is given by

$$S(f) = A^2 T_b \left(\frac{\sin \pi T_b f}{\pi T_b f}\right)^2 \tag{3.3}$$

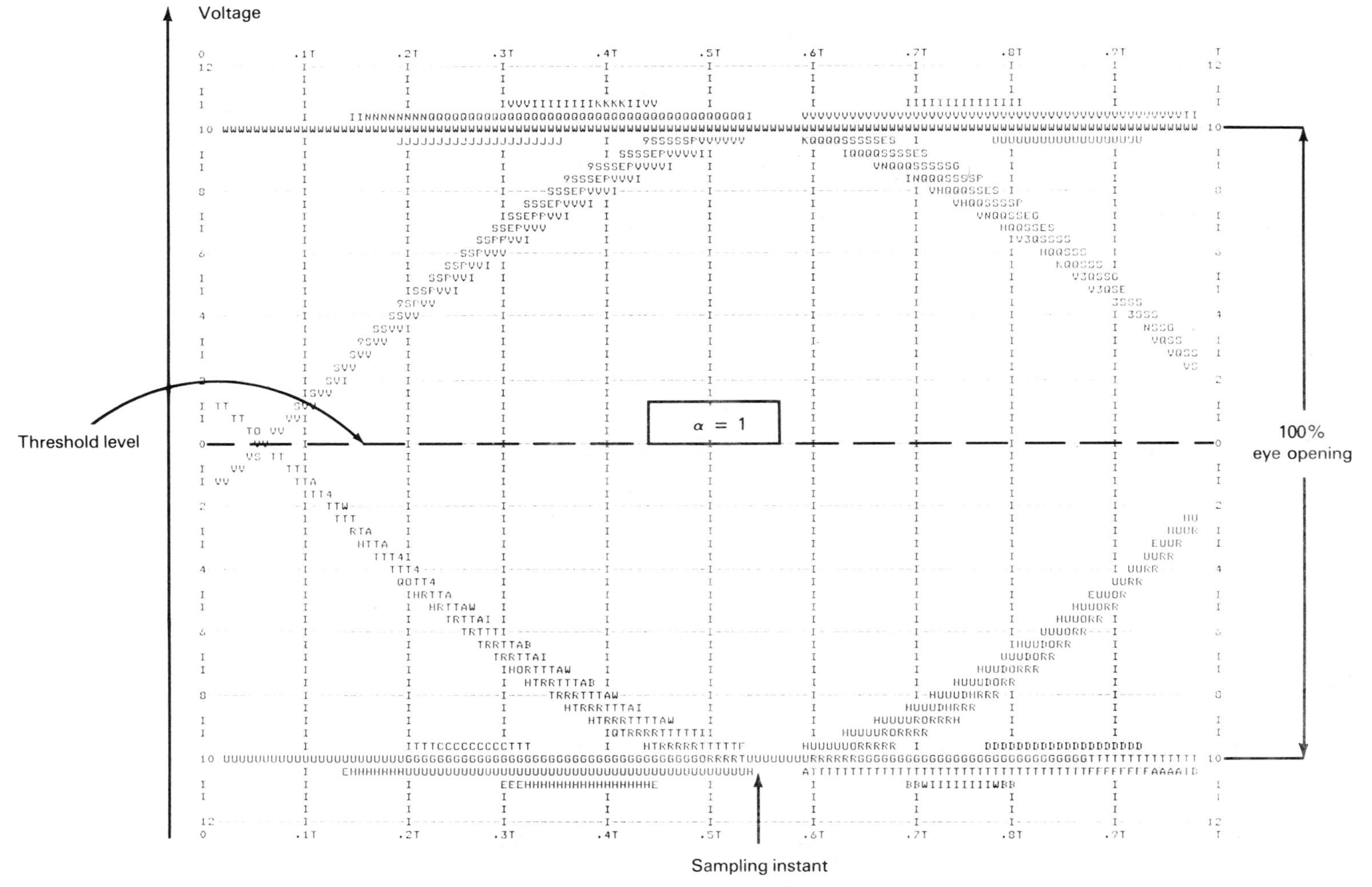

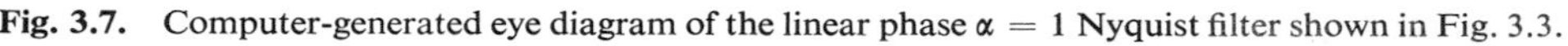

**Fig. 3.7.** Computer-generated eye diagram of the linear phase $\alpha = 1$ Nyquist filter shown in Fig. 3.3.

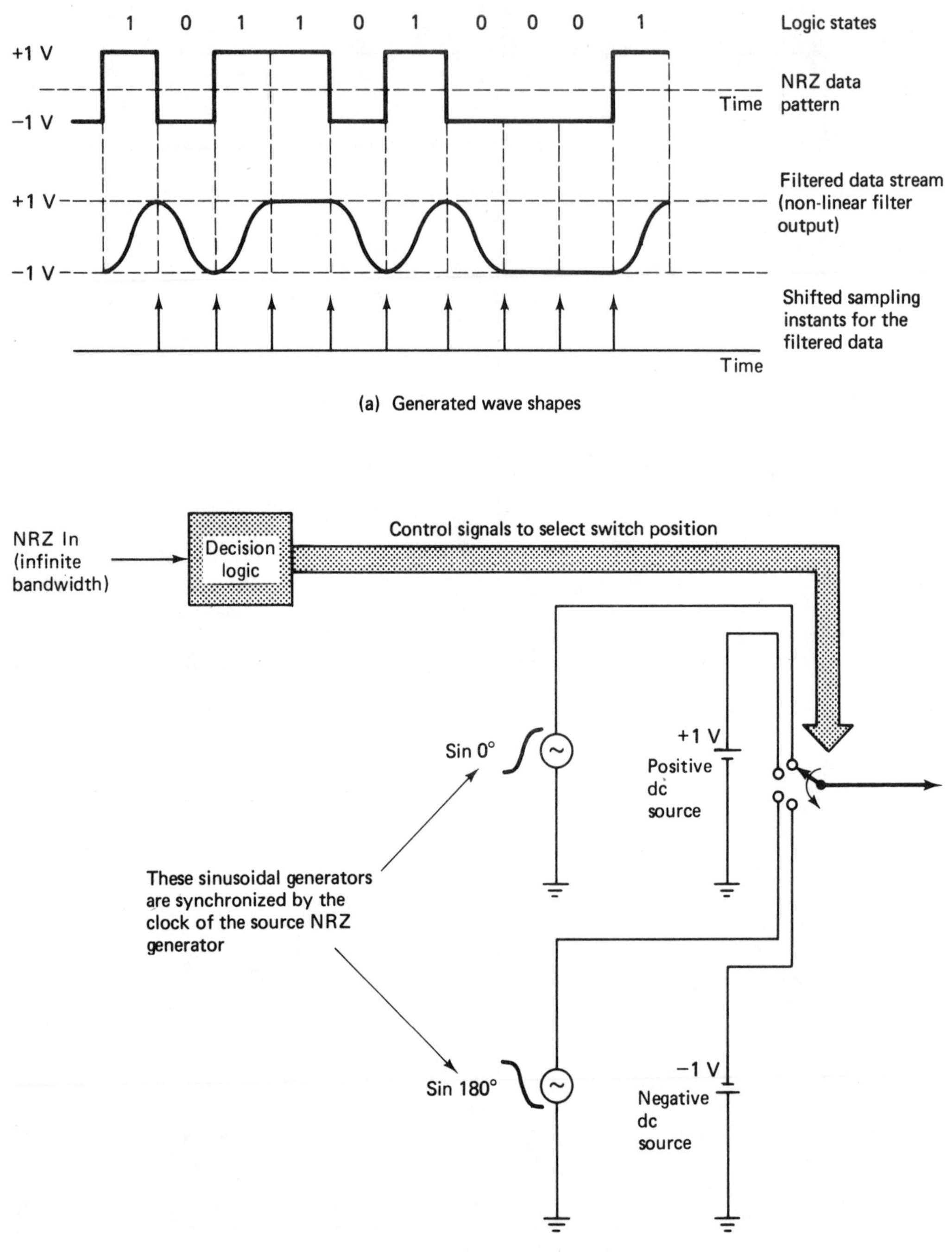


**Fig. 3.8.** Principle of operation of Feher's bandwidth-efficient ISI and jitter-free non-linear filter. (After References [3.14, 3.15 and 3.16])

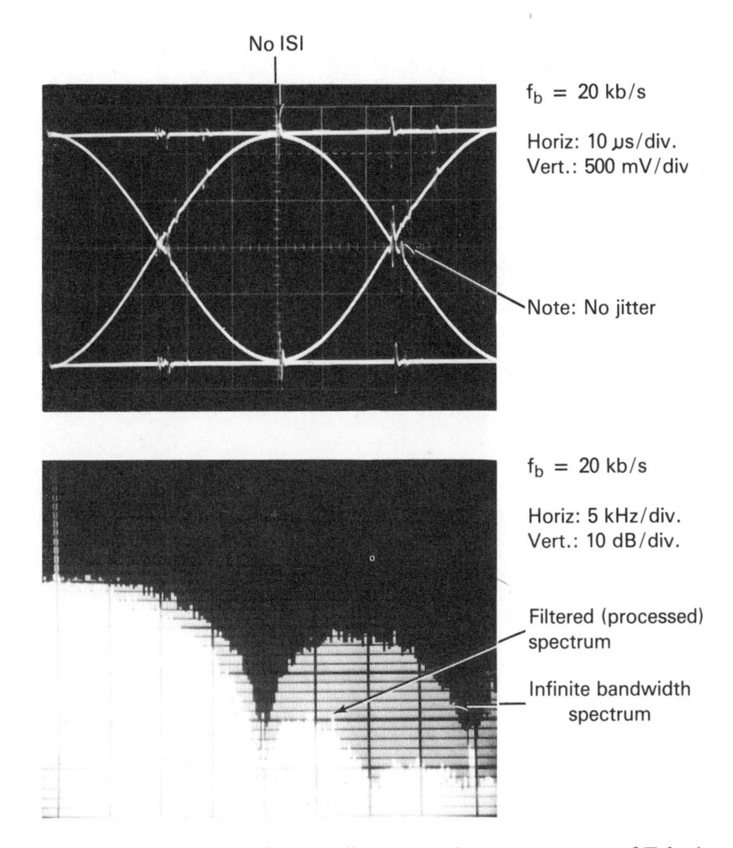


**Fig. 3.9.** ISI and jitter-free eye diagrams and power spectrum of Feher's non-linear filter.

where $A$ is the peak voltage, and $T_b$ is the bit duration ($T_b = 1/f_b$). Figure 3.11 shows a measured 45 Mb/s infinite bandwidth NRZ spectrum and a band-limited spectrum. The same $\alpha = 0.3$ seventh-order filter used to obtain Fig. 3.5 was employed in these measurements. **(Solve Problems 3.6 and 3.7.)**

For many applications it is necessary to transmit at a rate of more than 2 b/s/Hz. A conversion from binary NRZ to multi-level pulse amplitude modulated (PAM) signals, such as shown in Fig. 3.12, will achieve this goal. An NRZ (2-level) to 4-level PAM converter, by pairing the incoming bits, generates an $M =$ 4-level signal. Each 4-level symbol contains 2 bits of information. The symbol duration $T_s$ of the output PAM signal is double that of the incoming bit; thus, $T_s = 2T_b$. The spectrum of this signal is compressed by a factor of two. Based on the Nyquist theorem, it is theoretically possible to transmit, without ISI, 2 symbols/s/Hz. As each symbol contains 2 bits of information this means that with $M = 4$-level PAM it is possible to transmit 4 b/s/Hz. Each $M = 8$-level PAM symbol contains 3 bits of information; thus, it is possible with this scheme to transmit at a rate of three times of that of NRZ, that is, 6 b/s/Hz.

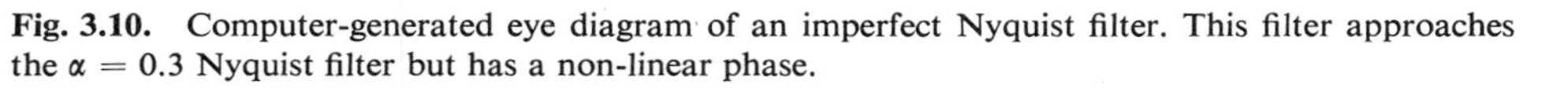


**Fig. 3.10.** Computer-generated eye diagram of an imperfect Nyquist filter. This filter approaches the $\alpha = 0.3$ Nyquist filter but has a non-linear phase.

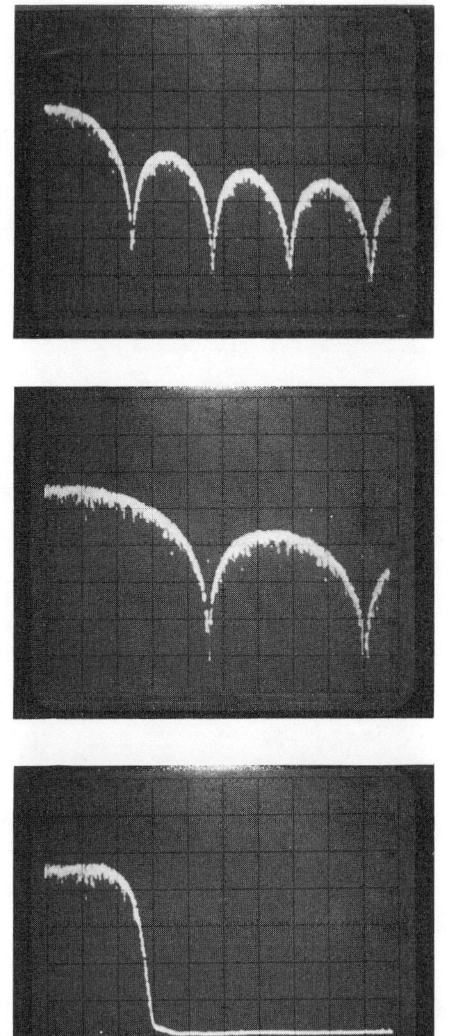

(a) H: 20 MHz/div.,
V: 10 dB/div.

Infinite bandwidth.

(b) H: 10 MHz/div.,
V: 10 dB/div.

Infinite bandwidth same as photograph (a) but expanded to 10 MHz/div.

(c) H: 10 MHz/div.,
V: 10 dB/div.

Band-limited with an $\alpha = 0.3$ filter.

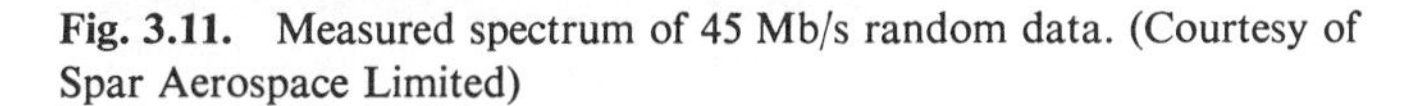

**Fig. 3.11.** Measured spectrum of 45 Mb/s random data. (Courtesy of Spar Aerospace Limited)

The eye diagram of an $M = 4$-level PAM data stream, having a transmission rate of $f_b = 200$ Mb/s, corresponding to a symbol rate of $f_s = f_b/2 = 100$ M symbols per second = 100 M Baud is shown in Fig. 3.13. Two independent (in phase $I$ and quadrature $Q$) $M = 4$-level eye diagrams are illustrated. In Chapter 6 (Fig. 6.10), it will be shown that these eye diagrams correspond to the demodulated baseband eye diagrams of an $M = 16$-ary modem. The combined transmission rate of the $I$ and $Q$ channels is 400 Mb/s [3.17]. **(Solve Problem 3.8.)**

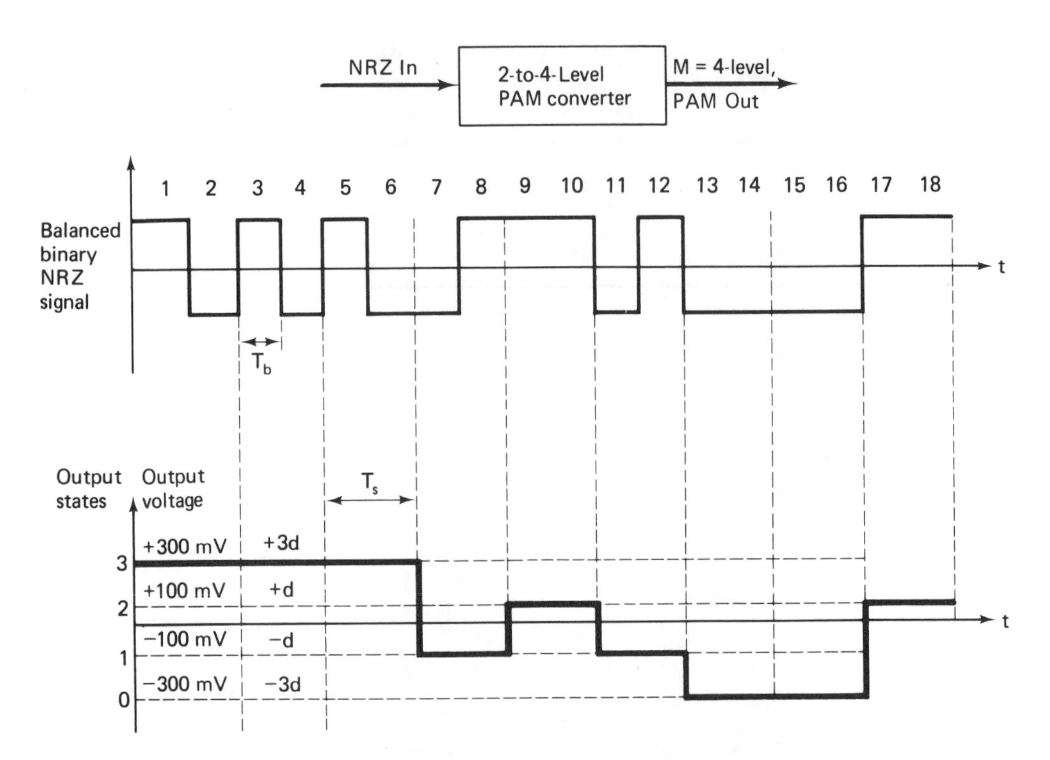


Fig. 3.12. 2- and 4-level random PAM baseband signals.

Fig. 3.13. Measured eye diagram of a 100 M Baud (200 Mb/s). $M =$ 4-level PAM data stream. (Courtesy of H. Ishio, Nippon Telegraph and Telephone Public Corporation)

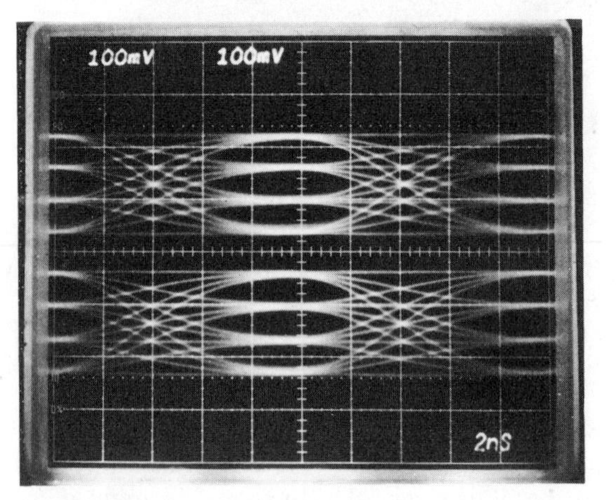


Vert.:
100 mV/div.
Horiz:
2 ns/div.

## 3.2 $P(e)$ PERFORMANCE OF $M$-LEVEL PAM AND GENERALIZED DUOBINARY (PARTIAL RESPONSE) BASEBAND SYSTEMS

In $M$-level baseband transmission an error occurs if at the sampling instant $\eta$ the noise exceeds in amplitude the distance from the nominal received level to the nearest decision threshold level $d$; that is, $|\eta| > d$. The *nominal* signal level is the value of the sampled received signal when there is no intersymbol interference or noise in the transmission system. The two outside levels are in error only if the additive noise sample has an opposite polarity to that of the signal. Thus, the probability of error is

$$P(e) = \left(1 - \frac{1}{M}\right), \qquad P(|\eta| > d) \tag{3.4}$$

where $P(|\eta| > d)$ is the numerical value of the probability distribution function of the noise sample for $|\eta| > d$. The $\left(1 - \frac{1}{M}\right)$ factor is required to weight, for the two outside levels, the probability of noise exceeding $d$.

The $P(e)$ for the additive white gaussian (AWGN) channel having a noise density $N_0$ is derived next.

The nominal received levels are equally likely to assume any of the $M$-possible levels. These levels are given by $\pm d, \pm 3d, \pm 5d, \ldots, \pm(M-1)d$ and are illustrated in Fig. 3.14. In most practical systems symbols occurring at different times are statistically independent. For these systems the average ac symbol power is computed from equation (2.13), which, for our discrete PAM signal, is given by

$$\begin{aligned}\bar{a}^2 &= \sum_{m=1}^{M} x_m^2 p_m(x_m) \\ &= \frac{2}{M} \sum_{i=1}^{M/2} [d(2i-1)]^2 = \frac{d^2}{3}(M^2 - 1)\end{aligned} \tag{3.5}$$

In PAM transmission systems the transmit and receive filters are frequently partitioned equally. If the channel characteristics are specified by equation (3.1) and the channel is normalized to have a 1 Hz bandwidth, then the receive filter is given by $\sqrt{H(j\omega)}$, where $H(j\omega)$ is the overall Nyquist transfer function. In this case the variance of the noise voltage at the input of the threshold comparators is given by

$$\sigma^2 = \frac{N_0}{2\pi} \int_{-\infty}^{\infty} |\sqrt{H(j\omega)}|^2 \, d\omega = N_0 \tag{3.6}$$

The probability of error can be expressed by

$$P(e) = 2\left(1 - \frac{1}{M}\right) Q\left(\frac{d}{\sigma}\right) \tag{3.7}$$

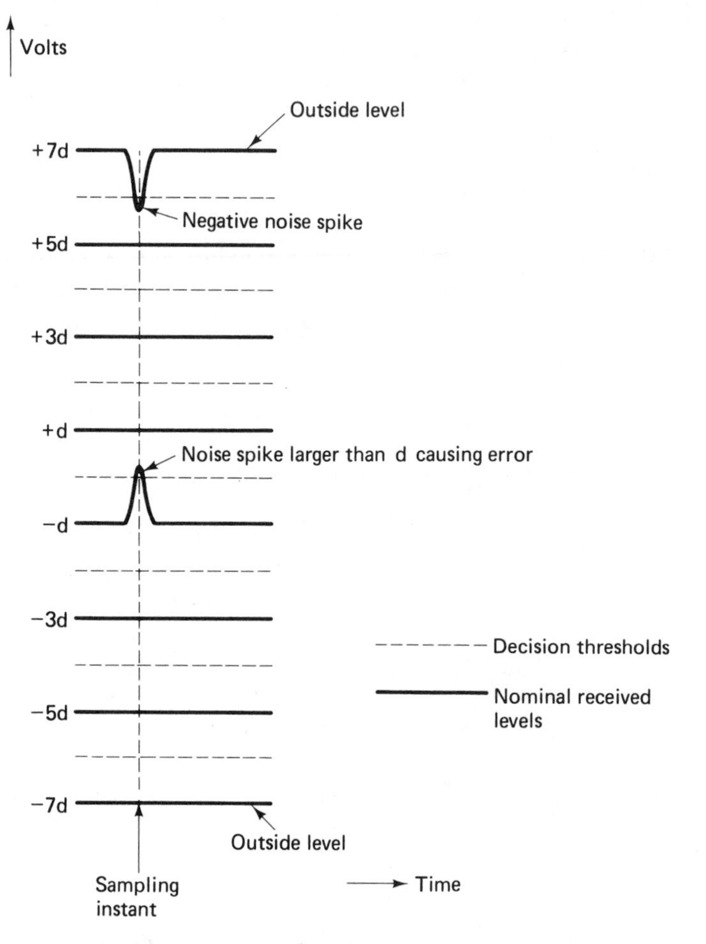


**Fig. 3.14.** Nominal received signal levels and decision threshold levels in an $M = 8$-level PAM baseband system.

or, in terms of average signal-to-noise ($S/N$) power ratio, by

$$P(e) = 2\left(1 - \frac{1}{M}\right)Q\left(\sqrt{\frac{3}{M^2 - 1}\frac{S}{N}}\right) \tag{3.8}$$

where $M = 2, 4, 8 \ldots,$

$$Q(x) = \frac{1}{\sqrt{2\pi}}\int_x^\infty e^{-t^2/2}\,dt \tag{3.9}$$

In equation (3.8) the $S/N$ term represents the average signal-to-noise power ratio in the Nyquist band, that is, in one-half of the symbol rate band. The $Q(x)$ function, equation (3.9), is the complement of the normal cumulative distribution function, shown in graphical form in Fig. 2.3(b).

The $P(e)$ performance of $M$-level PAM systems is shown in Fig. 3.15. The solid lines represent the theoretical curves computed from equations (3.8) and (3.9); the dashed line illustrates the measured results for an $f_b = 10$ Mb/s rate $M = 2$-level baseband transmission system. The dashed line is shifted approximately 3 dB to the right when compared with the ideal $M = 2$-level curve. This performance degradation has been caused by ISI.

The $M = 4$-level PAM system requires an 8 dB higher $S/N$ ratio than the $M = 2$-level system, whereas the $M = 8$-level system requires a 14 dB higher $S/N$ ratio than the $M = 2$-level system. By increasing the number of transmission levels $M$, a higher spectrum efficiency is achieved, but unfortunately a considerably higher $S/N$ ratio is required to attain the same $P(e)$ as in binary systems. **(Solve Problem 3.9.)**

Figure 3.16 shows the spectrum efficiency, in bits/second/hertz, (b/s/Hz) of baseband transmission systems as a function of the available root-mean-square $S/N$ ratio. The theoretical curve given by

$$R = \log_2 \left(1 + \frac{S}{N}\right) \tag{3.10}$$

represents the theoretical *Shannon limit* [3.10]. Based on Shannon's work, it should be possible to find coding and modulation schemes which would approach his theoretical curve, which represents the lowest possible $S/N$ requirement for error-free, that is, $P(e) = 10^{-\infty}$ transmission.

For the same b/s/Hz efficiency, as given by the Shannon limit, the PAM baseband system having $M = 2, 4, 8, 16, \ldots$ number of levels for a $P(e) = 10^{-4}$ and $P(e) = 10^{-8}$ performance requires considerably higher $S/N$ ratios. In order to allow comparison with Dr. Lender's duobinary and generalized duobinary (partial response) baseband systems, the performance of these systems is shown with dashed lines in Figs. 3.15 and 3.16. Partial response systems are described in more detail in Chapter 7. From the curves presented in Fig. 3.16 we conclude that, for all $M$-level PAM and partial response systems, a $P(e) = 10^{-8}$ performance requires approximately a 4 dB higher $S/N$ ratio than for a $P(e) = 10^{-4}$. The information presented in Fig. 3.16 is intended to provide data to the system designer for a fast system comparison, based on bit efficiency in a 1 Hz normalized channel bandwidth; Fig. 3.15 presents detailed $P(e) = f(S/N)$ curves. **(Solve Problem 3.10.)**

## 3.3 PRINCIPLES OF PHASE SHIFT KEYED (PSK) SYSTEMS

The principles and the most important performance characteristics of baseband transmission systems were presented in the previous section. Here we concentrate on modulated systems and, in particular, we describe the principle of operation of an $M = 4$-ary (4-phase) phase shift keyed (PSK) modulator and demodulator (modem). This modem is widely used in digital terrestrial microwave and satellite systems. It is essential, prior to the study of more complex systems, to understand

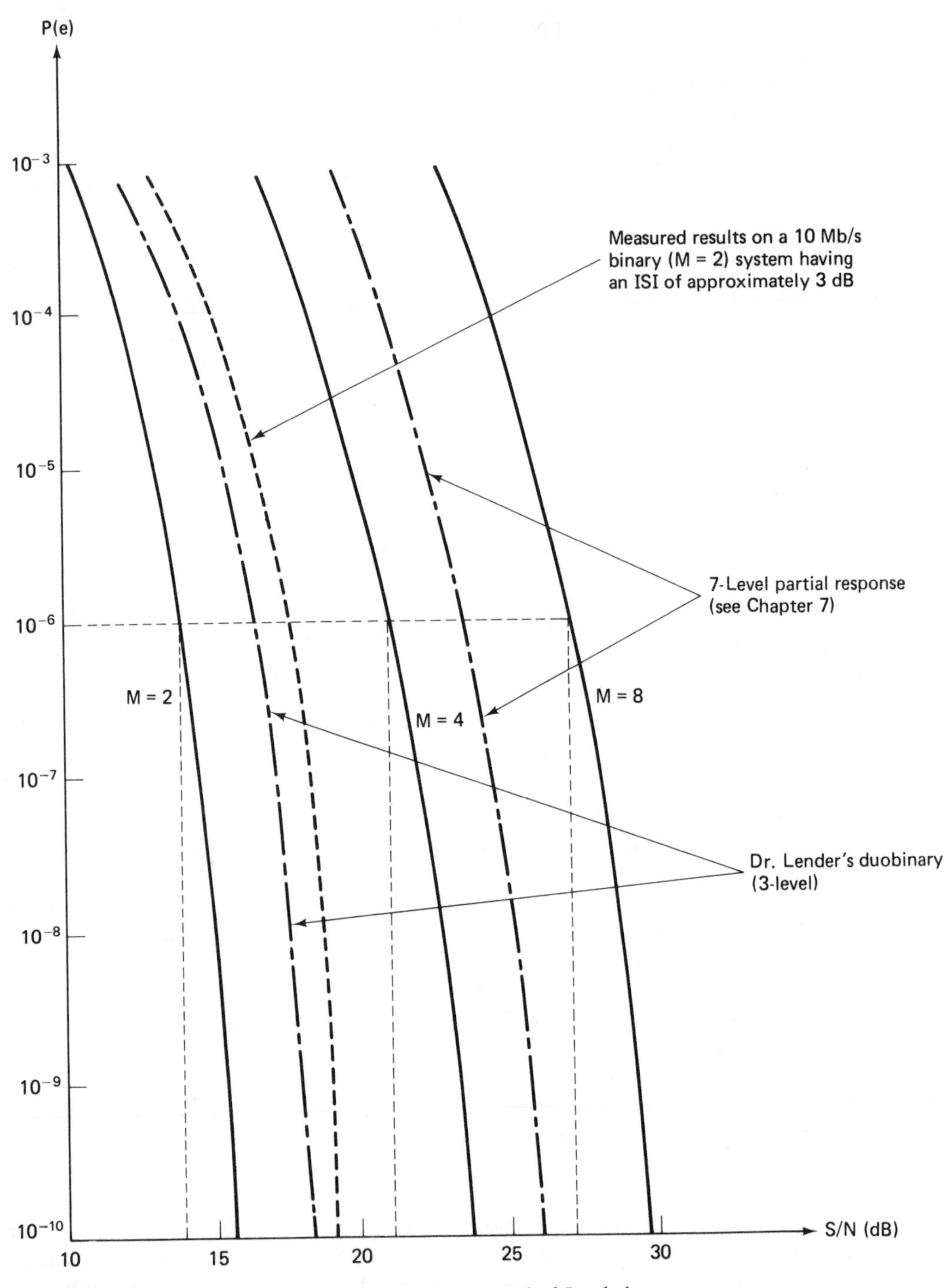


**Fig. 3.15.** Probability of error, $P(e)$, of $M$-level PAM and of Lender's generalized duobinary (partial response) baseband systems. The rms $S/N$ is measured in the Nyquist bandwidth, after the receive LPF, at the regenerator input. Dashed lines show the measured results of an $L = 2$ binary 10 Mb/s system.

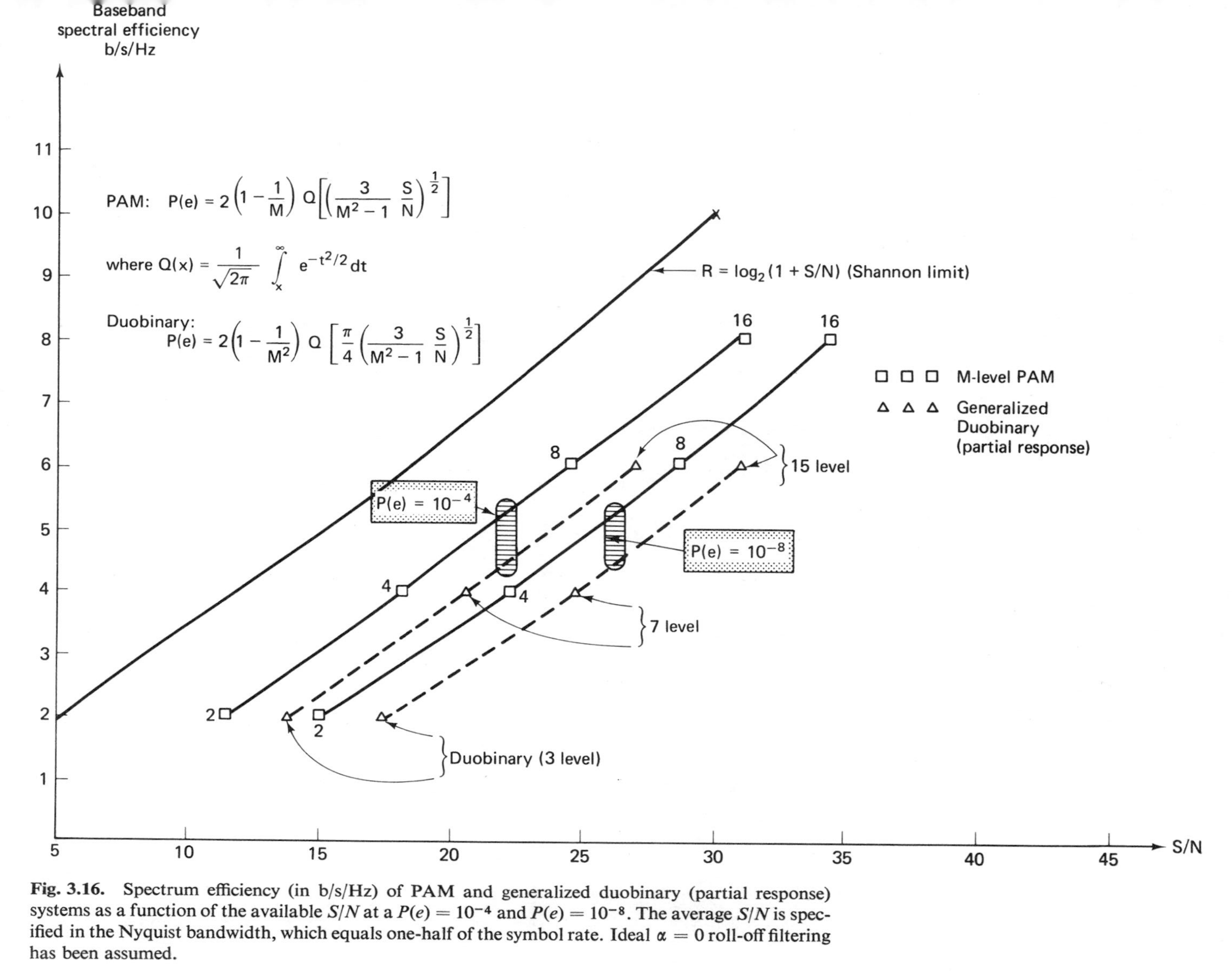


**Fig. 3.16.** Spectrum efficiency (in b/s/Hz) of PAM and generalized duobinary (partial response) systems as a function of the available $S/N$ at a $P(e) = 10^{-4}$ and $P(e) = 10^{-8}$. The average $S/N$ is specified in the Nyquist bandwidth, which equals one-half of the symbol rate. Ideal $\alpha = 0$ roll-off filtering has been assumed.

the theory of operation of this fundamental modulation technique. The description of modems having a higher number of signal states and employing combined amplitude and phase modulation methods, such as in an amplitude phase keyed (APK) system, is presented in later chapters.

The block diagram of a conventional 4-phase PSK modulator—known as a *quadrature*, or *quaternary*, *PSK* (*QPSK*) *modulator*—is shown in Fig. 3.17. The

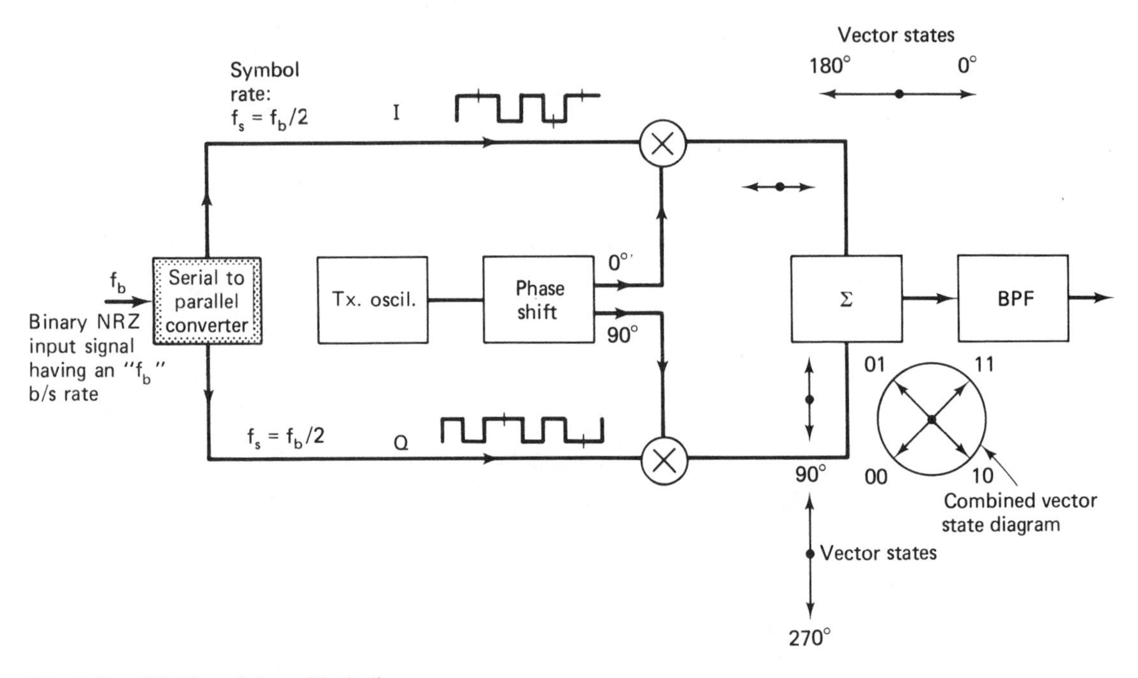

**Fig. 3.17.** QPSK modulator block diagram.

serial-to-parallel converter transforms the incoming $f_b$-rate binary stream into two, parallel, $f_s = f_b/2$ data rates. The baseband spectrum of the parallel $I$ and $Q$ baseband branches has the same shape as that of the incoming data stream, but as the symbol rate of these branches is one-half of the bit rate ($f_s = f_b/2$), the width of these lobes becomes one-half of the original $f_b$-rate lobe. The transmit oscillator generates the unmodulated carrier frequency, which is passed through a 0° and 90° phase splitter. The $I$ and $Q$ baseband NRZ symbol streams are time domain multiplied by the carrier signals. This multiplication in the time domain results in frequency translation (convolution); that is, the baseband signals modulate the carrier in a double-sideband-suppressed carrier (DSB-SC) mode.

The baseband signals are symmetrical and can take only the normalized $+1$ or $-1$ voltage values, as illustrated by the $v_i(t)$ signal in Fig. 3.4. Multiplication of a carrier wave $\cos w_c t$ by a "1" symbol state, which corresponds to a normalized $+1$ V value, does not change the phase of the unmodulated carrier. If a logic "0" symbol state, which corresponds to a normalized $-1$ V value, is multiplied by the cos $w_c t$ carrier, then we obtain $-1 \cos w_c t = \cos(w_c t + 180°)$, that is, a 180° phase shift. An alternate sequence of ones and zeros shifts the carrier instantaneously from 0° to 180°. The modulated wave at the output of the $I$ channel multiplier (mixer) is a binary phase shift keyed (BPSK) signal. The scenario of the $Q$ channel, Fig. 3.17, is similar to the $I$ channel with the exception that the unmodulated carrier frequency is now shifted by 90° through the phase shifter network. The modulated $I$ channel and the modulated $Q$ channel BPSK signals are said to be *orthogonal* because there is a 90° shift in the $I$ and $Q$ modulated path. After linear addition of the corresponding BPSK vector-state space diagrams, a four-phase PSK (QPSK) signal is obtained. The spectral shape of this QPSK signal is identical to the spectral shape of the individual binary PSK signals.

The QPSK signal might be bandlimited by the transmit band-pass filter. Based on the equivalent performance of linearly modulated systems with that of baseband systems, it can be shown, [3.1 and 3.4], that the minimum bandwidth of an ideal double-sideband brick-wall Nyquist band-pass filter, which will cause no ISI in QPSK transmission, equals one-half of the bit rate ($f_b/2$). This means that an ideal *minimum bandwidth QPSK modem can transmit 2b/s/Hz.* For example, if it is necessary to transmit at a data rate of $f_b = 90$ Mb/s, then the minimum theoretical transmission bandwidth requirement of a QPSK system is 45 MHz. **(Solve Problem 3.11.)**

The block diagram of a QPSK demodulator is shown in Fig. 3.18. The receive BPF eliminates the out-of-band noise and the adjacent channel interference. The filtered modulated wave is split into the $I$ and $Q$ main demodulation paths and the carrier recovery path. The carrier recovery subsystem is essential to obtain from the modulated band-limited received signal an unmodulated carrier wave which tracks the frequency and phase variation of the transmitter and of the channel. A number of carrier recovery subsystem design techniques have been described by

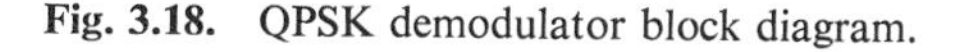
**Fig. 3.18.** QPSK demodulator block diagram.

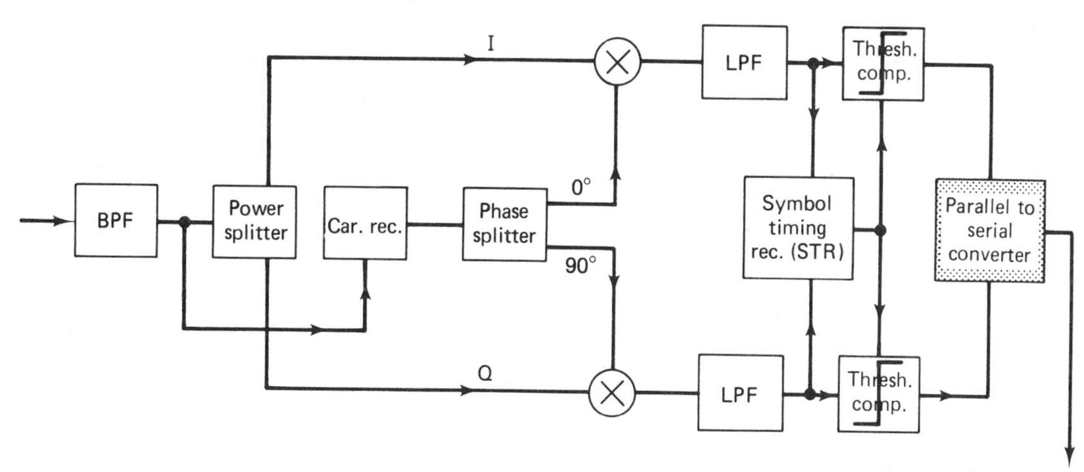

Spilker [3.11]. The recovered carrier wave is passed through a phase splitter, which provides 0° and 90° phase shifts. Coherent linear demodulation is the inverse process of the modulation; that is, the modulated $I$ and $Q$ signals are multiplied by the recovered carrier wave. This multiplication is easily achieved by balanced mixers. The low-pass filters eliminate the second and higher harmonics of the carrier wave. At the output of these filters the band-limited $I$ and $Q$ baseband signals are obtained. **(Solve Problem 3.12.)**

The threshold comparators sample these baseband signals and provide a logic one output state if the sampled value is positive; otherwise, they provide a logic zero state. As each transmitted symbol has to be sampled, the sampling rate equals the symbol rate $f_s$ that is one-half of the bit rate. The symbol rate clock is obtained from the symbol-timing recovery (STR) circuitry by means of non-linear signal processing. Conventional implementation techniques of STR circuits have been presented by Spilker [3.11] and fast synchronization methods by Feher [3.12]. Finally, the parallel-to-serial converter logic circuitry provides the output bit stream.

## 3.4 *P(e)* PERFORMANCE OF *M*-ARY PSK, QUADRATURE PARTIAL RESPONSE (QPR), AND AMPLITUDE PHASE KEYED (APK) SYSTEMS

In this section we derive the $P(e)$ of ideal, coherent, $M$-ary PSK systems in an additive white gaussian noise (AWGN) environment. This derivation is followed by a summary of the performance characteristics of various modulation techniques. By following carefully the derivation of the $P(e)$ function we will get an insight into the AWGN-caused errors. For an AWGN and co-channel or adjacent-channel interference environment, the derivation is more elaborate. You are referred to [3.1] for the study of these systems.

The following $P(e)$ derivation is illustrated on a 4-phase QPSK-state space diagram but applies also to binary and, in general, to $M$-ary systems, where $M = 2, 4, 8, 16, \ldots$, that is, $M = 2^n$. In the signal-state space diagram of Fig. 3.19 each equal amplitude phase state represents one symbol; each symbol contains $n = 2$ bits of information. Let's assume that the $\phi = 0°$ vector has been encoded at the transmitter to represent the 00 logic state, while the 90°, 180°, and 270° vectors represent the 01, 11, and 10 logic states, respectively. We will assume that each transmitted vector has the same probability; that is, the input data to the modulator has been scrambled and thus has an equiprobable distribution of the random binary zero and one states.

The signal space diagram illustrates that the $M$-ary modem has a circular symmetry. Because of this symmetry we can assume that in a noise-free environment the $\phi = 0°$ vector representing the 00 state has been transmitted. It is also assumed that an ideal Nyquist channel shaping is available; that is, in the sampling instant there is no intersymbol interference (ISI). The theoretically optimum phase

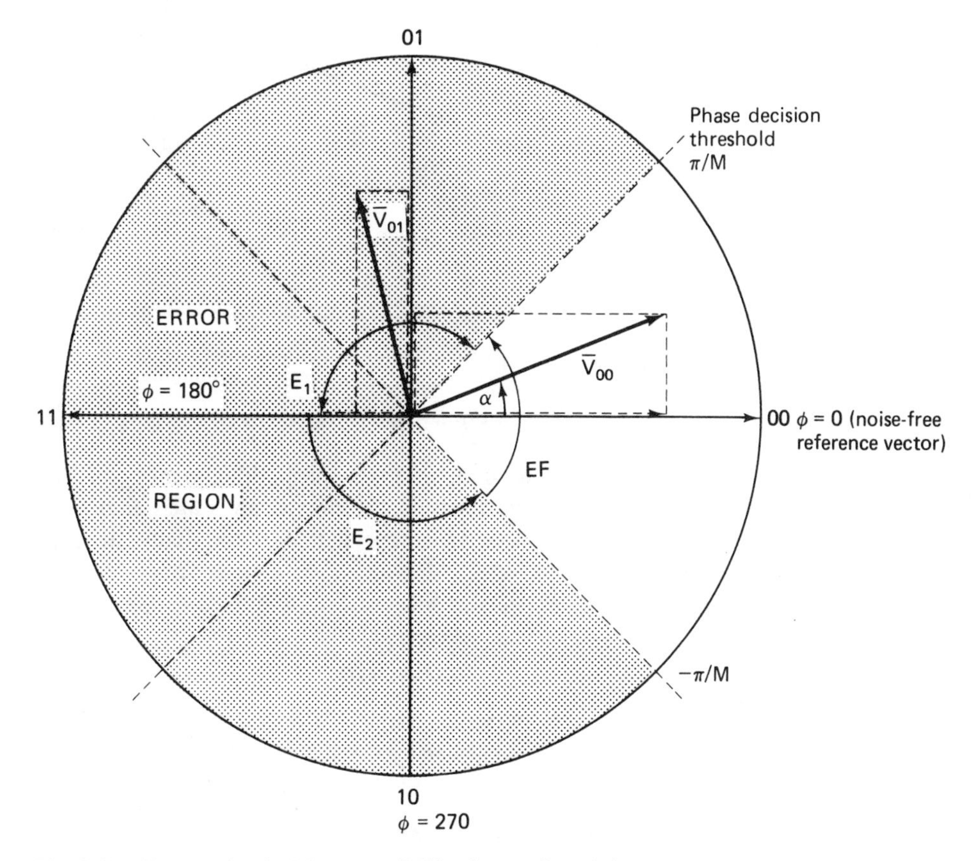


**Fig. 3.19.** Error region in $M = 4$-ary PSK coherent demodulators.

demodulator will detect the 00 phase state correctly if the received carrier plus noise vector, in the sampling instant, is within the $-\pi/M$ to $\pi/M$ error-free (EF) region. As an example see vector $r(t) = \bar{\mathbf{V}}_{00}$. If this vector is within the $\pi/M$ to $\pi$ region (error region $E_1$) or within the $\pi$ to $-\pi/M$ region (error region $E_2$), then the transmitted vector having a $\phi = 0°$ phase will be erroneously detected. In the example of a received vector shown in the position $r(t) = \bar{\mathbf{V}}_{01}$, the demodulator will decide that a 01 vector has been transmitted (instead of a 00), and thus the detected phasor will be erronous.

The received carrier and noise wave, $r(t)$, of the $M$-ary PSK signal is given by

$$r(t) = A \cos (w_c t + \phi) + n_c(t) \cos (w_c t + \phi) + n_s(t) \sin (w_c t + \phi) \quad (3.11)$$

where $A$ is the peak value of the received carrier, and $n_c(t)$ and $n_s(t)$ represent the instantaneous in-phase and quadrature-phase gaussian noise components. Without loss of generality it can be assumed that $\phi = 0$. In Fig. 3.20 the vector diagram of the composite carrier and noise wave is depicted. From Fig. 3.19 and Fig. 3.20

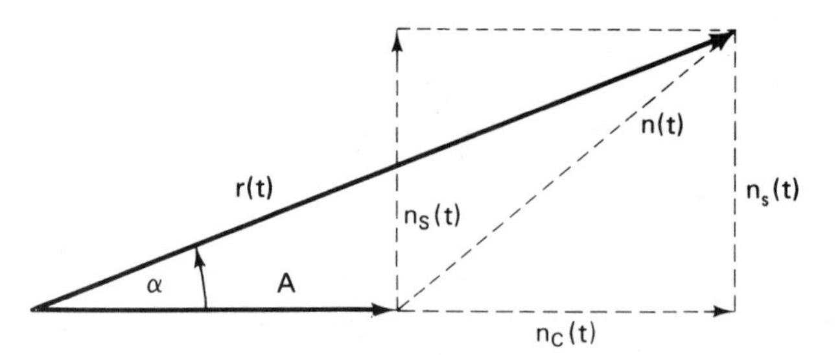


**Fig. 3.20.** Vector diagram of a received carrier and noise wave.

we conclude that an error will occur if

$$|\alpha| > \frac{\pi}{M} \quad \text{(modulo-}2\pi\text{ arithmetic)} \tag{3.12}$$

To derive the $P(e)$ we have to find, first, the probability density of $\alpha$. The probability distribution function of $\alpha$ within the previously stated error regions $E_1$, $\pi/M$ to $\pi$, and region $E_2$, $\pi$ to $-\pi/M$, is represented by the shaded area in Fig. 3.19 and is the $P(e)$ of the system.

The received phase $\alpha$ is given by

$$\alpha = \tan^{-1} \frac{n_s(t)}{A + n_c(t)} \tag{3.13}$$

The $P(e)$ of the $M$-ary PSK system is

$$P(e) = \int_{\pi/M}^{\pi} p(\alpha)\, d\alpha + \int_{-\pi}^{-\pi/M} p(\alpha)\, d\alpha = 2 \int_{\pi/M}^{\pi} p(\alpha)\, d\alpha \tag{3.14}$$

where $p(\alpha)$ is the probability density function of $\alpha$. This function for the AWGN channel has been derived in [3.8] and is given by

$$p(\alpha) = \frac{1}{2\pi} e^{-C/N}\left[1 + \sqrt{4\pi\left(\frac{C}{N}\right)} \cos\alpha \, e^{(C/N)\cos^2\alpha} Q\left(\sqrt{2\left(\frac{C}{N}\right)} \cos\alpha\right)\right], \quad (-\pi \leq \alpha \leq \pi) \tag{3.15}$$

where

$$Q(x) = \frac{1}{\sqrt{2\pi}} \int_x^{\infty} e^{-t^2/2}\, dt \tag{3.16}$$

In equation (3.15) the $C/N$ term represents the mean-carrier power to mean-noise power ratio specified in the double-sided Nyquist bandwidth which equals the symbol rate bandwidth. As there is no known closed-form equation that satisfies (3.15) and (3.16), it is necessary to use numerical methods to evaluate the $P(e)$ function. The $P(e)$ can also be estimated by the simple equation (3.17),

$$P(e) \simeq e^{-C/N \sin^2 \pi/M} \tag{3.17}$$

This approximation for high $C/N$ ratios ($C/N > 15$ dB) is accurate to within 1 dB. The computed values of the $P(e) = f(C/N)$ curve, based on the accurate equa-

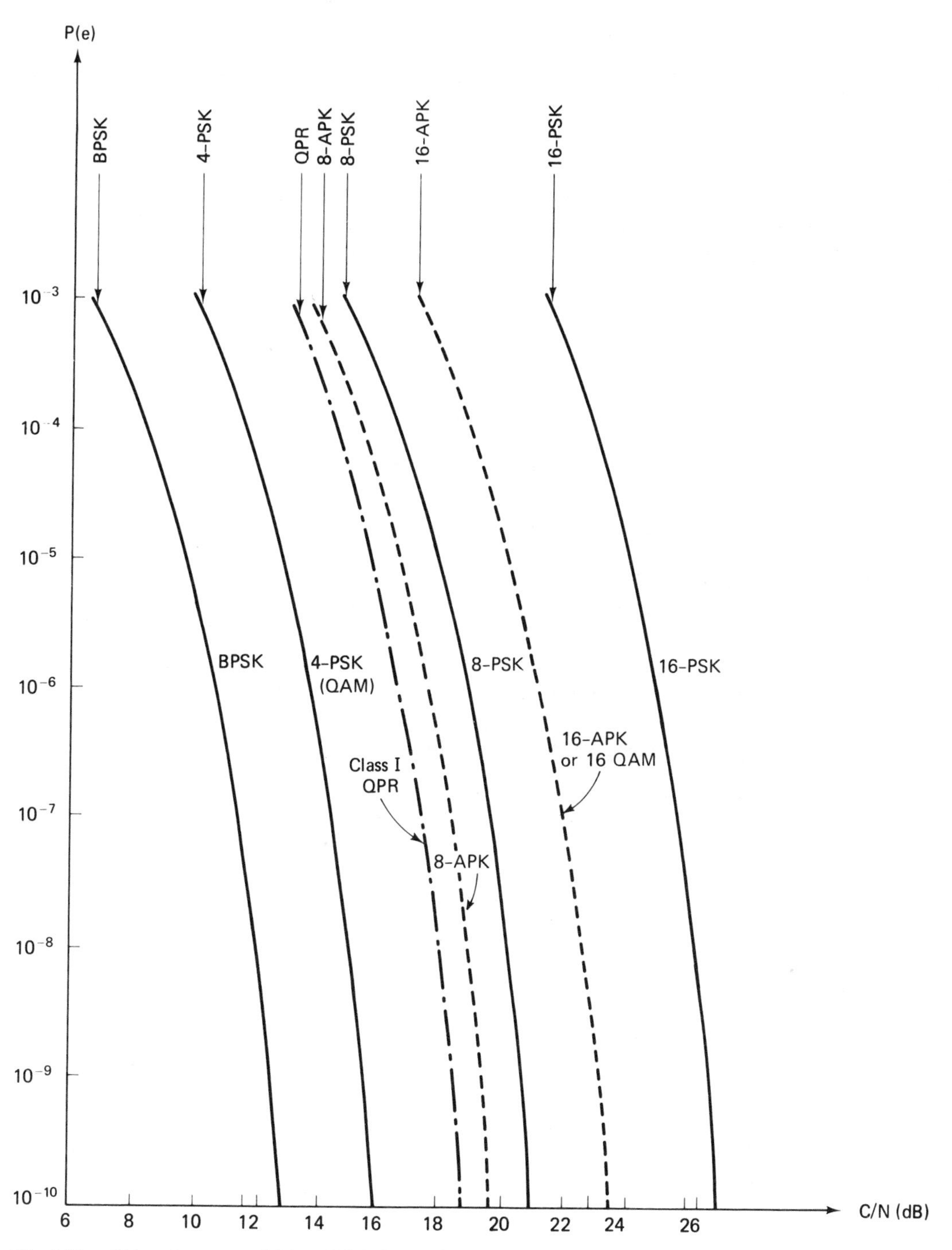


**Fig. 3.21.** $P(e)$ performance of $M$-ary PSK, QAM, QPR, and $M$-ary APK coherent systems. The rms $C/N$ is specified in the double-sided Nyquist bandwidth.

tions (3.14), (3.15), and (3.16), have been plotted in Fig. 3.21. **(Solve Problems 3.13 and 3.14.)**

In most practical systems the receiver noise bandwidth is larger than the double-sided Nyquist bandwidth. In order to provide a comparison of the minimum bandwidth theoretical system with the wider-band practical systems, equation (3.18) is frequently used:

$$\frac{E_b}{N_0} = \left(\frac{C}{N}\right)_{\text{bw}} \frac{\text{BW}}{f_b} \tag{3.18}$$

In this equation:

$E_b$ = average energy of a bit = $CT_b$
$f_b$ = transmitted bit rate $f_b = 1/T_b$
$T_b$ = unit bit duration
$C$ = average carrier power
$N_0$ = noise power spectral density, that is, average noise power in 1 Hz bandwidth
BW = noise bandwidth of the receiver.

**(Solve Problem 3.15.)**

**EXAMPLE 3.1.** A number of operational microwave systems employ 8-ary PSK modulation techniques. What is the theoretical $C/N$ ratio requirement if a $P(e) \leq 10^{-5}$ is required? (a) Assume that the receive band-pass-filter (BPF) noise bandwidth is 30 MHz. (b) Assume that this bandwidth has been increased to 45 MHz. (c) How much is the $C/N$ requirement if the noise is measured prior to the receive BPF in a bandwidth equaling the bit rate? (d) How much is the $E_b/N_0$ requirement in decibels for the case (a) to (c)?

***SOLUTION:*** (a) In this case, the noise bandwidth equals the minimum double-sided Nyquist bandwidth (90 Mb/s: 30 MHz = 3b/s/Hz – theoretical limit of 8-ary PSK). The $C/N$ requirement for a $P(e) = 10^{-5}$ is (reading from Fig. 3.21) equal 18.5 dB.

(b) The $E_b/N_0$ requirement is computed first. From equation (3.18) we obtain:

$$\frac{E_b}{N_0} = \left(\frac{C}{N}\right)_{30\text{ MHz}} + 10 \log \frac{30\text{ MHz}}{90\text{ Mb/s}}$$
$$= 18.5\text{ dB} - 4.8\text{ dB} = 13.7\text{ dB}$$

That is,

$$\frac{E_b}{N_0} = 13.7\text{ dB} \quad \text{for } P(e) = 10^{-5}$$

Now, the $C/N$ ratio in a 45 MHz bandwidth is calculated:

$$\left(\frac{C}{N}\right)_{45\text{ MHz}} = \frac{E_b}{N_0}(\text{dB}) + 10 \log \frac{f_b}{\text{BW}}$$
$$= 13.7\text{ dB} + 3\text{ dB} = 16.7\text{ dB}$$

(c) In this case, BW $= f_b$; thus,

$$\frac{E_b}{N_0} = \left(\frac{C}{N}\right)_{90\text{ MHz}} = 13.7\text{ dB}$$

(d) The $E_b/N_0$ requirement equals 13.7 dB in all three cases. You should attempt to explain why the $E_b/N_0$ requirement is independent of the noise bandwidth. ■

Terrestrial microwave system $P(e)$ performance is most frequently specified in terms of $C/N$ ratio, whereas satellite systems performance is specified in terms of $E_b/N_0$. For a convenient comparison of these specifications in Fig. 3.22, the $P(e) = f(E_b/N_0)$ performance of $M$-ary PSK systems is given. The coherent modems having built-in carrier recovery circuits have a better performance than the modems which employ differential phase detection ($M$-ary DPSK) [3.1].

**Fig. 3.22.** Error probability performance for coherent and differentially coherent detection of differentially encoded $M$-ary PSK. (Redrawn by permission from Reference [3.1])

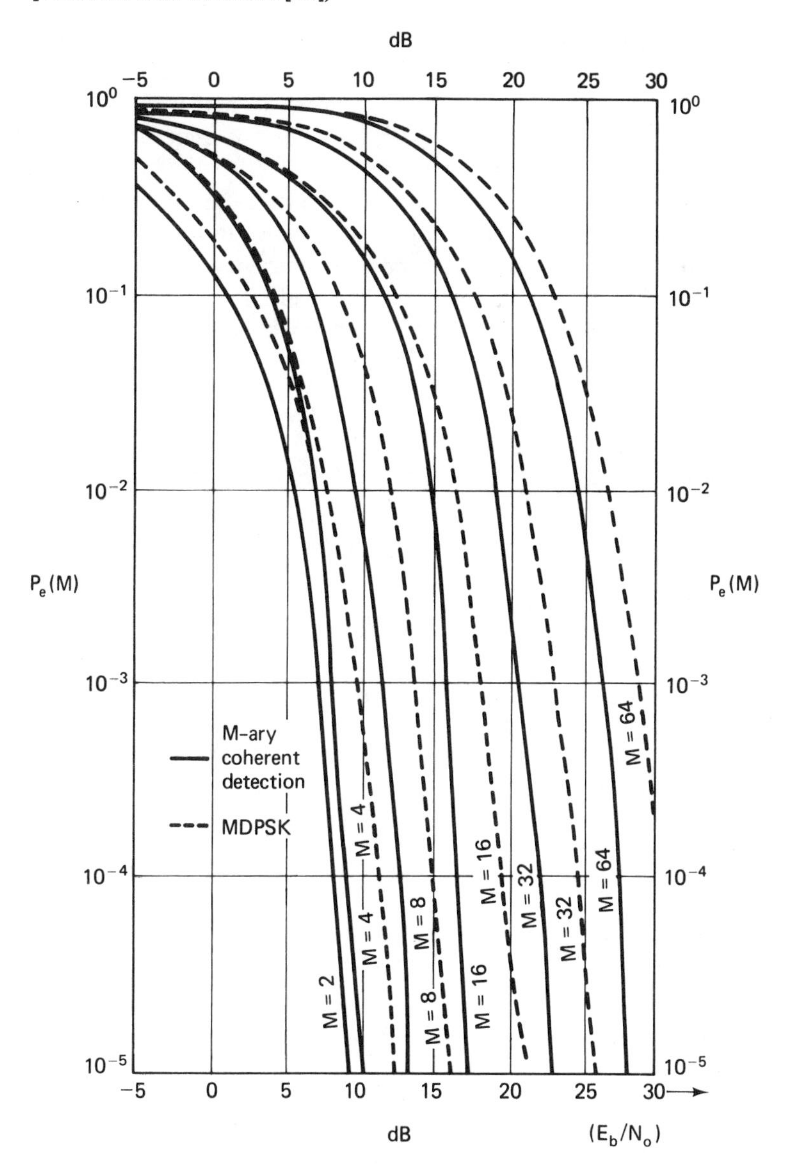

In addition to the $P(e)$ performance of $M$-ary PSK systems, the $P(e)$ performance of coherent quadrature partial response (QPR), quadrature amplitude modulation (QAM), and 8-ary and 16-ary amplitude phase keyed (APK) systems are presented in Fig. 3.21. These systems are described in later chapters. However, for a comparative reference it is useful to include their curves in this figure.

The b/s/Hz spectral efficiency of modulated systems, as a function of available $C/N$ ratio, is shown in Fig. 3.23. This representation is useful for fast system comparisons. From this figure, we note that if a 4 b/s/Hz efficiency and a $P(e) = 10^{-8}$ is required, then it could be achieved by digital vestigial-sideband (VSB) suppressed carrier quadrature AM-SC, 16-ary APK or 16-ary PSK modulation methods. The required $C/N$ would be only 21.5 dB for the first two methods, and it would be 23 dB and 26 dB for the 16-ary APK and PSK systems. Even though these latter systems have a higher $C/N$ requirement than the other modulation techniques, they are stronger candidates in a number of digital microwave systems due to their simpler hardware implementation.

In later chapters we will often return to the performance curves of various modulated systems. The presentations shown in Figs. 3.21 and 3.23 are frequently used in the literature. The bandwidth efficiency term expressed in terms of transmitted b/s/Hz of radio frequency bandwidth is now a standard term used in various FCC regulations, CCIR recommendations, and other regulations.

## PROBLEMS

**3.1** On a baseband cable system it is necessary to transmit binary random data at a rate of $f_b = 100$ Mb/s. Determine the minimum cable bandwidth required if this information has to be transmitted without intersymbol interference (ISI).

**3.2** Sketch the amplitude and phase characteristics of a Nyquist channel if it is assumed that infinitesimally narrow random impulses are transmitted at a rate of 10 kb/s. Is this a practical transmission method?

**3.3** Sketch the amplitude and phase characteristics of an ideal channel if it is necessary to transmit a 10 kb/s binary non-return-to-zero (NRZ) data stream: (a) in the smallest possible bandwidth, (b) in a channel having 30% higher bandwidth than the minimum Nyquist bandwidth.

**3.4** Sketch the eye diagram of a 100 kb/s binary NRZ random baseband system. Assume that the ideal brick-wall linear-phase low-pass filters employed have the following cut-off frequencies: (a) 10 MHz, (b) 300 kHz, (c) 100 kHz, (d) 50 kHz, (e) 30 kHz.

**3.5** Estimate the intersymbol interference and the peak-to-peak jitter for the filtered NRZ information of Problem 3.4.

**3.6** The root-mean-square voltage of a 40 Mb/s balanced random NRZ data stream is 100 mV. The characteristic impedance of the transmission system is 75 ohms. How much is the power spectral density in dBm/Hz around the dc value, and how much is it at 60 MHz?

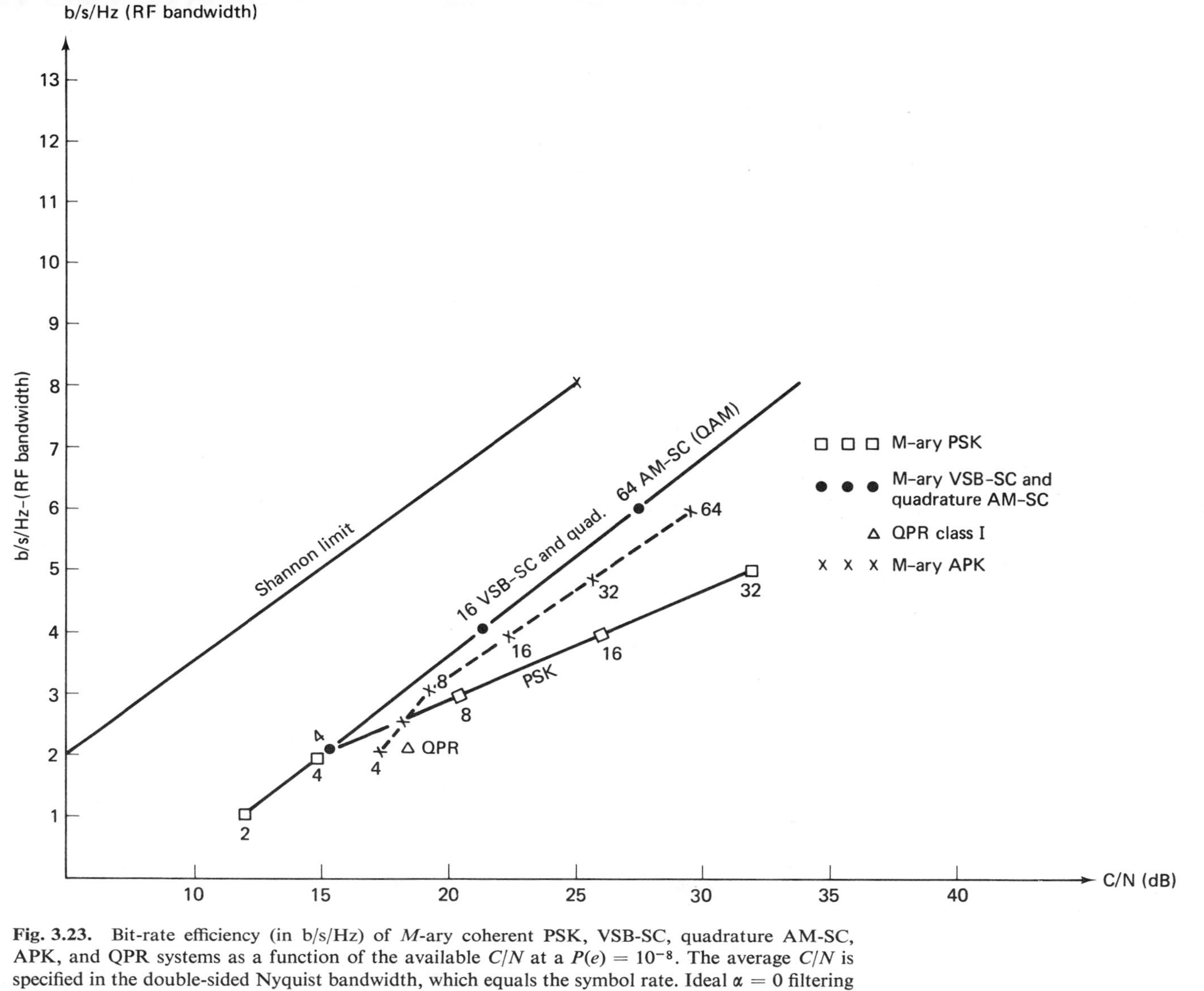


**Fig. 3.23.** Bit-rate efficiency (in b/s/Hz) of $M$-ary coherent PSK, VSB-SC, quadrature AM-SC, APK, and QPR systems as a function of the available $C/N$ at a $P(e) = 10^{-8}$. The average $C/N$ is specified in the double-sided Nyquist bandwidth, which equals the symbol rate. Ideal $\alpha = 0$ filtering has been assumed.

**3.7** If the total power of a 20 Mb/s balanced random NRZ signal is 0 dBm, then how much power would you measure with a selective mean power meter which is centered at 10 MHz and has a filter bandwidth of 3 kHz? Note that in a laboratory environment a selective root-mean-square voltmeter could be used.

**3.8** What is the theoretically minimum baseband bandwidth required of a coaxial cable system if transmission is to be at a data rate of 300 Mb/s? Assume that $M = 4$- and $M = 16$-level PAM hardware designs are available for this project.

**3.9** Given that it is necessary to have a $P(e) \leq 10^{-8}$ on the transmission facility described in Problem 3.8, what is the minimum $S/N$ ratio requirement at the PAM decoder input? Assume that the $S/N$ ratio has been measured after the minimum bandwidth receive Nyquist filter. Estimate the practical $S/N$ requirements.

**3.10** In the operational Bell Data Under Voice microwave system for 1.544 Mb/s data transmission, a 600 kHz baseband bandwidth has been made available. Which baseband transmission method would you consider for this microwave system application? As a practically oriented systems engineer you should allow a 30% higher bandwidth than stipulated by the minimum bandwidth Nyquist channel.

**3.11** Sketch the power spectral density of a 90 Mb/s QPSK modulated random-data stream. Assume that (a) there has been no band-limiting applied after modulation, (b) the transmit band-pass filter is a minimum bandwidth Nyquist filter.

**3.12** Sketch the power spectral density and the eye diagram of 10 Mb/s BPSK and 10 Mb/s QPSK minimum bandwidth demodulators at the input points of their threshold comparators.

**3.13** Write the exact $P(e) = f(C/N)$ equations for $M = 8$-ary coherent PSK systems. Given that, in a 90 Mb/s 8-PSK system, the available $C/N$ in the 30 MHz receiver bandwidth is 21 dB, what is the theoretically expected $P(e)$ performance?

**3.14** Compare the $C/N$ ratio requirements for a $P(e) = 10^{-8}$ for binary, 4-phase, 8-phase and 16-phase PSK systems. For this comparison use equation (3.17). Afterward, compare the computed $C/N$ ratios with the values given in Fig. 3.21.

**3.15** What is the $P(e)$ of a 10 Mb/s $M = 4$-ary PSK (QPSK) system if the measured $C/N$ ratio at the receiver input is 10 dB? Assume that the system has been corrupted by additive white gaussian noise (AWGN) and the receiver bandwidth is 15 MHz. Compare the computed results with the curves shown in Fig. 3.21.

## REFERENCES

[3.1] Feher, K., *Digital Modulation Techniques in an Interference Environment*, *EMC Encyclopedia*, Vol. 9, Don White Consultants, Inc., Gainesville, VA, 1977.

[3.2] Welch, H. E., "Applications of Digital Modulation Techniques to Microwave Radio Systems," Proc. IEEE International Conference on Communications, ICC-77, Chicago, June, 1977.

[3.3] Bennet, W. R., J. R. Davey, *Data Transmission*, McGraw Hill Book Company, New York, 1965.

[3.4] Lucky, R., J. Salz, J. Weldon, *Principles of Data Communication*, McGraw-Hill Book Company, New York, 1968.

[3.5] Kurematsu, H., K. Ogawa, T. Katoh, "The QAM2G-10R Digital Radio Equipment Using a Partial Response System," Fujitsu Scientific and Technical Journal, June, 1977.

[3.6] Juroshek, J. R., "An Approximate Method for Calculating the Performance of CPSK and NCFSK Modems in Gaussian Noise and Interference," U.S. Department of Commerce, Office of Telecommunications, OTR-77-109, Boulder, Colo., January, 1977.

[3.7] Thomas, C. M., M. Y. Weidner, S. A. Durrani, "Digital Amplitude Phase Keying with M-ary Alphabets," IEEE Trans. Communications, February, 1974.

[3.8] Panter, P. F., *Modulation, Noise and Spectral Analysis*, McGraw-Hill Book Company, New York, 1965.

[3.9] Feher, K., "Digital/Analog Microwave Transmission Study," Ph.D. Thesis, Electrical Engineering, University of Sherbrooke, Canada, April, 1974.

[3.10] Wozencraft, J. M., I. M. Jacobs, *Principles of Communication Engineering*, John Wiley & Sons, Inc., New York, 1967.

[3.11] Spilker, J. J., *Digital Communications by Satellite*, Prentice-Hall, Inc., Englewood Cliffs, N.J., 1977.

[3.12] Feher, K., G. Takhar, "A New Symbol Timing Recovery Technique for Burst Modem Applications," IEEE Trans. Communications, January, 1978.

[3.13] Ward, C. G., "The Why and How of PCM Microwave Use by Manitoba Hydro," Proc. IEEE Canadian Communications and Power Conference, Montreal, October, 1976.

[3.14] Feher, K., "Jitter and ISI Free Nyquist Filtering of Data Signals by Means of Feher's Processor (Filter)," Canadian Patent Disclosure, Ottawa, May, 1979.

[3.15] Gendron, M., K. Feher, "Une Nouvelle Famille de Filtre Nonlineaire," Canadian Electrical Engineering Journal, January, 1979.

[3.16] Huang, J. C. Y., K. Feher, M. Gendron, "Techniques to Generate ISI and Jitter Free Bandlimited Nyquist Signals and a Method to Analyze Jitter Effects," IEEE Trans. Communications, November, 1979.

[3.17] Ishio, H., et al., "A New Multilevel Modulation and Demodulation System for Carrier Digital Transmission," Proceedings of the IEEE International Conference on Communications, ICC-76, Philadelphia, June, 1976.

# 4

# MICROWAVE AMPLIFIERS

**DR. WOLFGANG J.R. HOEFER**

*Chairman, Department of Electrical Engineering,*
*University of Ottawa*

> *Dr. Wolfgang J.R. Hoefer is a well known professor and research engineer in the field of electromagnetic engineering and microwave devices. I wish to thank him for his effort and valuable contribution.*
>
> *Dr. K. Feher*

Inevitably, the communications systems engineer will encounter microwave amplifiers of some kind when designing or evaluating a microwave system. In a typical digital microwave system the amplifiers contribute more to the overall $P(e)$ performance and system gain (described in the next chapter) than up-converters, down-converters, oscillators, or other active elements. In this chapter we therefore describe the most common types of microwave amplifiers; their characteristics, specifications, and limitations are presented, and a survey of the state of the art is included. Our purpose in this chapter is to enable the systems engineer to understand the significance of amplifier specifications, to evaluate such a product, and to specify the desirable characteristics of an amplifier required for a given system.

The requirements imposed on microwave amplifiers depend on their purpose. Two fundamental types of amplifiers can be distinguished: the microwave power amplifier and the small-signal amplifier.

The *power amplifier* must deliver a microwave signal of sufficient power to produce an easily detectable output at the end of a transmission channel. This signal should be produced with maximum efficiency and reliability and with minimum distortion. In contrast, the *small-signal amplifier* must increase the power of a weak signal sufficiently for further processing. In this application, it is crucial that the amplifier add as little noise as possible to the signal. Efficiency is usually of secondary concern in this application, but reliability and linearity requirements are as stringent as for the power amplifier.

## 4.1 MICROWAVE POWER AMPLIFIERS

Power amplifiers for the microwave range are described in terms of the following characteristics:

1) Output power level and flatness
2) Gain
3) Operating bandwidth
4) Overall efficiency
5) Harmonic and intermodulation distortion
6) AM to PM conversion
7) Noise

The *output power* is always specified in one of two ways: minimum output or nominal output. These values are, in general, different from each other because the output power varies more or less over the *operating bandwidth.* Figure 4.1 illustrates these definitions in the power vs. frequency diagram. The input power $P_{\text{in}}$ is kept constant over the whole frequency range. The *saturated output power* level is reached when a further increase in input power will no longer increase the output power.

The minimum and nominal *gains* of an amplifier are defined as

$$g_{\min} = 10 \log \left(\frac{P_{\text{out min}}}{P_{\text{in}}}\right) \quad \text{dB} \tag{4.1}$$

and

$$g_{\text{nom}} = 10 \log \left(\frac{P_{\text{out nom}}}{P_{\text{in}}}\right) \quad \text{dB} \tag{4.2}$$

respectively.

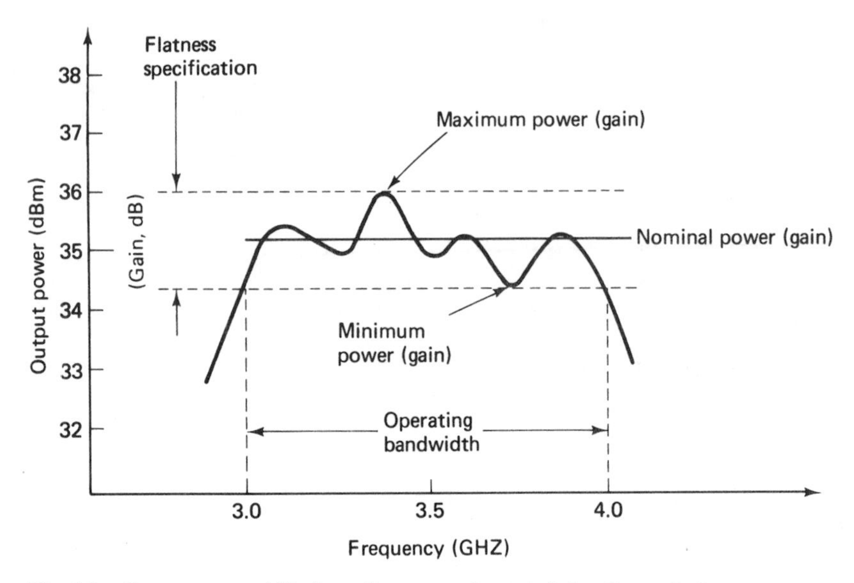


**Fig. 4.1.** Output power (dBm) vs. frequency characteristic of a typical microwave amplifier for constant input power. The ordinate can represent the amplifier gain as well (dB).

Some manufacturers represent the gain instead of the output power vs. frequency, which results in a diagram that has the same shape as the output power characteristic (Fig. 4.1).

The gain of solid-state amplifiers is quite sensitive to *temperature* changes. If the gain of such an amplifier must remain constant over a wide temperature range, the installation of a temperature-compensating circuit is required. See Figs. 4.2(a) and 4.2(b).

The *overall efficiency* of an amplifier is defined as follows:

$$\eta = \left(\frac{P_{\text{out}} - P_{\text{in}}}{P_{\text{dc}}}\right) 100\% \tag{4.3}$$

where $P_{\text{in}}$ and $P_{\text{out}}$ are the RF input and output powers, respectively, and $P_{\text{dc}}$ is the power supplied to the amplifier by its power supply.

Another important characteristic of an amplifier is the diagram showing the output power as a function of the input power level: the so-called *power transfer characteristic* (Fig. 4.3). The noise generated by the amplifier determines the lower limit of its *dynamic range*.

In a linear amplifier, the output power increases linearly with increasing input power, as shown in Fig. 4.3. However, saturation inevitably occurs and limits the output in such a way that it departs from the linear relationship. The 1 *dB compression point* refers to the power level at which the actual output power drops 1 dB below the predicted power. The 3 *dB compression point* is defined in an analogous way.

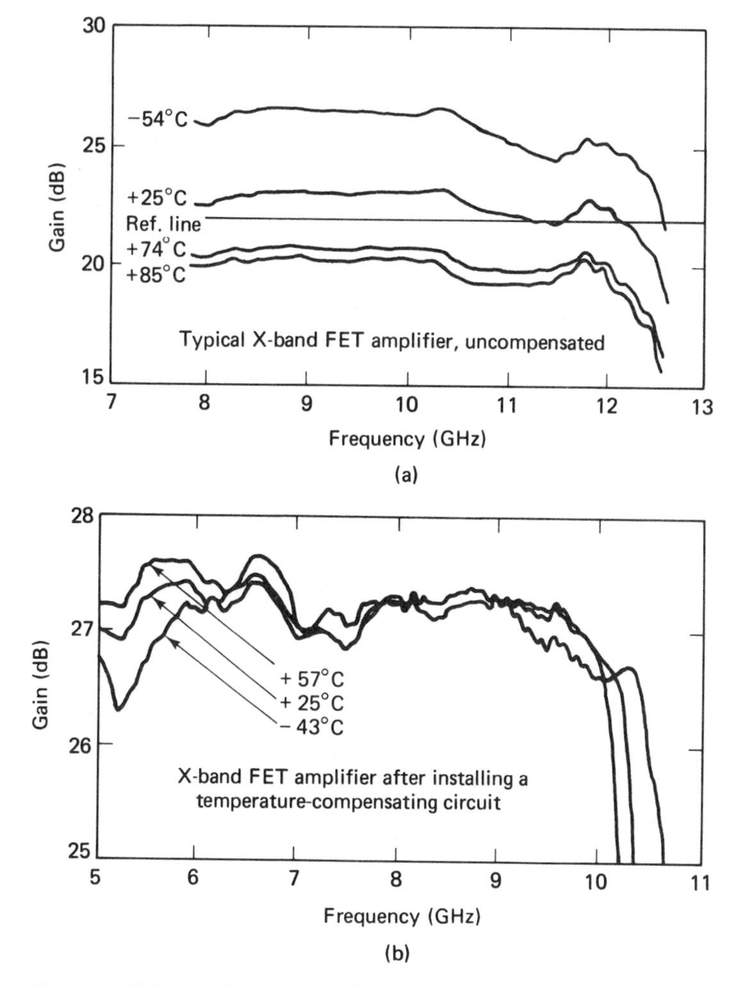


**Fig. 4.2.** Gain vs. frequency and temperature for a typical X-band FET amplifier. (Reprinted with permission of Aertech Industries, Reference [4.4])

The non-linearity of the transfer characteristic causes *non-linear distortion* of the amplified signal, resulting in the generation of harmonics. If two or more input signals of different frequencies are present, intermodulation products are generated.

While harmonic generation is only of concern if the bandwidth of the amplifier exceeds one octave, intermodulation products usually fall within the passband of most amplifiers.

*Intermodulation distortion* is specified by using the *third-order intercept point.* Let two signals at frequencies $f_1$ and $f_2$ be incident at the input of a microwave

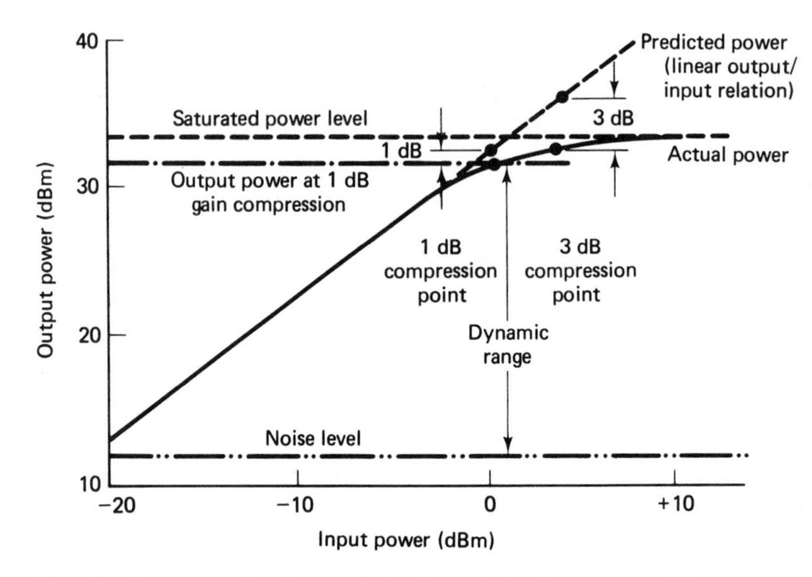


**Fig. 4.3.** Power transfer characteristic of a typical microwave amplifier. Saturation produces gain compression at high power levels.

amplifier. Due to intermodulation, the output contains additional signals at frequencies $nf_1 \pm mf_2$, where $n$ and $m$ are positive integers ($n, m = 1, 2, 3, 4\ldots$). The sum $n + m$ defines the order of an intermodulation product. Thus, the signals of frequencies $2f_1 - f_2$, $2f_2 - f_1$, $2f_1 + f_2$, and $2f_2 + f_1$ are the third-order intermodulation products. Obviously, only the first two signals are of interest in a microwave amplifier of less than an octave of bandwidth. (See Fig. 4.4.)

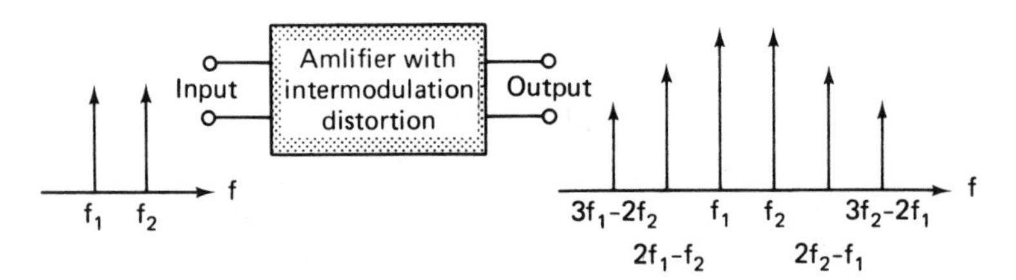


**Fig. 4.4.** Input and output spectrum of a microwave amplifier with intermodulation distortion. The output spectrum shows third-order and fifth-order intermodulation products.

The concept of the third-order intercept point is demonstrated in Fig. 4.5. Intermodulation products appear as soon as the transfer characteristic becomes non-linear. If the non-linearity is cubic and the two input signals are of equal amplitude, the third-order intermodulation product power increases three times as quickly as the signal output. The intercept point is identified as the intersection of the asymptotes to the characteristics of the signal and the intermodulation power

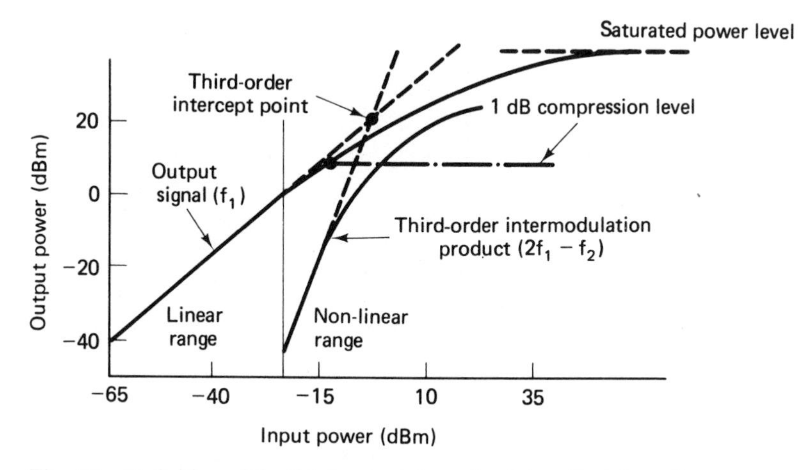


**Fig. 4.5.** Definition of the third-order intercept point as the intersection of the asymptotes to the characteristics of the signal and the intermodulation power outputs.

outputs. Figure 4.6 shows a series of output spectra demonstrating the fast growth of the intermodulation products with increasing signal amplitude. Thus, the slope of the third-order transfer characteristic is much steeper than that of the main transfer characteristic.

The amplitude of the intermodulation products can be calculated from the third-order intercept point and the desired signal output levels as follows [4.4]:

If $P_{im3}$ = output power in dBm of third-order intermodulation product
$P_1$ = output power in dBm at frequency $f_1$
$P_2$ = output power in dBm at frequency $f_2$
$P_{3i}$ = third-order intercept level in dBm

then

$$P_{im3} = 2P_1 + P_2 - 2P_{3i} \quad (\text{for } 2f_1 \pm f_2) \quad (\text{dBm}) \tag{4.4}$$

$$P_{im3} = 2P_2 + P_1 - 2P_{3i} \quad (\text{for } 2f_2 \pm f_1) \quad (\text{dBm}) \tag{4.5}$$

**EXAMPLE 4.1.** An amplifier has a gain of $g = 15$ dB. The third-order intercept point occurs at +23.5 dBm. Calculate the third-order intermodulation products in the output spectrum if the following two signals are incident simultaneously at the input:

$$\text{S1: } f_1 = 1300 \text{ MHz}, \qquad P_{i1} = -20 \text{ dBm}$$

$$\text{S2: } f_2 = 1320 \text{ MHz}, \qquad P_{i2} = -22 \text{ dBm}$$

***SOLUTION:*** First, the signal output power at the frequencies $f_1$ and $f_2$ is calculated:

$$P_1 = P_{i1} + g = -5 \text{ dBm}$$

$$P_2 = P_{i2} + g = -7 \text{ dBm}$$

Second, the intermodulation products are evaluated, using equations (4.4) and (4.5) as follows:

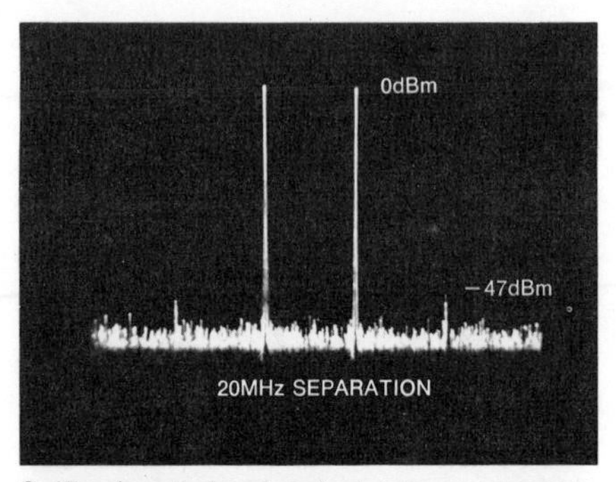


0 dBm (small signal region)

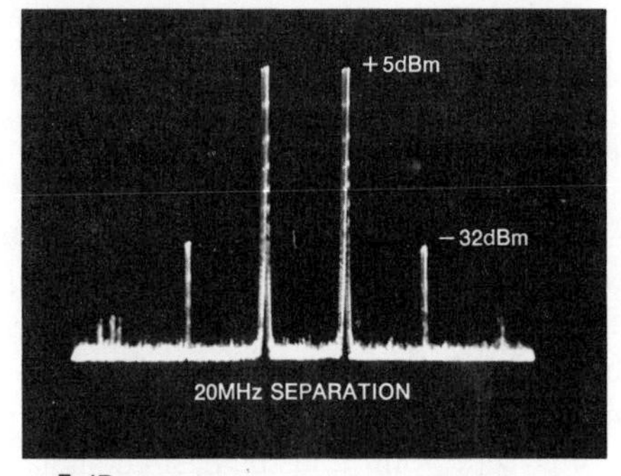


+ 5 dBm

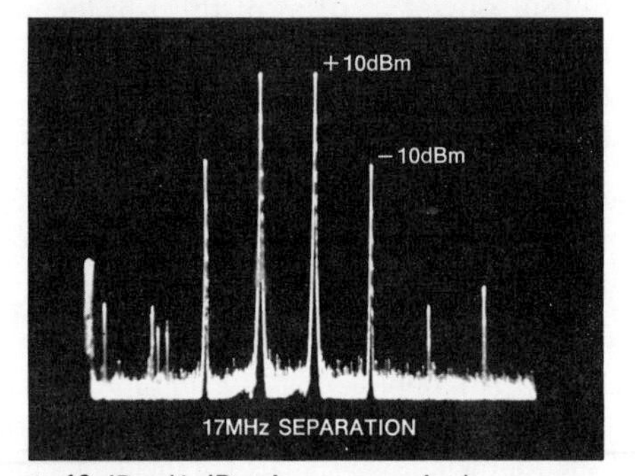


+ 10 dBm (1 dB gain compression)

**Fig. 4.6.** Third-order intermodulation products in the output spectrum of a typical X-band FET amplifier for two equal output tones. (Reprinted with permission of Aertech Industries, Reference [4.4])

At $f = 2f_1 - f_2$ (1280 MHz):

$$P_{\text{im3}} = 2(-5\text{ dBm}) + (-7\text{ dBm}) - 2(23.5\text{ dBm})$$

$$P_{\text{im3}} = -64\text{ dBm}$$

At $f = 2f_2 - f_1$ (1340 MHz):

$$P_{\text{im3}} = 2(-7\text{ dBm}) + (-5\text{ dBm}) - 2(23.5\text{ dBm})$$

$$P_{\text{im3}} = -66\text{ dBm} \quad \blacksquare$$

Typically, the third-order intercept point for IMPATT microwave amplifiers lies at the saturated power output level. In amplifiers containing GUNN devices or transistors, the intercept usually occurs 6–10 dB above saturation.

Another parameter of considerable interest to the communications engineer is the *AM to PM conversion factor*. This parameter indicates the phase shift of the amplified signal caused by a 1 dB change in input power. Figure 4.7 shows a typical AM to PM conversion factor together with the power transfer characteristics of a class of 6 GHz power amplifiers [4.5]. From the AM to PM conversion curve it is evident that the conversion factor varies significantly with the input level.

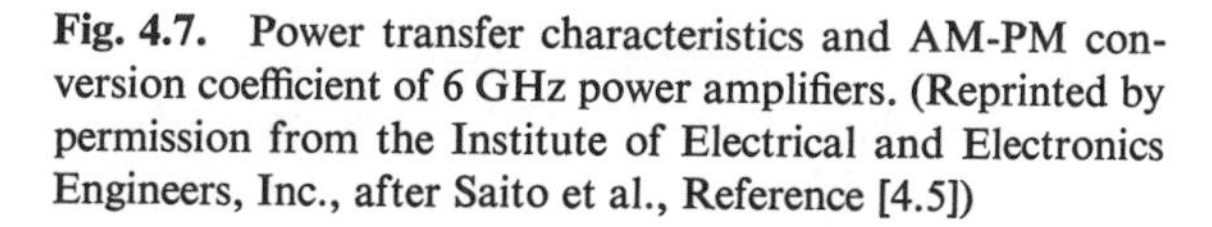

**Fig. 4.7.** Power transfer characteristics and AM-PM conversion coefficient of 6 GHz power amplifiers. (Reprinted by permission from the Institute of Electrical and Electronics Engineers, Inc., after Saito et al., Reference [4.5])

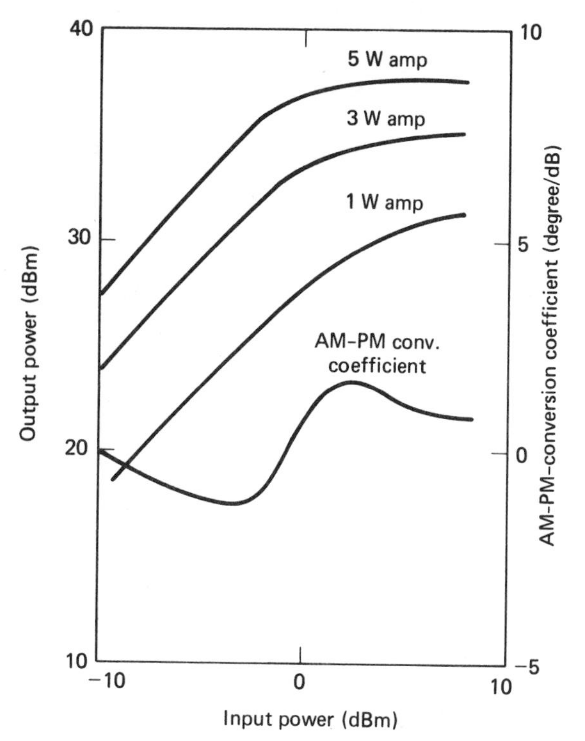

## 4.2 SMALL-SIGNAL AMPLIFIERS

Small-signal amplifiers operate practically always in the linear range of the transfer characteristic. Their purpose, and consequently their specifications, are quite different from those discussed for power amplifiers. Small-signal amplifiers are usually evaluated in terms of the following characteristics:

1) Gain
2) Operating bandwidth
3) Noise level specified by the noise figure (NF), noise temperature ($T_n$) or noise measure (M)

The third specification is of particular importance if the microwave signal power is commensurate with the level of accompanying noise (low signal-to-noise ratio at the input of an amplifier).

The *noise figure* (NF) describes the deterioration of the signal-to-noise ratio due to the presence of an amplifier. It is defined as follows [4.1]:

$$\text{NF (dB)} = 10 \log \frac{P_{si}/P_{ni}}{P_{so}/P_{no}} \tag{4.6}$$

where $P_{si}$ = available input signal power, in watts
$P_{so}$ = available output signal power, in watts
$P_{ni}$ = available input noise power, in watts
$P_{no}$ = available output noise power, in watts.

The output noise power is composed of the amplified input noise and the inherent amplifier noise $P_{inh}$ originating in its active and passive elements:

$$P_{no} = G\,P_{ni} + P_{inh} \tag{4.7}$$

Here $G$ is the absolute amplifier gain,

$$G = \frac{P_{so}}{P_{si}} \tag{4.8}$$

whereas the amplifier gain in dB is defined as

$$g(\text{dB}) = 10 \log G \tag{4.9}$$

A combination of (4.6), (4.7), and (4.8) yields for the noise figure:

$$\text{NF (dB)} = 10 \log \frac{P_{no}}{GP_{ni}} = 10 \log \left(1 + \frac{P_{inh}}{GP_{ni}}\right) \tag{4.10}$$

An ideal amplifier which does not add any noise to the amplified signal has a noise figure of 0 dB. The closer the noise figure is to this value, the higher the quality of an amplifier and the better its ability to amplify small signals. This, in turn, leads to a higher overall system gain.

The inherent noise of an amplifier is often expressed in terms of its *noise temperature* ($T_n$). It is the absolute temperature of a matched load, at the input of the amplifier, that would produce the noise power $P_{inh}$ at its output if the amplifier itself were ideal:

$$P_{inh} = GP_n \tag{4.11}$$

where $P_n$ is the thermal noise power produced by the matched input load at the temperature $T_n$ such that

$$P_n = kT_n \Delta f \tag{4.12}$$

where $k$ = Boltzmann's constant ($1.38 \cdot 10^{-23}$ joules/degree Kelvin)
$T_n$ = noise temperature, in degrees Kelvin
$\Delta f$ = bandwidth of the amplifier, in hertz.

Assuming that the input noise power $P_{ni}$ of a real amplifier is produced by the same matched load at room temperature of 290°K, such that

$$P_{ni} = k(290°\text{K})\Delta f \tag{4.13}$$

the noise figure [equation (4.10)] becomes, with (4.11), (4.12), and (4.13):

$$\text{NF (dB)} = 10 \log \left(1 + \frac{T_n}{290°\text{K}}\right) \tag{4.14}$$

Conversely, the noise temperature of the amplifier is related to its noise figure by the following expression:

$$T_n = 290°\text{K}(10^{\text{NF}/10} - 1) \tag{4.15}$$

In many applications, microwave systems contain several cascaded stages of similar noise characteristics. If the noise figure of an infinite cascade of identical stages is calculated,* the so-called *noise measure* $M$ results. It is related to the noise figure NF and the gain $G$ of one stage by the following expression [4.4]:

$$M\,(\text{dB}) = 10 \log \frac{\text{NF} - 1}{1 - \frac{1}{G}} \tag{4.16}$$

If the gain of the individual stages is specified in dB, the noise measure is

$$M\,(\text{dB}) = 10 \log \left(\frac{\text{NF} - 1}{1 - 10^{-g/10}}\right) \tag{4.17}$$

where $g$ (dB) = 10 log $G$.

In order to achieve minimal noise characteristics, amplifiers are often cooled down to temperatures as low as 4.2°K (liquid helium), resulting in noise temperatures as low as 3–30°K.

## 4.3 TECHNOLOGY OF MICROWAVE AMPLIFIERS

### *4.3.1 Microwave Amplification Devices*

Microwave amplification devices generally belong to one of the following two broad categories:

a) Tubes
b) Semiconductor devices.

*In practice, three to four stages in cascade approach this condition.

Devices using quantum-mechanical effects (masers), Cerenkov effect, Doppler effect, or plasma oscillations are not usually found in microwave communication systems, even though they are of considerable scientific interest.

Among the microwave tubes, gridded devices with electrostatic current control (such as triodes and tetrodes), klystrons of the reflex and multi-cavity type, crossed field devices (magnetrons), traveling-wave (TWT) and backward wave (BWT) tubes are most frequently employed.

Microwave semiconductor devices include three-terminal devices such as bipolar and field effect transistors (FETs), and two-terminal devices such as avalanche diodes (IMPATTs and TRAPATTs), transferred electron devices (GUNNs, LSA devices), tunnel diodes, and varactors. Figure 4.8 gives an overview of the microwave devices most commonly found in modern communications systems.

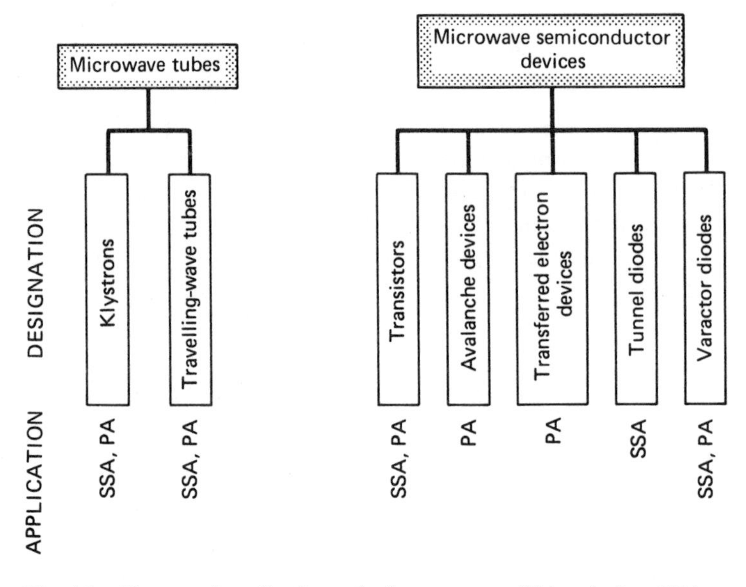


**Fig. 4.8.** Types and applications of microwave amplifying devices (SSA = small-signal amplifier, PA = power amplifier).

### *4.3.2 Basic Amplifier Configurations*

Three-terminal devices are commonly used to build two-port or transmission-type amplifiers with separate input and output ports. Impedance transformers match the signal source and the load to the device, as shown in Fig. 4.9(a). In the case of two-terminal devices, a circulator usually separates the incoming from the amplified signal. Such a circuit is called a *single-port*, or *reflection-type*, *amplifier* and is shown in Fig. 4.9(b).

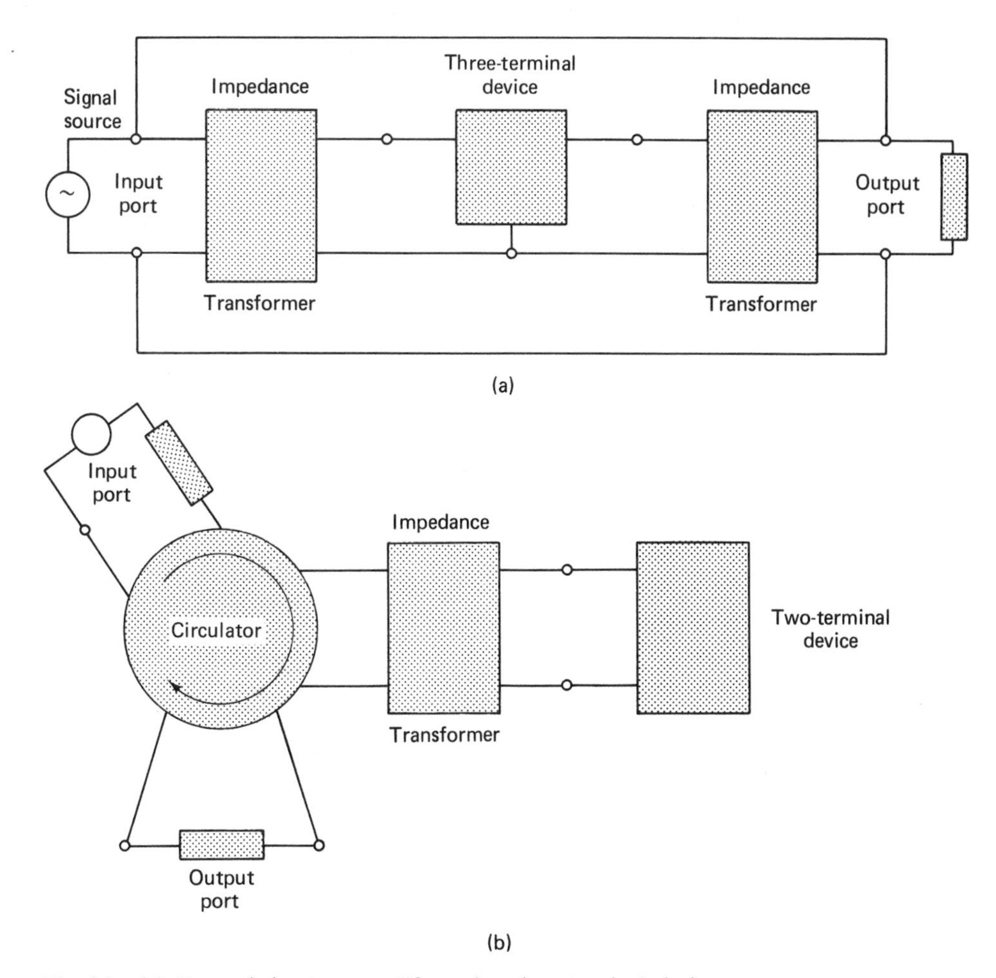


**Fig. 4.9.** (a) Transmission-type amplifier using three-terminal device. (b) Reflection-type amplifier using two-terminal device and a circulator to separate input and output.

### *4.3.3 Power Amplifier Performance*

The average output power limits of solid-state and of tube power sources are compared in Fig. 4.10. This figure shows that, for the highest power levels at high frequencies, the tubes are superior to solid-state sources, but in the 5 to 20 GHz range, GaAs FET transistors play an increasingly important role in intermediate power applications and are taking over the functions traditionally performed by microwave tubes. GaAs FET devices are capable of producing 5 W of CW power at 6 GHz [4.5] and 1 W at 10 GHz with 27% efficiency [4.7]. Among the two-terminal devices, IMPATTs will probably play the most important role in tomor-

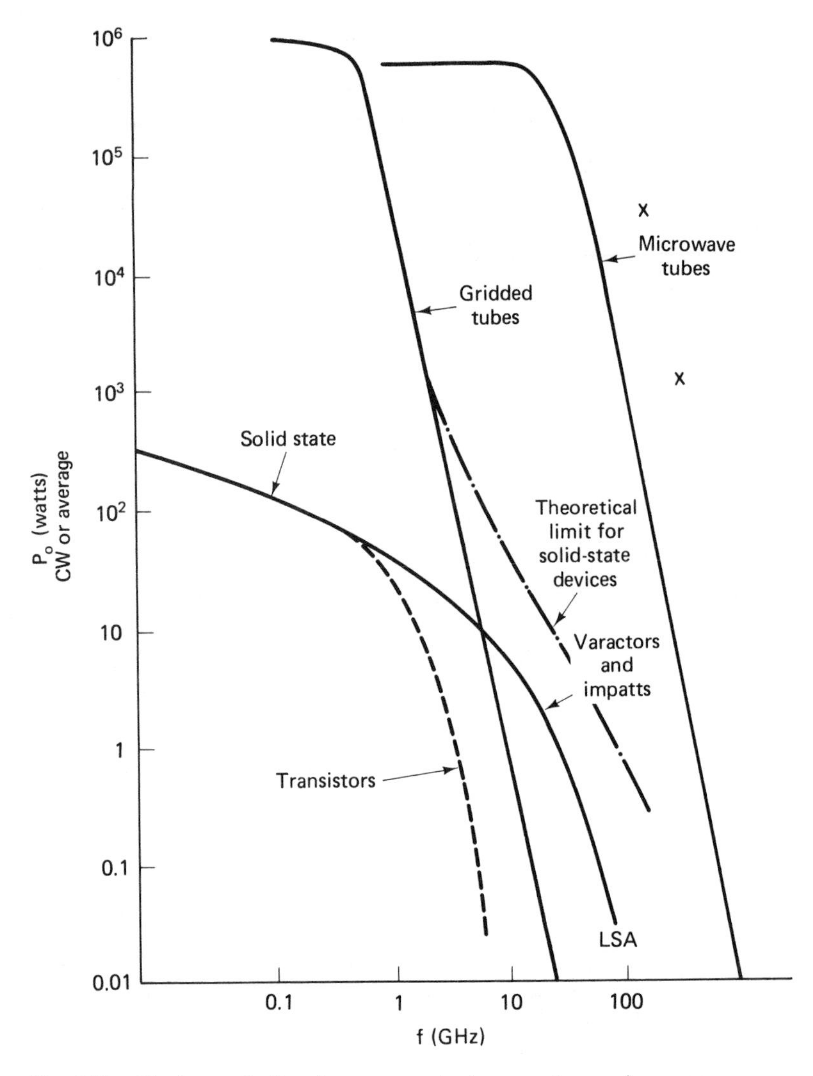


**Fig. 4.10.** Maximum limits of average output power from microwave power sources. (Reprinted by permission from Robert W. Biering, Reference [4.8])

row's communications systems. Presently, double-drift IMPATTS generate up to 20 W of CW power with 20% efficiency at 10 GHz [4.8].

The theoretical limit for semiconductors shown in Fig. 4.10 is based on transit time and voltage breakdown phenomena [4.8].

Among the microwave tubes, the traveling-wave tube (TWT) is the most interesting device for communications applications. It possesses wide signal bandwidth and high reliability and combines efficiency (which is predicted to reach 84% by the year 2000) with output powers of the order of 1-kW in the X band and 200 W in the Ku band [4.8]. Multi-kilowatt levels above 30 GHz have already been generated with so-called fast-wave tubes such as the Soviet gyrotron [4.9]. This performance is indicated in Fig. 4.10 by crosses to the right of the microwave tube curve.

### *4.3.4 Small-Signal Amplifier Performance*

In communications systems having low noise figure requirements, parametric devices such as varactor diodes were most frequently employed. However, significant advances in the realization of low-noise GaAs FET and Si bipolar transistors [4.13] have made these devices extremely competitive, Si bipolars providing lower noise below 3 GHz and FETs being superior above 3 GHz. Wide-band GaAs FET amplifiers with noise figures below 2 dB ($T_n = 170°K$) have been built to operate in the 3.7–4.2 GHz region with 10 dBm output power capability [4.14]. A typical 7 GHz GaAs FET amplifier with 25 dB gain has a noise figure of 4 db ($T_n = 438°K$) and a third-order intercept point of 20 dBm. This performance is sufficient to qualify GaAs FET amplifiers for application in digital communication systems. Uncooled and cooled parametric amplifiers will continue to dominate in applications such as low-power satellite ground stations, deep space communications, and radioastronomy. Figure 4.11 summarizes the noise figures of various solid-state microwave devices [4.2].

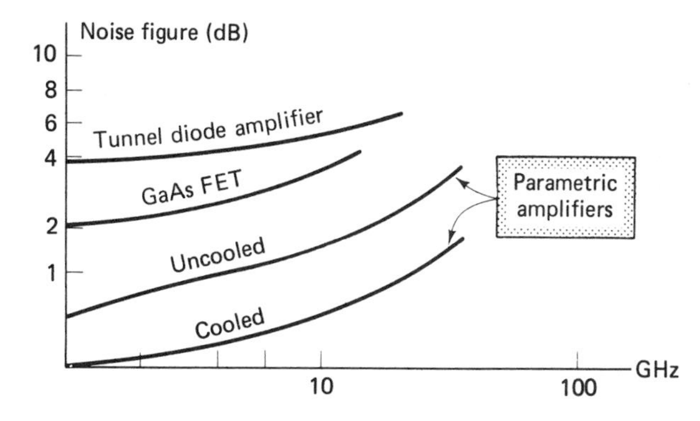


**Fig. 4.11.** Noise figure performance of microwave devices.

## 4.4 SUMMARY AND CONCLUSIONS

Digital microwave communication systems require reliable amplifiers which must fullfill the following main requirements:

The power amplifier at the transmitter end must have a flat gain over the useful bandwidth to avoid altering the overall transfer characteristic of the system. It must also be as linear as possible to avoid restoration of sidelobes in the power spectrum and to limit interference with adjacent channels. Finally, low AM to PM conversion is necessary to limit the $P(e)$ performance degradation caused by this non-linearity.

The small-signal amplifier must, in addition to fulfilling the same requirements as the power amplifier, exhibit sufficiently low inherent noise to amplify the received signal without additional degradation.

Traveling wave tubes (TWT) and GaAs field effect transistors (FET) are the most versatile microwave devices, offering excellent performance in both power and small-signal applications. It can be expected that these devices will have a significantly higher efficiency, power, and frequency capability in the near future.

Parametric devices (varactors) will continue to offer lowest noise performance for small-signal application, while IMPATT diodes are the most powerful solid-state devices to qualify for successful application in digital microwave systems.

## REFERENCES

[4.1] Lebedev, I., *Microwave Electronics*, Mir Publishers, Moscow, 1974.

[4.2] Howes, M. J., D. V. Morgan, *Microwave Devices*, John Wiley & Sons, Ltd., London, 1976.

[4.3] Young, L., *Advances in Microwaves*, Vol. 7, Academic Press, Inc., New York, 1971.

[4.4] Aertech Industries: "Solid State Microwave Amplifiers." Brochure published by Aertech Industries, a subsidiary of TRW, Catalog No. 5978, 1978.

[4.5] Saito, Y., S. Akasaka, S. Fukuda, I. Haga, "6 GHz 5 W GaAS FET Power Amplifier for 78 Mbits/s 8-Phase PSK Signal Transmission," 1978 IEEE MTT-S, Intl. Microwave Symposium, Ottawa, June 27–29, pp. 67–69.

[4.6] Ho, P. T., "A 7 Watt C-Band FET Amplifier Using Serial Power Combining Techniques," 1978 IEEE MTT-S, Intl. Microwave Symposium, Ottawa, June 27–29, pp. 142–144.

[4.7] Rector, R. M., G. D. Vendelin, "A 1.0 Watt GaAs MESFET Oscillator at X-Band," 1978 IEEE MTT-S, Intl. Microwave Symposium, Ottawa, June 27–29, pp. 145–146.

[4.8] Bearse, S. V., "Impatts GaAs FETs and TWTs Deemed Most Likely to Succeed," Microwaves, Vol. 15, No. 7, July, 1976, pp. 14–17.

[4.9] Jory, H. R., F. Friedlander, S. J. Hegji, J. F. Shively, R. S. Symons, "Gyrotrons for High Power Millimeter Wave Generation," 1977 IEEE Intl. Electron Devices Meeting, Washington, D.C. December 5–7, pp. 234–237.

[4.10] Tserng, H. Q., H. M. Macksey, "Microwave GaAs Power FET Amplifiers with Lumped-Element Impedance Matching Networks," 1978 IEEE MTT-S, Intl. Microwave Symposium, Ottawa, June 27–29, pp. 282–284.

[4.11] Yuan, H. T., Y. S. Wu, "A 1.5 Watt 9 GHz Silicon Transistor Power Amplifier," 1978 IEEE MTT-S, Intl. Microwave Symposium, Ottawa, June 27–29, pp. 378–379.

[4.12] Kajiwara, Y., K. Horikiri, Y. Yukimoto, G. Nakumara, M. Aiga, "A New Microwave High Power Transistor (Static Induction Transistor)," 1978 IEEE MTT-S, Intl. Microwave Symposium, Ottawa, June 27–29, pp. 380–382.

[4.13] Okean, H. C., A. J. Kelly, "Low-Noise Receiver Design Trends Using State-of-the-Art Building Blocks," IEEE Trans. on Microwave Theory and Techniques, Vol. MTT-25, No. 4, April, 1977, pp. 254–267.

[4.14] Emery, F. E., "Low-Noise GaAs FET Amplifiers," Microwave Journal, Vol. 20, No. 6, June, 1977, pp. 79–82.

# 5

# SYSTEM GAIN: THE CONCEPT AND ITS APPLICATIONS

The reliability of communications systems is an important factor in design considerations. In this context, the *system gain* is a very useful concept since it aggregates into a single, convenient measure many of the significant factors which affect reliability.

In this chapter we first present a brief survey of reliability objectives, after which system gain requirements necessary to meet these objectives are defined and displayed graphically. The factors which contribute to overall system gain are examined.

There follows a discussion of the mechanism of multi-path fading, its impact on unprotected, single-channel system, and the options available to designers to compensate for this phenomenon.

Co-channel interference, resulting from the "two-frequency plans" favored by regulatory authorities for frequency spectrum conservation, is a major cause of degradation in system gain. The term *co-channel interference* refers to interference from a source having a frequency close to that of the desired carrier. Its effects on system design are examined, and the compromises inherent in various digital modulation schemes are outlined.

Finally, there is a preliminary discussion of frequency-selective fading and its practical effects on system implementation. This section includes a survey of published quantitative values for amplitude and delay distortions caused by frequency-selective fading.

## 5.1 RELIABILITY OBJECTIVES FOR COMMUNICATIONS SYSTEMS

Operators of communications systems naturally expect reliability. Public utilities such as telephone, electric, oil, and gas companies, because of the nature of their business, require highly reliable systems. Their "reliability objectives" are usually specified in terms of the maximum allowable time of failure due to all causes, expressed as a percentage of total service time during a given period, over a given route length.

The reliability objectives of U.S. telephone companies for short-haul systems limit the two-way service failure time caused by propagation effects to *0.01% annually over a 400 km route* [5-16]. The Canadian standard calls for a 0.02% annual maximum, two-way, over the same route length for protected systems and all causes of unavailability. Some of this allocation could be divided between equipment failure, atmospheric multi-path fading, and rainfading. It is assumed that the antenna heights and sight locations are set so that obstruction ("earth bulge") and terrain reflections are of no consequence. Obstruction fading can be decreased by using higher towers or shorter hops or by increasing the hop fade margin. Where obstruction fading is known or expected to occur, increased clearances or shorter path lengths are assumed to be used. Consequently, no allocation to obstruction fading is made, and the entire annual allocation is applied to multi-path fading. A two-way annual fading allocation of 0.01% over a 400 km route is equivalent to 53 minutes (3200 seconds) per year; for a hop $d$ km long, it is $3200 \times d/400$ seconds per year. In the average 50 km hop, this is 400 seconds, or just under 7 minutes per year. Such reliability can be achieved by unprotected space or frequency diversity system design. Detailed Canadian and U.S. long-haul system design objectives are given in references [5.36 and 5.37].

Electric, oil, and gas utilities, because of the large amounts of energy or energy commodities flowing through their transmission systems, have more stringent reliability standards. Their allocation to fading is 0.01% for a non-diversity, unprotected system during the worst month. For some specific systems, an additional requirement of a maximum monthly outage of 0.0001% per hop for a diversity system is specified—a diversity improvement of 100 times. This subject is discussed in detail in Chapter 10.

## 5.2 SYSTEM GAIN

### *5.2.1 Definition of System Gain*

System gain is a useful measure of performance because it incorporates many parameters of interest to the designer of microwave systems. In its simplest form, applying only to the equipment, it is the difference between transmitter output power and the receiver threshold sensitivity for a given bit error rate (BER). Its value must be greater than or at least equal to the sum of the gains and losses which are external to the equipment. Mathematically, it is

$$G_s = P_t - C_{\min} \geq \text{FM} + L_p + L_f + L_b - G_t - G_r \tag{5.1}$$

where $G_s$ = system gain (dB)

$P_t$ = transmitter output power (dBm), excluding antenna branching network

$C_{\min}$ = received carrier level (dBm) for a minimum quality objective. The $C_{\min}$ in dBm is usually specified for a BER $= 10^{-6}$. This is also called the *receiver threshold.*

$L_p$ = free space path loss attenuation between isotropic radiators

$$L_p = 92.4 + 20 \log d + 20 \log f \tag{5.2}$$

where $d$ = path length, in km, and $f$ = carrier frequency (GHz)

$L_F$ = feeder loss. (Loss factors for commonly used feeders are shown in Table 5.1.)

$L_B$ = branching loss, that is, the total filter and circulator loss when transmitters and receivers are coupled to a single line. In an unprotected or

**TABLE 5.1 System Gain Parameters**

| Mid-band Frequency (GHz) | Diversity Spacing ($\Delta f/f$ %)* | Feeder ($L_f$) | | $L_B$ | Antenna ($G_T = G_R$) | |
|---|---|---|---|---|---|---|
| | | Type | Loss/200 m (dB) | Freq. diversity (dB)* | Size (m) | Gain (dB) |
| 1.8 | 2.33 | Air-filled coaxial cable | 10.8 | 5.0 | 2.4<br>3<br>3.7 | 31.2<br>33.2<br>34.7 |
| 7.4 | 4.24 | EWP 64 elliptical waveguide | 9.5 | 3.0 | 2.4<br>3<br>3.7 | 43.1<br>44.8<br>46.5 |
| 8.0 | 2 | EWP 71 elliptical waveguide | 13.0 | 3.0 | 2.4<br>3<br>3.7 | 43.8<br>45.6<br>47.3 |

*Frequency diversity systems and the definition of diversity spacing are discussed in Chapter 10.

space diversity system, the branching loss is typically about 2 dB. For frequency diversity systems, see Table 5.1.

$G_T, G_R$ = gain of transmitter and receiver antennas over an isotropic radiator. Although antenna gains are frequency-dependent, for the sake of simplicity, mid-band gains as published in manufacturers' catalogs are shown in Table 5.1.

FM = hop fade margin (dB) of a non-diversity system required to meet the reliability objective. This parameter is part of the Barnett-Vigant reliability formulas found in references [5.12, 5.13, 5.14].

### 5.2.2 *Fade Margin Requirements for a Specified System Availability*

The Barnett-Vignant reliability equations mentioned in the previous section may be solved explicitly to determine the maximum allowable fade margin for a specified annual system availability. Equation (5.3) indicates the solution for an unprotected non-diversity system.

$$\text{FM} = 30 \log d + 10 \log (6ABf) - 10 \log (1 - R) - 70 \tag{5.3}$$

where $1 - R$ = reliability objective (one way) for a 400 km route

$A$ = roughness factor
= 4 for very smooth terrain, including over water
= 1 for average terrain with some roughness
= $\frac{1}{4}$ for mountainous, very rough terrain

$B$ = factor to convert worst-month probability to annual probability
= $\frac{1}{2}$ for Great Lakes or similar hot, humid areas
= $\frac{1}{4}$ for average inland areas
= $\frac{1}{8}$ for mountainous or very dry areas.

This fade margin is for availabilities on an annual basis. It may be used on a worst-month basis by setting $B = 1$.

Table 5.2 summarizes and reformulates the reliability objectives given previously.

**TABLE 5.2 Reliability Objectives**

| Operator | Case | Reliability Objective $(1 - R)$ |
|---|---|---|
| Common carriers | Two-way | $\frac{0.0001d}{400}$ (U.S.A.) |
| | One-way | $\frac{0.0002d}{400}$ (Canada) |
| Utilities | Worst month (per hop, non-diversity) | 0.0001 |
| | Worst month (per hop, diversity protected) | 0.000001 |

By substituting these objectives into equation (5.3), we may obtain the fade margin for an unprotected utility having 99.99% service reliability per hop. (Service outage $= 1 - R = 0.01\% = 0.0001$, corresponding to $10 \log 0.0001 = -40$ dB.) Thus, a fade margin of

$$\text{FM} = 30 \log d + 10 \log (6Af) - 30 \text{ dB} \tag{5.4}$$

is required. *Note that a 10 dB increase in fade margin gives an order-of-magnitude improvement in reliability.*

Substituting equation (5.4) into (5.1), we obtain the required system gain:

$$\begin{aligned} G_s = {} & 50 \log d + 30 \log f + 10 \log (6A) \\ & + 62.4 + L_F + L_B - G_T - G_R \end{aligned} \tag{5.5}$$

To illustrate this relationship, the required system gain is shown as a function of path length in Fig. 5.1. Here it is assumed that the reliability requirement is $1 - R = 0.01\%$ for a 7.4 GHz non-diversity system planned for a power utility. The system is to operate over average terrain with some roughness, that is, $A = 1$. Inserting these values into equation (5.3), with $d = 50$ km and $B = 1$, we obtain FM = 37.5 dB. Using equation (5.5) and Table 5.1, we obtain the results shown in Fig. 5.1. (In the calculations, it was assumed that the transmitter and receiver antennas were the same size.) Using this procedure, we can easily obtain the system gain requirements for arbitrary path length, antenna size, and reliability objectives. **(Solve Problem 5.1.)**

In subsequent sections, the effect of co-channel interference on system gain is examined. It will be shown that it is necessary to determine fade margin from known system gain, path loss, feeder and branching losses, and antenna gains. The relationship for the fade margin is obtained by rearranging equation (5.1), thus:

$$\text{FM} = G_s - L_P - L_F - L_B + G_T + G_R \tag{5.6}$$

### *5.2.3 Discussion of Results*

For an unprotected common-carrier system, a 5 dB increase in system gain allows a hop to be 25% longer and still provide the same reliability. This conclusion can be used to effect significant savings in cost. For example, consider a 400 km system having (nominally) eight 50 km hops. A 5 dB increase in $G_s$ means that the same reliability can be obtained using 62.5 km hops, which translates, in practice, to seven hops of average length 57.1 km (62.5 km maximum). This is an outright saving of one site, including the tower, building, access roads, etc., and possibly another by adjusting antenna sizes.

Alternatively, for the same number of hops, smaller antenna dishes can be used throughout the system, thus reducing wind loads and, as a result, tower costs. For example, a 200 kph wind (design worst-wind velocity) creates a frontal thrust of 3540 kg on a 4 m parabolic antenna. Reducing the antenna size to 3 m results in a 2450 kg thrust—a 31% reduction. Considering that a tower may hold several antennas, a reduction in loading of this magnitude results in a substantial reduction in cost. **(Solve Problems 5.1 and 5.2.)**

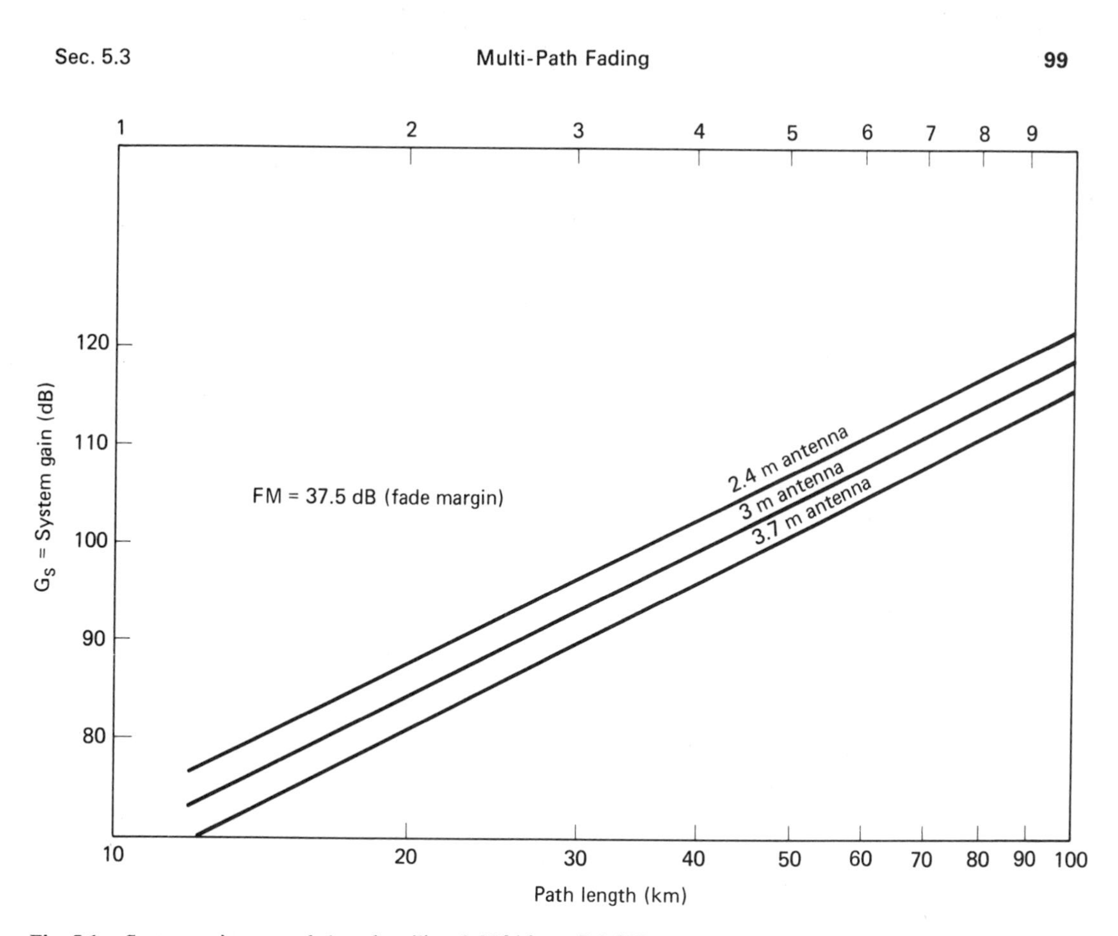


**Fig. 5.1.** System gain vs. path length utility, 0.01% hop, 7.4 GHz non-diversity. For 0.001%, add 10 dB to $G_s$; for mountainous or dry, subtract 6 dB ($A = \frac{1}{4}$); for smooth or humid, add 6 dB ($A = 4$).

## 5.3 MULTI-PATH FADING

### *5.3.1 System Engineering Considerations*

From equations (5.1) and (5.3), it is seen that when the magnitude of a multi-path fade exceeds the fade margin (FM), a condition of potential service failure exists. Protection will be required if the duration of the fade exceeds the time limit imposed by the reliability specifications. $L_P$, the line-of-sight path attenuation, although constant in time, is a function of carrier frequency and path length. The fade depth is a time-varying term, which accounts for all the usual causes of fading and signal loss, that is, atmospheric multi-path, rainfall, and anomalous propagation disturbances, reflections, obstructions, and insufficient path clearance.

Except for multi-path disturbances, these factors will not be discussed since they are well covered in the FDM/FM literature [5.1, 5.2, 5.3]. They are applicable to digital microwave radio systems because they all cause signal fading or attenuation [5.4], thus increasing the system gain requirement by adding to the fade margin in a manner dependent on the type of disturbance. Good engineering judgement is also required since, for example, attenuation due to rainfall and multi-path fading will not normally occur simultaneously. Digital microwave systems have dual-polarization possibilities. It should be noted that polarization decoupling due to rain is a limiting feature. Particular attention has to be given to systems operating above the 6 GHz band [5.38].

### *5.3.2 Geometry of Multi-Path Fading*

As a transmission medium for electromagnetic radiation, the atmosphere is inhomogenous. Spatial variations in temperature, pressure, humidity, turbulance, etc., cause variations in the index of refraction. Figure 5.2 illustrates a simple model of two rays being emitted from a transmitter antenna [5.11]. The two rays will

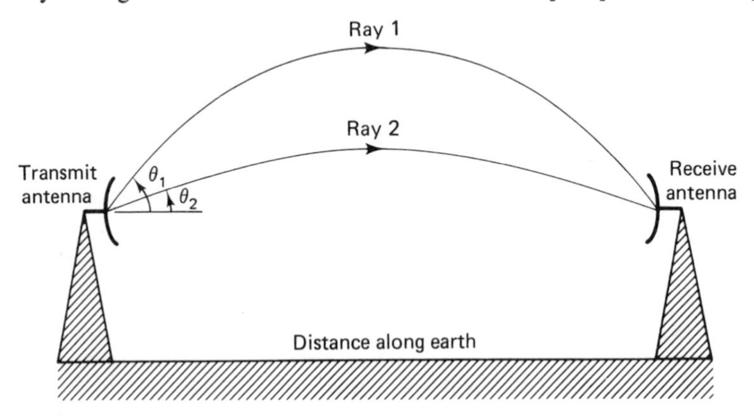


**Fig. 5.2.** Refraction from a single layer.

both arrive at the receiver but, because of differential refraction, will have traveled over different path lengths, be out of phase on arrival, in general, and interfere with each other since the received signal is their vector sum. Reduction of the received signal below its free-space value, as a result of this phenomenon, is called *multiple-path fading*. Since the meteorological parameters also change with time, the observed result is fluctuations of the received signal.

Most severe multi-path fading occurs during clear summer nights when temperature inversions and associated meteorological effects produce negative gradients of the atmospheric index of refraction; that is, it increases with altitude. Figure 5.2 shows a profile of a simplified case: In this example, the gradient of the index of refraction is such that two rays, emitted at angles $\theta_1$ and $\theta_2$, both arrive at the receiver, having traveled paths of different lengths. If the gradient were zero, both rays would undergo the same amount of refraction, with the result that the ray emitted at the angle $\theta_1$ would miss the receiving antenna and there would be no interference.

It is not necessary that the atmosphere be layered; a continuum of path may exist between transmitter and receiver, with the signal components arriving at the receiver antenna with different phase angles. Statistically, it is possible that the aggregate of phase angles is such that the net signal amplitude is zero or near zero. This phenomenon is called a *deep multi-path fade.*

### *5.3.3 Duration of Multi-Path Fading*

The time during which a signal fades below a given level $L$ is called the *duration of fade* of that level; levels in decibels relative to normal are determined in the usual manner, that is, 20 log $L$. Figure 5.3 shows an example in which the free-space signal strength is $-30$ dBm, and a single, idealized fade reduces it temporarily to a minimum of $-80$ dBm. The duration of a 40 dB fade is also illustrated in Fig. 5.3. In general, the average durations of fades are independent of frequency but are proportional to $L$, the depth of fade.

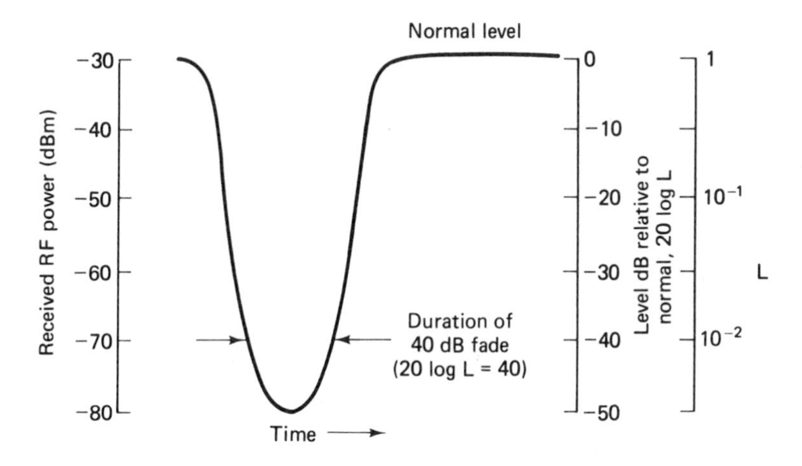


**Fig. 5.3.** Definitions of $L$ and fade duration ($-30$ dBm assumed normal as an example).

A convenient formula for determining the average duration $\tau$ of a fade is:

$$\tau = 410 \cdot L \quad \text{seconds,} \qquad (L \leq 0.1) \tag{5.7}$$

See also Fig. 5.4.

A useful approach to the study of fading due to multi-path interference is to plot the cumulative amplitude distribution of deep fades $P(V \leq L)$ against fade depth (in dB) on logarithmic graph paper, as shown in Fig. 5.5 [5.10]. Examination of large volumes of experimental data indicate that, in general, a straight line with a negative slope of *10 dB per decade* of cumulative probability is a good approximation of most deep fades in non-diversity systems. Algebraically, this is given by

$$P(V \leq L) = EL^2, \qquad (L_{up} > L > 0) \tag{5.8}$$

where $V$ is the envelope voltage of the randomly fading signal normalized to its

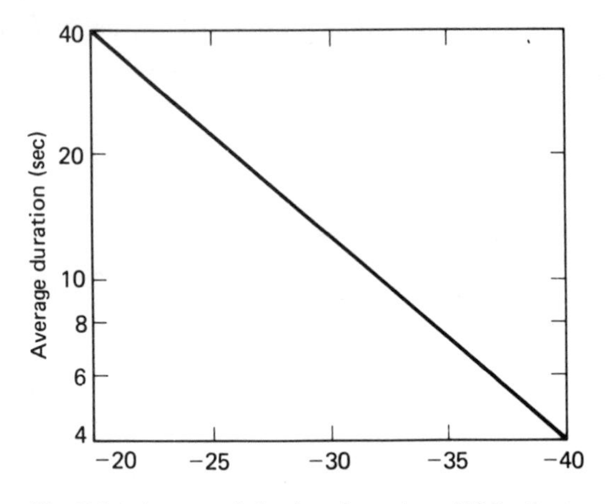


**Fig. 5.4.** Average fade durations ($t = 410\,L,\ L \leq 0.1$).

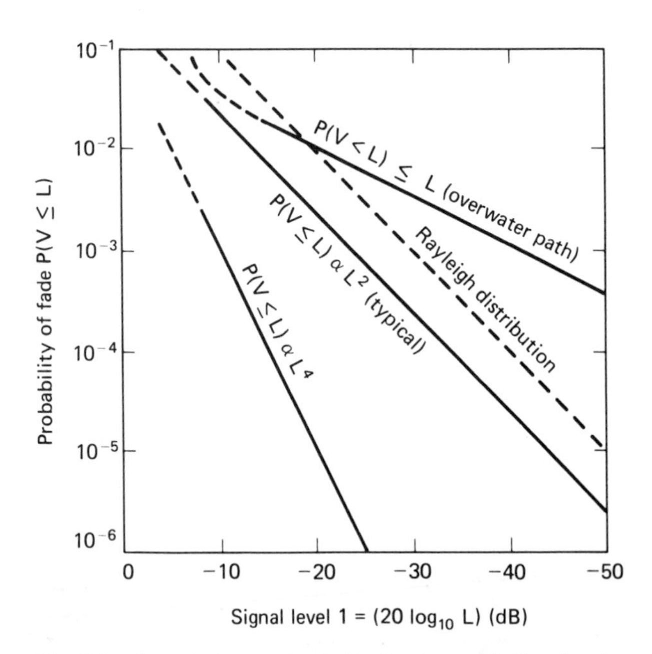


**Fig. 5.5.** Cumulative amplitude distributions of fading signals.

unfaded level, $L$ is any specified reference level, $E$ is a parameter depending on the fading environment, and $L_{up}$ is the upper bound of validity of the straight-line approximation of $P(V \leq L)$.

This empirical result implies that the amplitude distributions of most deep fades in non-diversity systems vary directly as the square of the reference level,

$$P(V \leq L) \propto L^2, \qquad (L_{up} \geq L > 0) \tag{5.9}$$

in spite of the great variability of fading environments and test conditions. This "square law" of Fig. 5.5 is known as *Rayleigh fading*. The duration of a simultaneous fade is shown in Fig. 5.6. In Chapter 10 we present a discussion of the simultaneous fade.

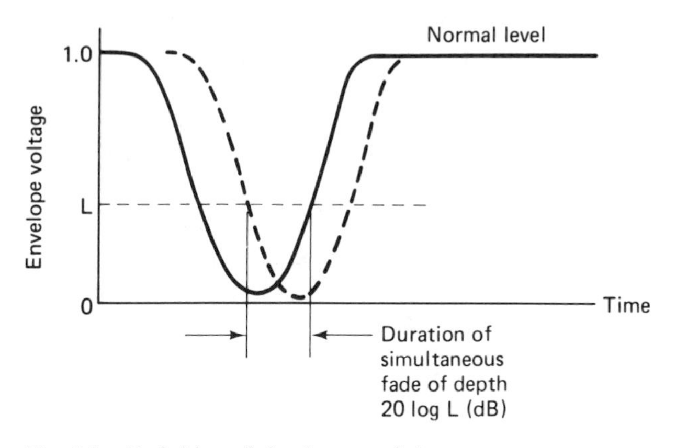


**Fig. 5.6.** Definition of simultaneous fade.

## 5.4 EFFECTS OF FREQUENCY CONTROL SCHEMES

In the interest of frequency spectrum conservation, regulatory authorities show a preference for *two-frequency plans* for multi-hop, two-way, microwave communications systems. In this scheme, the same pair of transmitting/receiving frequencies are used in all hops, resulting in two major co-channel interference exposures per receiver. Figure 5.7 is a schematic representation of a system with three sites, *A*, *B*, and *C*, using parabolic antennas. At point *B*, where the receiving antenna of site *B* faces site *C*, interfering signals $I_{AB}$ and $I_{CB}$ are received from sites *A* and *C*,

**Fig. 5.7.** Two-frequency plan interference.

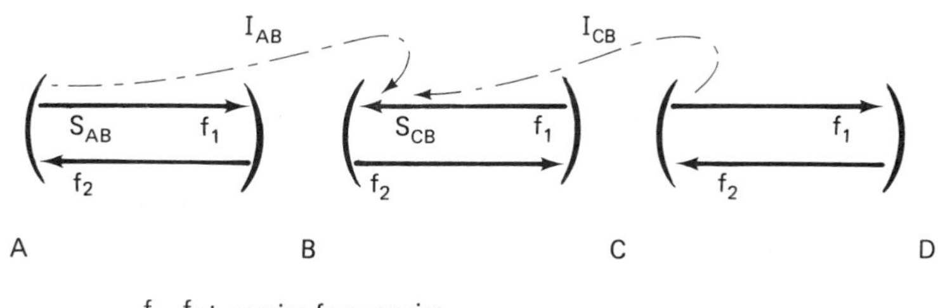


$f_1$, $f_2$: carrier frequencies

$S_{CB}$: victim carrier at site B from site C

$I_{AB}$: interfering carrier from site A (on frequency $f_1$)

$I_{CB}$: interfering carrier from site C (on frequency $f_1$)

respectively. For the purposes of this example the hop lengths between all sites are the same, and the feeder lengths, antenna sizes, and equipment power output are identical at all sites. The same signal level is then received at each site. In practice, of course, this situation seldom exists, and the desired and interfering carrier levels must be adjusted accordingly.

In the system illustrated, $I_{AB}$ traverses path *A–B*, while $I_{CB}$ and $S_{CB}$ (the signal being transmitted from *C* to *B*) both traverse path *C–B*. Since the incidences of fading on successive hops of a multi-hop microwave system are most frequently uncorrelated, the signal-to-interference ratio $S_{CB}/I_{AB}$, from received backside radiation, changes as $S_{CB}$ fades, whereas $S_{CB}/I_{CB}$, from transmitted backside radiation, does not.

Consider first the transmitted backside radiation. When both transmitters at sites *A* and *C* are operating, the ratio $S_{CB}/I_{CB}$ is simply the front-to-back ratio of the antennas used. For the smallest antennas normally employed at 1.8 GHz (2.4 m), this ratio is 39 dB. A carrier-to-interference ratio of this value causes a maximum of 0.2 to 0.3 dB degradation for QPSK, 8 PSK, and QPR modulation [5.17, 5.18, 5.19]. The degradation in threshold for 8-level, PAM-FM, non-coherent detection is approximately 0.8 dB [5.19]; for 16 PSK/APK, it is estimated to be 1 dB [5.18]. The result of this degradation is to raise the receiver sensitivity threshold, thus reducing the available system gain.

A front-to-back ratio of 65 dB is the minimum antenna requirement for the 7.1–7.7 GHz and 7.7–8.2 GHz frequency bands. A carrier-to-interference ratio of this magnitude causes an insignificant amount of degradation with respect to all digital modulation techniques in current use.

If a transmitter ceases to operate, the undesired signal must be sufficiently below (typically 6 dB) the victim receiver threshold that the PCM channel banks will be disabled on loss of the desired signal. The available fade margin for a 2.4 m antenna then becomes 39 dB − 6 dB, or 33 dB, which is generally sufficient for short hops.

The interference signal from received backside radiation ($I_{AB}$) causes maximal degradation when $S_{CB}$ fades to the design threshold value. At this level, the receiver demodulator makes more erroneous decisions than would be caused by thermal noise alone; consequently, $P(e)$ is increased to a value greater than the desired $10^{-6}$. For QPSK, the least sensitive of the modulation techniques discussed here, $P(e)$ increases somewhat more than an order of magnitude (from $10^{-6}$ to $10^{-5}$) when the carrier-to-interference ratio is 18 dB.

In the example being considered (Fig. 5.7), when $S_{CB}$ has faded and the interfering signal $I_{AB}$ has not, the only protection against the interference is the front-to-back ratio of the antenna located at site *B*, facing site *C*. Thus, the minimum front-to-back ratio required for this antenna is the sum of the fade margin between 30 and 40 dB and the threshold $C/I$ ratio.

This value must be at least 50 to 60 dB when QPSK modulation is used; up to 10 dB more is necessary, otherwise. Generally, such values can be achieved by using the high-performance (and highly priced) shrouded antennas that are available for the 6 to 8 GHz bands. At 1.8 GHz, these front-to-back ratios are difficult to obtain even when high-performance antennas are used; they have not been achieved with the simple, low-cost antennas normally used for this band.

### *5.4.1 Effect of Co-Channel Interference on Gain of Digital System*

The key to solving the problem mentioned at the end of the last section is to recognize that, from the overall system point of view, a decrease in system gain is equivalent to an increase in receiver threshold, for a given carrier-to-interference ratio. Thus, a given $P(e)$ can be maintained in the presence of interference by increasing the carrier-to-noise ratio, or the received carrier amplitude, of the victim receiver. This not only overcomes the difficulty found, as mentioned above, in the 1.8 GHz band but may also result in the ability to use smaller antennas in the 6–8 GHz range.

In Fig. 5.8 the approximate increase in carrier-to-noise ratio required to maintain a specified error rate, plotted against carrier-to-interference ratio for 2-PSK, 4-PSK, 8-PSK, QPR (class I duobinary), 8-level, PAM-FM, and 16-PSK modulated carriers is shown [5.19, 5.29, 5.31, 5.39]. Note that the increases are all less than 10 dB. It should be possible to accommodate small values in the design as a decrease in system gain, in much the same way as is allowed for conventional feeder losses or decreases in transmitter power output.

Greater values of degradation, in higher-ary modulation schemes, will compromise the system design more and will, as discussed earlier, lead to higher equipment and circuit costs.

## 5.5 FREQUENCY SELECTIVE FADING

Deep fading causes a significant amount of both amplitude and delay distortion in the channel; in turn, this leads to intersymbol interference and a resulting decrease in system gain and, with it, the fade margin. This occurs at a time when the maximum system fade margin is desired. A degradation of the cross-polarization discrimination has also been observed during deep fading. This causes an increase in channel interference; the net result is, once again, a reduction in system gain [5.16, 5.19, 5.21].

Some quantitative observations of the variation of signal amplitude with frequency have been made. [5.22, 5.23]. These can be approximated by functions having both linear and quadratic components, as shown in Fig. 5.9.

In Fig. 5.10, the dependence of phase distortion on frequency is shown. This empirical result is derived from observation over one path of a non-diversity system [5.24]. The graph indicates, for example, that fades of 40 dB are accompanied by a linear time delay distortion which exceeds 1 ns/MHz for 50% of the fades.

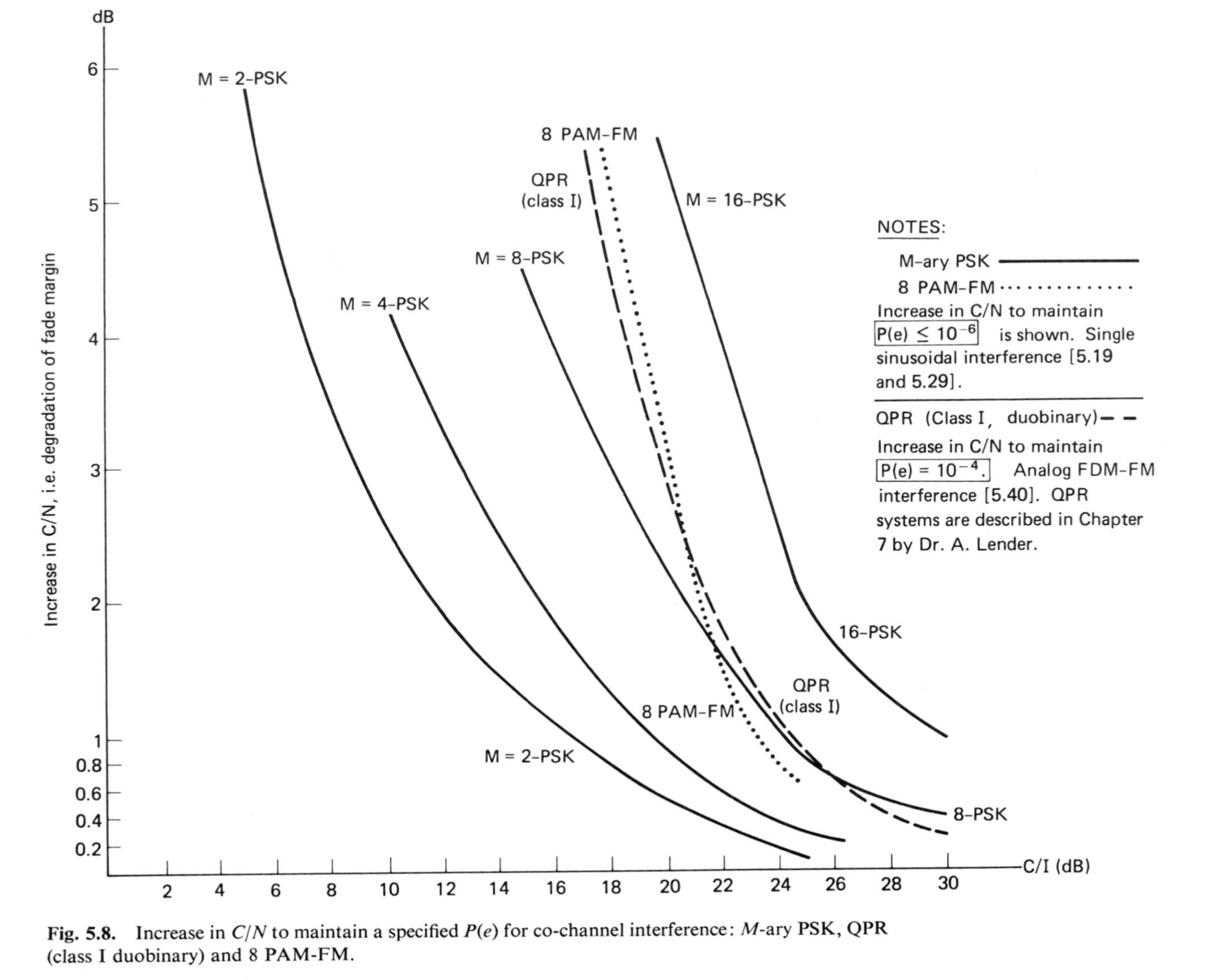


**Fig. 5.8.** Increase in $C/N$ to maintain a specified $P(e)$ for co-channel interference: $M$-ary PSK, QPR (class I duobinary) and 8 PAM-FM.

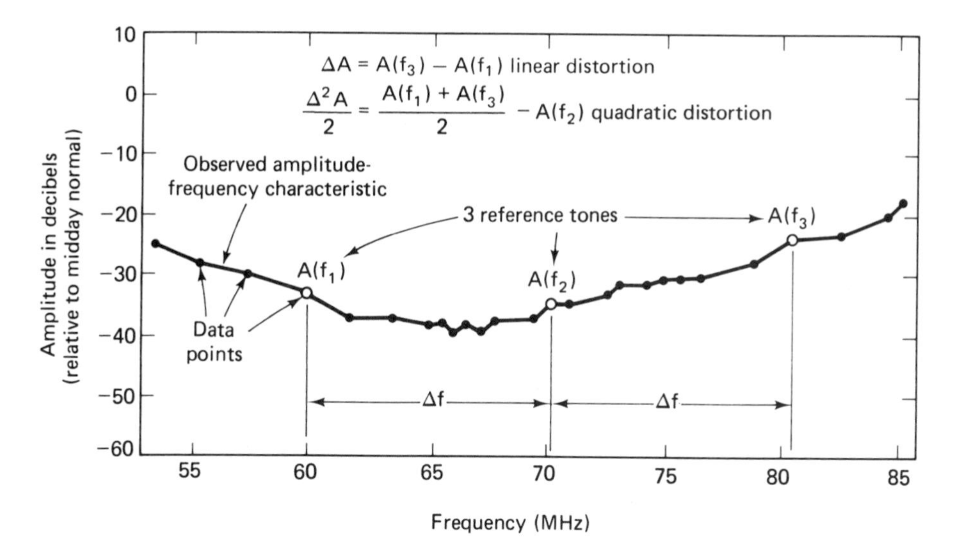


**Fig. 5.9.** Selectivity characterization of the observed amplitude-frequency characteristic. (Redrawn with permission from the *Bell System Technical Journal*, Copyright 1972, The American Telephone and Telegraph Company, References [5.22 and 5.23])

Although there is some experimental work reported in the literature, for most system studies computer simulations are required in order to determine the intersymbol interference due to amplitude and delay distortions [5.19, 5.26, 5.27, 5.30].

The effects of the amplitude-slope distortion (linear distortion) on $C/N$ degradation are illustrated in Fig. 5.11. In this figure computer-calculated $C/N$ degradations of 22.5 M Baud (67.5 Mb/s) 8-PSK and of 22.5 M Baud (44.5 Mb/s) 45 Mb/s QPSK and *offset keyed* QPSK systems are presented. In offset QPSK (O-QPSK) systems the binary symbols in the quadrature channel are one-half of a symbol interval shifted in reference to the symbols in the in-phase channel. Offset QPSK signals have a lower sideband regeneration when transmitted through non-linear output amplifiers. From Fig. 5.11 it is evident that the higher-ary 8-PSK system having a higher bit rate (67.5 Mb/s) is much more sensitive to the amplitude-slope imperfection than the lower-speed (45 Mb/s) QPSK system. However, for amplitude slopes less than 0.45 dB/MHz, the performance of the 45 Mb/s 8-PSK system is better than the performance of the 45 Mb/s QPSK system.

The measured $C/N$ degradation results due to amplitude and delay slope on a Farinon Canada Ltd., 45 Mb/s O-QPSK system as well as computer generated results are shown in Fig. 5.12. The cause of added degradation in the measured results is due to carrier recovery jitter and hardware imperfections which were not taken into account in the computer program.

Both computer simulations and experimental work clearly indicate that higher-speed multi-level systems (e.g., QPR and 8-phase PSK systems) are more sensitive to amplitude and phase distortions than lower-speed QPSK systems [5.27, 5.28,

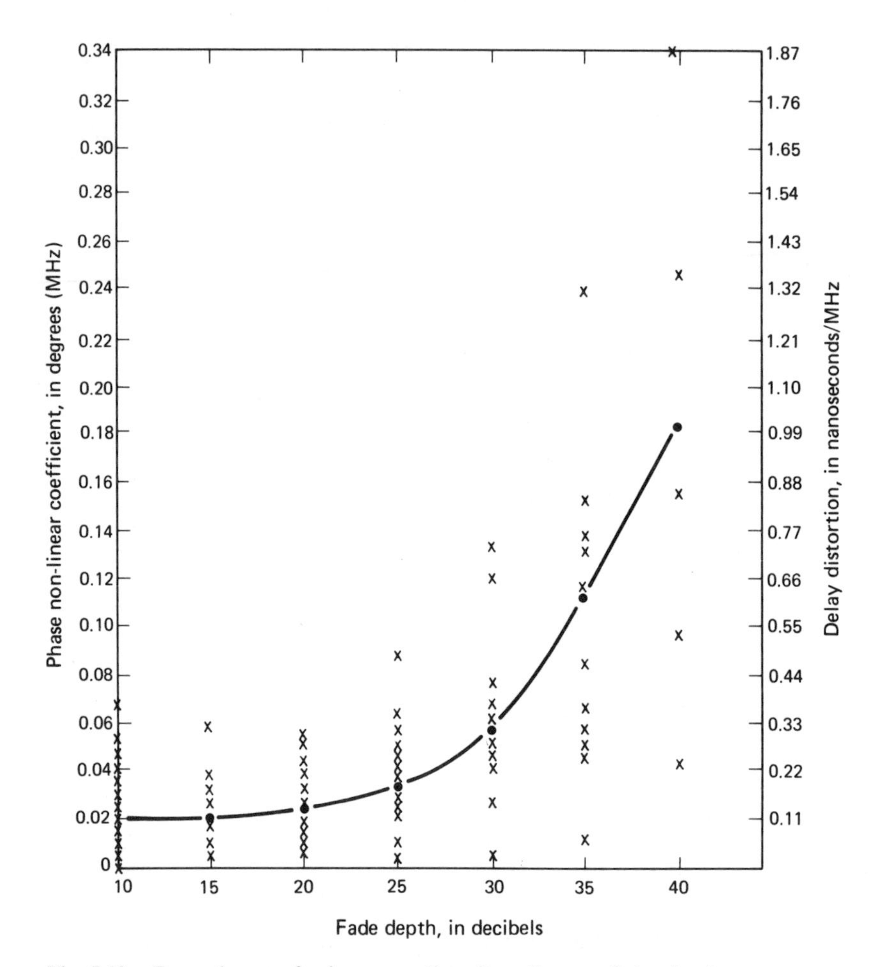


**Fig. 5.10.** Dependence of phase non-linearity, $C_\phi$, on fade depth. (Redrawn by permission from the *Bell System Technical Journal*, copyright 1972, The American Telephone and Telegraph Company, Reference [5.24])

5.31, 5.32]. For digital systems operating in an environment which produces frequency-selective fading, particularly where hop lengths exceed about 30 km, it appears that adaptive equalization is desirable at data rates of 45 Mb/s and essential at 90 Mb/s. **(Solve Problems 5.3 and 5.4.)**

## 5.6 SUMMARY AND CONCLUSIONS

The fade margin requirements for each hop of a digital microwave communications system are fixed by that portion of the operator's reliability objective which is allocated to propagation effects. The system gain relates the fade margin to the radio and antenna characteristics.

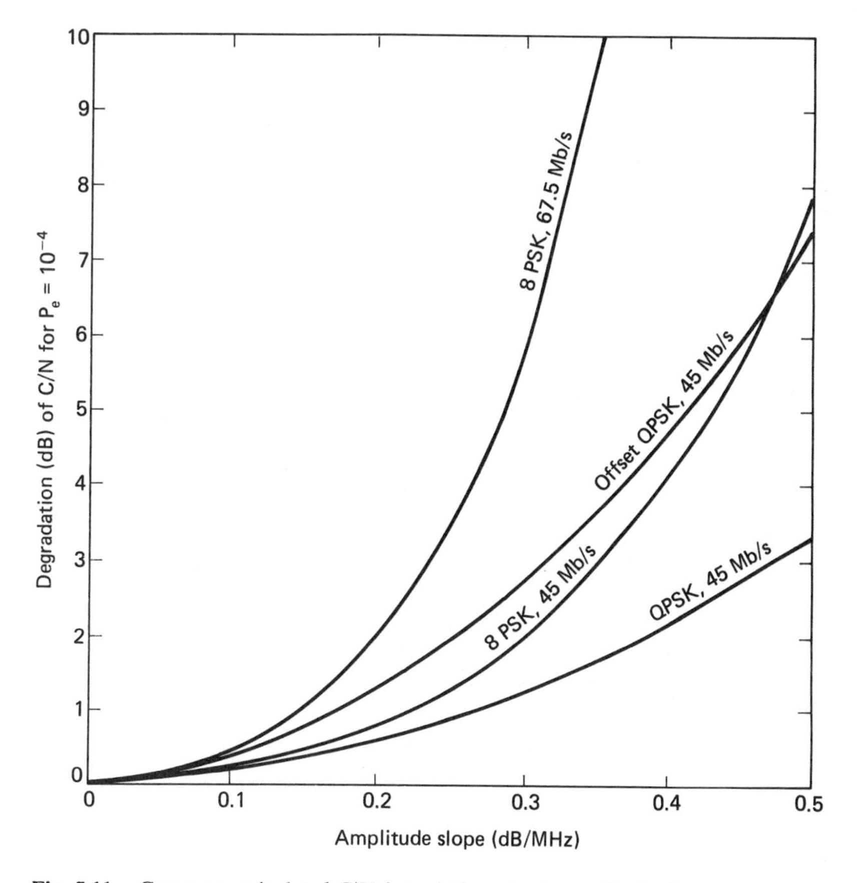


**Fig. 5.11.** Computer-calculated *C/N* degradations due to amplitude slope distortion. (Redrawn by permission from Reference [5.30])

Given the available system gain, the reliability objective, and the antenna characteristics, the maximum path length can be calculated. The only type of propagation-caused outage which is significant in such considerations is multi-path or Rayleigh fading since other sources can effectively be eliminated by good path design. Use of the Barnett-Vigants equation enables the determination of system gain requirements for various physiographic and climatological regimes.

The formulas given are empirical, being based on experimental observations of multi-path fading. Most of the observed effects can be explained by a simple atmospheric layering model, where the layers through which the signals propagate have different indices of refraction. The cumulative distributions of fading amplitudes are well approximated by straight lines having negative slopes of about 10 dB per decade of probability, when plotted on log-log graph paper.

Multi-path fading, because of its frequency-selective nature, causes some reduc-

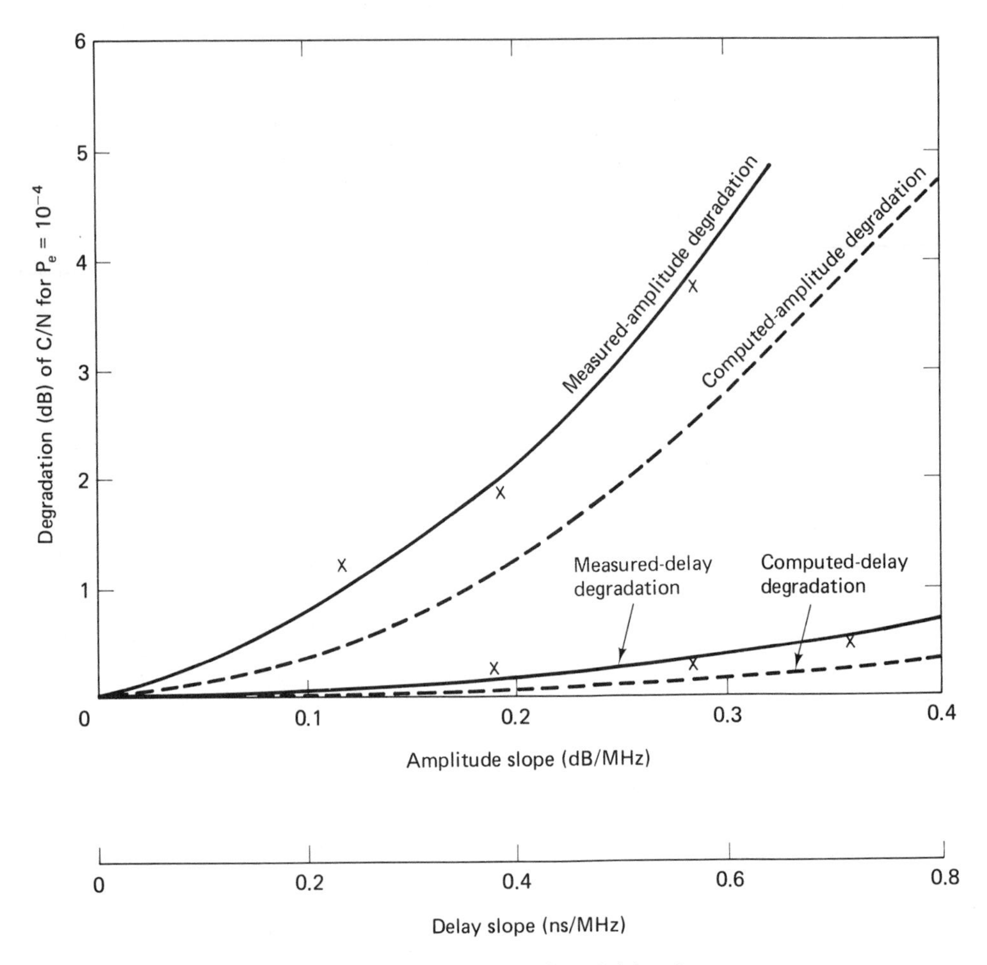


**Fig. 5.12.** Measured $C/N$ degradation due to amplitude and delay slope on a 45 Mbit/s offset QPSK, 50% raised-cosine system. (Redrawn by permission from Reference [5.30])

tion in available system gain in medium-capacity systems operating in the 6 to 8 GHz range. The amplitude and group delay distortions resulting from fading cause intersymbol interference. The threshold bit-error-rate limit of the receiver increases by 10 to 15 dB, thus reducing the overall available system gain. To avoid this significant system gain, reduction-adaptive equalization techniques have been developed [5.32].

QPSK/QAM systems, which usually have a higher gain to start with, are affected less than those using 8-PSK or QPR modulation. As usual, the reduction in available system gain increases costs because shorter hops (heading to more sites) and more complex antenna systems (larger antennas, space diversity) are required.

## PROBLEMS

**5.1** The reliability requirement of a one-hop non-diversity system is 99.99% per hop. Assuming that this system will operate on average terrain with some roughness and will have a carrier frequency of 1.8 GHz, calculate the maximum path length between hops if the system gain is 105 dB and the receive and transmit antenna diameters are 3 m.

**5.2** The permissible service outage for an operating company is 0.001% per hop. What is the required system gain if the transmission is in the lower 2 GHz band, the transmit and receive antennas have 2.4 m diameters, and a hop length of 40 km is desired?

**5.3** The transmitter output power of a digital microwave system is 33 dBm. The system is employed for the transmission of four T-1 data streams (6.3 Mb/s). This system has a QPSK modem operating in a 3.5 MHz RF bandwidth. The center of the RF bandwidth is at 1.8 GHz, and the system operates in a non-diversity mode. The receiver sensitivity for a $P(e) = 10^{-6}$ is $-80$ dBm. Calculate the maximal path length of a hop if the system is intended to have a reliability of 0.001% and will operate on mountainous terrain. If the receiver noise figure is 6 dB, estimate the total degradation of the modem due to intersymbol interference and other causes. If an adaptive transversal filter could eliminate all intersymbol interference degradation, then estimate the maximum hop length.

**5.4** The purchase of a 7.4 GHz non-diversity system is considered by an electric utility. This system would operate in a very humid area. It is required that the system carry 45 Mb/s. If a QPSK system is considered, having a 3 dB degradation from the theoretical additive white gaussian $P(e)$ curve, determine the maximal hop length if 99.99% reliability per hop is required. Assume that the transmit power is 32 dBm, the transmit and receive antennas have 2.4 m diameters, and the receive noise figure is 7 dB.

## REFERENCES


[5.1] White, R. F., "Engineering Considerations for Microwave Systems." Report by GTE Lenkurt, Inc., San Carlos, CA., 1975.

[5.2] Lin, S. H., "From Rain to Attenuation Application to 11 GHz Radio," Proc. IEEE International Conference on Communications, ICC-77, Vol. 1, Chicago, June, 1977.

[5.3] Laine, R. U., "Blackout Fading in Line-of-Sight Microwave Links," 1975 PIEA-PESA-PEPA Conference, Dallas, April 22–24, 1975.

[5.4] Gill, W. J., "Transmission Engineering Considerations for Digital Microwave," Telephony, October 11, 1976, pp. 24–28.

[5.5] DeLange, O. E., "Propagation Studies at Microwave Frequencies by Means of Very Short Pulses," B.S.T.J., Vol. 31, No. 1, January, 1952, pp. 91–103.

[5.6] Crawford, A. B., W. C. Jakes, "Selective Fading of Microwaves," B.S.T.J., Vol. 31, No. 1, January, 1952, pp. 68–90.

[5.7] Sharpless, W. M., "Measurement of the Angle of Arrival of Microwaves," Proc. IRE, Vol. 34, No. 11, November, 1946, pp. 837–845.

[5.8] Crawford, A. B., "Further Observations of the Angle of Arrival of Microwaves," Proc. IRE, Vol. 34, No. 11, November, 1946, pp. 845–848.

[5.9] Kaylor, R. L., "A Statistical Study of Selective Fading of Super-High Frequency Radio Signals," B.S.T.J., Vol. 32, No. 9, September, 1953, pp. 1187–1202.

[5.10] Lin, S. H., "Statistical Behavior of a Fading Signal," B.S.T.J., Vol. 50, No. 10, December, 1971.

[5.11] Ruthroff, C. L., "Multiple-Path Fading on Line-of-Sight Microwave Radio Systems as a Function of Path Length and Frequency," B.S.T.J., Vol. 50, No. 7, September, 1971.

[5.12] Barnett, W. T., "Occurrence of Selective Fading As a Function of Path Length Frequency, Geography," Proc. IEEE International Conference on Communications, ICC-70.

[5.13] Barnett, W. T., "Microwave Line-of-Sight Propagation With and Without Frequency Diversity," B.S.T.J., October, 1970, pp. 1827–1871.

[5.14] Vigants, A., "Number and Duration of Fades at 6 and 4 GHz," B.S.T.J., March, 1971, pp. 815–841.

[5.15] Department of Communications (DOC), Canada, Ottawa, RSP 113, Issue 2, Final Draft, March 26, 1975.

[5.16] Vigants, A., "Space Diversity Engineering," B.S.T.J., Vol. 54, No. 1, January, 1975, pp. 103–142.

[5.17] Prabhu, V. K., "Error Rate Considerations for Coherent Phase-Shift Keyed Systems with Co-channel Interference," B.S.T.J., March, 1969, pp. 743–767.

[5.18] Jurasek, J. R., "Performance of Digital Modems with Co-channel Interference and Gaussian Noise," U.S. Office of Telecommunication, Institute of Telecommunications Science, publ. #PB 251 961, February, 1976.

[5.19] Feher, K., "Digital Modulation Techniques in an Interference Environment," *EMC Encyclopedia*, Vol. 9, Don White Consultants, Inc., Gainesville, VA, September, 1977.

[5.20] Zenko, W., "Digital Microwave Communications for the Power Utilities," A.P.P.A., Engineering and Operations Workshop, Seattle, February 25, 1975.

[5.21] Giger, A. J., T. L. Osborne, "3A-RDS 11 GHz Radio System," Proc. IEEE International Conference on Communications, ICC-75, June, 1975.

[5.22] Babler, G. M., "A Study of Frequency-Selective Fading for a Microwave Line-of-Sight Narrowband Radio Channel," B.S.T.J., March, 1972, p. 731.

[5.23] Babler, G. M., "Selectively Faded Non-Diversity and Space Diversity Narrowband Microwave Radio Channels," B.S.T.J., February, 1973, p. 239.

[5.24] Subramanian, M., K. O'Brien, P. J. Puglis, "Phase Dispersion Characteristics During Fade in a Microwave Line-of-Sight Radio Channel," B.S.T.J., December, 1973, p. 1877.

[5.25] Lundquist, L., M. Lopriore, F. M. Gardner, "Transmission of 4 Ø—Phase-Shift Keyed Time-Division Multiple Access Over Satellite Channels," IEEE Trans. Communications, September, 1974, p. 1354.

[5.26] Sunde, E. D., "Pulse Transmission by AM, FM and PM in the Presence of Phase Distortion," B.S.T.J., Vol. 40, No. 2, March, 1961, pp. 353–422.

[5.27] El-Torky, M. A., K. Feher, "Analysis and Design of Band-Limiting Filters to Meet FCC Restrictions for Digital QPSK Radio Systems in an Interference Environment," Proc. IEEE International Conference on Communications, ICC-78, Toronto, June, 1978.

[5.28] Huang, J., K. Feher, "On Partial Response Transmission Systems," Proc. IEEE International Conference on Communications, ICC-77, June, 1977.

[5.29] Spilker, J. J., *Digital Communications by Satellite*, Prentice-Hall, Inc., Englewood Cliffs, N.J., 1977.

[5.30] Morais, D. H., A. Severinson, K. Feher, "The Effects of Amplitude and Delay Slope Distortions on an 8 GHz Offset QPSK Digital Radio System," IEEE Canadian Communications and Power Conference, Montreal, October, 1978, and in a revised form in the IEEE Transactions on Communications, December, 1979.

[5.31] Wachira, M., "Partial-Response Transmission Systems," M.Sc.A. Thesis, Department of Electrical Engineering, University of Ottawa, Ottawa, March, 1979.

[5.32] Hartman, P., "Adaptive Equalizer for 6 GHz Digital Radio," Proc. IEEE International Conference on Communications, ICC-79, Boston, June, 1979.

[5.33] Prabhu, V. K., L. J. Greenstein, "Analysis of Multipath Outage with Applications to 90 Mb/s PSK Systems at 6 & 8 GHz," Proc. IEEE International Conference on Communications, ICC-78, Toronto, June, 1978.

[5.34] Barnett, W. T., "Measured Performance of a High Capacity 6 GHz Digital Radio System," Proc. IEEE International Conference on Communications, ICC-78, Toronto, June, 1978.

[5.35] Trans-Canada Telephone Systems, "Short Haul Systems," TCTS, TG. 2.006, Ottawa, August, 1973.

[5.36] Trans-Canada Telephone Systems, "Long Haul Systems," TCTS, TG. 2.005, Ottawa, August, 1973.

[5.37] Sartori, H. J., "Path Availability in Microwave Radio System Design," Rockwell International, Collins Transmission Systems Division, 523-0602739-101A3R, Dallas, September, 1978.

[5.38] Stretten, A., "Digital Microwave Fundamentals." Course No. 48391, Saskatchewan Telephones, March, 1979.

[5.39] Hartmann, P. R., E. W. Allen, M. Ramadan, "Effects of Interference, Cross-Polarization, Rain, and Multipath on Digital Systems," Rockwell International, Collins Transmission Systems Division, 523-0602754-101A3R, Dallas, September, 1978.

[5.40] Transmission Division, Radio Systems Design Group, Bell Northern Research Ltd., "A Determination of Technical Criteria for the Coordination of Digital and Analogue Microwave Systems." Vol. II: *Interference into Digital Systems*, The Department of Communications, Government of Canada, DSS-16ST., 36100-7-0748, Ottawa, March, 1978.

# 6

# *M*-ARY PSK AND QAM MICROWAVE SYSTEMS

In Chapter 3, we describe the principles of simple modulation techniques and we also give a performance summary for a large class of modulated systems in a linear additive white gaussian noise (AWGN) environment. Chapter 4 deals with the characteristics of linear and non-linear microwave amplifiers. Chapter 5 features the system gain concept, and its applications are also introduced.

Now, as a well equipped reader, you should find it relatively easy to understand the principles of operation and the performance characteristics of the more sophisticated $M$-ary phase shift keyed (PSK) and $M$-ary quadrature amplitude modulated (QAM) digital radio systems presented in this chapter. Following the description of a multichannel digital radio transmitter and receiver, the theory of operation of bandwidth-efficient $M$-ary PSK and QAM systems is presented. These systems frequently have a spectral efficiency of 3b/s/Hz or higher. The filtering requirements and a practical optimization procedure designed to meet FCC or other regulatory constraints are described in Section 6.3. In Chapter 4 it is pointed out that microwave power amplifiers (PA) operate more efficiently in the non-linear mode, close to saturation, which implies that in this operating mode a higher transmitted power can be obtained. Unfortunately, a non-linear amplifier causes spectral spreading; also, due to the AM to AM and AM to PM non-linearities, a $P(e)$ degradation exists. These effects are highlighted in Section 6.4. Finally, in the last two sections of this chapter, digital radio system performance design guidelines are presented, and the performance characteristics of typical $M$-ary PSK and QAM systems analyzed.

## 6.1 BLOCK DIAGRAM OF A DIGITAL TRANSCEIVER

Figure 6.1 shows the major functional building blocks of a multichannel digital radio transmitter intended to operate in a frequency plan in which all adjacent channels are cross-polarized. This frequency plan has been adopted in Canada in the 8 GHz band to ease receiver filtering requirements [6.22]. Here we use the same nomenclature as in the description of the single-channel heterodyne transceiver block diagram (Fig. 1.8).

In a multichannel system, such as shown in Fig. 6.1, the spectrum of the transmitted signal outside the authorized bandwidth must be controlled. This is required in order that adjacent channel interference be limited to the specifications imposed by regulatory agencies. A number of methods exist to control the spectrum of a transmitted signal. For a specified bit rate and emission limits, multi-state signaling combined with steep filtering is frequently required. To control the spectrum by means of filtering, the designer has to decide whether to use pre-modulation low-pass (LPF) filters, IF band-pass Filters ($BPF_1$), RF band-pass filters ($BPF_2$) preceding the PA or RF band-pass Filters ($BPF_3$) after the output PA. For some IF and RF frequencies and non-linear output stages it might be advantageous to use a combination of all of these filters. **(Solve Problem 6.1.)**

An example of spectral control is illustrated in Fig. 6.2, where the FCC-authorized bandwidth at 6 GHz is shown. In order to avoid excessive adjacent-channel interference, the transmitted spectrum must be confined within the illustrated 30 MHz-wide FCC mask. If it is required to transmit two multiplexed DS-3 data streams (approximately 90 Mb/s) within the boundaries of this authorized bandwidth, then a modulation technique having an efficiency of at least 3 b/s/Hz is required. The spectrum of an $M$-ary PSK system, for an equiprobable binary random-data ($f_b = 1/T_b$) rate, is

$$S(f) = A^2 T_s \left\{ \frac{\sin [\pi T_s(f - f_c)]}{\pi T_s(f - f_c)} \right\}^2 \tag{6.1}$$

where $T_s$ is the unit symbol duration given by

$$T_s = (\log_2 M) T_b \tag{6.2}$$

$f_c$ is the unmodulated carrier frequency, and $A^2$ is a constant proportional to the total $M$-ary PSK power. From Chapter 3 we conclude that, in order to achieve the stipulated 3b/s/Hz bandwidth efficiency, an $M = 8$ or higher-ary modulation technique is required. For our 90 Mb/s application, we choose an $M$ = 8-phase

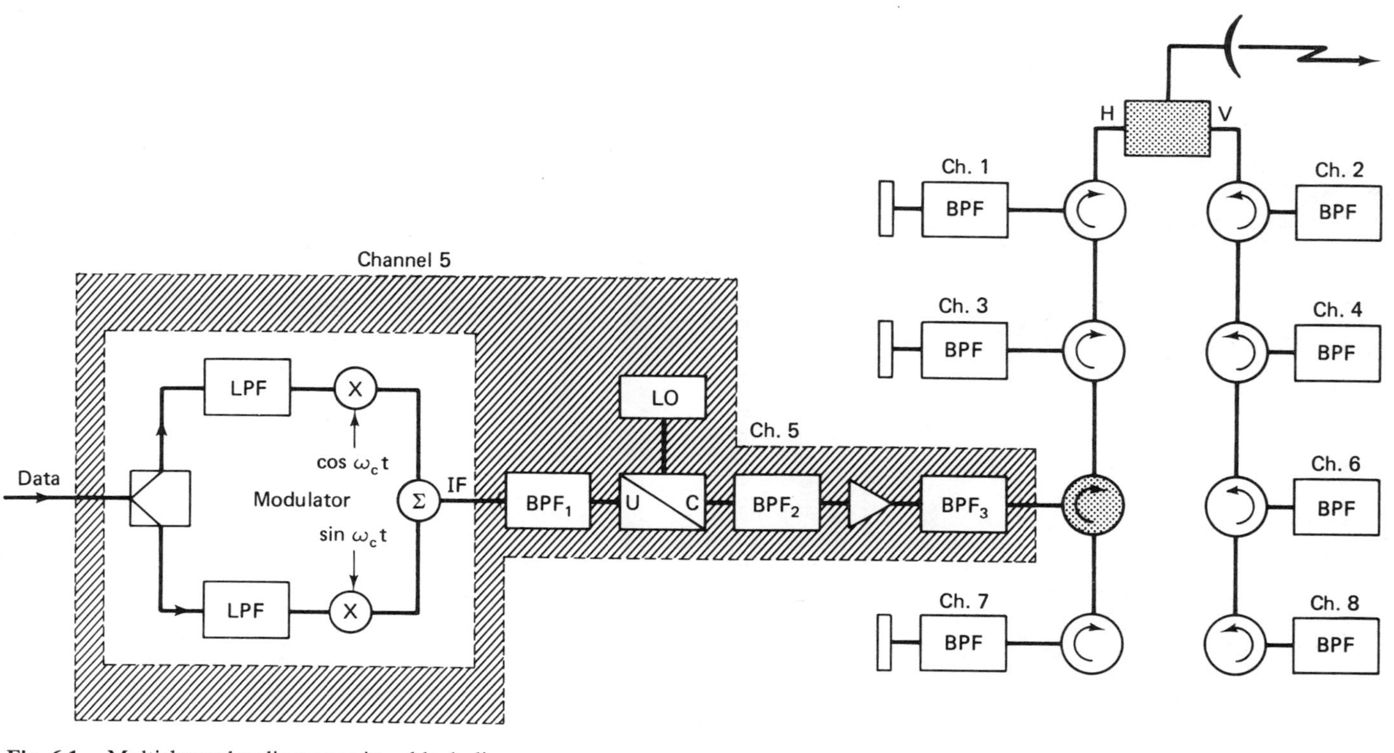


Fig. 6.1. Multichannel radio transmitter block diagram.

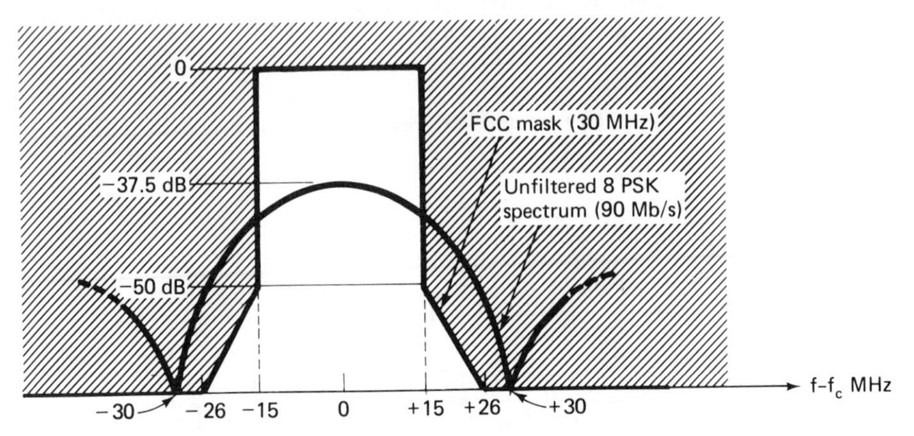


**Fig. 6.2.** FCC mask in relation to the 30 MHz bandwidth allocation at 6 GHz and the unfiltered spectrum of $M = 8$-ary 90 Mb/s PSK data.

PSK system. From the shape of the unfiltered 8-PSK spectrum, shown in Fig. 6.2, and the authorized mask, it is seen that very tight filtering is required to satisfy the emission limits. This filtering might be achieved by a combination of the filters illustrated in Fig. 6.1.

The multichannel radio receiver, shown in Fig. 6.3, has a radio frequency and intermediate frequency band-pass filter designed to reduce noise and adjacent channel interference [6.6]. In addition to these filters, a post-demodulation low-pass filter may be used to achieve the same ends.

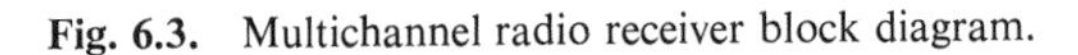

**Fig. 6.3.** Multichannel radio receiver block diagram.

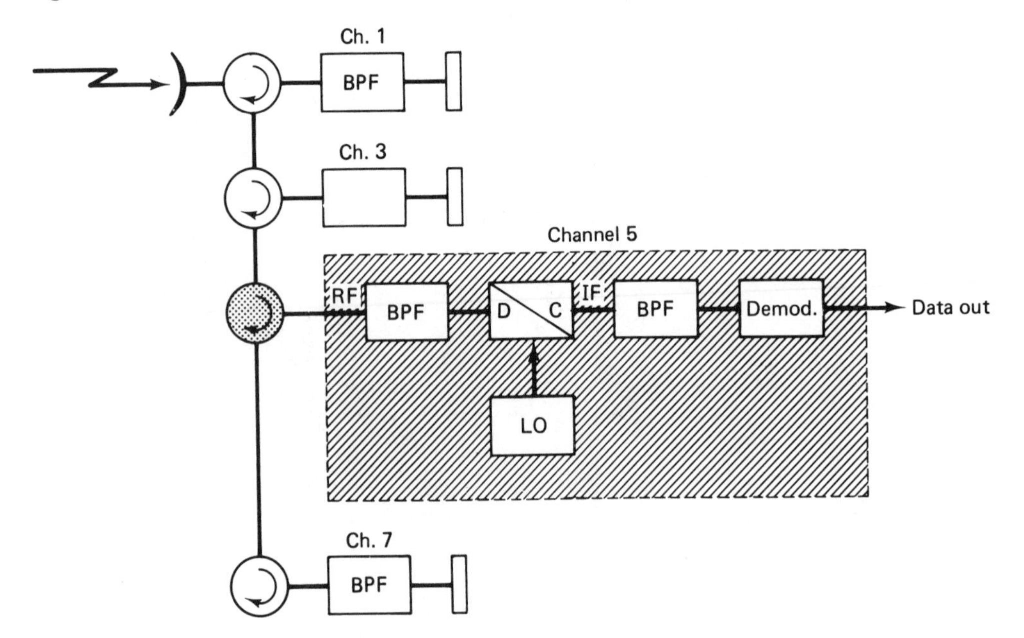

In summary, for bandwidth-efficient radio transmission (e.g., $\geq$ 3b/s/Hz) it is necessary to use higher-ary modulation techniques ($M \geq 8$) and design filters which approach the Nyquist limit. In the following section we describe $M$-ary PSK and QAM modulation techniques which satisfy these requirements. **(Solve Problem 6.2.)**

## 6.2 BANDWIDTH-EFFICIENT DIGITAL RADIO SYSTEMS

In this section 8-phase 8-PSK systems and 16-ary quadrature amplitude modulated (QAM) systems are described. The 8-PSK systems are frequently employed for 15 to 100 Mb/s range radio transmission requirements. The 16-ary QAM systems were developed for highly efficient (4 b/s/Hz) transmission requirements.

### *6.2.1 8-Phase 8-PSK Systems*

The 8-PSK modulation technique can be viewed as an extension of the QPSK system, which is described in Chapter 3. In the classical 8-PSK modulator block diagram, shown in Fig. 6.4, the $f_b$ rate data is split into three binary parallel streams, each having a transmission rate of $f_b/3$. The 2-level to 4-level converter provides one of the four possible levels of a polar baseband signal at $a$ and $b$. If the binary symbol $A$ is a logic one (zero), then the output level $a$ has one of the two possible (positive, negative) signal states. The logic state of the $C$ bit determines whether the larger or smaller signal level should be present at $a$ or at $b$. When $C = 1$, then the amplitude of $a$ is greater than that of $b$; if $C = 0$, then the converse is true [6.4]. The 4-level polar baseband signals at $a$ and $b$ are used to double-sideband suppressed-carrier (DSB-SC) amplitude modulate the two quadrature carriers. The polar baseband signal and the modulated 8-PSK signal-state space diagrams are also shown in Fig. 6.4. The detailed construction of these signal state-space diagrams is suggested in Problem 6.4. **(Solve Problems 6.3 and 6.4.)**

A modern approach in the design of an 8-PSK modulator for high-speed (90 Mb/s) transmission, using only digital devices, has been reported in [6.1]. The principle of operation of such an 8-PSK modulator is illustrated in Fig. 6.5. The $f_b$ rate binary baseband information is *serial-to-parallel* converted in the data distributor unit. These parallel $f_b/3$ rate data streams switch on and off the logic gates of the high-speed commutative IF multiplexer. Depending on the baseband logic states, one of the eight digital IF vectors is connected to the digital IF output. This digital phase-shifted 8-PSK carrier is filtered by means of a conventional BPF; thus, a band-limited 8-PSK signal is obtained. Figure 6.6 shows the digitally implemented, 90 Mb/s, 8-PSK printed circuit board used by Raytheon Data Systems in their 6 and 11 GHz microwave systems. The eye diagram of these 8-PSK systems, prior to threshold comparisons, is shown in Fig. 6.7. There was no fading present in the system when this eye diagram photograph was taken.

The structure of a coherent 8-PSK demodulator is more complex than that of the QPSK demodulator. The functional block diagram of a theoretically optimal

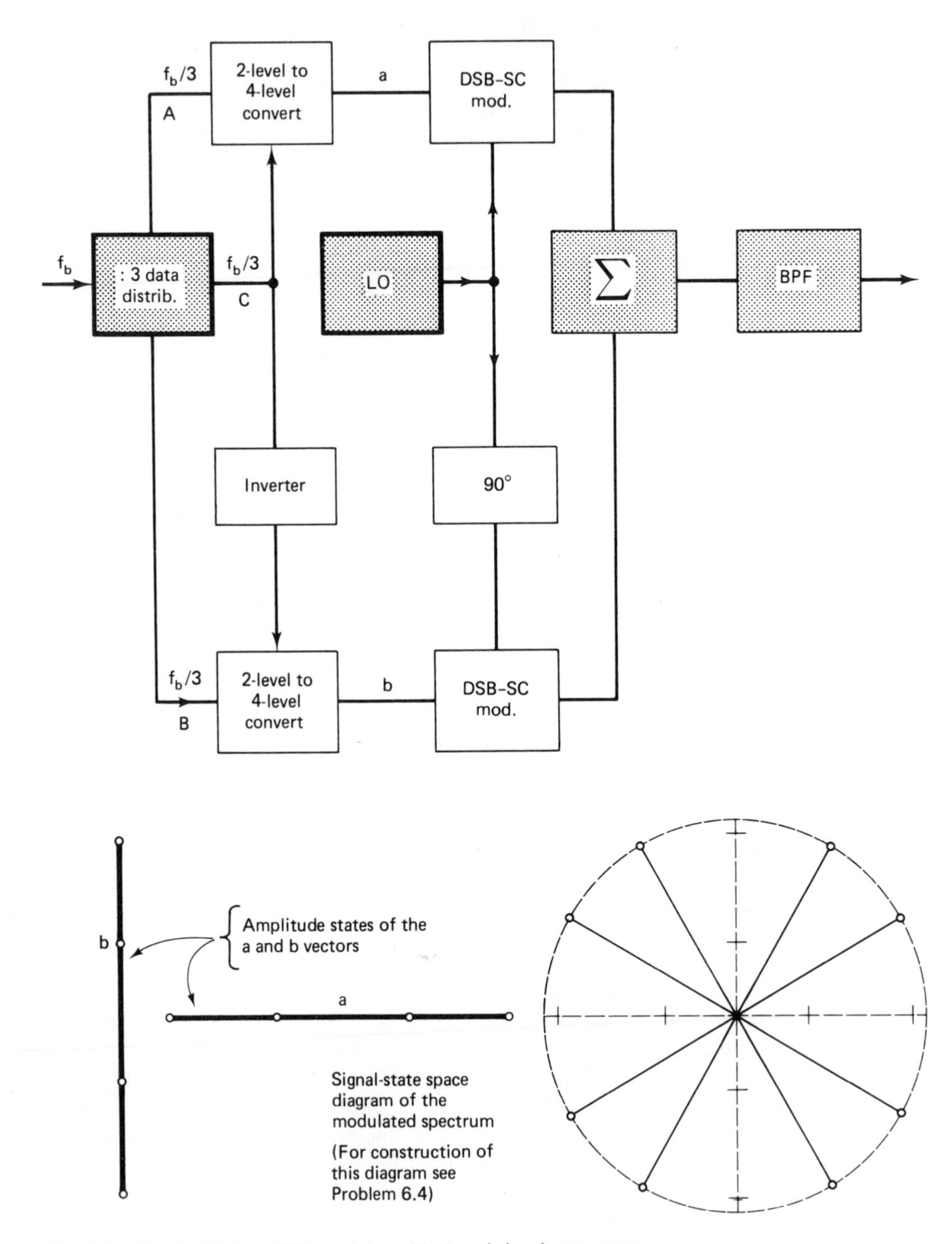


**Fig. 6.4.** Classical 8-phase PSK modulator block and signal-state space diagrams.

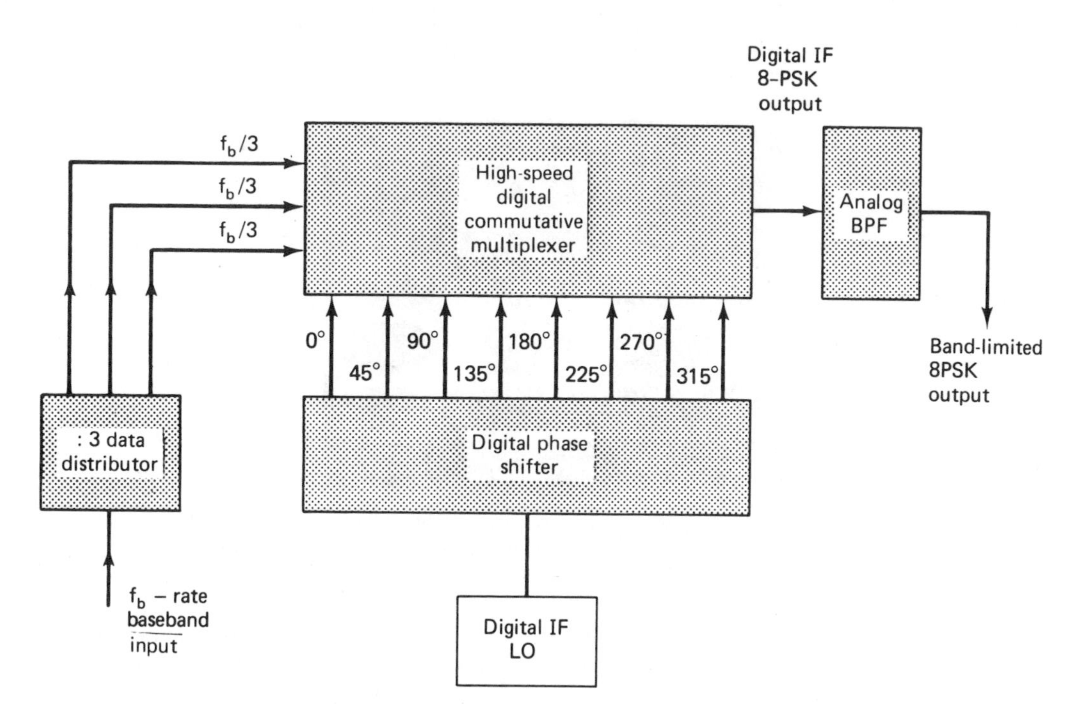


**Fig. 6.5.** High-speed 8-PSK modulator using digital subsystems.

**Fig. 6.6.** Printed circuit board of a 90 Mb/s all-digital 8-PSK modulator. (Courtesy of Raytheon Data Systems)

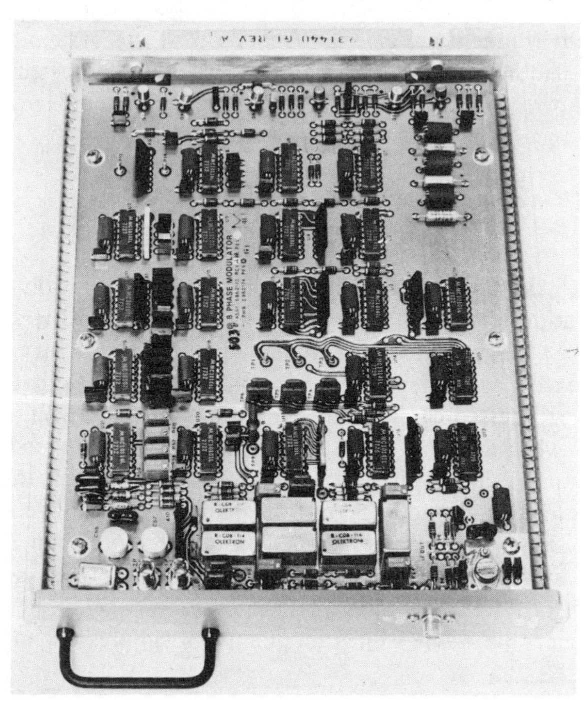

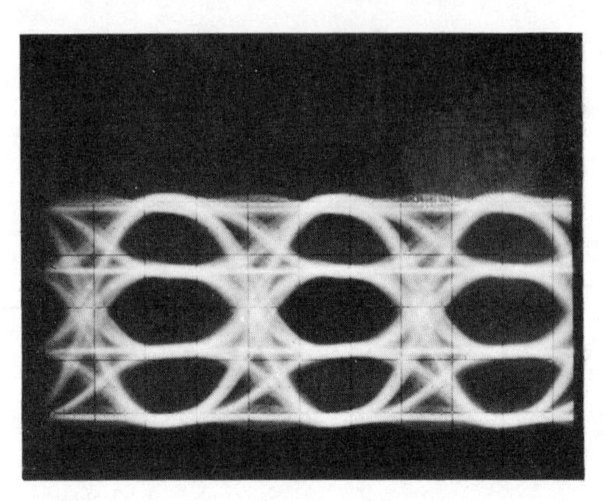

Vertical:
100 mV/div.
Horizontal:
10 ns/div.

**Fig. 6.7.** Demodulated eye diagram of a 90 Mb/s band-limited 8-PSK system prior to threshold comparisons. (Courtesy of Raytheon Data Systems)

$M$-ary PSK demodulator is described in [6.31], and various implementation techniques of 8-PSK demodulators are presented in [6.1, 6.7, 6.8, 6.18, 6.24]. The major blocks, and the operation of these demodulators, resemble that of the $M$-ary QAM demodulator structure. For this reason we defer the description of the demodulator until the next section, where the operation of the $M$-ary QAM and PSK demodulators are described simultaneously.

The $P(e) = f(C/N)$ curves of 8-PSK systems in an additive white gaussian noise environment are given in Chapter 3. If this system operates in the presence of gaussian noise and, also, in a sinusoidal interference environment, the resulting system performance is degraded. The performance degradation caused by these disturbances is illustrated in Fig. 5.8.

### *6.2.2 Quadrature Amplitude Modulated (QAM) $M = 16$-State Radio Systems*

A large class of digitally modulatable signals, specifically those which carry their information content in their phase angle and/or in the amplitude of the carrier wave, can be generated in a similar manner. The binary PSK modulated signal-state space diagram, shown in Fig. 6.8, is identical to that of a binary AM signal, with a suppressed carrier. The quadrature PSK (QPSK) signal is identical to two binary AM signals, with suppressed carriers, modulated in quadrature. In the description of the 8-phase PSK modulator we showed that an 8-PSK signal can be obtained by the addition of two quadrature modulated 4-level baseband PAM signals. In order to achieve an efficiency of more than 3 b/s/Hz, offered by the 8-PSK system, an extension to $M$-ary QAM or PSK systems having a higher number of states is required.

A generalized block diagram of a QAM suppressed-carrier modulator is shown

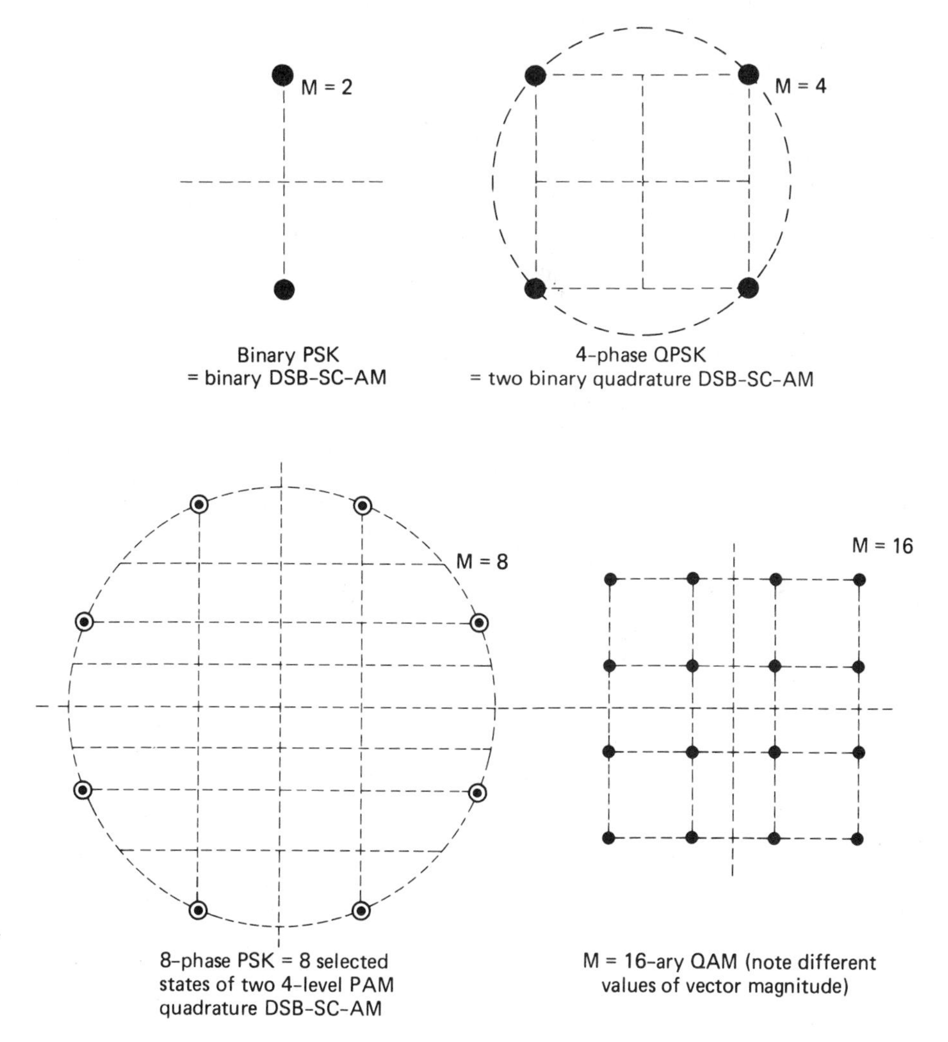


**Fig. 6.8.** Signal-state space diagrams of $M$-ary PSK and QAM signals.

in Fig. 6.9. This type of modulator is also known as an *amplitude phase keyed* (APK) modulator. The $f_b$ rate binary source is commuted into two binary symbol streams, each having a rate of $f_b/2$. The following 2-to-$L$-level baseband converter converts these $f_b/2$ rate data streams into $L$-level AM signals having a symbol rate of

$$f_s = (f_b/2) : (\log_2 L) \quad \text{symbols/sec} \tag{6.3}$$

For example, if the source bit rate is $f_b = 10$ Mb/s, then the commuted binary baseband streams have an $f_b/2 = 5$ Mb/s rate. If an $M = 16$-ary QAM modulated signal is desired, which has a theoretical efficiency of 4b/s/Hz, then these commuted

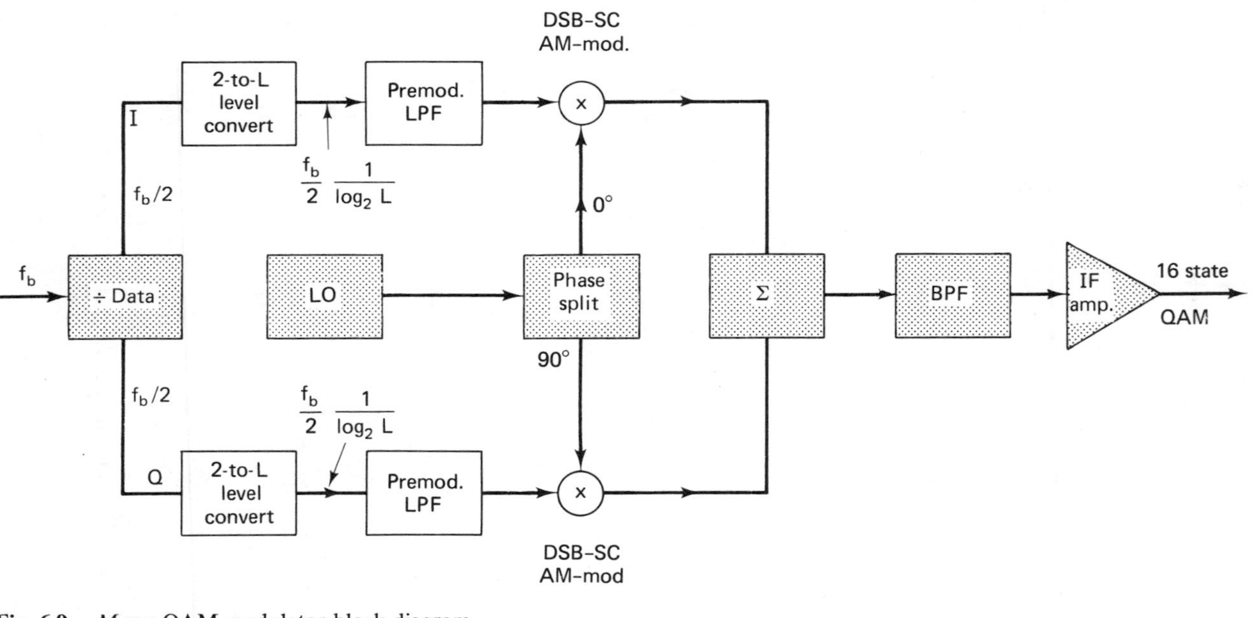


**Fig. 6.9.** *M*-ary QAM modulator block diagram.

binary streams are converted into $L = 4$-level baseband streams. The resultant 4-level symbol streams of the $I$ and $Q$ channels are 5 Mb/s: $\log_2 4 = 2.5$ M symbols/sec. If pre-modulation LPFs are used, as shown in Fig. 6.9, then the minimum bandwidth (Nyquist bandwidth with $\alpha = 0$) of these filters is 1.25 MHz. The minimum IF bandwidth requirement equals the double-sided minimum baseband bandwidth, that is, 2.5 MHz. This example illustrates that a 10 Mb/s, $M =$ 16-ary QAM signal can be transmitted in a theoretical minimum bandwidth of 2.5 MHz; thus, a spectral efficiency of 4b/s/Hz has been obtained. Practical, high-speed, 400 Mb/s, 16-ary systems have been achieving a bandwidth efficiency of approximately 3.7 b/s/Hz [6.32].

The block diagram of a coherent $M$-ary QAM demodulator is shown in Fig. 6.10. This demodulator incorporates the major building blocks of $M$-ary PSK demodulators. For this reason, with only minor modifications in the signal processing circuity, this demodulator structure could be employed for the demodulation of $M$-ary PSK signals, such as 8-PSK or 16-PSK signals. For optimum performance it is essential to recover the carrier and the symbol rate frequencies. This is achieved in the carrier recovery (CR) and symbol timing recovery (STR) blocks. A detailed description of these blocks is given in [6.6, 6.27, 6.31]. To distinguish between the $L$-demodulated baseband levels, $L - 1$ threshold comparators are required in each of the $L$-to-2-level PAM converters. Individual threshold comparators provide a logic 1 state if, in the sampling instant, the received signal plus noise vector is larger than the preset threshold level. Otherwise, they provide a logic 0 state. Sampling is performed at the symbol rate, at the maximum eye opening instants. This rate equals $f_b/[2(\log_2 L)]$. The $L$-to-2-level converter logic circuitry accepts the $L - 1$ parallel binary outputs of the threshold comparators and provides the x2 data combiner inputs with the $f_b/2$ rate binary signal from the $I$ channel. A similar input to the data combiner is received from the $Q$ channel. Finally, the data combiner, which is a parallel-to-serial converter, provides the desired $f_b$ rate binary signal output. **(Solve Problem 6.5.)**

The $P(e)$ performance of $M$-ary QAM systems is summarized in Chapter 3. From that chapter we note that, given an $M =$ 16-ary QAM modem (same as a 16-APK modem), which operates in an additive white gaussian noise environment, a theoretical average $C/N = 23$ dB is required for a $P(e) = 10^{-8}$. In this case, the noise is specified in the symbol rate bandwidth. **(Solve Problem 6.6.)**

An illustrative example of $M =$ 16-ary QAM systems is the 2 GHz radio equipment which has been developed by a number of manufacturers [6.17 and 6.33], for use by common carriers. For 2 GHz systems, the FCC-authorized bandwidth is 3.5 MHz. Theoretically, in this bandwidth, with a 16-ary system, it is possible to transmit 3.5 MHz $\times$ 4b/s/Hz $=$ 14 Mb/s. Practical roll-off factors range between $\alpha = 0.3$ and 1. We assume that an $\alpha = 0.5$ roll-off factor is employed. With this filter, an excess bandwidth of 50% is required; thus, the practical transmission rate is approximately 14 Mb/s: 1.5 $\approx$ 9.5 Mb/s. This rate corresponds to a data capacity of six DS-1 signals, with the allowance for multiplex bit stuffing.

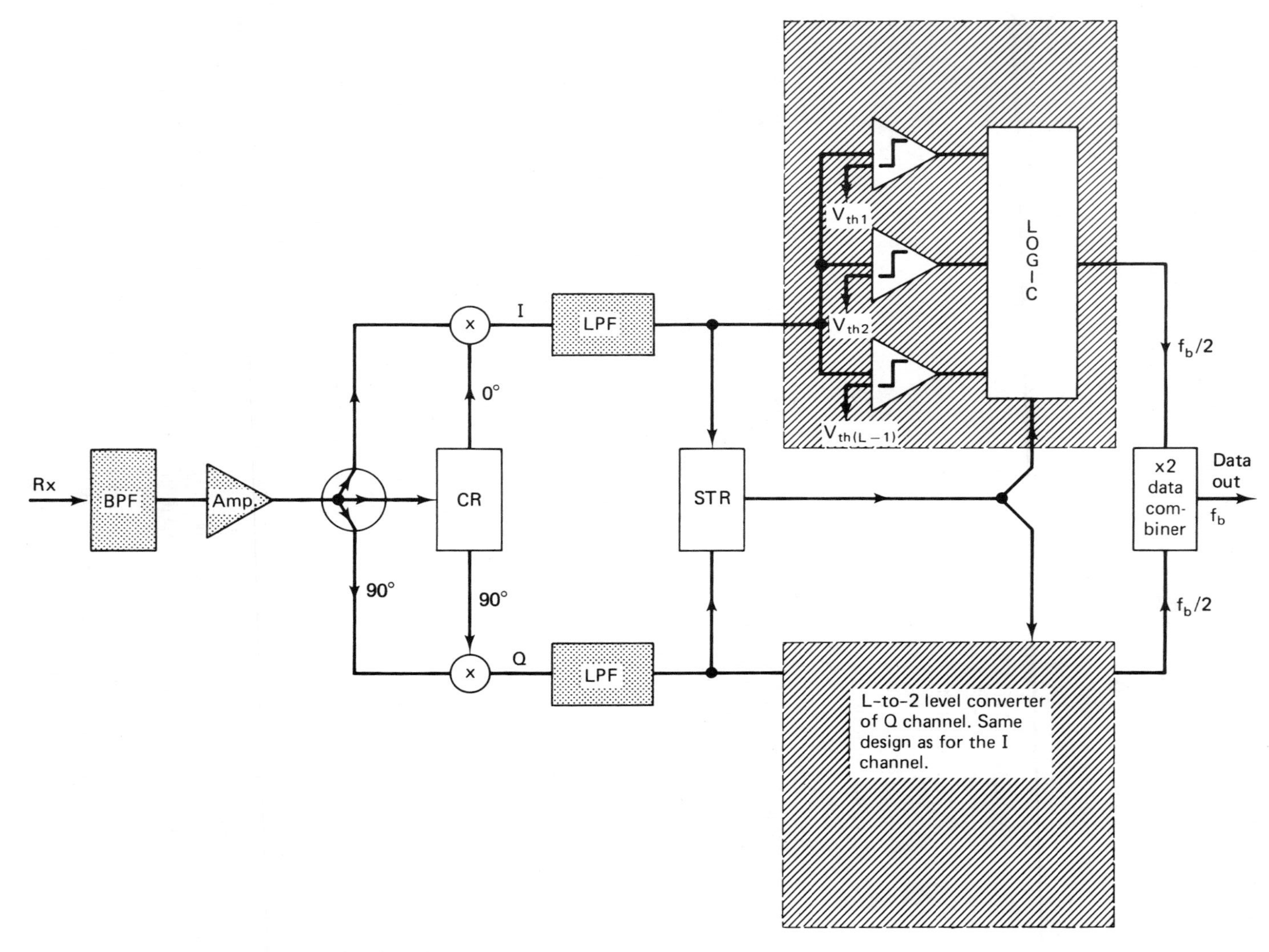


**Fig. 6.10.** *M*-ary QAM or *M*-ary PSK demodulator block diagram.

## 6.3 FILTERING REQUIREMENTS IN DIGITAL RADIO SYSTEMS

In the design of a bandwidth-efficient digital radio system, which satisfies the emission limits imposed by regulatory agencies and which performs well in a severe adjacent-channel interference environment of multichannel radio systems, it is imperative that special attention be paid to the filter design problems. The filters have to be as narrow as possible to optimize performance in a faded environment, but they should be wide enough so that the intersymbol interference-caused system gain degradation is minimal.

The channel filtering in the radio transmitter and receiver can be achieved by means of pre-modulation low-pass transmit filtering, post-modulation intermediate-frequency (IF) or radio-frequency (RF) band-pass filtering or a combination of these filtering techniques. The equivalance of these filters, considering the $P(e)$ performance and the occupied spectrum, is shown in [6.6]. In the design of digital radio systems particular care has to be given to the proper choice of the IF frequency [6.28].

In Fig. 6.11 the IF filters for a simplified multichannel radio system are shown. It has been assumed that all channel filtering is performed at IF. The modulated power spectrum $S_A(f)$ is band-limited by the $H_A(f)$ transmit filter, equalized, up-converted to RF, transmitted through the medium, down-converted at the receive end to IF, filtered by the $H_B(f)$ filter, and demodulated. In the case illustrated, the relatively wide-band up-and-down converters do not contribute to signal distortion, so they are not shown. In a deeply faded system, the noise caused by the front-end noise figure of the receiver is simulated by an AWGN source. In addition to the AWGN signal impairment, the adjacent interfering signals $S_C(f)$ and $S_D(f)$ contribute also to the system degradation. The system designer has to find a compromise between the ideal $\alpha = 0$ roll-off Nyquist filter, having a nearly infinite cost, and the cost-effective filter which will satisfy the overall system requirements. Most designers tend to use standard filters such as Chebyshev, Butterworth, or elliptic filters, and add to them the required number of equalized stages.

Elliptic filters are frequently chosen because they provide more attenuation closer to the pass-band. After choosing the type and order of filter, the designer has to verify whether the transmitted spectrum, $S_E(f)$ is within the authorized frequency mask. This spectrum is given by

$$S_E(f) = S_A(f)\,|H_A(f)|^2 \tag{6.4}$$

Using an iterative computer program [6.11], the designer finds the lowest-order filter (simplest implementation), which ensures that, for the chosen bit rate and modulation method, the spectral limits are still satisfied. The receive filter is chosen so that within the preassigned channeling plan (even in the deepest fades of the desired channel) the adjacent channels are sufficiently suppressed. A frequently used number for the *permissible system gain degradation*, resulting from adjacent channel interference, is *about* 1 dB. In the next stage the designer verifies whether

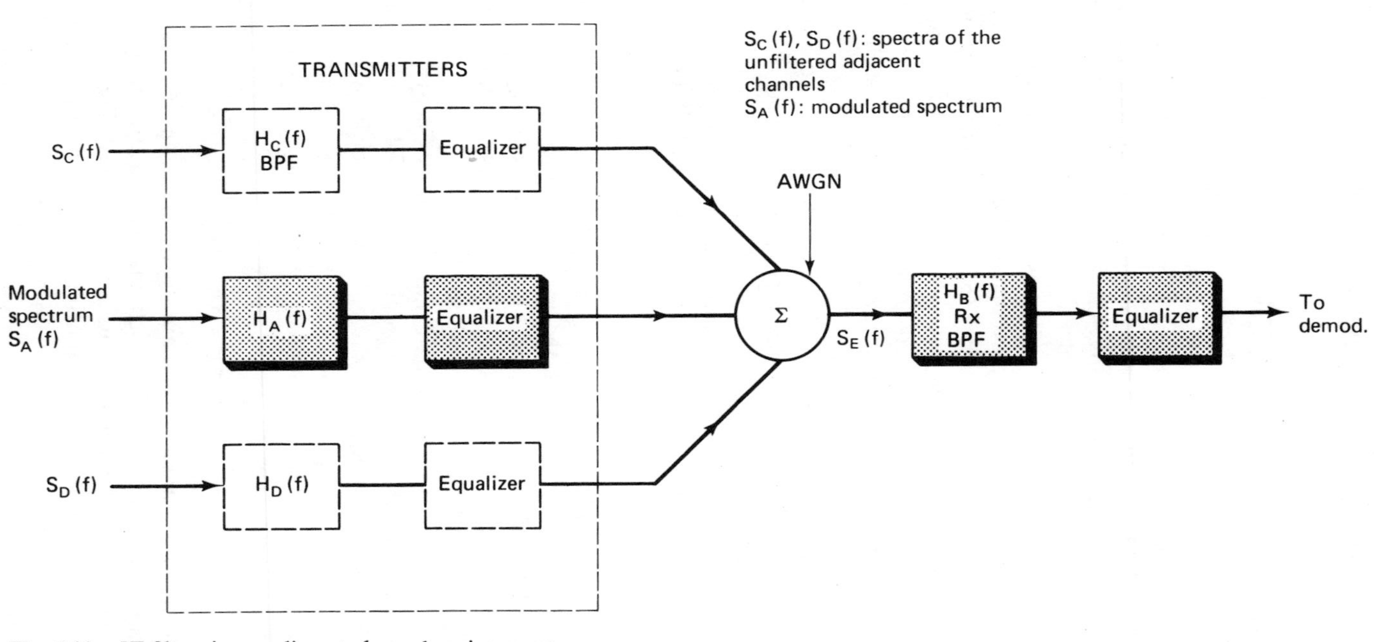


Fig. 6.11. IF filters in an adjacent-channel environment.

the overall ISI degradation is within the design objectives. If this is not the case, the number of filter stages and equalizers are iteratively increased until satisfactory system performance is obtained. This design procedure requires several computer programs. It is illustrated in the following example, which is taken from a practical Canadian system specification.

**EXAMPLE 6.1.** Specify the transmit and receive filters for a QPSK system which has to transmit six multiplexed DS-1 data streams (9.264 Mb/s) in a 7 MHz authorized bandwidth. This bandwidth is shown in Fig. 6.12. Assume that elliptic filters are the most cost-effective for this design [6.11].

***SOLUTION:*** The unfiltered 9.264 Mb/s QPSK spectrum and the 7 MHz authorized Canadian bandwidth are shown in Fig. 6.12. From this figure it is evident that severe band-limiting is required to satisfy the constraints on the radiated spectrum. With the aid of an iterative computer program it was found that a 5-pole elliptic filter having a 0.5 dB ripple and a 3 dB double-sided bandwidth of 6.4 MHz will satisfy the requirements [6.12]. The resultant filtered spectrum is also shown in Fig. 6.12.

The overall system specification allows for an approximate 1 dB degradation as a result of the adjacent channel interference. The performance of a QPSK system in an AWGN environment and adjacent two-channel interferers is shown in Fig. 6.13 [6.6 and 6.12]. From this figure it is concluded that for a 1 dB degradation the permissible carrier-to-interference ratio is approximately $C/I = 20$ dB. Thus, the $C/I$ should exceed 20 dB under all conditions, including the case of severe fading. If a practical fade margin of 40 dB is allowed, then the $C/I$ provided by filtering, under normal propagation conditions, should be 60 dB. Assuming that a 20 dB attenuation is provided by cross-polarization, the remaining 40 dB of attenuation must be provided by filtering.

The designer obtains the receive filter selectivity requirements by using an iterative computer program, which computes the $C/I$ ratio of two adjacent interfering transmitters, given by

$$C/I = 10 \log_{10} \left\{ \frac{\int_0^\infty S_A(f)\,|H_A(f)|^2\,|H_B(f)|^2\,df}{\int_0^\infty [S_C(f)\,|H_C(f)|^2 + S_D(f)\,|H_D(f)|^2]\,|H_B(f)|^2\,df} \right\} \text{ (dB)} \qquad (6.5)$$

The terms in equation (6.5) represent the spectra and functions shown in Fig. 6.11. In this example the designer found that a receive filter identical with the transmit filter will meet the system selectivity requirements. Finally, from computer-generated eye diagrams the designer concluded that three equalization stages are required to reduce the overall system ISI budget to a practical 1.5 dB. ■

## 6.4 *P(e)* PERFORMANCE DEGRADATION AND SPECTRAL SPREADING CAUSED BY NON-LINEAR RF DEVICES

Radio-frequency (RF) devices operate frequently in a non-linear mode, close to saturation. This mode of operation is required to achieve a higher efficiency and output power. Cost considerations are also important. For example, a 2 GHz amplifier having an output power of 2 W (+33 dBm), operating in a non-linear

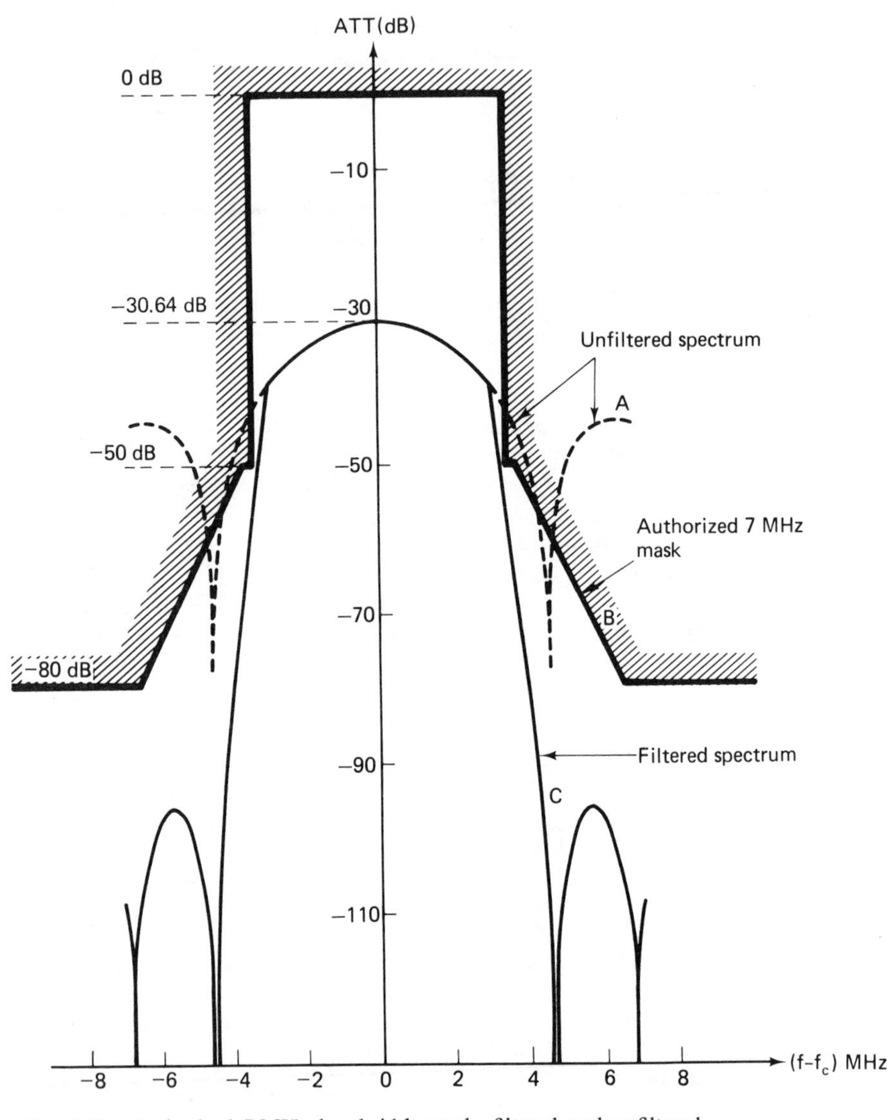


**Fig. 6.12.** Authorized 7 MHz bandwidth mask, filtered and unfiltered QPSK spectrum.

mode, costs approximately the same amount as a 0.5 W (+27 dBm) amplifier, which operates in a linear mode. Unfortunately, non-linear amplifiers are frequently the cause of severe $P(e) = f(C/N)$ degradation and spectral spreading. Thus, we can see that the judicious use of non-linear amplifiers requires special attention of the system designer.

Closed-form equations, by which the $P(e)$ degradation or the spectral spreading

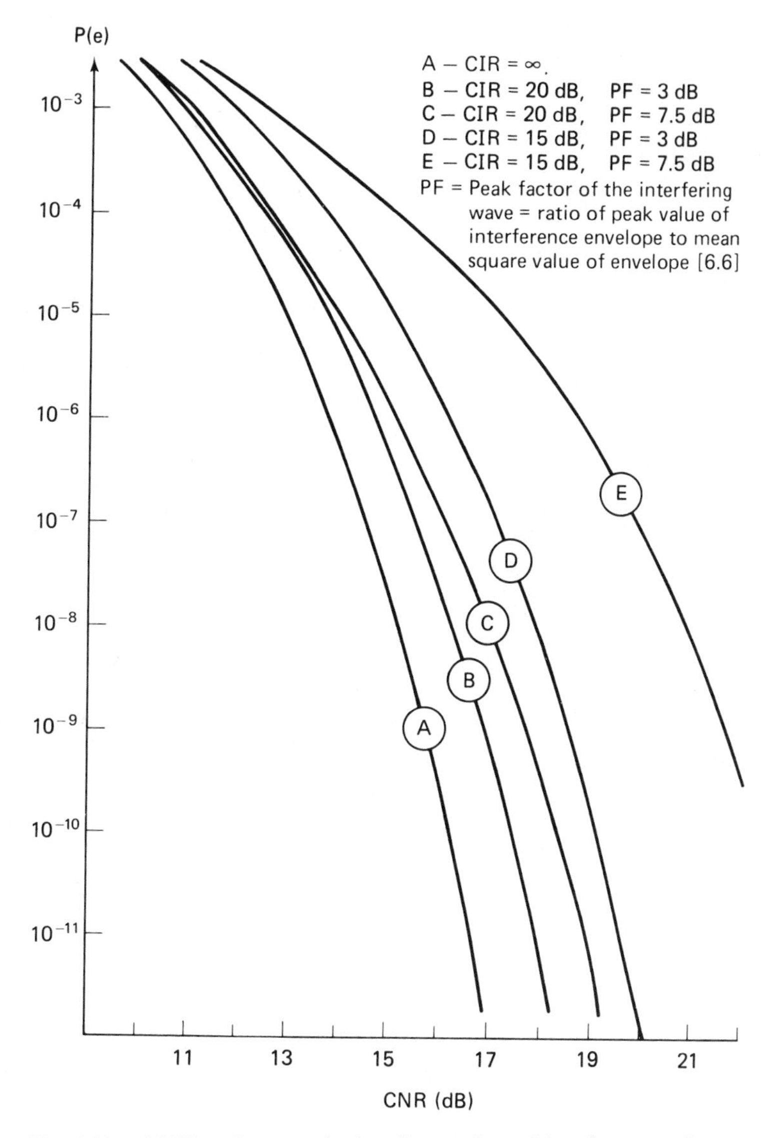


**Fig. 6.13.** QPSK performance in the adjacent-channel interference environment of two interferers.

caused by non-linear elements could be evaluated, have not been derived. System calculations are frequently performed by means of computer simulations, such as in references [6.2, 6.12, 6.13, 6.19]. Involved experimental results might also be used for performance predictions of operational non-linear systems [6.26].

The $P(e)$ degradations of a QPSK modulated signal, caused by a non-linear PA and obtained by computer simulations, are illustrated in Fig. 6.14. In this

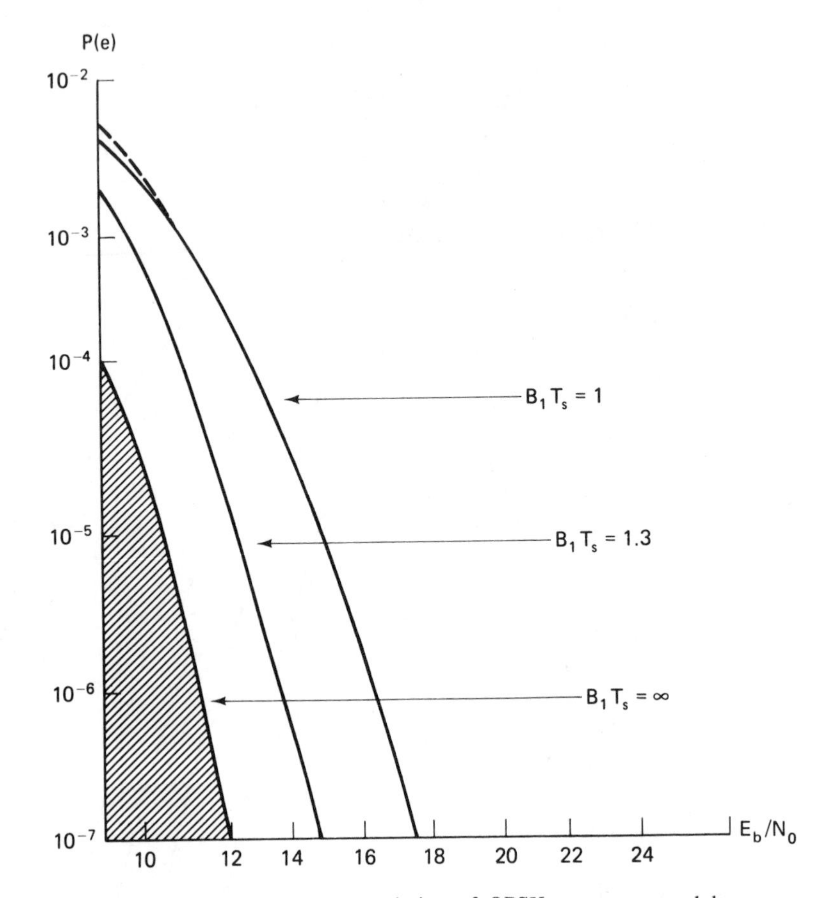


**Fig. 6.14.** *P(e)* performance degradation of QPSK systems caused by TWT non-linearities (only 1 dB back-off).

example it has been assumed that the traveling-wave tube (TWT) power amplifier operates in a highly non-linear mode, having an only 1 dB back-off, and that the QPSK signal is band-limited by a fourth-order Chebychev filter which precedes the TWT. The double-sided 3 dB RF bandwidth of this filter is $B_1$ Hz, and the symbol duration is $T_s$ seconds. This symbol duration corresponds to an $f_b = 2/T_s$ bit rate (there are two bits per symbol).

The normalized, minimum bandwidth filter, having a $B_1T_s = 1$, causes a large envelope fluctuation and a large $E_b/N_0$ degradation. The $E_b/N_0$ requirement for a $P(e) = 10^{-7}$ is increased from 12 dB (for $B_1T_s = \infty$) to 17.5 dB. This is equivalent to a system fade margin degradation of 5.5 dB.

The effect of the TWT and the up-converter amplifier non-linearity on an 8-PSK digital radio system is illustrated in the experimental results, shown in Fig. 6.15 [6.26]. In this system an 11 dB output power back-off of the 6 GHz TWT amplifier corresponds to a 2 W output power. In this nearly linear mode of operation, it is seen that for a $P(e) = 10^{-6}$ a $C/N = 24$ dB is required. This system also

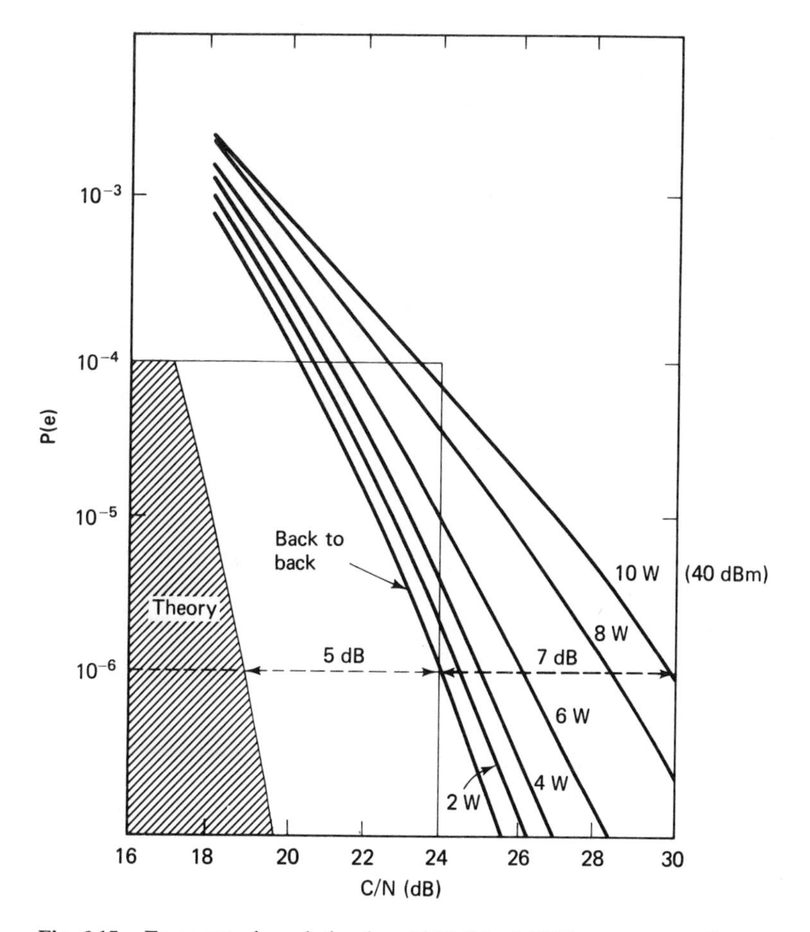


**Fig. 6.15.** Error-rate degradation in a 108 Mb/s, 8-PSK system, caused by TWT amplifier non-linearities. (Redrawn by permission from Reference [6.26])

achieves a transmission rate of 108 Mb/s in a 36 MHz RF channel. Because of this tight band-limitation (3b/s/Hz) and imperfect equalization of the channel filters, it becomes necessary to increase the $C/N$ ratio an extra 5 dB over the theoretical $C/N$ ratio requirement of 19 dB. If the TWT output power is increased to 10 W, then an additional increase of 7 dB in the $C/N$ ratio is required to achieve a $P(e) = 10^{-6}$. That is to say, given that the $C/N$ ratio at the demodulator input is limited to 24 dB, then a $P(e) = 10^{-6}$ could be achieved if the TWT amplifier transmits 2 W in a linear mode. With the same $C/N$ ratio of 24 dB, the $P(e)$ increases to $10^{-4}$ if the TWT transmits 10 W in a non-linear mode. *Note* that the $P(e) = f(C/N)$ curves are not as steep as those resulting from operation in a linear additive white gaussian noise environment.

The previously mentioned $P(e)$ degradation for a given $C/N$ ratio, or the increase in the $C/N$ ratio required, to maintain a specified $P(e)$ is caused by the transmission of the band-limited $M$-ary PSK signal (8 PSK in this case), having a large envelope fluctuation, through the AM/AM non-linearities and the AM/PM transfer effects of the TWT amplifier [6.21 and 6.27]. One way to avoid this degradation is to *band-limit the modulated signal only after the non-linear amplifier*. In this case a nearly constant envelope signal is fed to the output TWT; thus, the AM/AM and AM/PM effects become negligible. This approach has been used successfully in a number of 90 Mb/s digital microwave systems [6.20, 6.22]. However, one distinct disadvantage of this approach is that it prevents the use of pre-modulation baseband and IF filtering for final spectral shaping. For certain bit rates and radio frequencies the design of a bandwidth-efficient Nyquist RF filter might be a very difficult task.

An other disadvantage of a non-linear output amplifier is that it causes spectral spreading, that is, a restoration of the filtered sidelobes. In Fig. 6.16 the band-limited spectrum of a QPSK random-data signal is shown in [6.12]. If this signal is transmitted through a non-linear TWT amplifier, operating with only 4 dB back-off, a spectral spreading, as shown, is expected to occur.

In conclusion, a non-linear output stage has better power efficiency (more output power) and, for most applications, is less expensive than a linear amplifier. However, the $P(e)$ degradation and the spectral spreading effects might force the

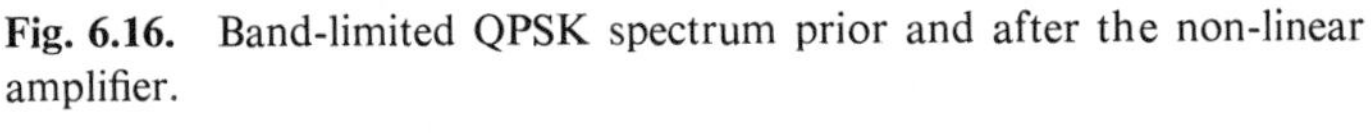

**Fig. 6.16.** Band-limited QPSK spectrum prior and after the non-linear amplifier.

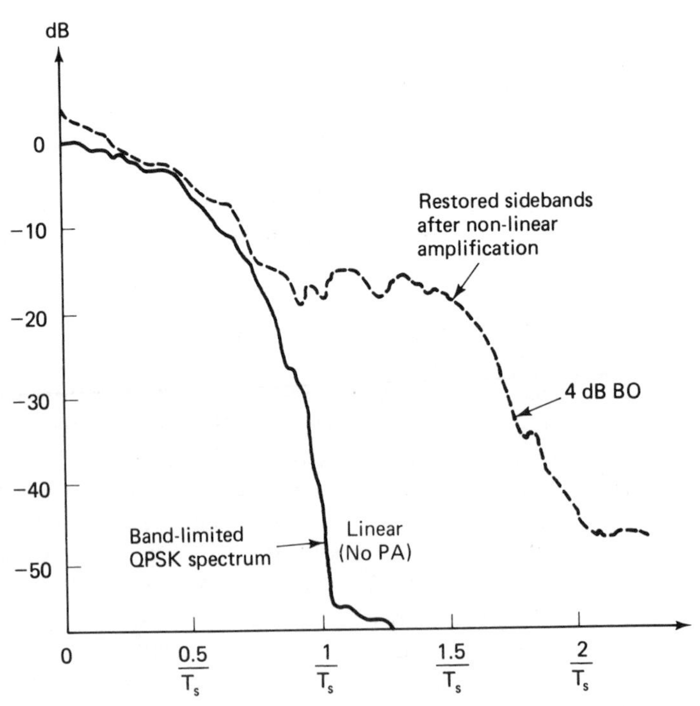

system designer to have the spectral shaping filters implemented at RF. For relatively low-bit-rate (less than 15 Mb/s) microwave systems this might require complex filter designs. Thus, the decision whether to use a non-linear output amplifier or a linear amplifier has to be based on system performance and cost tradeoffs of the particular digital microwave system.

## 6.5 RADIO SYSTEM PERFORMANCE DESIGN GUIDELINES

In this section information necessary for the systems engineer to evaluate the expected performance of an unprotected microwave channel is presented. Material required for performance and reliability evaluation of complete-diversity and protection-switched microwaves is described in Chapter 10. As an illustrative design procedure, the noise and interference budget of a typical 8-PSK radio system, operating in the 11 GHz band and used for 90 Mb/s transmission (two multiplexed DS-3 rate signals), is derived. These kinds of systems are currently being manufactured by the Collins, Nippon, and Raytheon companies. The method used in the derivation of the system characteristics is general and can readily be adapted for other radio frequencies, bit rates, or modulation techniques.

**EXAMPLE 6.2.** An unprotected microwave channel, having a length of 400 km, for the transmission of 1344 digitized telephony channels is required. It is expected that a commercially available 8-PSK radio, operating in the 11 GHz band, will be purchased. As this system will be installed in the United States, it has to meet the FCC emission limits; that is, in the 11 GHz band the transmitted spectrum has to be confined to 40 MHz. This system is required to meet the standard reliability objectives of U.S. telephone companies. As the system designer, you must determine the required system parameters.

***SOLUTION:*** In the initial specifications an engineer assumes a number of system characteristics. For the more detailed analysis (which is not presented in this book) detailed specifications are obtained from the suppliers and calculations are modified in accordance with the exact characteristics of their equipment.

Even though it is well known that frequency selective fading can reduce the system gain by as much as 15 to 20 dB, in the initial calculations the effect of selective fading is not taken into account here [6,15; 6.16; 6.29]. It is assumed that the manufacturer has various adaptive equalizers or other methods to analyze the effects of the selective fade on the loss of the system gain. A field-proven design, in which the damaging effect of selective fading across a 40 MHz bandwidth of a radio receiver has been successfully eliminated, employs adaptive IF equalizers and decision-feedback baseband equalizers as reported in reference [6.22].

The following is an outline of a recommended procedure for obtaining the required system parameters.

***Step 1:*** *C/N Requirement*

Assume that the system is considered out-of-service when the $P(e)$ of the system exceeds $10^{-8}$. Thus, for an 8-PSK system, the theoretical $C/N$ requirement for a $P(e) = 10^{-8}$, as obtained from Chapter 3, equals 20.5 dB. In a practical system, a higher $C/N$ ratio is required because of various degradations. A listing of a typical degradation budget is shown in Table 6.1. In this example, the total degradation caused by the back-to-back modem and RF channel imperfections is 5.5 dB. This degradation, when added to the theoretical 20.5 requirement, increases the practical, required $C/N$ to 26 dB.

**TABLE 6-1 System Degradation Budget in a Typical High-speed (90Mb/s) Radio System**

| Degradation Caused By | Degradation (dB) |
|---|---|
| 1. *Modem imperfections—AWGN back-to-back:* | |
| 1.1 Phase and amplitude errors of the modulator | 0.1 |
| 1.2 Intersymbol interference caused by the filters in a back-to-back modem | 1.0 |
| 1.3 Carrier recovery phase noise | 0.1 |
| 1.4 Differential encoding/decoding | 0.3 |
| 1.5 Jitter (imperfect sampling instants) | 0.1 |
| 1.6 Excess noise bandwidth of receiver (demodulator) | 0.5 |
| 1.7 Other hardware impairments (temperature variations, aging, etc.) | 0.4 |
| *Modem total:* | 2.5 dB |
| 2. *RF channel imperfections:* | |
| 2.1 AM/PM conversion of the quasi-linear output stage | 1.5 |
| 2.2 Band-limitation and channel group delay | 0.3 |
| 2.3 Adjacent RF channel interference | 1.0 |
| 2.4 Feeder and echo distortion | 0.2 |
| *Channel total:* | 3.0 dB |
| *Total modem and channel degradation:* | 5.5 dB |

***Step 2:*** *Receiver Noise Figure and Noise Power*

The total noise power present at the demodulator input is directly proportional to the receiver noise figure (F). Thus, it is desired to have a receiver having the lowest possible F. Modern 11 GHz systems have noise figures in the 5 to 10 dB range. Here we assume F = 8 dB. The total noise power $N_T$ at the demodulator input is given by the following well-known equation [6.6, 6.21, 6.22]:

$$N_T = kTBF \tag{6.6}$$

where $k$ = Boltzman constant (−228.6 dBW sec/°K)
$T$ = absolute temperature in degrees Kelvin
$B$ = double-sideband bandwidth of the receiver
$F$ = receiver noise figure.

*Note:*

$$kT = -174 \text{ dBm/Hz}$$

at a 17°C (290°K) room temperature. The total noise power in the receiver, assuming a minimum receiver bandwidth of 30 MHz (remember for an 8-PSK signal the efficiency is 3b/s/Hz; thus, 90 Mb/s: 3 = 30 MHz) is given by:

$$N_T = -174 \text{ dBm} + 10 \log 30 \text{ MHz} + 8 \text{ dB} = -91.2 \text{ dBm} \approx -91 \text{ dBm}$$

***Step 3:*** *Required Received Carrier Level* ($C_{min}$)

In Chapter 5 [equation (5.1)] the required received carrier level for a minimum quality objective is defined. In this example that minimum corresponds to $P(e) = 10^{-8}$. The value of $C_{min}$ is obtained from the total noise power and the practical C/N requirement. It is given by

$$C_{min} = N_T + \text{C/N} \quad \text{(dB)} \tag{6.7}$$

In this example,

$$C_{min} = -91 \text{ dBm} + 26 \text{ dB} = -65 \text{ dBm}$$

***Step 4:*** *Transmit Power* ($P_t$)

The system gain is directly proportional to the transmitted output power. As described in Chapter 5, it is desirable to have the highest possible system gain. In order to avoid performance degradation caused by AM/PM conversion of the transmit power amplifer, the bandwidth limitation might be performed after the RF amplifier stage [6.22], or direct baseband to RF modulation could be employed [6.7, 6.30]. The 8-PSK signal generated and amplified by GUNN and IMPATT diodes, in this later system, has an output power of $P_t = +30$ dBm (1 W). For our subsequent calculations we shall use this number.

***Step 5:*** *System Gain*

The system gain $G_s$ is obtained by

$$G_s = P_t - C_{min} \quad \text{[dB]} \tag{6.8}$$

In our example,

$$G_s = +30 \text{ dBm} - (-65 \text{ dBm}) = 95 \text{ dB}$$

This is a somewhat low system gain. Some recently developed and planned 11 GHz systems have a higher output power, lower noise figure, and less degradations than we assumed. Systems gains as high as 108 dB have been reported [6.4]. With new modem design techniques and advancements made in high-gain amplifier design, it is expected that the system gain of 90 Mb/s, 11 GHz systems will reach a value of about 115 dB within a few years.

***Step 6:*** *Repeater Spacing*

From the calculated system gain, the chosen transmit and receive antenna size, the reliability objectives (e.g., service outage to be limited to 0.01%

annually), and the methods presented in Chapter 5 the system designer is able to calculate the required repeater spacing. This last step is a straightforward application of the material presented in Chapter 5; thus, further elaboration is not required. ■

## 6.6 PERFORMANCE CHARACTERISTICS OF TYPICAL *M*-ARY PSK AND QAM MICROWAVE SYSTEMS

In this section the most important performance characteristics of *M*-ary PSK and QAM microwave systems are presented. Two well-known, operational, low-capacity, and three high-capacity systems have been selected to illustrate practical system specifications.

The characteristics of certain Avantek and Farinon microwave systems are summarized in Table 6.2 [6.4 and 6.5]. These are examples of low-capacity systems. It should be noted that some of the entries are approximate and do not necessarily represent the latest manufacturer specifications.

**TABLE 6-2 Performance of the Avantek and Farinon Electric 1.7 to 2.3 GHz Low-capacity Digital Microwave Systems**

| System Parameter | Avantek | Farinon Electric |
|---|---|---|
| Radio-frequency range | 1.7 to 2.3 GHz | 1.7 to 2.3 GHz |
| Capacity | 2 Tl or 4 Tl<br>3.152 or 6.312 Mb/s | 2 Tl or 4 Tl<br>3.152 or 6.312 Mb/s |
| Transmitter output power (dBm): highest option | 32 | 33 |
| Receiver noise figure (dB) | 5 | 6 |
| Antenna duplexer loss (dB) | 0.4 | 2.2 |
| Receiver sensitivity for $10^{-6}$ BER (dBm) | 2 Tl: −89<br>4 Tl: −82 | 2 Tl: −89<br>4 Tl: −85 |
| System gain at $10^{-6}$ BER (antenna duplexer loss included) (dB) | 2 Tl: 120.6<br>4 Tl: 113.6 | 2 Tl: 119.8<br>4 Tl: 115.8 |
| Type of modulation | QAM (QPSK)<br>4 Tl: QPR | QAM (QPSK) |
| Occupied bandwidth (MHz) | 3.5 | 3.5 |
| Spectrum utilization per polarization (b/s/Hz) | 2 Tl: 0.9<br>4 Tl: 1.8 | 2 Tl: 0.9<br>4 Tl: 1.8 |

These systems are used for the transmission of two or four DS-1 rate multiplexed signals (3.152 Mb/s or 6.312 Mb/s, respectively). In the case of the Avantek radio system, it is possible, by a simple change of the baseband signal processor, to convert the binary baseband drive signals of the modulator from a binary to a 3-level partial response signal. This signal processing modifies the modulation from binary QAM to quadrature partial response (QPR). (For the equivalence of QAM and QPSK see Chapter 3). By using QPR modulation, which is studied further in Chapter 7, the spectrum utilization per polarization is increased from 0.9 b/s/Hz to 1.8 b/s/Hz. This increase in the spectral efficiency has an effect on the system gain; specifically, it contributes to system gain reduction. The radio equipment built by Farinon Electric has characteristics similar to that of the Avantek equipment. It is now obvious that an increased bit rate, given a constant bandwidth (that is, increased spectrum utilization) reduces the system gain.

To illustrate the system parameters of high-speed (90 Mb/s) 8-phase PSK radio systems, planned for operation (in some cases already operational) in the 6 GHz and 11 GHz bands, we consider the characteristics of certain Rockwell International (Collins), Nippon Electric, and Raytheon Systems. The 6 GHz Raytheon system (Table 6.3 and reference [6.4]) has the highest spectral efficiency,

**TABLE 6-3 System Parameters of Certain Raytheon, Rockwell International (Collins), and Nippon 90Mb/s Systems (6 and 11 GHz)**

| System Parameter | Raytheon | Collins | NEC (11 GHz) |
|---|---|---|---|
| Frequency band (GHz) | 6 | 11 | 11 |
| Type of modulation | 8-PSK | 8-PSK | 8-PSK |
| Bit rate (Mb/s) | 90 | 90.258 | 90 |
| Capacity | 56 Tl | 56 Tl | 56 Tl |
| Transmitter output power (dBm) | +40 | +40 | +37 |
| Receiver sensitivity for $10^{-6}$ BER (dBm) | −65.5 | −68 | −68 |
| System gain at $10^{-6}$ BER (dB) | 105.5 | 108 | 105 |
| Receiver noise figure (dB) | 6.5 | 8 | 8 |
| Noise power (in bit rate BW) (dBm) | −88.0 | −86.4 | −86.5 |
| Practical required $C/N$ (in bit rate BW) for $10^{-6}$ BER (dB) | 22.5 | 18.4 | 18.5 |
| Theoretical required $C/N$ (in bit rate BW) for $10^{-6}$ BER (dB) | 13.8 | 13.8 | 13.8 |
| Occupied RF bandwidth (MHz) | 30 | 40 | 40 |
| Spectral efficiency (b/s/Hz) | 3 | 2.25 | 2.3 |

3b/s/Hz. This efficiency is required from 6 GHz systems which have to operate within the 30 MHz FCC-authorized channel plan, and is also the theoretical limit of 8-PSK systems. To achieve this efficiency, very steep filtering is required. Due to intersymbol and adjacent-channel interference, a significant $C/N$ penalty has to be paid, as seen from Table 6.3. The 11 GHz, 90 Mb/s systems operate in an FCC-authorized bandwidth of 40 MHz. In this case a 2.25 b/s/Hz efficiency is sufficient [6.23].

## PROBLEMS

**6.1** The authorized bandwidth for a DS-2 rate (6.312 Mb/s) QPSK digital radio system, operating in the 2 GHz band, is 3.5 MHz. If the spectral shaping is achieved by means of pre-modulation low-pass filters (LPF), sketch the amplitude mask of these filters. If the spectral shaping is achieved by post-modulation band-pass filters (BPF), sketch the amplitude mask of the BPF. Compare the masks of the LPF and BPF for both cases. Explain the conditions required to perform the spectral shaping solely by pre-modulation filters. If direct baseband to RF modulation is used, would you recommend the baseband low-pass filtering or the RF band-pass filtering method?

**6.2** Is it essential to have a post-demodulation low-pass filter built into a coherent demodulator? What would happen to the $P(e)$ performance of this demodulator if this LPF were bypassed?

**6.3** The 8-PSK modulator, shown in Fig. 6.4, is fed by an $f_b = 30$ Mb/s random-data stream. The local oscillator frequency is $f_0 = 140$ MHz. Sketch the spectrum at the modulator output. Indicate the minimum bandwidth double-sided Nyquist mask.

**6.4** Assume that the four discrete baseband levels at the outputs of the 2- to 4-level converters, shown in Fig. 6.4, can have one of the following values: $+1.307$ V, $-1.307$ V, $+0.541$ V, $-0.541$ V. Sketch the resultant modulated signal-state space diagram for all possible phase states. Determine the resultant phase angles. Would these phase angles be the same if the baseband levels had equidistant spacings?

**6.5** Describe the amplitude mask of an $\alpha = 0.3$ roll-off Nyquist baseband LPF if an $f_b = 100$ Mb/s rate is transmitted. Assume that an $M = 16$-ary QAM system is used and that the demodulator structure is the same as shown in Fig. 6.10. Indicate the threshold levels and the sampling instants.

**6.6** A 6.3 Mb/s, 16-ary coherent QAM digital radio system operates in an additive white gaussian noise environment. What is the required $C/N$ ratio if a $P(e) = 10^{-10}$ is required? It should be assumed that, due to imperfect phase equalization, the intersymbol interference will increase the $C/N$ requirement by 3 dB.

## REFERENCES

[6.1] Wood, W. A., "Modulation and Filtering Techniques for 3 Bits/Hertz Operation in the 6 GHz Frequency Band," Proc. IEEE International Conference on Communications, ICC-77, Chicago, June, 1977.

[6.2] Yokoyama, S., K. Hinoshita, Y. Tan, T. Ryu, R. Mitchell, "An Eight-Level PSK Microwave Radio for Long Haul Data Communications," Proc. IEEE International Conference on Communications, ICC-75, San Francisco, June, 1975.

[6.3] DeWitt, R. G., "Digital Microwave Radio—Another Building Block for the Integrated Digital Network," Proc. IEEE International Conference on Communications, ICC-75, San Francisco, June, 1975.

[6.4] Wachira, M., H. Yazdani, K. Feher, W. Steenaart, "A Survey of Eight-Phase PSK and QPRS Digital Radio Systems," Proc. 1978 IEEE Canadian Communications and Power Conference, Montreal, October, 1978.

[6.5] Morais, D., and K. Feher, "A Survey of North American 2 GHz Digital Radio Systems," Proc. Intelcom-77, Atlanta, October, 1977.

[6.6] Feher, K., *Digital Modulation Techniques in an Interference Environment*, *Multi-Volume EMC Encyclopedia*, Vol. 9, Don White Consultants, Inc., Gainesville, VA, 1977.

[6.7] Ramadan, M., "Practical Considerations in the Design of Minimum-Bandwidth, 90 Mb/s, 8-PSK Digital Microwave Systems," Proc. IEEE International Communications Conference ICC-76, Philadelphia, June, 1976.

[6.8] Tan, Y., et al., "The 8-Level PSK Modem with Cosine Roll-off Spectrum for Digital Microwave Communications," Proc. IEEE International Conference on Communications, ICC-76 Vol. 2, Philadelphia, June, 1976.

[6.9] Takeuchi, E., P. Tobey, "A 6 GHz Radio for Telephony Applications," Proc. IEEE International Conference on Communications, ICC-76, Vol. 2, Philadelphia, June, 1976.

[6.10] Tracey, R. J., "A 90 Megabit Per Second Modem for Microwave Radio Links," Proc. IEEE International Conference on Communications, ICC-77, Chicago, June, 1977.

[6.11] El-Torky, M., K. Feher, "Design of Bandlimiting Filters for Digital QPSK Radio Systems in an Interference Environment," Proc. IEEE International Conference on Communications, ICC-78, Toronto, June, 1978.

[6.12] El-Torky, M., K. Feher, "The Effects of Transmitter Power Amplifier Nonlinearity on QPSK Radio Transmission," Proc. 1978 IEEE Canadian Communications and Power Conference, Montreal, October, 1978.

[6.13] Morais, D., K. Feher, "MSK and Offset QPSK Modulation in Line of Sight Digital Radio Systems," Proc. IEEE International Conference on Communications, ICC-77, Chicago, June, 1977.

[6.14] Nippon Electric Co. Ltd., "NEC Digital Radio System (11 GHz 1344-CH) System Application Manual," Nippon Electric Co. Ltd., MSD-3902; 7509-02, Tokyo, 1975.

[6.15] Barnett, W. T., "Measured Performance of a High Capacity 6 GHz Digital Radio System," Proc. IEEE International Conference on Communications, ICC-78, Toronto, June, 1978.

[6.16] Prabhu, V. K., L. J. Greenstein, "Analysis of Multipath Outage with Applications to 90 Mb/s PSK Systems at 6 and 11 GHz," Proc. IEEE International Conference on Communications, ICC-78, Toronto, June, 1978.

[6.17] Penwarden, K., S. C. Chu, "Improving Digital Radio Efficiency," Telephony, June 6, 1977.

[6.18] Asahara, M., H. Nakamura, T. Sugiura, "8-Phase and 16-Phase High-Speed PSK Modems for PCM-TDMA Satellite Communications," Fujitsu Scientific and Technical Journal, December, 1977.

[6.19] Huang, J., K. Feher, "Performance of QPSK, OKQPSK and MSK Signals Through a Satellite Channel," Proc. 1978 IEEE Canadian Communications and Power Conference, Montreal, October, 1978.

[6.20] Hartmann, P. R., E. W. Allen, "Design Considerations for a 3 Bit/Hertz Digital Radio at 6 GHz," Proc. IEEE International Conference on Communications, ICC-78, Toronto, June, 1978.

[6.21] Technical Staff, American Telephone and Telegraph Company, Bell Telephone Companies and Bell Telephone Laboratories, *Telecommunications Transmission Engineering*, Vol. 2, Bell System for Technical Education, Winston-Salem, N.C., 1977.

[6.22] Barber, S. G., C. W. Anderson, "Modulation Considerations for the DRS-8 91 Mb/s Digital Radio," Proc. IEEE International Conference on Communications, ICC-77, Chicago, June, 1977.

[6.23] Federal Communications Commission: "FCC Docket 19311," Washington, D.C., November 1, 1974.

[6.24] Bennet, W. R., J. Davey, *Data Transmission*, McGraw-Hill Book Company, New York, 1965.

[6.25] Hogge, Jr., C. R., "Carrier and Clock Recovery for 8 PSK Synchronous Demodulation," IEEE Trans. Communications, May, 1978.

[6.26] Chakraborty, D., L. S. Golding, "Digital Transmission over Analog Radio Relay Links," IEEE Trans. Communications, November, 1975.

[6.27] Spilker, J. J., *Digital Communications by Satellite*, Prentice-Hall, Inc., Englewood Cliffs, N.J., 1977.

[6.28] CCIR, "Choice of Intermediate Frequencies for High-Capacity Digital Radio-Relay Systems," Draft Report AE/9, Study Programme 12 B/9, Conclusions of the Interim Meeting of Study Group 9 (Fixed Service Using Radio-Relay Systems), Part I, C.C.I.R., Doc. 9/196-E, Geneva, July, 1976.

[6.29] Jakes, W. C., "An Approximate Method to Estimate an Upper Bound on the Effect of Multipath Delay Distortion on Digital Transmission," Proc. IEEE International Conference on Communications, ICC-78, Vol. 3, Toronto, June, 1978.

[6.30] Hartmann, P. R., "A 90 Mb/s Digital Transmission System at 11 GHz Using 8-PSK Modulation," Proc. IEEE International Conference on Communications, ICC-76, Philadelphia, June, 1976.

[6.31] Lindsey, W. C., M. K. Simon, *Telecommunication Systems Engineering*, Prentice-Hall, Inc., Englewood Cliffs, N.J., 1973.

[6.32] Ishio, H., et al., "A New Multilevel Modulation and Demodulation System for Carrier Digital Transmission," Proc. IEEE International Conference on Communications, ICC-76, Philadelphia, Iune, 1976.

[6.33] Byington, M., C. J. Pallemaertz, "Design and Performance of 16 State Digital Modem," Proc. IEEE International Conference on Communications, ICC-79, Boston, June, 1979.

# 7

# CORRELATIVE (PARTIAL RESPONSE) TECHNIQUES AND APPLICATIONS TO DIGITAL RADIO SYSTEMS

**Dr. ADAM LENDER**

*GTE Lenkurt, Incorporated*
*San Carlos, CA.*

> *It is a pleasure to have Dr. Adam Lender as the author of this important chapter. He discovered the concept of correlative transmission techniques and developed many operational duobinary and other partial response systems. Dr. Lender is recognized as an authority in the digital communications field.*
>
> *Dr. K. Feher*

Duobinary, modified duobinary, and correlative techniques were originated in 1962 and 1963 [7.1, 7.2]. *Duo*-means doubling the speed of binary. *Correlative* implies correlation or finite-memory systems rather than zero-memory. Subsequently [7.3], in 1965 the term *partial response* was introduced. Correlative and partial response are synonymous; both terms are used in the literature.

This chapter is an in-depth treatment of many aspects of the correlative techniques, as applicable to digital microwave systems. However, the same techniques are used widely in data transmission and cable PCM and may find applications in fiber optics, satellite and tropo-scatter systems.

The Nyquist criteria for binary and multi-level signaling, postulated in 1924 [7.4], are based on the premise that each digit must be confined to its own time slot to as great an extent as possible. This implies that the intersymbol interference (ISI) in a particular time interval, due to the tails of preceding and succeeding pulses, should be eliminated or, at least, minimized. The Nyquist rate cannot be achieved in practice, even if the ideal rectangular filter were synthesized, because it is not possible to have a precise relationship between the cut-off frequency of the ideal filter and the bit rate. Thus, the Nyquist rate with the Nyquist-type *zero-memory* system cannot be achieved. Correlative techniques introduce, deliberately, a limited amount of ISI over a span of one, two, or more digits and capitalize on it. The net result is *spectral reshaping* of binary or multi-level pulse trains. The consequences are significant: For a given bandwidth and power input to the channel, correlative techniques permit the transmission of substantially more bits per second per hertz (b/s/Hz) than Nyquist-type zero-memory systems, for a specified probability of error criterion. With correlative techniques, the Nyquist rate and higher rates are possible. Also, owing to correlation between digits, correlative pulse trains have distinctive patterns. These patterns are monitored at the receiver; any violations due to noise or other causes result in errors which may be easily detected. Thus, error detection is accomplished without introducing redundant bits, such as parity checks, at the transmitter.

## 7.1 FUNDAMENTAL CONCEPTS OF CORRELATIVE TECHNIQUES AND REVIEW OF ZERO-MEMORY SYSTEMS

The key assumption stipulated in the Nyquist theorems [7.4] is that the ISI at the sampling and the transition points between successive digits can be eliminated. It follows that the digits are independent and uncorrelated, and that each digit can be recovered without resorting to the past history of the waveform. Such systems are often referred to as *zero-memory systems.*

Two criteria have been postulated for ISI-free transmission [7.4]. The first criterion requires that there be no ISI at the sampling instants $T$ seconds apart, where $1/T$ is the bit rate in b/s. To ensure that the minimum bandwidth requirement is met, the transmission filter is made rectangular, with a cut-off frequency at $1/2T$ Hz, resulting in the well-known $\frac{\sin \pi t/T}{\pi t/T}$ impulse response, which meets the above requirements. Such a filter is physically unrealizable. Even if it could be approximated satisfactorily, its practical use is precluded because of the excessive ISI at the transition points, caused by large overshoots of pulse tails which decay as $1/t$. As a result, even the slightest deviation from the bit rate of $1/T$ b/s at the sampling instant would render the system unusable.

The second Nyquist criterion [7 4; 7.5] is, precisely, that there be no such ISI at the transition points. It can be met by the (minimum bandwidth) filter having a frequency response $\cos \omega T/2$, with cut-off at $1/2T$ Hz. However, signaling at the $1/T$ b/s rate is now impossible because such a filter will not pass the frequency $1/2T$ Hz. Thus, a steady alternating pattern 010101010101 . . . , at the rate of $1/T$ b/s with fundamental frequency $1/2T$, cannot be transmitted through a filter satisfying only the second Nyquist criterion. Both criteria ensure minimum channel bandwidth, but systems with such minimum bandwidths do not permit signaling at the Nyquist rate of $1/T$ b/s. The first criterion, however, is still satisfied if any function that is odd about $1/2T$ Hz is added to the rectangular filter. Similarly, the second criterion is still satisfied if any function that is even about $1/2T$ Hz is added to the $\cos \omega T/2$ function. In both cases, the new bandwidth will considerably exceed the Nyquist bandwidth, but the systems can now be made "practical."

The raised-cosine channel characteristic with 100% roll-off, which is described in Chapter 3, has been employed frequently. It can be seen that, now, the Nyquist bandwidth is *doubled*, and the signaling rate is only one symbol per hertz of bandwidth. However, there is no ISI at the sampling and transition instants. Furthermore, the signaling over the "gentle" slope raised-cosine filter does not have to be precisely $1/T$ b/s but can be somewhat varied, with only gradual degradation of the system.

The correlative concept involves correlation between groups of digits or finite memory. Intersymbol interference is allowed in controlled amounts and is interpreted at the receiving end. The overall transfer function $F(\omega)$ of a correlative system (including transmitter and receiver) has the following general form:

$$F(\omega) = \sum_{k=0}^{n} a_k e^{-jk\omega T}$$

where $a_0 = 1$, and $a_k = \pm 1$ or 0. In the next section, two important members of the correlative family, duobinary and modified duobinary techniques as applied to binary pulse trains [7.2, 7.6, 7.7], are presented.

## 7.2 DUOBINARY WAVEFORMS: SPECTRAL RESHAPING AND ENCODING

First, we discuss the duobinary technique. Consider a binary input train consisting of 1's and 0's represented by impulses $+\delta(t)$ or $-\delta(t)$, as shown at $A$ in Fig. 7.1. For each $\delta(t)$ input at $A$, the output at $B$ is $[\delta(t) + \delta(t - T)]$ with the appropriate sign. We define the impulse response of $H_1(f)$ as $h_1(t)$:

$$h_1(t) = \mathfrak{F}^{-1}[H_1(f)] \text{ and } h_1(t) = \delta(t) + \delta(t - T) \tag{7.1}$$

where $\mathfrak{F}$ is the Fourier transform, and $h_1(t)$ the impulse response. Also,

$$\frac{1}{T} = \text{speed in b/s}$$

$$T = \text{bit interval in seconds}$$

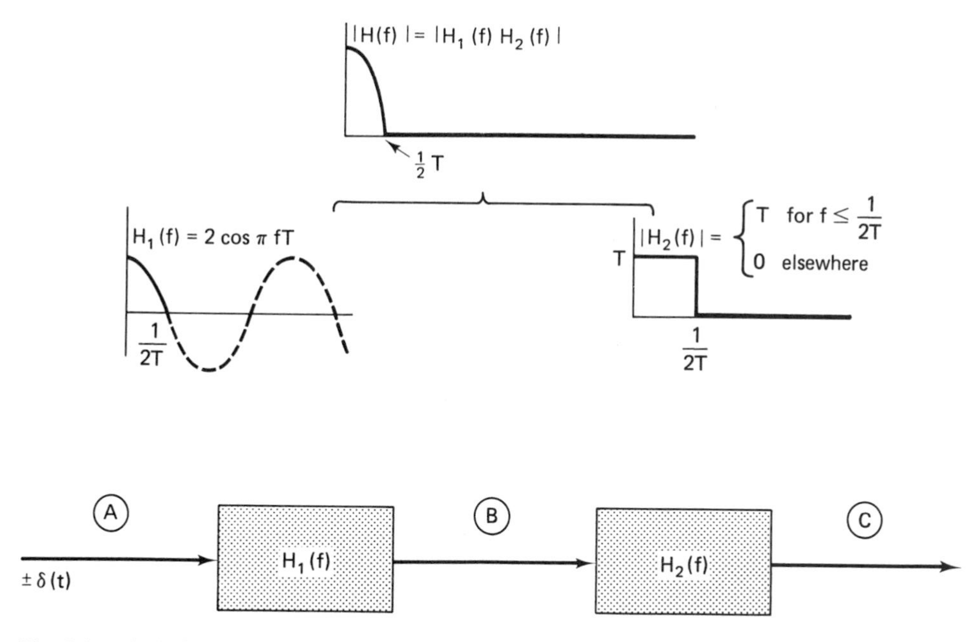


**Fig. 7.1.** Block diagram of duobinary system.

Since $H_1(f) = \mathfrak{F}[h_1(t)]$, then

$$H_1(f) = 1 + e^{-j2\pi fT} \quad \text{or} \quad |H_1(f)| = 2\cos \pi fT$$

To limit the bandwidth, we place the Nyquist rectangular filter $H_2(f)$ after $H_1(f)$, as shown in Figure 7.1, and specify $H_2(f)$ by the following equation: $H_2(f) = T$ for $|f| \leq 1/2T$ and zero elsewhere. The overall transfer function from $A$ to $C$ in Fig. 7.1 represents the duobinary conversion filter $H(f)$ and is given by:

$$|H(f)| = |H_1(f)H_2(f)| = 2T\cos \pi fT \quad \text{for } |f| \leq \frac{1}{2T} \tag{7.2}$$

and zero elsewhere.

The impulse response of $H(f)$ is obtained from equation (7.2), and is

$$h(t) = \frac{\sin \pi t/T}{\pi t/T} + \frac{\sin \pi(t-T)/T}{\pi(t-T)/T} \tag{7.3}$$

Hence, for every input impulse $\delta(t)$ at $A$, the output at $C$ is $h(t)$, with an appropriate polarity. Since the bit interval is $T$ seconds, there will be overlap or ISI between the digits over a correlation span of one. If so, then at the sampling instants there will be three rather than two distinct amplitude levels: $+2$, $0$, or $-2$, as illustrated in Fig. 7.2. It is assumed that the input at $A$ of Fig. 7.1 consists of two successive binary 1's represented by the delta function $\delta(t)$ followed by $\delta(t - T)$. The output at $C$ in Fig. 7.1, assuming no delay in the system, is $h(t)$ followed by $h(t - T)$, shown in Fig. 7.2. Clearly, both $h(t)$ and $h(t - T)$ consist of two sin $x/x$ type pulses

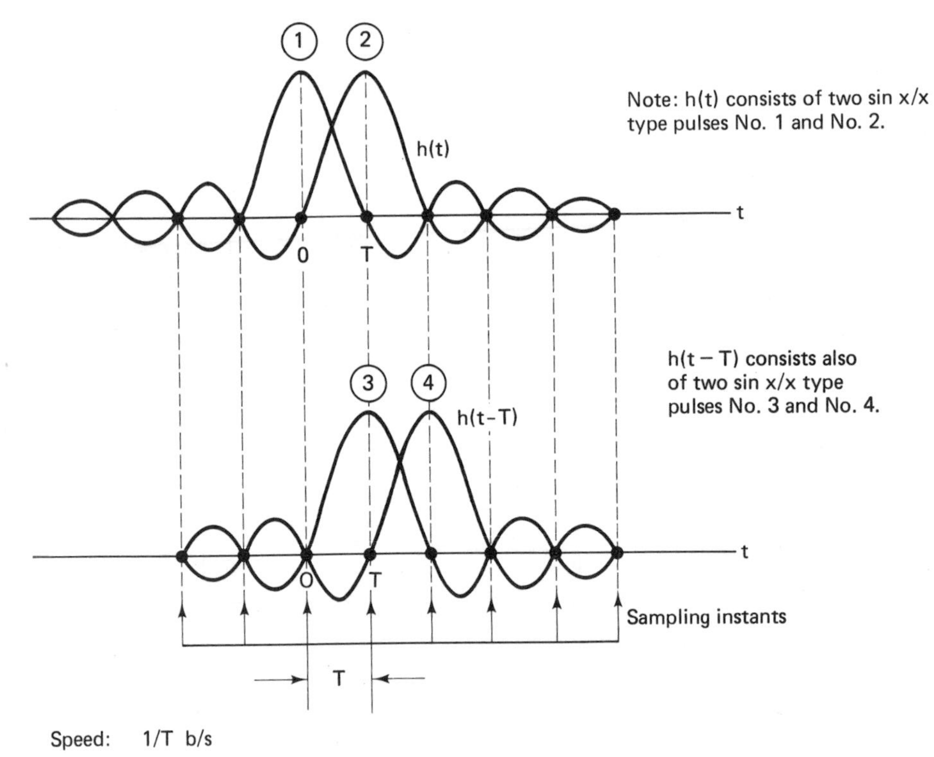


**Fig. 7.2.** Impulse patterns in duobinary process.

numbered 1 and 2 for $h(t)$ and 3 and 4 for $h(t - T)$ in Fig. 7.2. Each of the four pulses has unity amplitude at the sampling instant. In effect, pulse 2 constitutes ISI for pulse 3. Since the system is linear and the pulses appear at the same instant of time $t = T$, they add algebraically. If so, then their sum at the sampling time $t = T$ is $+2$ rather than unity. Figure 7.2 shows the time response to binary input 11. For binary input 00 represented by $-\delta(t)$ and $-\delta(t - T)$, the waveform of Fig. 7.2 would still be similar but with *negative* polarities. For such a case, the value at $t = T$ would be $-2$. Alternatively, for inputs 10 or 01, $h(t)$ and $h(t - T)$ would have *opposite* polarities, so that the value of the duobinary waveform at $t = T$ would be *zero*. Thus, the duobinary waveform has one of the three possible amplitudes at the sampling instants: $+2, 0$, or $-2$. However, the bandwidth [see equation (7.2)] is still the Nyquist bandwidth, and the Nyquist rate, or up to 43% higher transmission than that of the Nyquist rate, can be achieved [7.3]. For zero-memory binary systems the roll-off or excess bandwidth is, in many cases, 100% ($\alpha = 1$). Thus, for binary systems with $\alpha = 1$ filters, only *half* of the Nyquist transmission rate is achieved. Further, the cosine or, rather, the quarter-cycle cosine filter for duobinary can be easily approximated in practice.

The *modified duobinary* technique involves a correlation span of two digits. Its block diagram is the same as for the duobinary shown in Fig. 7.1. The *only* difference is in $H_1(f)$. In this case (for the modified duobinary),

$$\begin{aligned}
H_1(f) &= 1 - e^{-j4\pi fT} \\
h_1(t) &= \delta(t) - \delta(t - 2T) \\
|H_1(f)| &= 2 \sin 2\pi fT \\
H_2(f) &= T \quad \text{for } |f| \leq 1/2T \text{ and zero elsewhere} \\
|H(f)| &= |H_1(f)H_2(f)| = 2T \sin 2\pi fT \\
&\qquad \text{for } |f| \leq 1/2T \text{ and zero elsewhere}
\end{aligned} \tag{7.4}$$

The impulse response of $H(f)$ for the modified duobinary system is

$$h(t) = \frac{\sin \pi t/T}{\pi t/T} - \frac{\sin \pi(t - 2T)T}{\pi(t - 2T)/T} \tag{7.5}$$

Figure 7.3 shows an experimentally obtained impulse response of the modified duobinary filter described in equation (7.5). A specific modified duobinary 3-level

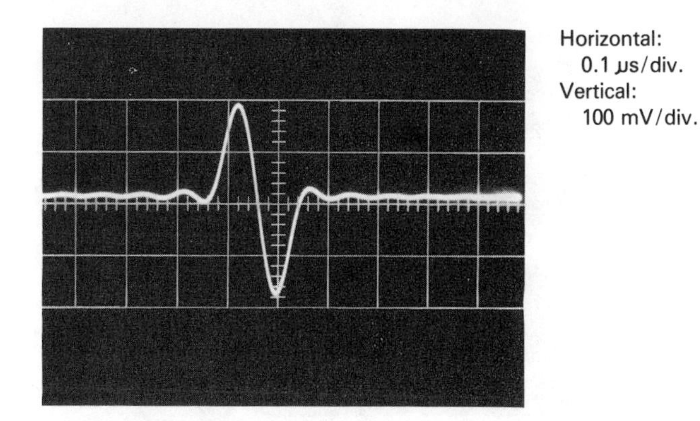


**Fig. 7.3.** Impulse response of modified duobinary filter.

pulse pattern is shown in Fig. 7.4. In both cases, the bandwidth is the Nyquist bandwidth, and the filter attenuation beyond the Nyquist cut-off frequency $1/2T$ Hz is 35 dB or more. Again, for every $\pm\delta(t)$ input at $A$, the output at $C$ is represented by expression (7.5), with the appropriate polarity. The waveform has *three* distinguishable levels at the sampling instants. In reference [7.3] it is shown that the Nyquist signaling rate and up to a 16% higher rate can be achieved. The modified duobinary system has *no* dc component. This is important since many transmission links cannot transmit dc. Both the duobinary and the modified duobinary techniques are employed in digital radio systems in conjunction with PSK and FM modulation techniques.

Figures 7.5 and 7.6 show, respectively, 3-level duobinary and modified duobinary eye patterns. The width of the eye of the modified duobinary is narrower

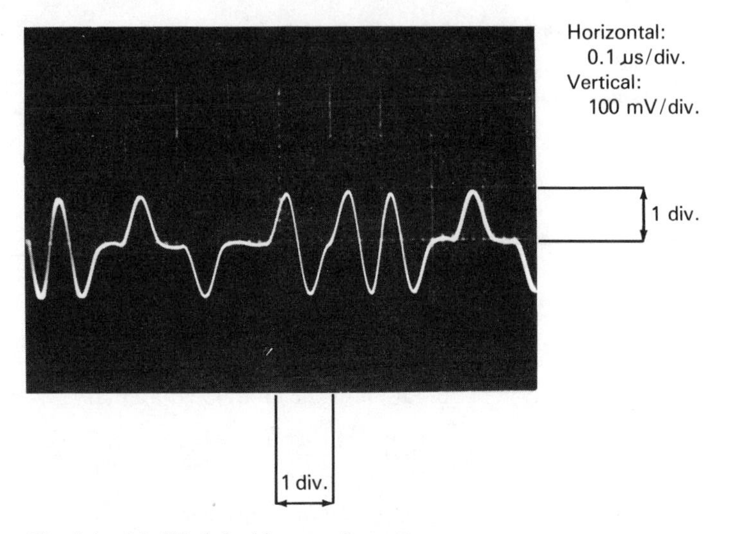


**Fig. 7.4.** Modified duobinary pulse pattern.

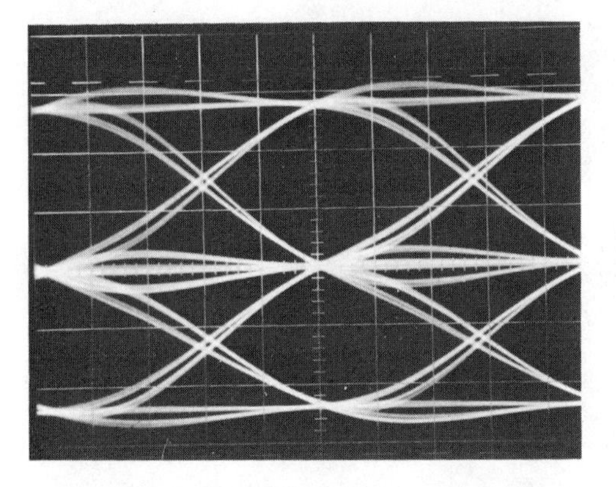


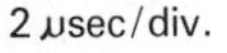


**Fig. 7.5.** Experimental eye diagram for duobinary (Redrawn by permission from Reference [7.22])

than that of the duobinary. This, in turn, indicates inherently higher ISI in the modified duobinary than in duobinary. The reason is that, although both permit signaling at the Nyquist rate or higher, in the duobinary the only transitions permitted in successive bits are between any two adjacent amplitude levels. For example, transition from the top level to the bottom one or vice versa does *not* occur in the duobinary between successive bits. Such a restriction does *not* exist in the modified duobinary pulse train, resulting in increased ISI.

A few words are in order about the modified duobinary filter in equation (7.4). Using conventional analog filter design methods, it is difficult to approximate such a filter characteristic. To get around this problem, we analyze again the filter

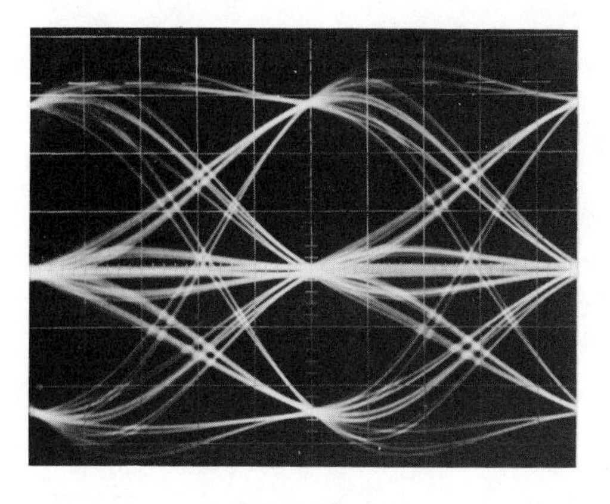

**Fig. 7.6.** Experimental eye diagram for a modified duobinary signal. (Redrawn by permission from Reference [7.22])

characteristic to find a relatively easy and practical design technique. We note that, for the modified duobinary system, the first part of the transfer function is given by $H_1(f) = 1 - e^{-j4\pi fT}$ and

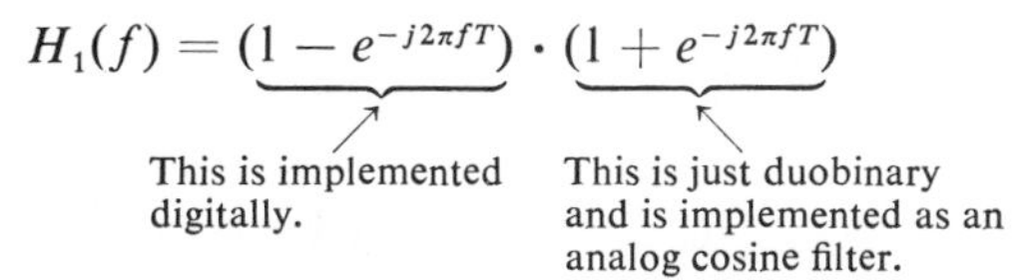

$$H_1(f) = \underbrace{(1 - e^{-j2\pi fT})}_{\text{This is implemented digitally.}} \cdot \underbrace{(1 + e^{-j2\pi fT})}_{\text{This is just duobinary and is implemented as an analog cosine filter.}}$$

The implementation of the modified duobinary filter is shown in Fig. 7.7. Point $C$ in Fig. 7.7 represents the transmitter output. If, for simplicity, we disregard

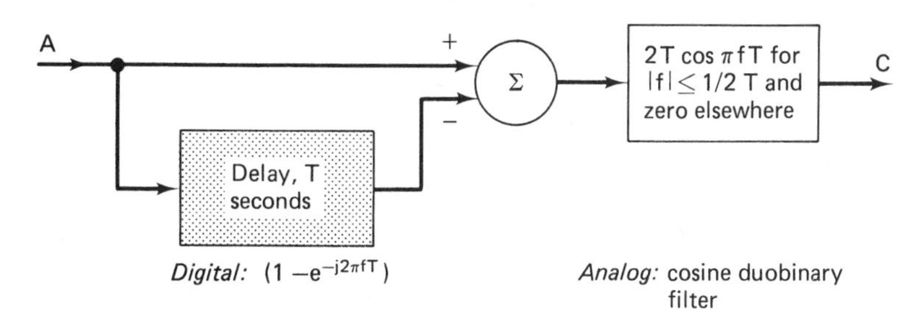


**Fig. 7.7.** Modified duobinary filtering.

errors due to noise in the transmission medium, the modified duobinary signal at $C$ represents also the received waveform ready for sampling and conversion to binary 1's and 0's. Decoding of this signal at the receiver is possible but not desirable. The signal at $C$ has three amplitude levels *at the sampling instants.* The top level could be interpreted as "1" and the bottom level as "0." The center level interpretation would have to be based on the previous bits, which could cause propagation of errors. The remedy is to encode as explained in the following paragraphs.

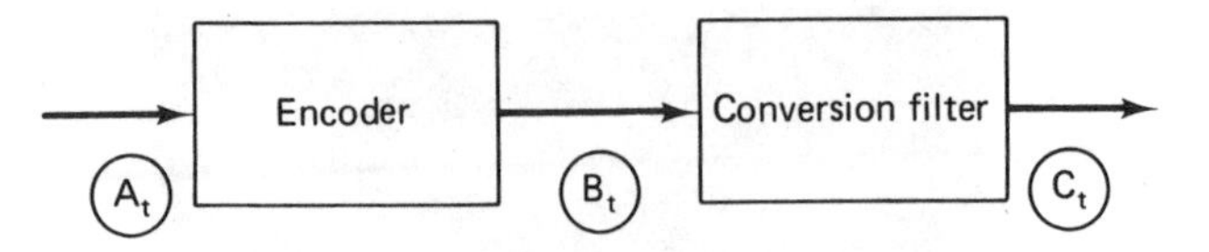


**Fig. 7.8.** Encoding of duobinary signals.

Figure 7.8 shows the system *with encoding to prevent error propagation.* We described previously the conversion filter from $B_t$ to $C_t$ for both the duobinary and the modified duobinary signals. Figure 7.9 depicts the actual circuit for encoding of the duobinary input sequence. The $T$ second delay is implemented by D-type

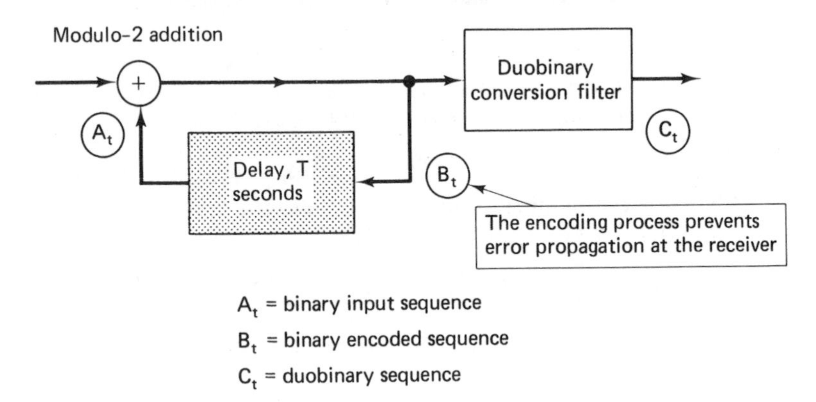


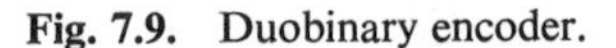

**Fig. 7.9.** Duobinary encoder.

flip-flops, and the modulo-2 addition by an EXCLUSIVE-OR gate. The input-output relationships of Fig. 7.9 can be expressed more precisely. For notational simplicity, we use the symbols $\Delta$ and $\Delta^2$, indicating in a practical sense *one* and *two* delay units, respectively, as

$$\Delta = e^{-j2\pi fT}, \qquad \Delta^2 = e^{-j4\pi fT}$$

For example, $\Delta B_t$ indicates that pulse train $B_t$ is delayed by one symbol interval of $T$ seconds. Similarly, $\Delta^2 B_t$ denotes a $2T$ second delay. Further, $\oplus$ indicates modulo-2 or EXCLUSIVE-OR addition, and the symbol $+$ the usual algebraic addition. Thus, the relationships in Fig. 7.9 are

$$A_t = B_t \oplus \Delta B_t \quad \text{modulo-2} \tag{7.6}$$

$$C_t = B_t + \Delta B_t \quad \text{algebraic} \tag{7.7}$$

Equation (7.6) can be rewritten as $B_t = A_t \oplus \Delta B_t$ in accordance with EXCLUSIVE-OR logic rules. The key point that follows from equations (7.6) and (7.7) is that $C_t \equiv A_t$, provided $C_t$ is interpreted modulo-2.

The duobinary conversion filter, in effect, delays the input by 1 bit and adds, algebraically, undelayed and delayed signals. Encoding from $A_t$ to $B_t$ is equivalent to differential encoding. In accordance with equations (7.6) and (7.7), each bit can be decoded without resorting to the previous history or previous bits, despite correlation properties.

**EXAMPLE 7.1. Duobinary.** The $A_t$ and $C_t$ sequences should be compared. $C_t$ has three amplitude levels 0, 1, and 2. If we interpret $C_t$ in a modulo-2 manner, then *amplitude* $2 = 0$ *modulo*-2. If so, then the sequence $C_t$ is identical to the sequence $A_t$. It is most important to note that every bit in $C_t$ is decoded into $A_t$ *without* resorting to a prior bit or bits. Should an error occur in $C_t$, it will affect only the erroneous bit and no other bits. Consequently, there is no possibility of error propagation. Without encoding from $A_t$ to $B_t$, as shown in Example 7.1, the pulse sequence could not possibly be decoded without resorting to prior bits which could be in error. Such a decoding would result in error propagation. ■

| | | | | | | | | | | | | | | | | | |
|---|---|---|---|---|---|---|---|---|---|---|---|---|---|---|---|---|---|
| $A_t$: | 0 | 0 | 0 | 1 | 1 | 1 | 1 | 0 | 1 | 0 | 1 | 0 | 0 | 1 | 0 | 1 | 1 |
| $B_t$: | 0 | 0 | 0 | 1 | 0 | 1 | 0 | 0 | 1 | 1 | 0 | 0 | 0 | 1 | 1 | 0 | 1 |
| $C_t$: | 0 | 0 | 0 | 1 | 1 | 1 | 1 | 0 | 1 | 2 | 1 | 0 | 0 | 1 | 2 | 1 | 1 |

The *encoding scheme* which prevents error propagation in the *modified duobinary* system is shown in Fig. 7.10. The governing equations for input-output relationships in the figure are

$$\left.\begin{aligned} A_t &= B_t(1 \oplus \Delta^2) \quad \text{modulo-2} \\ C_t &= B_t(1 - \Delta^2) \quad \text{algebraic} \end{aligned}\right\} \tag{7.8}$$

As a result of equations (7.8), $C_t \equiv A_t$, provided $C_t$ is interpreted as modulo-2.

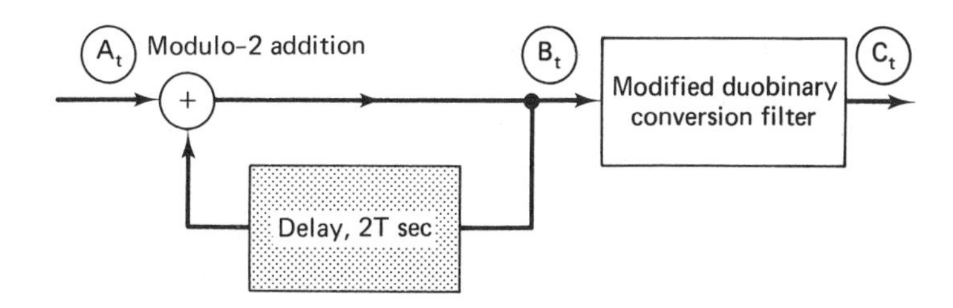


**Fig. 7.10.** Encoding in modified duobinary systems.

As an exercise in encoding the modified duobinary signal **Solve Problem 7.1.**

To summarize, *encoding* permits independent interpretation of each digit at the receiver, despite correlation properties between the digits. Thus, there is no possibility of error propagation.

## 7.3 POLYBINARY SIGNALS

The correlation span for binary signals can be extended to more than three digits, resulting in waveforms that have most of their energy at low frequencies. For duobinary and modified duobinary systems, the correlation span extends over two and three bits, respectively. Longer memories are possible; such systems have been termed *polybinary* [7.2].

Suppose a binary message with two signaling levels is transformed into a signal with *b signaling levels*, numbered consecutively from zero to $(b - 1)$, starting at the bottom. All even-numbered levels are identified as binary "0" and all odd-numbered ones as binary "1" (of course, this labeling can be reversed easily). Both the original message and the polybinary signal have an identical symbol duration of $T$ seconds. There are no restrictions on the number of $b$ levels.

A binary message is transformed into a polybinary signal in two steps. In the first step (encoding), the *original sequence* $a_n$, consisting of binary 1's and 0's, is converted into another *binary sequence* $d_n$ in such a manner that the present binary digit of sequence $d_n$ represents the modulo-2 sum of the $(b - 2)$ immediately preceding digits of sequence $d_n$ and the present digit $a_n$. For example, let

$$d_n = a_n \oplus d_{n-1} \oplus d_{n-2} \oplus d_{n-3}$$

Here, $a_n$ represents the input binary digits and $d_n$ the encoded bits. Since the encoding expression involves 3 bits preceding $d_n$, then $(b - 2) = 3$ and the number of levels will be $b = 5$. The second step involves transformation of the binary sequence $d_n$ into a *polybinary pulse train* $p_n$ by adding *algebraically* (not modulo-2) the present digit of sequence $d_n$ to the $(b - 2)$ preceding digits of sequence $d_n$. Consequently, $p_n$ modulo-2 $= a_n$. Thus, binary 1 and 0 in sequence $a_n$ are mapped into even- and odd-numbered levels, respectively, in the sequence $p_n$. This is significant since each digit in sequence $p_n$ can be independently detected, despite the strong correlation properties. The primary consequence of such properties is the *redistribution of the spectral density* of the original sequence $a_n$ so as to emphasize low frequencies. It is shown in reference [7.8] that the continuous component of the spectral density of the sequence $a_n$, consisting of uncorrelated binary signals, is

$$W_1(f) = \frac{1}{T} |G(f)|^2 pq$$

where $p$ is the probability of binary 1, $q = (1 - p)$ is the probability of binary 0, $G(f)$ is the Fourier transform of the pulse shape, and $1/T$ is the speed, in symbols per second. The spectral density for the $d_n$ sequence is given by [7.2]:

$$\left.\begin{aligned} W_2(f) &= W_1(f)Z_1 \quad \text{for } b = 3 \\ &= W_1(f)Z_2 \quad \text{for } b > 3 \end{aligned}\right\} \tag{7.9}$$

where

$$Z_1 = \frac{1}{(1 - 2p)^2 - 2(1 - 2p)^2 \cos 2\pi fT + 1} \tag{7.10}$$

$$Z_2 = \frac{1 + (1 - 2p)^2}{(1 - 2p)^4 - 2(1 - 2p)^2 \cos (b - 1)2\pi fT + 1} \tag{7.11}$$

Finally, the spectral density of the sequence $p_n$ is [7.2]:

$$\left.\begin{aligned} W_3(f) &= \frac{|G(f)|^2}{T}\left(\frac{\sin(b-1)\pi fT}{\sin \pi fT}\right) pqZ_1 \quad \text{for } b = 3 \\ &= \frac{|G(f)|^2}{T}\left(\frac{\sin(b-1)\pi fT}{\sin \pi fT}\right) pqZ_2 \quad \text{for } b > 3 \end{aligned}\right\} \tag{7.12}$$

The exact expression for the probability of error vs. normalized signal-to-noise ratio for the $b$-level polybinary system is derived in reference [7.2] and plotted for several values of $b$ in Fig. 7.11. Note that $b = 3$ represents the 3-level duobinary signal discussed in the previous section.

It is interesting to observe that the weighting factor $Z_2$ of the spectral density in equation (7.11) is a symmetrical function of $p$ and $q$; when $p \neq 0.5$, the energy density is more concentrated near low frequencies than for $p = 0.5$. The case for $b = 3$ is an exception.

The implementation of a polybinary system is similar to that of the duobinary. Encoding for a $b$-level system between points $A_t$ and $B_t$ requires $(b - 2)$ units of delay. This is accomplished by means of a shift register. Modulo-2 summation involves the data input $A_t$ as well as $(b - 2)$ digits from the $(b - 2)$ stage shift register. Subsequently, the transfer function between points $B_t$ and $C_t$ is approximated by a passive or active conversion and shaping filter. The number of delay units is, again, $(b - 2)$.

The recovery of the original binary data involves merely the interpretation of the $b$-level waveform at point $C_t$, at the sampling instants, in a modulo-2 manner.

## 7.4 CORRELATIVE TECHNIQUES FOR NON-BINARY SIGNALS

The correlative concept can be extended from binary to multi-level zero-memory non-binary signals [7.9]. The binary baseband correlative system, such as the duobinary and the modified duobinary, have a logical extension to non-binary waveforms where the *input pulse train has Q levels* and $Q = 2^n$, ($n$ being an integer greater than unity). The basic block diagram of a non-binary correlative system is similar to that of the duobinary (Fig. 7.8), except that at $A_t$ the data input is not binary but has $Q$ levels. A block diagram of such a system is depicted in Fig. 7.12.

At $A_t$ the data input appears in a non-binary form and has $2^n$ levels. The symbols are uncorrelated, and each represents two or more binary digits. The coder converts the $Q$-level input, consisting of independent digits, into a $Q$-level source with a memory extending over a fixed number of digits. Next, the level conversion is accomplished by using a level conversion filter. Such a filter causes overlap of pulses and introduces a controlled amount of intersymbol interference. As a consequence, the number of levels at $C_t$ is $2Q - 1$. Correlation properties are inherent in such a waveform. Nevertheless, it is possible to associate each level with the non-binary digit input at $A_t$. At the receiving end, the reconverter recon-

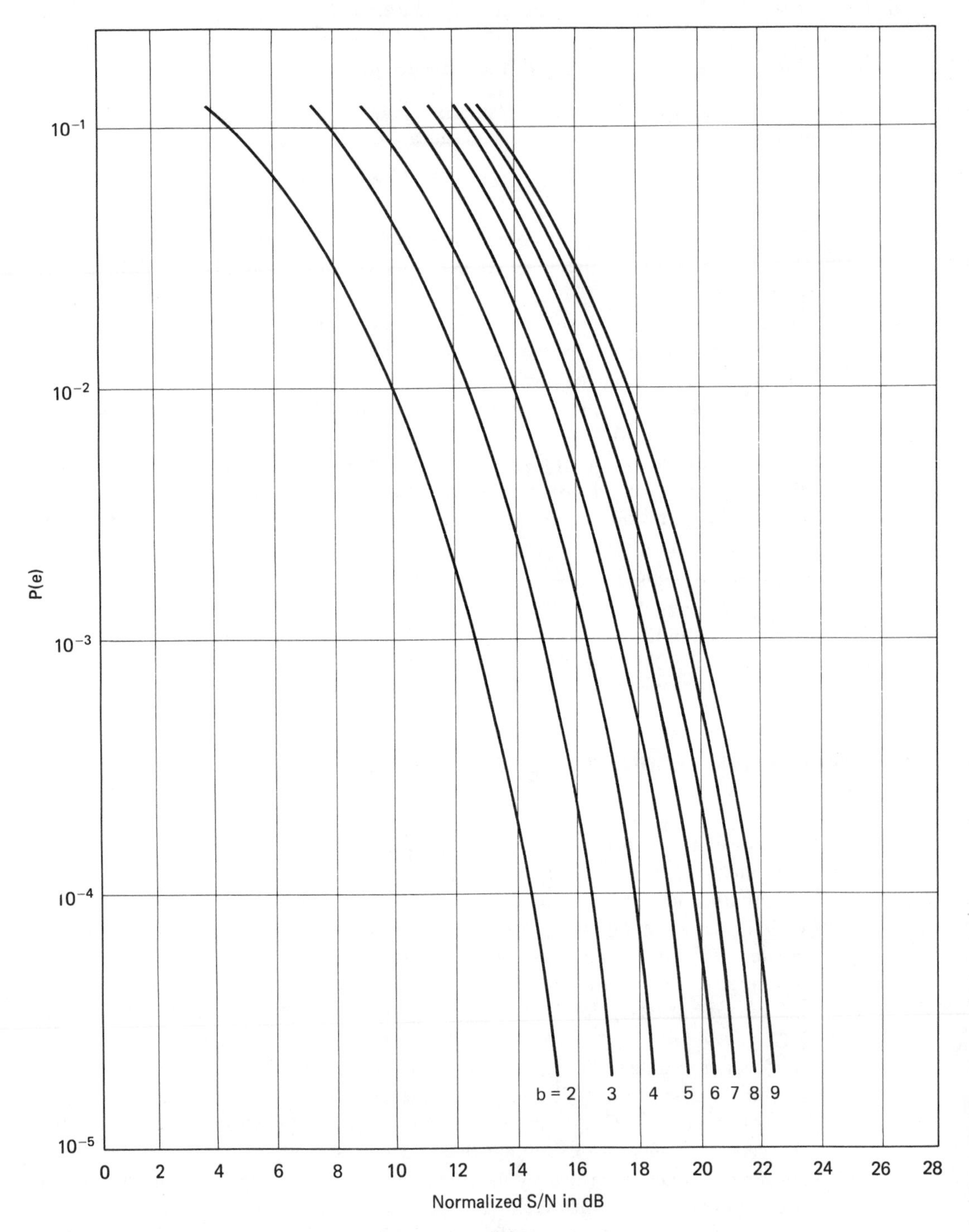


**Fig. 7.11.** Probability of error, $P(e) = f(S/N)$ of polybinary signals. (Reprinted by permission from the IEEE, Reference [7.2])

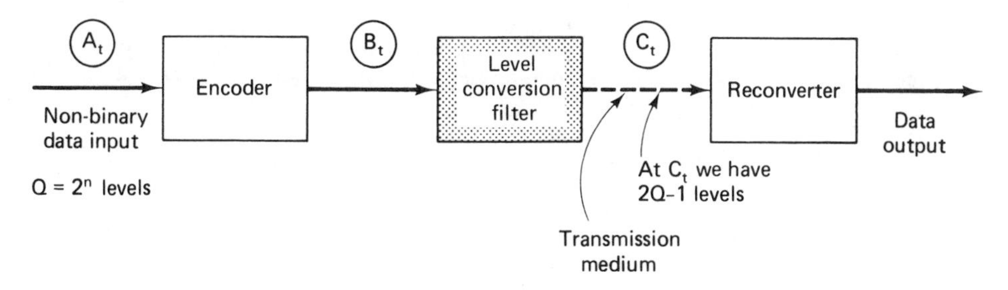


**Fig. 7.12.** Block diagram of the non-binary correlative system.

structs the original data input at $A_t$ by identifying each digit independently, without resorting to the past history of the correlative waveform.

Let us assume that, in Fig. 7.12, the level conversion filter is duobinary, namely $(1 + e^{-j\omega T})$ for $0 \leq \omega \leq \pi/T$ and zero elsewhere. Correspondingly, the non-binary symbol rate is $1/T$.

Before presenting the exact equations relating $A_t$, $B_t$ and $C_t$, we define the expression *modulo-Q* as applied to correlative encoding. We assume that any positive or negative integer $M$ is modulo-$Q$, where $Q$ is also an integer. For *positive* $M$, $M \bmod Q = M$ if $M < Q$. When $M \geq Q$, we subtract the *largest* multiple of $Q$ from $M$, but such a multiple must not be greater than $M$. The result of this subtraction is $M \bmod Q$, where *mod* stands for modulo. We note that the range of $M \bmod Q$ is $0 \leq (M \bmod Q) \leq (Q - 1)$. For example, $6 \bmod 4 = 2$, $17 \bmod 3 = 2$, or $4 \bmod 4 = 0$.

For *negative* $M$ we add to $M$ a multiple of $Q$ equal to or greater in magnitude than $M$, so that the result is a *positive* number. The next step is the same as for positive $M$. For example, $-3 \bmod 4 = 1$, $-2 \bmod 4 = 2$, $-5 \bmod 3 = 1$. One significant point is that in modulo-2 the minus sign can be replaced by plus sign, usually denoted by $\oplus$. Thus, $(x - y) \bmod 2 = (x \oplus y) \bmod 2$, which you can readily verify. Consequently, $z = x - y \bmod 2$ can be written as

$$z = x \oplus y \bmod 2 \quad \text{or} \quad y = x \oplus z \bmod 2 \quad \text{or} \quad x = y \oplus z \bmod 2$$

It must be emphasized that for mod $Q$, where $Q > 2$, the above *does not* apply, and care must be exercised in manipulating mod $Q$ expressions. Since the symbol $\oplus$ indicates mod 2 or EXCLUSIVE-OR addition, we do not use it for mod $Q$ when $Q > 2$. For such a case, we simply use $+$ or $-$ and specify whether it is mod $Q$ or merely an algebraic addition. The specific encoding and conversion process for the $Q$-level case is (duobinary type):

$$\left.\begin{aligned} A_t &= B_t + \Delta B_t \quad (\text{mod } Q) \\ C_t &= B_t + \Delta B_t \quad (\text{algebraic}) \\ \text{Then} \qquad C_t &\bmod Q = A_t \end{aligned}\right\} \tag{7.13}$$

The signal levels are interpreted at the receiver in the mod $Q$ sense, and consequently the data output is a replica of the data input at $A_t$. Non-binary correlative systems are analogous to the binary correlative, and the system of Fig. 7.12 is similar to the duobinary.

**EXAMPLE 7.2.** Suppose $Q = 4$, and the possible digit values are 0, 1, 2, or 3 volts at the sampling instants. The corresponding sequences $A_t$, $B_t$, and $C_t$ for $Q = 4$, in accordance with the set of equations (7.13), are:

| | | | | | | | | | | | | | | | | | | |
|---|---|---|---|---|---|---|---|---|---|---|---|---|---|---|---|---|---|---|
| $A_t$: | | 1 | 0 | 3 | 2 | 0 | 0 | 1 | 2 | 2 | 1 | 3 | 0 | 3 | 0 | 0 | 2 | 1 |
| $B_t$: | 0 | 1 | 3 | 0 | 2 | 2 | 2 | 3 | 3 | 3 | 2 | 1 | 3 | 0 | 0 | 0 | 2 | 3 |
| $C_t$: | | 1 | 4 | 3 | 2 | 4 | 4 | 5 | 6 | 6 | 5 | 3 | 4 | 3 | 0 | 0 | 2 | 5 |

Sequence $B_t$ is obtained from the equation $A_t = B_t + \Delta B_t \bmod 4$ or, equivalently, $B_t = A_t - \Delta B_t \bmod 4$. For example, the first symbol in $A_t$ is 1, and the *previous* symbol (denoted by $\Delta B_t$) in sequence $B_t$ is 0. Thus,

$$A_t - \Delta B_t \bmod 4 = 1 - 0 \bmod 4 = 1$$

so that the present symbol $B_t$ (right below present symbol $A_t$) is 1. Next,

$$A_t - \Delta B_t \bmod 4 = 0 - 1 \bmod 4 = 3$$

and the next one is

$$3 - 3 \bmod 4 = 0, \quad \text{etc.}$$

Sequence $C_t$ is obtained by the algebraic addition of two successive symbols $B_t$ since $C_t = B_t + \Delta B_t$. Thus, starting from the first two symbols of $B_t$: $0 + 1 = 1$; next, $1 + 3 = 4$; next, $3 + 0 = 3$, $0 + 2 = 2$, etc. Note that each symbol $C_t \bmod 4 = A_t$. For example, the first four symbols in $C_t$ are 1432 corresponding to 1032 mod 4 since $4 \bmod 4 = 0$. Similarly, $5 \bmod 4 = 1$, etc. The initial digit of $B_t$ can be either of the four symbols: 0, 1, 2, or 3, but $C_t \bmod 4$ always will be $A_t$. Problem 7.2 suggests verification that $B_t$ may assume any of the four values. ■

### *7.4.1 Correlative Non-binary Signaling without dc Component*

A non-binary correlative system that corresponds to a modified duobinary signal of the type $(1 - \Delta^2)$ is described next. This system has applications in a number of digital radio communication systems and is, therefore, described in detail. The system has a practical *speed efficiency* of $2 \log_2 Q$ b/s/Hz, both in baseband and SSB (single-sideband) modulated carrier system applications and has no dc component.

The input to the system, shown in Fig. 7.13 at point $A$, is the usual serial binary data consisting of binary 1 and 0. The bit rate is $(\log_2 Q)/T$ b/s, where $Q$ is the number of levels in the non-binary Nyquist-type (zero-memory) system at point $D$, and $T$ is the duration of the non-binary symbols in seconds. To convert the serial binary input data into a parallel binary stream, a shift register is employed between $A$ and $B$. There are $\log_2 Q$ parallel binary pulse trains, and the parallel binary symbol rate at point $B$ is $1/T$ symbols per second. Conceptually, the coding

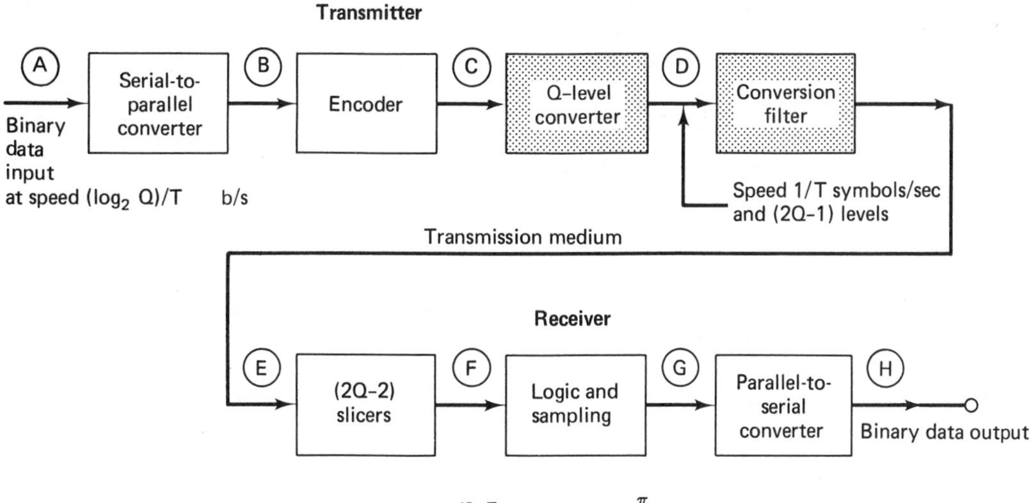


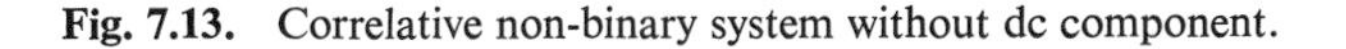
**Fig. 7.13.** Correlative non-binary system without dc component.

procedure is non-binary, but the encoder employs binary logic. A key parameter is $Q$, which is the number of non-binary levels.

The function of the encoder between $B$ and $C$ is to process the parallel binary signals as

$$B_t = C_t(1 - \Delta^2) \bmod Q \tag{7.14}$$

where $\Delta^2$ indicates a delay equal to two $Q$-ary symbol intervals. Next, the converter between $C$ and $D$ converts each parallel group of $\log_2 Q$ binary digits into one of the $Q$ levels. The output at $D$ is non-binary, with $Q$ amplitude levels, and each level corresponds uniquely to a group of $\log_2 Q$ binary digits at $C$. The conversion could be to a straight binary (binary-coded decimal) code or to a Gray code [7.10]. Finally, the filter between $D$ and $E$ transforms the $Q$-level waveform into a signal with $(2Q - 1)$ levels at $E$, at the rate of $1/T$ symbols per second. The shape of the conversion filter approximates a half-cycle sinusoid in accordance with the characteristic similar to modified duobinary, namely $(1 - e^{-j2\omega T})$ from zero to $1/2T$ Hz, and zero elsewhere. Each of the $(2Q - 1)$ levels at $E$ corresponds to a group of $\log_2 Q$ parallel binary digits at $B$. The correlation span of the signal at $E$ extends over three $Q$-ary symbols. Nevertheless, each digit at the receiving end can be uniquely identified without resorting to the past history of the waveform. Consequently, the receiver employs, in a straightforward manner, $(2Q - 2)$ slicers (threshold detectors) between $E$ and $F$, and the number of binary slicers is one less than the number of levels. The binary outputs of the slicers are combined by using standard logic gates between $F$ and $G$. Finally, a parallel-to-serial conversion takes place between $G$ and $H$. At $H$ the binary serial pulse train is a replica of the binary input data at $A$.

**EXAMPLE 7.3. Non-binary System with $Q = 4$ Input Levels.** To gain a better insight into the non-binary correlative techniques, particularly into the encoding and conversion operations, a practical example is given, using a specific value of $Q$.

***SOLUTION:*** Suppose the number of levels $Q$ is equal to four. Referring again to Fig. 7.13, we see that the serial-to-parallel converter between $A$ and $B$ has two stages. At $B$ each of the four possible levels is represented by two parallel binary digits.

In this case, Gray coding is assumed for the encoding between points $B$ and $C$. The encoding is performed as

$$C_t = B_t + \Delta^2 C_t \bmod 4 \tag{7.15}$$

In a practical system, binary elements must be employed. Consequently, $B_t$, $C_t$, and $\Delta^2 C_t$ are each represented by two binary digits labeled $X$, $Y$; $C_{t_1}$, $C_{t_2}$; and $Z$, $W$, respectively. All possible binary states must be considered in satisfying equation (7.15). In accordance with the *Gray code*, the four levels 0, 1, 2, and 3 are assigned binary states 00, 01, 11, and 10, respectively. Table 7.1 lists all possible states for $B_t$, $C_t$, and $\Delta^2 C_t$ in a manner that satisfies equation (7.15).

**TABLE 7.1 Encoding for $Q = 4$**

| $B_t$ | | $\Delta^2 C_t$ | | $C_t$ | |
|---|---|---|---|---|---|
| $X$ | $Y$ | $Z$ | $W$ | $C_{t_1}$ | $C_{t_2}$ |
| 0 | 0 | 0 | 0 | 0 | 0 |
| 0 | 0 | 0 | 1 | 0 | 1 |
| 0 | 0 | 1 | 0 | 1 | 0 |
| 0 | 0 | 1 | 1 | 1 | 1 |
| 0 | 1 | 0 | 0 | 0 | 1 |
| 0 | 1 | 0 | 1 | 1 | 1 |
| 0 | 1 | 1 | 0 | 0 | 0 |
| 0 | 1 | 1 | 1 | 1 | 0 |
| 1 | 0 | 0 | 0 | 1 | 0 |
| 1 | 0 | 0 | 1 | 0 | 0 |
| 1 | 0 | 1 | 0 | 1 | 1 |
| 1 | 0 | 1 | 1 | 0 | 1 |
| 1 | 1 | 0 | 0 | 1 | 1 |
| 1 | 1 | 0 | 1 | 1 | 0 |
| 1 | 1 | 1 | 0 | 0 | 1 |
| 1 | 1 | 1 | 1 | 0 | 0 |

States $C_{t_1}$ and $C_{t_2}$ are the two parallel outputs at point $C$ in Fig. 7.13 and, after minimization, appear as

$$\left.\begin{aligned} C_{t_1} &= X\bar{Z}\bar{W} + Y\bar{Z}W + \bar{X}ZW + \bar{Y}Z\bar{W} \\ C_{t_2} &= XZ\bar{W} + \bar{Y}ZW + \bar{X}\bar{Z}W + Y\bar{Z}\bar{W} \end{aligned}\right\} \tag{7.16}$$

**EXAMPLE 7.4.** Here we present a specific example of a digit pattern expressed in modulo-4 form. The letter designations are consistent with the block diagram of Fig. 7.13.

***SOLUTION:***

($B$) 0030333021032001221303002 1

($C$) 0030231330331310320100002 1

($E$) 0030-13-102-303-200-322-3-10-10021

($G$) The same as ($B$), except for errors caused by transmission impairments

Seven levels appear at point $E$, ranging from $-3$ to 3. Each level is uniquely interpreted at the receiver. There are six slicers between points $E$ and $F$. The signal levels are indicated by solid lines and the slicing levels by dashed lines in Fig. 7.14. The slicing levels are

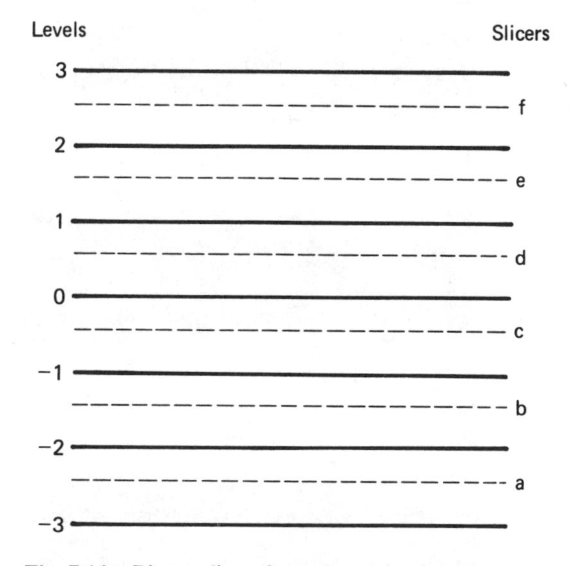


**Fig. 7.14.** Binary slicers for a $Q = 4$-level system.

denoted by $a$, $b$, $c$, $d$, $e$, and $f$, starting from the bottom. The general rule for logic between $F$ and $G$ in Fig. 7.13 is that, for the extreme levels, the adjacent single slicer provides an indication and is "up" for the top level and "down" for the bottom level. Any intermediate level is uniquely determined by the two adjacent slicers. The one above must be down and the one below up. Hence, in this case the logic consists of seven AND gates or, in general, $(2Q - 1)$ AND gates. For the example discussed, the logic is as follows:

$$\left.\begin{array}{ll} \text{level } 3 = f, & \text{level } -1 = b\bar{c} \\ \text{level } 2 = e\bar{f}, & \text{level } -2 = a\bar{b} \\ \text{level } 1 = d\bar{e}, & \text{level } -3 = \bar{a} \\ \text{level } 0 = c\bar{d}, & \end{array}\right\} \tag{7.17}$$

### *7.4.2 Comparison with Zero-Memory Systems*

At this point it is interesting to notice the experimental eye patterns for the non-binary systems. Figure 7.15 shows the modified duobinary 7-level eye pattern for $Q = 4$, and Fig. 7.16 shows a 15-level modified duobinary eye pattern for $Q = 8$.

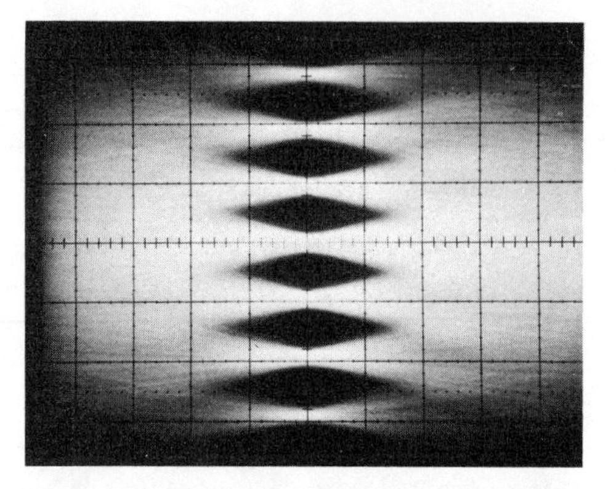


**Fig. 7.15.** 7-level modified duobinary eye pattern.

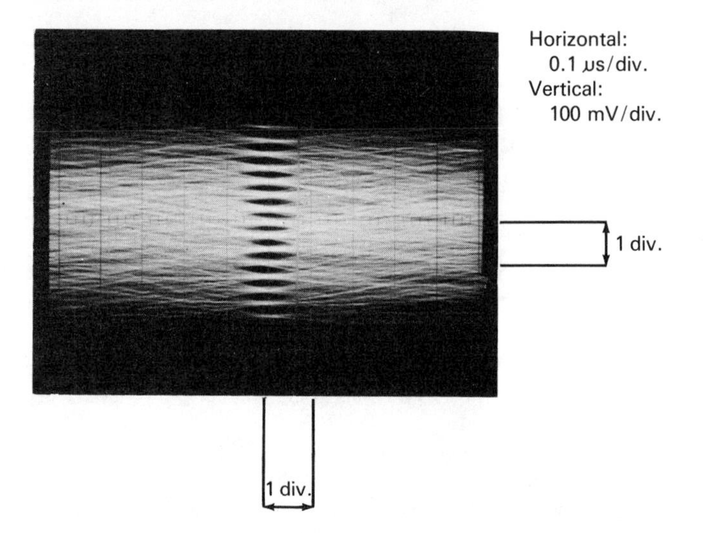


**Fig. 7.16.** 15-level modified duobinary eye pattern.

It should be noted that the extreme-level eyes are wider than the eyes near the center level. This phenomenon is due to greater intersymbol interference near the center because of the triangular probability distribution of levels for random binary-data input.

The advantages of correlative systems over zero-memory multi-level systems can now be shown, and are more dramatic for non-binary than for binary inputs. For comparison purposes, it is assumed that the transmission medium is a raised-cosine low-pass filter with $\alpha = 1$ corresponding to 100% rolloff, such as described in Chapter 3. Such a filter has been employed for zero-memory binary and multi-level PAM systems, and its characteristic is given by:

$$A(f) = \frac{\cos^2 \pi f T}{2} \quad \text{for } 0 \leq f \leq 1/T \text{ and zero elsewhere} \tag{7.18}$$

The assumed signaling rate is $1/T$ symbols per second for binary or multi-level systems. A conventional binary system is a good frame of reference and accommodates one binary channel or, equivalently, has a speed capability of 1 bit/s per Hz of bandwidth. Let $N$ represent the number of bits/s sent per 1 Hz of bandwidth (b/s/Hz). The correlative systems assumed are of the $(1 + \Delta)$ or $(1 - \Delta^2)$ type. Table 7.2 provides a comparison between correlative and zero-memory systems for the channels described by (7.18). The *number of levels* for *zero-memory* and *correlative* systems is represented by $R_z$ and $R_c$, respectively. Since the bandwidths are identical as per equation (7.18), and the binary data input rate is $1/T$ b/s, it turns out that

$$R_z = 2^N \tag{7.19}$$

$$R_c = 2^{(N/2)+1} - 1 \tag{7.20}$$

**TABLE 7.2 Comparison of Correlative with Zero-memory ($\alpha$ = 1) Systems**

| $N$ (b/s/Hz) | Number of Levels $R_z$ in Zero-memory Systems, with $\alpha = 1$ | Number of Levels $R_c$, in Correlative Systems |
|---|---|---|
| 1 | 2 | |
| 2 | 4 | 3 |
| 3 | 8 | |
| 4 | 16 | 7 |
| 5 | 32 | |
| 6 | 64 | 15 |
| 7 | 128 | |
| 8 | 256 | 31 |

For example, the zero-memory system requires more than twice as many levels to send 4 bits per hertz of bandwidth, or more than four times as many levels to send 6 b/s/Hz. Alternatively, when 15 or 16 levels are permitted on a particular channel, the zero-memory system sends 4 b/s/Hz, and the correlative system 6 b/s/Hz. It is stressed that this is based on a zero-memory channel with $\alpha = 1$, as expressed in equation (7.18).

## 7.5 ERROR DETECTION IN CORRELATIVE SYSTEMS

Another advantage of correlative systems compared to zero-memory systems is their error-detection capability [7.11, 7.12]. Error detection in zero-memory systems requires redundancy. Correlative systems, however, have finite memory, and this memory can be utilized to monitor and detect errors without introducing redundant digits at the transmitter.

Distinctive patterns exist in the $(1 + \Delta)$ or $(1 - \Delta^2)$ correlative waveforms.

The *duobinary* $(1 + \Delta)$ system has three levels: top and bottom (referred to as *extreme levels*) and a center level. These patterns follow the unique rule: The polarities of two successive bits at the extreme levels are opposite if the number of intervening bits at the center level is odd. Otherwise, they have the same polarity.

The *modified duobinary system* $(1 - \Delta^2)$ also has three levels. The pulse train is divided into *odd* and *even* bits. Both *odd* and *even* pulse trains follow the same patterns. The rule for odd as well as even bits is as follows: Two successive bits at the extreme levels always have opposite polarity. This phenomenon is indicated below, in sequence $C_t$ for the even bits.

**EXAMPLE 7.5. Modified Duobinary.**

$A_t$: 0 0 0 1 0 1 0 1 1 0 0 1 1 1 0 0 0 1 0 1 0

$B_t$: 0 0 0 1 0 0 0 1 1 1 1 0 0 1 0 1 0 0 0 1 0

$C_t$: 0 + 0 − 0 + + 0 0 − − + 0 0 0 − 0 + 0

Any time the above rules are violated, errors result that can readily be detected. The generalized diagram for the error-detection process [7.9] for binary and non-binary signals is shown in Fig. 7.17.

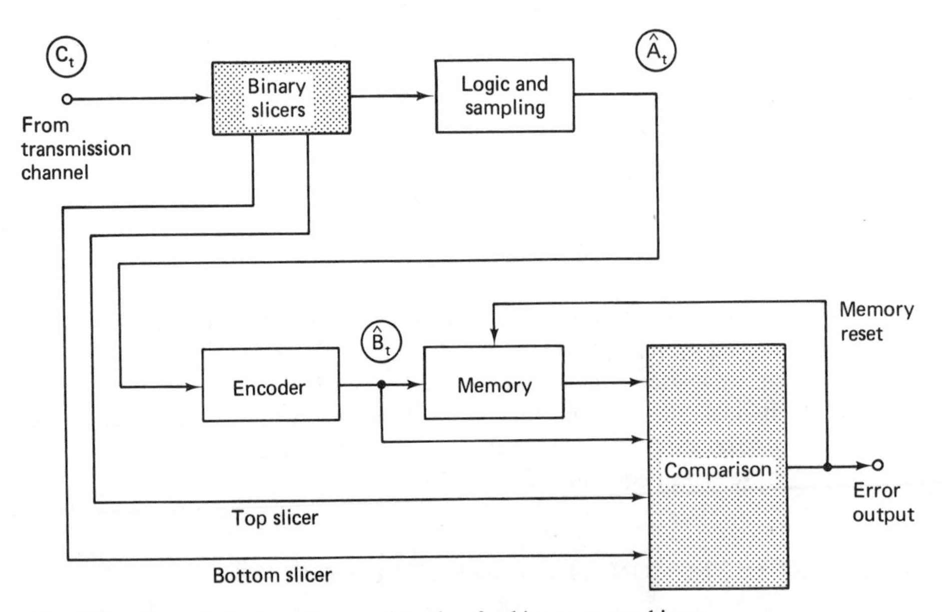


**Fig. 7.17.** General diagram of error detection for binary or non-binary correlative systems. (Reprinted by permission from the IEEE, Reference [7.9])

In Fig. 7.17 the two blocks at the top contain binary slicers and logic and sampling. The incoming waveform, with $(2Q - 1)$ levels, is $C_t$. Logic and sampling circuits provide a replica of the binary input data $A_t$ in parallel form, except for errors that might have occurred in the transmission medium. This binary data is encoded in exactly the same way as in the transmitter, resulting in $B_t$. The principle is to ascertain whether the extreme levels (top and bottom) correspond to the present and past digits originating from the encoder and digital memory. A comparison is made at the sampling instants of the extreme level digits of $C_t$. If there is disagreement, an error is indicated, and the memory is reset to the correct state. Such a comparison is done when the extreme levels are present because only the extreme levels are formed in a unique way in correlative systems. Intermediate levels may be formed in more than one way and are, therefore, not suitable for detection or errors. (**Solve Problem 7.4.**)

Each of the $(2Q - 1)$ levels on the line represents $\log_2 Q$ binary digits. An error implies that the particular level at the sampling instant is not the level that was originally transmitted; such an error results in at most $\log_2 Q$ erroneous bits. The terminology used here refers to a single error and implies a level error. ■

**EXAMPLE 7.6. Error Detection for $Q = 4$.** A detailed diagram of the *error-detection logic* circuit appears in Fig. 7.18 for $Q = 4$, or a 7-level correlative system. The two blocks at the upper left-hand corner, namely the slicers and logic and sampling, are actually an integral part of the receiver. The slicers provide two inputs from the threshold detectors, which monitor only the top and bottom levels of the 7-level correlative waveform. The logic and sampling block delivers $\log_2 Q$, which is in this case just two, regenerated, binary digits in parallel that represent the replica of the original data input in parallel form, except for possible errors. The AND gates G-6 through G-13, the OR gates G-14 and G-15, and both two-stage shift registers, which provide 2-digit delay and feedback to gates G-6 through G-13, form the encoder of the type $(1 - \Delta^2)$ mod 4. This encoding is exactly the same as at the transmitter. Our purpose is to compare the regenerated and encoded data, which may possibly contain errors, at the instants of time when the incoming correlative input waveform reaches one of the extreme levels (top or bottom) since these are the only levels that are uniquely formed from the encoded binary data at the transmitter.

In particular, the outputs of G-14 and G-15 are binary digits $C_1$ and $C_2$. These digits are delayed, using shift registers, by two unit intervals and provide $\Delta^2 C_1$ and $\Delta^2 C_2$. Combinations of $C_1$, $C_2$, $\Delta^2 C_1$, $\Delta^2 C_2$ provide a check during an instant of time when either the top or the bottom level is present. Knowing that these levels can only be formed in unique way, it is necessary to verify certain specific patterns of $C_1$, $C_2$, $\Delta^2 C_1$, and $\Delta^2 C_2$ that depend on the original binary coding at the transmitter. Since $Q = 4$ and Gray coding is assumed, levels 0, 1, 2, and 3 correspond to binary 00, 01, 11, and 10, respectively. Correlative encoding $(1 - \Delta^2)$ mod 4 and the assumed conversion filter result in a $(1 - \Delta^2)$-type of level conversion, so that the correlative levels at the input to the error detector are 3, 2, 1, 0, $-1$, $-2$, and $-3$. Consequently, the top level, 3, could have been formed in only one way, such that the four binary values of $C_1$, $C_2$, $\Delta^2 C_1$, and $\Delta^2 C_2$ must have been 1000. This corresponds to the assignment of a binary value of 10 to level 3, as per the original assumption. Similarly, for the bottom level, $-3$, the patterns of the four digits $C_1$, $C_2$, $\Delta^2 C_1$, and $\Delta^2 C_2$ should be 0010, which results in a binary value of 01. The binary value 01 corresponds to $-3 = 1$ mod 4. The appearance of any other patterns will indicate an error or errors, so that a signal will appear at the output of G-5. Gates G-1 and G-3 comprise the logic that compares the top-level pattern with the encoder output and, similarly, for gates G-2 and G-4. Consequently, G-3 and G-4 provide error indication, and the two outputs are combined in G-5. Should an error occur, it will be necessary

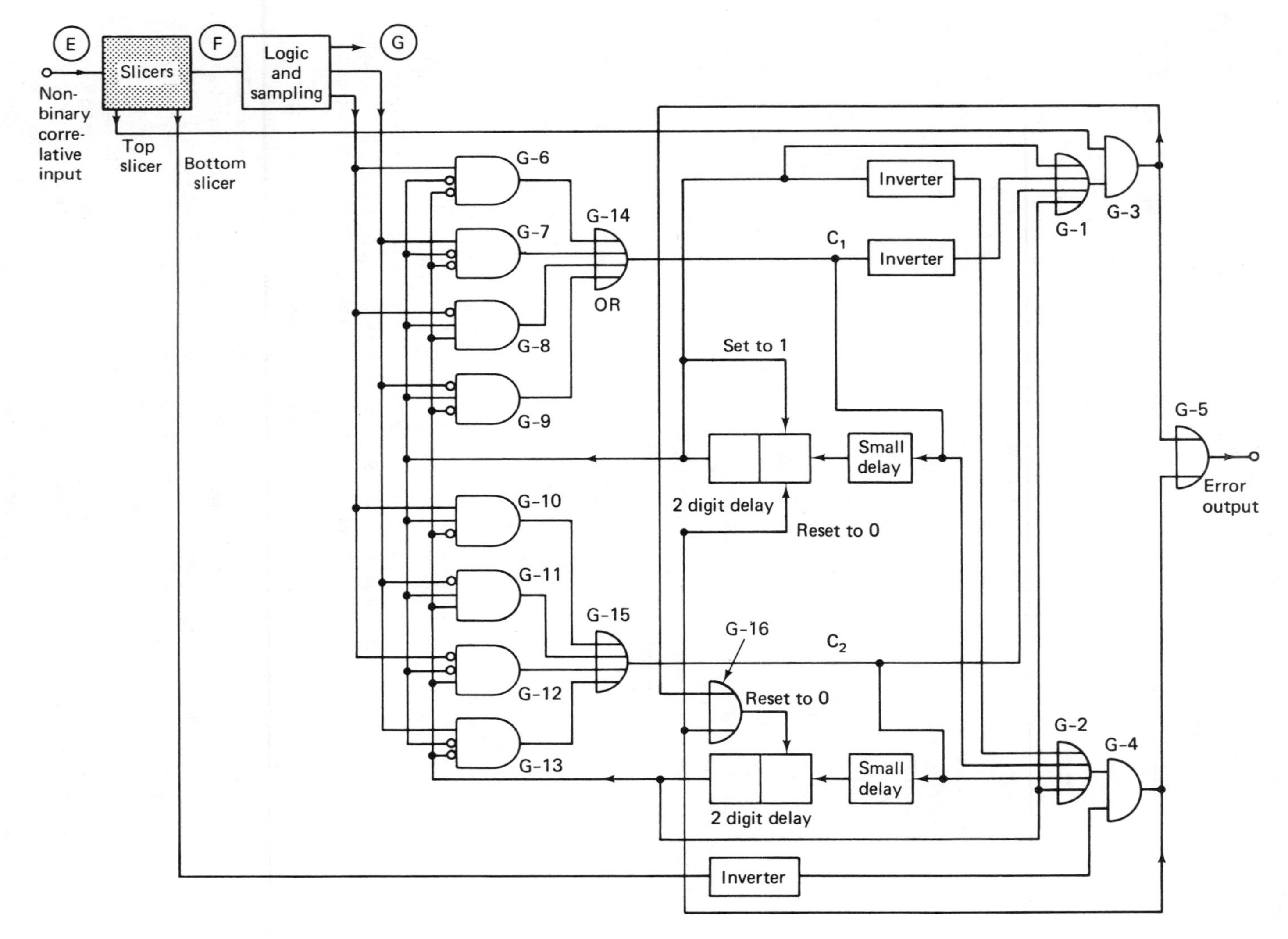


**Fig. 7.18.** Error detection for $Q = 4$.

to erase the memory in one of the two shift registers, which provide 2-digit delay, and to set it to the correct state. This is accomplished by gating the output of G-3, G-4, and G-16 directly to the two-stage registers.

An example of a single and double error-detection process, consistent with Fig. 7.18, is shown in Fig. 7.19 for $Q = 4$. The system is the $(1 - \Delta^2)$ type. A pattern of 23 digits is considered, and the digit positions in time at $A$ in Fig. 7.19 are consecutively labeled from 1 to 23. The original data input at the transmitter, before encoding, appears at $B$. After encoding and conversion to a 7-level waveform, the signal is transmitted as shown

**Fig. 7.19.** Error detection patterns for $Q = 4$.

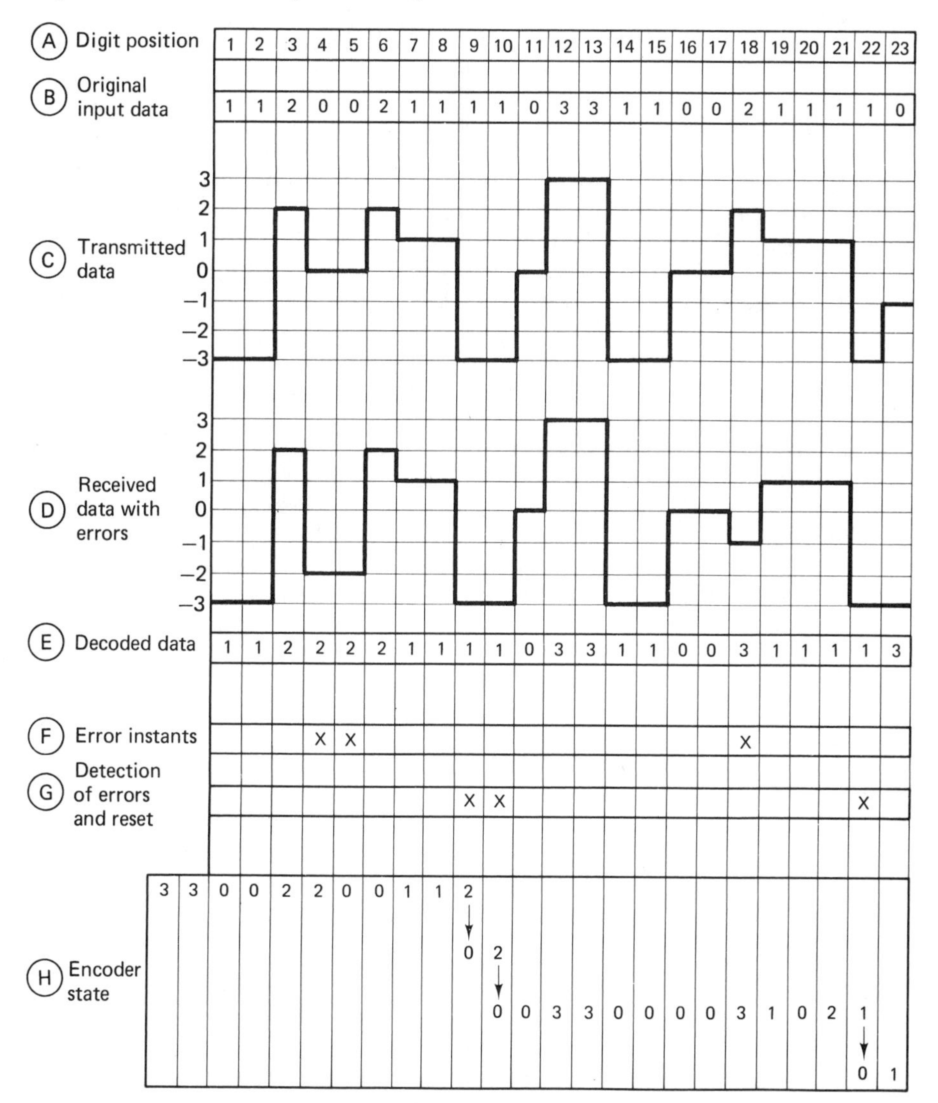

at $C$. For clarity the waveforms are shown in rectangular rather than in the form that they actually appear at the transmitter output.

At the receiver waveform $C$ is received with errors, as depicted at $D$. A double error occurs at digit positions 4 and 5, and a single error at position 18. This is apparent from a comparison of the waveforms $C$ and $D$. The received 7-level signal at $D$ is interpreted and decoded in a mod-4 manner, and the decoded data is shown at $E$. A comparison of the data at $B$ and $E$ indicates that the sequence 00 at positions 4 and 5 was altered to 22, and the digit 2 at position 18 becomes 3 after decoding. These error instants are identified at $F$; the time instants when they were detected are shown at $G$. An integral part of the error-detection system, as shown in Fig. 7.18, is the encoder, which is similar to the one shown at the transmitter. Its initial state, which is entirely arbitrary, is 33, shown at $H$ in Fig. 7.19, in the two time slots preceding digit position 1. The succeeding digits of the encoder are obtained by adding mod 4, the decoded data digit at $E$, to the encoder state at $H$, two digits back. For example, the digit at $H$ in digit position 4 is 2 and represents the sum mod 4 of the digit in position 4 at $E$, which is 2, and the digit in position 2 at $H$, which is 0.

To detect errors, we compare the received data $D$ with the state of the encoder at $H$ *only* at the time instants at which the waveform at $D$ reaches one of the extreme levels in Fig. 7.19. For example, comparisons are made only at digit positions 1, 2, 9, 10, 12, 13, 14, 15, and 22. Thus, detection of errors and resetting of the encoder to its correct state at $G$ can take place only at those digit positions. The double error at positions 4 and 5 is detected at digit positions 9 and 10 at $G$. At position 9 the extreme level at $D$ is $-3$. Since the conversion filter at the transmitter is $(1 - \Delta^2)$ and its input originates from the encoder, the present state of the encoder at the transmitter is 0, and the previous one (two digits back) is 3. These two states would result in level $-3$. Examination of the encoder state at $H$, however, indicates a discrepancy. The prssent digit at position 9 is 2, and the previous (two digits back) at position 7 is 1. Since this is inconsistent with level $-3$ at position 9 at $D$, error indication appears at $G$ at position 9. At the same time, the encoder state is reset from 2 to 0 as shown at $H$.

A similar situation prevails at digit position 10 in Fig. 7.19, so the second consecutive error is detected, and the encoder at $H$ is reset from 2 to 0. Finally, a single error occurs at position 18 and is detected at position 22. Then entire process is repeated again. ■

## 7.6 CODING AND MODULATION FOR CORRELATIVE SYSTEMS

In conjunction with some modulation systems, certain aspects of correlative techniques are interesting in that they involve a direct combination of digital coding and modulation, completely bypassing the baseband stage. Such an arrangement permits a significant simplification of the overall digital transmission system. Further, such combinations reveal unusual and useful properties of correlative methods when integrated with modulation. One such combination is the duobinary AM-PSK modulation which, after processing, results in an AM binary on-off system. Discussion of AM-PSK is important because AM-PSK constitutes an integral part of QPRS (quadrature partial response systems) discussed later.

The second system mentioned in this section is a correlative PSK orthogonal system with an absolute reference. Encoding and modulation are integrated in such a manner that, after processing, the two channels carrying information as well as the reference appear in the form of a serial stream of pulses, followed by a bandpass conversion filter. As a result, the system is rather simple, both from the conceptual and implementation points of view.

### *7.6.1 The Correlative AM-PSK Process*

A rather interesting signal characteristic results from the unique combination of the duobinary technique with AM-PSK modulation. In AM-PSK modulation as described here, the carrier is amplitude modulated as well as phase modulated in a binary manner. Such phase modulation is usually referred to as *phase shift keying* (PSK) to stress the discrete phase reversals of the carrier. Suppose the center level of the duobinary signal corresponding to a binary 1 is represented by the absence of a carrier, the upper level by a constant-amplitude carrier, and the bottom level by the same carrier reversed by 180°. The last two conditions correspond to the binary 0. This process is completely analogous to the baseband duobinary process, except for carrier modulation. There is a 180° reversal of the carrier if the number of intervening binary 1's (in this case represented by the absence of a carrier) is odd; otherwise, there is no reversal. The very fact that the waveform has carrier phase reversals that follow predetermined duobinary rules compresses the bandwidth, as we shall show, by a factor of two compared to a simple on-off AM, where no carrier reversals take place. This is so since the channel bandpass conversion filter is merely a bandpass version of the duobinary low-pass filter $(1 + \Delta)$. The conversion process, therefore, can be viewed as an algebraic addition of the encoded binary PSK waveform to its replica, delayed by one digit interval. Consequently, the addition of two successive digits, having an in-phase carrier, results in a carrier twice the amplitude either in 0° or 180° phase. When the carrier phases in two successive digits are 180° apart, cancellation results, and the amplitude is zero. This process is equivalent to the baseband duobinary conversion with a $(1 + \Delta)$ low-pass filter. Assuming a channel bandwidth between the 25 dB points, the capacity of the correlative AM-PSK system is 1 b/s/Hz of bandwidth, while the capacity of a conventional on-off binary AM system with $\alpha = 1$ roll-off is only 1/2 b/s/Hz.

Since, in the AM-PSK system, the presence of the carrier in either phase represents a binary 0 condition, there is no need, at the receiver, to distinguish between the phases to identify a binary 0. Consequently, the demodulator at the receiving end is arranged to disregard phase reversals and to detect only the envelope of the carrier. The AM-PSK duobinary system has two carrier amplitude states, yet it requires only one-half the bandwidth of a conventional on-off AM system which has an $\alpha = 1$ roll-off. Conversely, for a fixed bandwidth, the AM-PSK duobinary system has twice the bit capacity of a conventional $(\alpha = 1)$ binary AM system. In fact, there is a 3 dB noise advantage on a normalized basis over straight binary AM since the AM-PSK duobinary system still has two amplitude levels but requires only half the bandwidth.

The entire AM-PSK process, and the corresponding block diagram, are shown in Fig. 7.20. The encoder converts the original binary sequence at *A* into a binary sequence with a correlation span of two digits at *B*. Carrier modulation with 180° phase reversals is accomplished in a strictly binary manner and follows the reversals of waveform *B*. Although any number of integral carrier cycles per bit is possible, for this particular case there is only one cycle per bit. The conversion process of waveform *D* is accomplished by a filter that is a bandpass version of the duobinary ($1 + \Delta$) low-pass filter and centered at the carrier frequency. In a

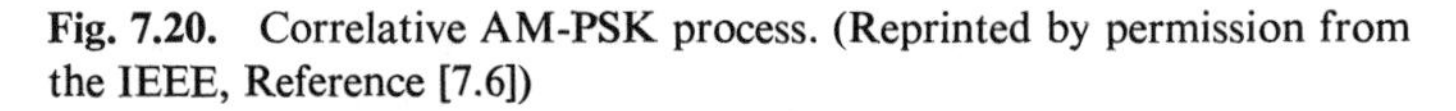

**Fig. 7.20.** Correlative AM-PSK process. (Reprinted by permission from the IEEE, Reference [7.6])

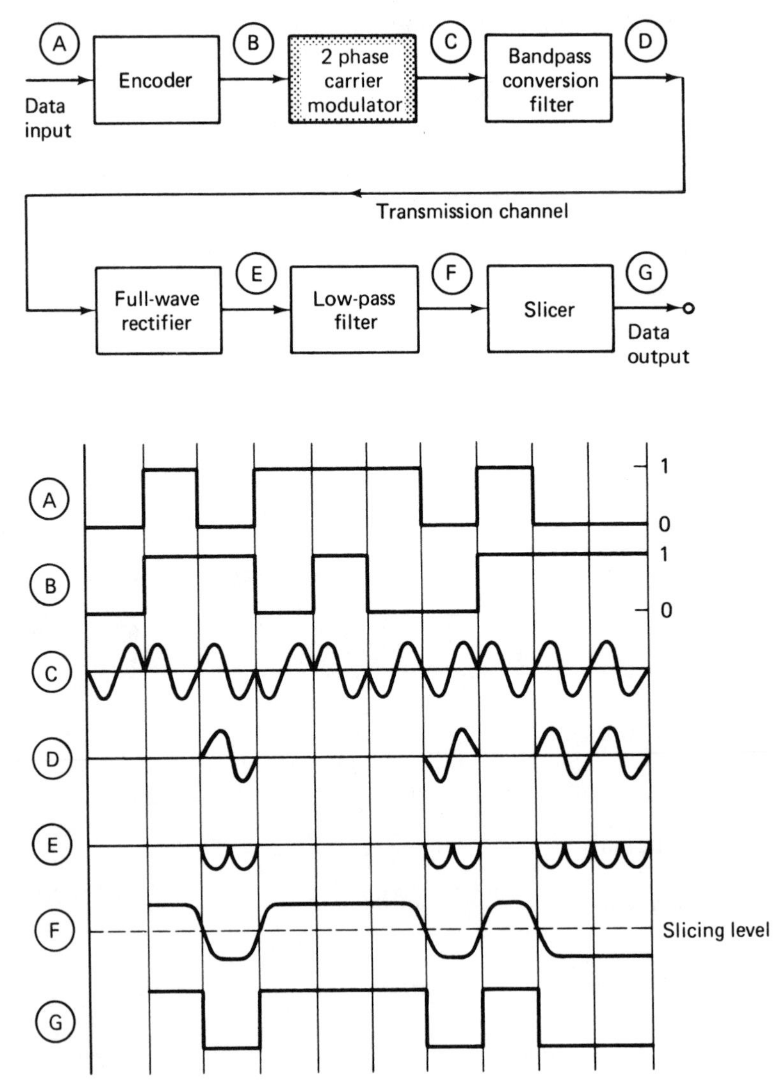

practical system, the symmetrical bandpass filter has 3 dB points at $\pm 1/4T$ Hz and 25 dB or more loss at and beyond $\pm 1/2T$ Hz from the carrier; the speed is $1/T$ b/s. The net effect of the conversion filter is to add the waveforms at $C$ in each two successive time slots, resulting in an on-off signal with phase reversals at $D$. The processing of such a signal at the receiver follows the conventional routine of envelope detection, as indicated in Fig. 7.20, and is self-explanatory; obviously, the phase reversals are completely ignored. It should be emphasized again that inasmuch as the conversion process in the system described is accomplished after the carrier modulation, there is a two-to-one bandwidth compression relative to the conventional binary on-off AM system having a roll-off factor $\alpha = 1$.

### *7.6.2 The Correlative Orthogonal PSK System*

In this system, digital encoding forms an integral part of the carrier modulation. Modulation is PSK and is combined with the modified duobinary signal of the type $(1 - \Delta^2)$. The system employs time orthogonality for two signals which are in quadrature. These signals occupy the same bandwidth at an overall speed of $2/T$ b/s. Since the signal is a modified duobinary, the baseband required is $1/T$ Hz between, for example, 25 dB points. In double-sideband PSK modulation (with $\alpha = 1$), twice as much bandwidth would be required, namely, $2/T$ Hz per channel. For two orthogonal channels, therefore, the bandwidth is the same as for the baseband, ($1/T$ Hz), and the system has the capability of transmitting 2 b/s/Hz. While the overall speed is $2/T$ b/s, the speed per channel is $1/T$ symbols per second, and each symbol carries two information bits. The carrier frequency $f_c$ must be related to the digit speed in that there must be an integral number of cycles per symbol; that is,

$$f_c = \frac{k}{T}, \qquad (k = 1, 2, \ldots) \tag{7.21}$$

Such a restriction is not serious since in many systems (e.g., microwave radio or cable) heterodyning to the desired frequency band does not present any difficulties and is often a routine matter.

To convey the concept the generalized process, in terms of a block diagram, is shown in Fig. 7.21. The data input in serial form at $2/T$ b/s is applied at $A$. Partial encoding $(1 + \Delta)$ mod 2 as well as serial-to-parallel conversion is accomplished between $A$ and $B$. Orthogonality between the two channels, each at $1/T$ b/s, is introduced by means of clock pulses $\phi_1$ and $\phi_2$, which drive the two encoders between $B$ and $C$. To assure orthogonality, the clock pulses $\phi_1$ and $\phi_2$, which determine the time instants of digits between $B$ and $C$ in Fig. 7.21, must be separated by an odd multiple of one-quarter of a carrier cycle. If the digit time interval is $T$ seconds and $\phi_1$ is always placed at the beginning of this interval at $t = 0$, then the time instants of $\phi_2$ relative to $\phi_1$, and denoted by $t_{\phi_2}$, are

$$t_{\phi_2} = \frac{nT}{4k}, \qquad \begin{pmatrix} n = \text{odd} \\ k = \text{any integer} \end{pmatrix} \tag{7.22}$$

Equation (7.22) is consistent with (7.21). The two encoders between $B$ and $C$ in

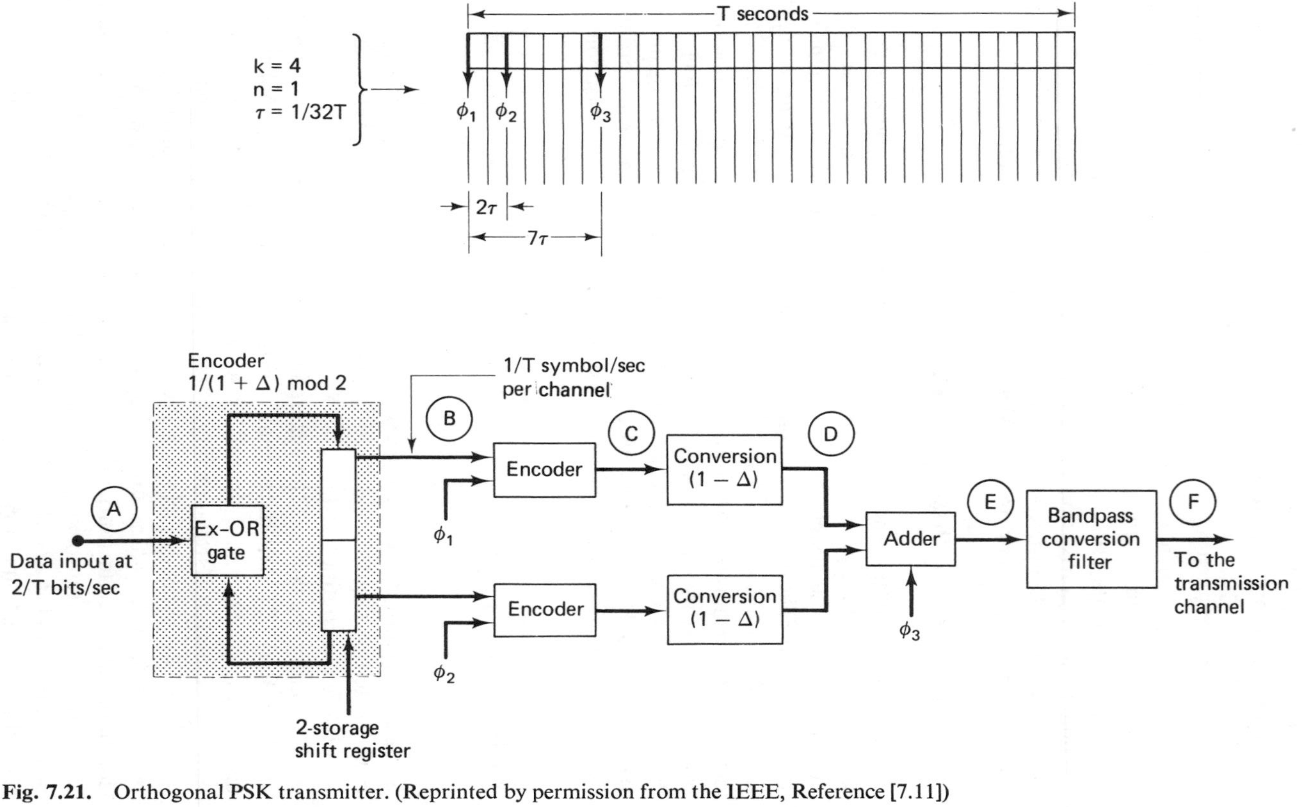


**Fig. 7.21.** Orthogonal PSK transmitter. (Reprinted by permission from the IEEE, Reference [7.11])

Fig. 7.21 are $(1 + \Delta)$ mod 2, so that the overall encoding between $A$ and $C$ is $(1 - \Delta^2)$ mod 2, which is consistent with the modified duobinary signal. Furthermore, orthogonality already exists at point $C$ as mentioned above.

The next step involves a modified duobinary conversion filter with the characteristic $(1 - \Delta^2)$. This process is accomplished by splitting filter $(1 - \Delta^2)$ into two filters, namely $(1 - \Delta)$ and $(1 + \Delta)$. The conversion filter $(1 - \Delta)$ is merely approximated by the simple RC differentiator between points $C$ and $D$ of Fig. 7.21. This splitting of filters into baseband and band-pass is justified since the system is linear between $C$ and $F$. RC differentiation converts the binary NRZ (non-return-to-zero) waveforms at $C$ into positive and negative narrow pulses corresponding to the instants of positive and negative transitions of the binary signal.

The outputs of the conversion filters at $D$ are added algebraically in the resistive adder. At the same time a periodic clock pulse $\phi_3$, at the bit rate $1/T$ pulses per second, it also added between $D$ and $E$. This clock pulse represents the absolute carrier-reference pilot signal, which eventually will be extracted at the receiver to aid the coherent demodulation of the two orthogonal channels. The time position of the periodic clock $\phi_3$, with respect $\phi_1$, is any odd multiple of one-eighth of the carrier period. If $\phi_1$ is positioned at $t = 0$, then the time position of $\phi_3$ relative to $\phi_1$, and denoted by $t_{\phi_3}$, is

$$t_{\phi_3} = \frac{nT}{8k}, \qquad \begin{pmatrix} n = \text{odd} \\ k = \text{any integer} \end{pmatrix} \tag{7.23}$$

Figure 7.21 depicts the relative time positions of $\phi_1$, $\phi_2$, and $\phi_3$, in a digit interval of $T$ seconds and with parameters $k = 4$ and $n = 1$, in equations (7.21), (7.22), and (7.23).

As a result of the waveform processing between points $A$ and $E$, three time-multiplexed signals appear at point $E$. The waveforms corresponding to Fig. 7.21 are shown in Fig. 7.22. For clarity, Fig. 7.22 has been simplified in that the time positions of $\phi_2$ and $\phi_3$ relative to $\phi_1$, at $E$, merely convey the concept and are not exact.

The input data pattern at $A$ in Fig. 7.22 is split into odd and even bits; the bit position numbers appear above the waveform $A$. Assuming that the initial states of the encoders between points $A$ and $C$ in Fig. 7.21 are all zero, the outputs at $C$ after encoding are shown in Fig. 7.22. The subscripts $\phi_1$ and $\phi_2$ refer to the "odd" and "even" bits, respectively. The waveforms resulting from RC differentiation at $D_{\phi_1}$ and $D_{\phi_2}$ are essentially 3-level. There are three possibilities: a positive spike, a negative spike, or zero. Finally, at $E$ the waveforms $D_{\phi_1}$ and $D_{\phi_2}$ are combined. In addition, a periodic clock $\phi_3$ is also added within each digit interval of $T$ seconds. Pulses $\phi_3$ at $E$ are shown as negative pulses, shorter than the information-carrying pulses. The processing from waveform $A$ to waveform $E$ is accomplished almost entirely in a digital manner.

Waveform $E$, shown in Fig. 7.22, constitutes the input to the bandpass filter between $E$ and $F$ in Fig. 7.21. This conversion filter is merely a band-pass version of the duobinary filter $(1 + \Delta)$ and is centered at frequency $f_c$. The overall conversion process becomes clearer with the aid of Fig. 7.23. Conversion $(1 - \Delta)$

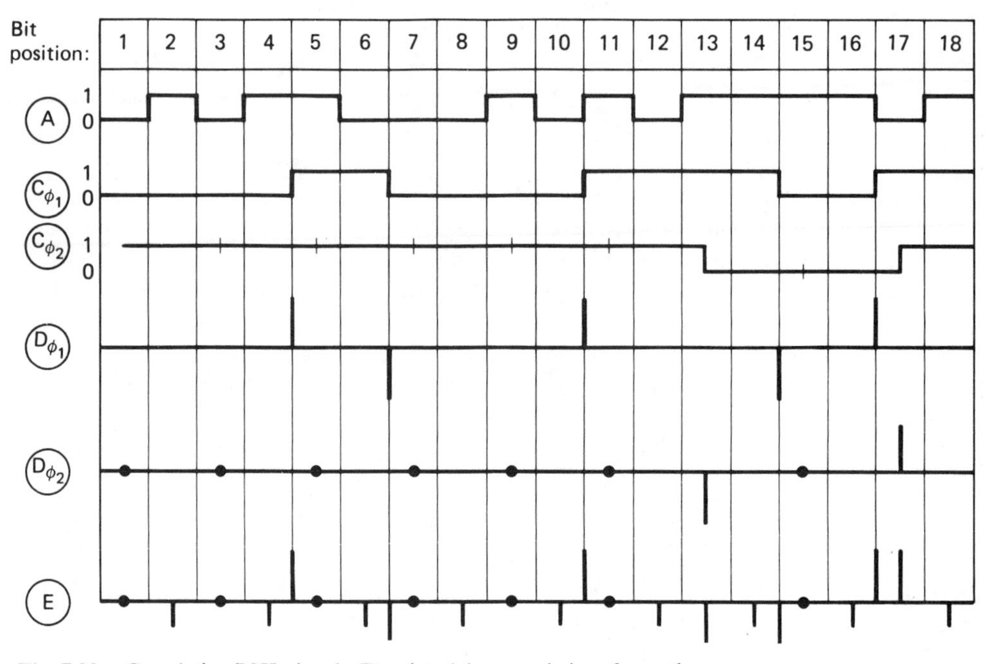


**Fig. 7.22.** Correlative PSK signal. (Reprinted by permission from the IEEE, Reference [7.11])

between points $C$ and $D$, in Fig. 7.21, has frequency bands $|1 - \Delta|$ as shown in Fig. 7.23, with nulls at all frequencies that are integral multiples of the bit speed $1/T$. The next conversion step between points $E$ and $F$ in Fig. 7.21 results in frequency bands $|1 + \Delta|$, also shown in Fig. 7.23, with nulls at frequencies equal to *odd* multiples of one-half the bit speed. The band-pass filter between $E$ and $F$ in Fig. 7.21 has an attenuation characteristic approximating any $|1 + \Delta|$ frequency band, in Fig. 7.23, between frequencies $n/2T \leq f \leq (n + 2)/2T$, with $n$ an odd number, and zero elsewhere.

**Fig. 7.23.** Frequency bands for $|1 - \Delta|$ and $|1 + \Delta|$.

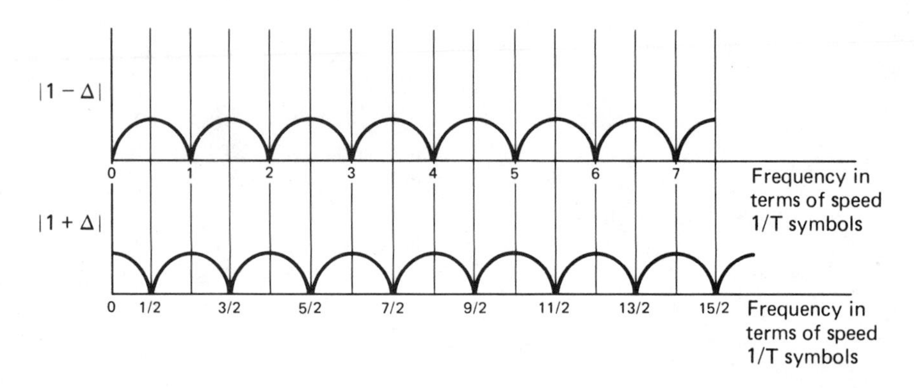

This characteristic is consistent with the desired overall transfer function $(1 - \Delta^2)$ between $C$ and $E$ in Fig. 7.21, for a speed of $1/T$ b/s. This function has nulls in the frequency domain at multiples of $1/2T$ Hz. The first lobe of the function $(1 - \Delta^2)$ between dc and $1/2T$ Hz is merely the baseband signal, and each pair of successive lobes represents the same baseband signal in a double-sideband form. Consequently, the carrier frequency must be as in (7.21). The carrier, however, is suppressed since $(1 - \Delta^2)$ has nulls at $f_c = k/T$. These nulls permit insertion of the carrier pilot in the form of one of the harmonics of the clock pulses $\phi_3$. Since the clock pulses $\phi_3$ have a repetition rate of $1/T$ pulses per second, their harmonics appear at frequencies $k/T$ Hz, which are the suppressed carrier frequencies $f_c$. As a result, the carrier pilot appears at the center of the band-pass conversion filter in Fig. 7.21. The center poistion of the reference pilot is the most advantageous position from the point of view of phase equalization. Also note that the nulls at the center of each double-sideband band are already introduced at point $D$ in Fig. 7.21 by the $(1 - \Delta)$ processing.

Each orthogonal signal is a modified duobinary waveform with three possible states. Conceptually, this waveform modulates the phase of the carrier. The actual phase-modulated signal appears explicitly only at $F$ in Fig. 7.21 and has nine possible states. If the pilot were disregarded, then one possible state is zero, and the remaining states are represented by the carrier in one of the eight possible phases, equally spaced. With a steady pilot tone present, positioned originally at the pulse $\phi_3$ in the time diagram of Fig. 7.21, the nine possible signal states are shown in Fig. 7.24 in a vector diagram form. This signal represents the output at point $F$ in Fig. 7.21, while the input is depicted by the waveform $E$ in Fig. 7.22.

**Fig. 7.24.** Geometrical representation of signal states (at point $F$ of Fig. 7.21).

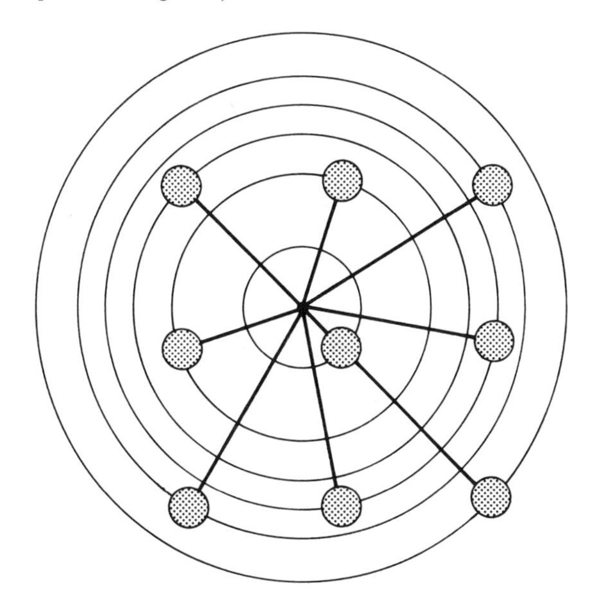

The geometrical representation of the signal states in Fig. 7.24 indicates that the correlative orthogonal PSK signal has both phase and amplitude modulation. The detection process involves coherent demodulation, using absolute carrier reference extracted from the center of the band. Since this process is conventional, no further discussion is necessary.

## 7.7 PRACTICAL APPLICATIONS IN DIGITAL MICROWAVE RADIO TRANSMISSION

Present-day digital radio systems frequently employ either 8-phase PSK modulation or a duobinary technique sometimes termed *quadrature partial response signal* (QPRS). It merely represents two 3-level duobinary signals of the $(1 + \Delta)$ type, phase modulated in quadrature. Here again $\Delta = e^{-j\omega T}$, where $1/T$ is speed in b/s. At present, at least four types of digital radios, at 2 GHz and 8 GHz, employ duobinary 3-level techniques [7.13, 7.14, 7.15]. There is one digital radio, at 2 GHz, that uses a 7-level modified duobinary method [7.16].

Why are correlative techniques employed in digital radios? Perhaps the most important reason is the simplicity of implementation which is comparable to 4-phase radios, yet less complex than the implementation of 8-phase digital radio [7.14]. At the same time, correlative-QPRS, for example, easily accommodates 2 bits per hertz in carrier modulation, or even 2.25 bits/Hz [7.15]. From a performance point of view, the 3-level QPRS requires 3 dB more signal power than the 4-phase. On the other hand, the 8-phase signal is 5.3 dB poorer than the 4-phase (see the performance curves in Chapter 3).

Another reason for using correlative, modified duobinary [7.16], for example, is that a service channel and other supervisory signals can be made completely independent of the main traffic bit stream. That is, should the data stream be lost, the service (order) channel will still exist; this will be described later. In the following sections we discuss practical examples of 3-level duobinary and 7-level modified duobinary applications.

### *7.7.1 QPRS Phase-Modulation Example*

The QPRS signal can be regarded as two AM-PSK 3-level duobinary signals (previously discussed) in quadrature, as shown in Fig. 7.25. Each such signal has three states—extreme at the tip of the vectors representing binary 0 and the center state (absence of carrier) representing binary 1. When the in-phase and quadrature waveform are combined as in QPRS, the resultant is nine possible states, as indicated in Fig. 7.25. This signal-space diagram forms the basis of the digital radio equipment, at 2 GHz, for transmission of 96 PCM channels at a 6.3 Mb/s rate described in reference [7.13]. The efficiency achieved is 2 b/s/Hz.

There are inherent symmetries in the QPRS signal that are sufficiently significant in carrier acquisition for *coherent* demodulation [7.13]. Such symmetries are

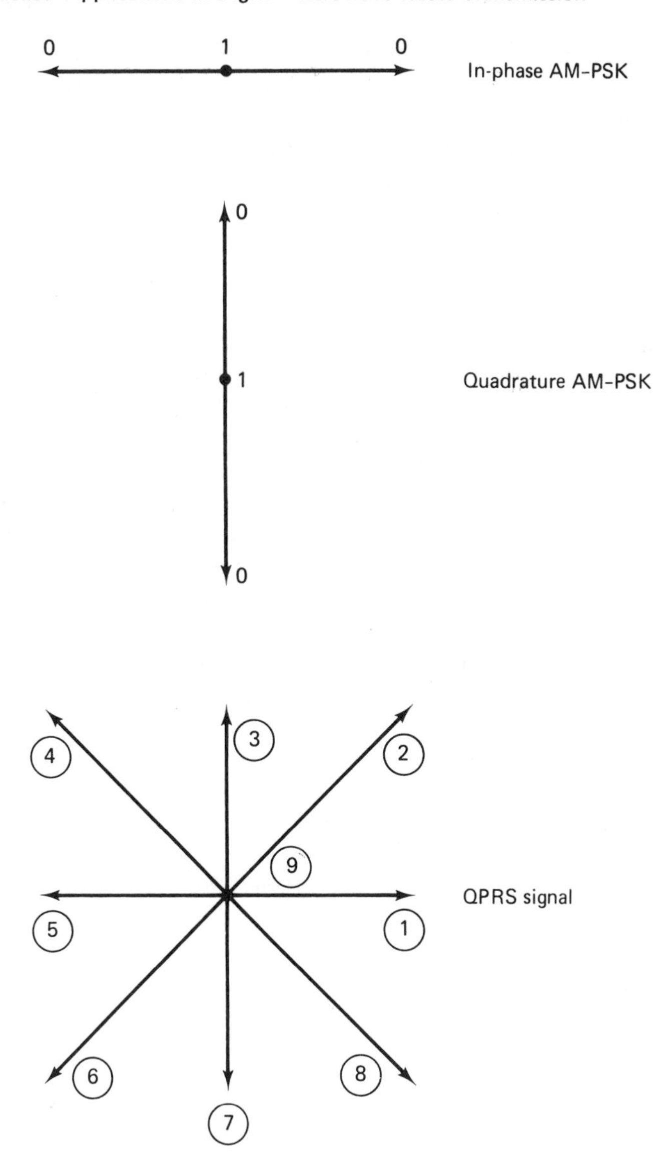


**Fig. 7.25.** QPRS modulation.

apparent in Fig. 7.25. Remembering that the tips of the vectors represent "0" and the center "1," states 2, 4, 6, and 8 always represent the same pattern, namely (0, 0), both on the $I$ and $Q$ channels. $I$ and $Q$ stand, respectively, for in-phase and quadrature channels. Further, states 1 and 5 represent (0, 1) and 3 and 7 represent (1, 0). Thus, for the *odd-numbered* states (except for state 9), carrier ambiguity of 180° is immaterial. All *even-numbered* states are invariably (0, 0). Finally, the absence of carrier state 9 represents (1, 1). The probability distribution of the nine signal states is the subject of Problem 7.5. The coherent carrier is always locked to one of the odd-numbered states, (except for state 9) and may be acquired by using the modified Costas loop [7.17].

The general block diagram and the implementation of QPRS systems is very similar to the implementation of 4-phase QPSK modems described in previous chapters. The one, and essential, difference is filtering. Clearly, filtering must be duobinary of $(1 + \Delta)$ type, either low-pass in baseband *before* modulation or band-pass *after* modulation. In the case of the 2 GHz, 96 PCM, channel radio [7.13], the filtering is low-pass, followed directly by RF modulation and power amplification. The output power is 0.5 W, and the receiver threshold for a $10^{-6}$ error rate is $-82.7$ dBm. An alternative and interesting implementation can be found in references [7.14] and [7.15]. This digital radio operates at 91 Mb/s, accommodating 1344 PCM channels at 8 GHz. Again, its signal is duobinary phase modulation with $I$ and $Q$ channels. It has two unusual characteristics. The first one is related to more effective bandwidth compression to achieve 2.25 b/s/Hz. The interesting solution is the introduction of decision feedback [7.17] to eliminate ISI primarily due to lagging echoes resulting from such an efficient bandwidth compression over and above 2 b/s/Hz. The second interesting and distinctive feature is duobinary band-pass filtering *after* power amplification. Such a strategy circumvents potential problems due to non-linearities. In effect, the signal can be regarded as 4-phase PSK until, *after* saturated power amplification, the combined characteristics of the transmit and receive filters convert the waveform into QPRS. The output of the power amplifier is 10 W [7.14, 7.15, 7.19].

### *7.7.2 FM Example*

The digital radio described here [7.16, 7.20] accommodates 96 PCM channels in the 3.5 MHz authorized bandwidth at 2 GHz, thus achieving 2 b/s/Hz. It consists of a standard FM radio terminal that operates at 2 GHz, as well as a digital modem. The digital modem has a 7-level modified duobinary signal processor providing 4 b/s/Hz in baseband and 2 b/s/Hz at RF frequencies. The system block diagram is depicted in Fig. 7.26. Binary data input at 6.312 Mb/s, representing 96 PCM channel passes through a self-synchronizing scrambler [7.21]. The duobinary 7-level encoder provides four parallel binary outputs at the symbol rate of 3.156 Megasymbols per second. Each symbol represents 2 bits. The next block directly converts the binary signal into the 7-level modified duobinary signal, in a strictly digital manner. To limit the bandwidth a raised-cosine filter is employed with $\alpha = 0.25$. This low-pass filter is split equally between transmitter and receiver, as shown in Fig. 7.26. The baseband signal is fed into the FM radio transmitter. Here, an unusual and interesting aspect is that a band of 10 kHz is "carved out" from the baseband of the modified 7-level duobinary waveform. This has no effect on the signal for two reasons: First, there is no energy at dc and a negligible amount at low frequencies. Secondly, 10 kHz bandwidth at the low end has hardly

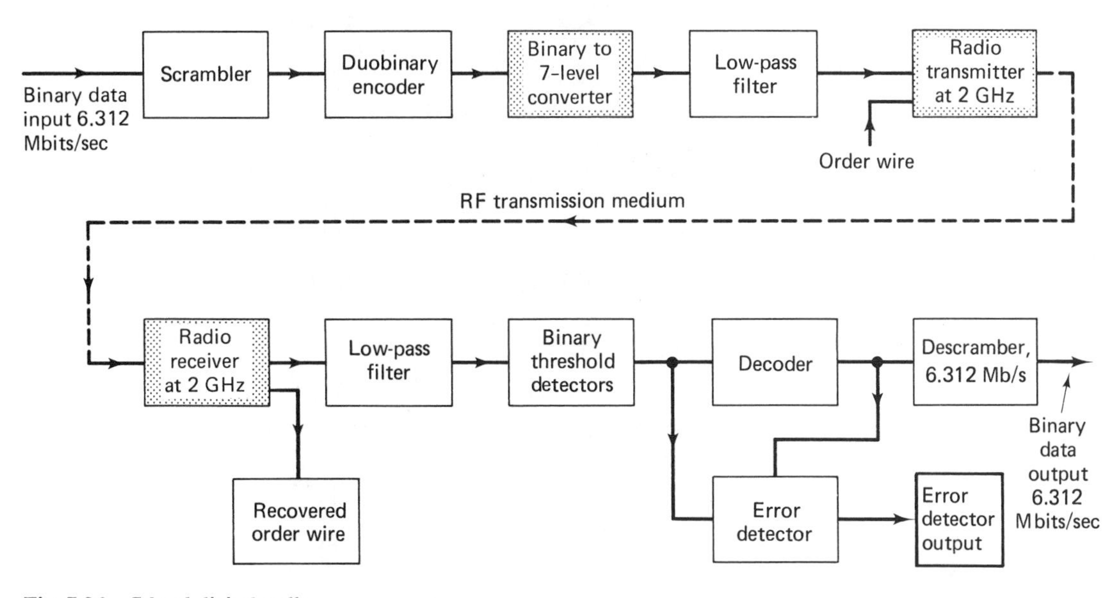


**Fig. 7.26.** 7-level digital radio.

any effect, considering that the signal baseband bandwidth is about 1.6 MHz and the spectral density is proportional to (omitting raised-cosine filtering for simplicity):

$$H(f) = 2T \sin 2\pi f T \quad \text{for } |f| \leq \frac{1}{2T},$$

and zero elsewhere

The 10 kHz accommodates analog order wire, which constitutes a separate input along with the baseband signal to the FM radio transmitter, as shown in Fig. 7.26. There is a significant advantage in having order wire completely independent of the digital data bits rather than as part of it. At the receiving end, the order wire is extracted separately as part of the baseband. The error detector appearing in Fig. 7.26 is based on the correlative properties of the 7-level waveform and triggers an alarm when the average error rate exceeds the predetermined error criterion. The overall system gain for $10^{-6}$ error rate is 110 dB. Linearity in power amplification is no problem since FM modulation is used. To accommodate the FCC mask for 2 GHz, the deviation ratio is 0.7. However, outside the United States, for any possible applications where bandwidth is not strictly specified, the deviation ratio can be increased by converting the extra available bandwidth into signal-to-noise ratio advantage, as is well-known in FM modulation. This digital radio, known as the 79F1D, appears as Fig. 7.27.

An interesting aspect of this radio application is in multi-hop systems. Because of the unique design, the digital modem can be omitted at non-dropping repeater sites, greatly simplifying repeater arrangements. Further, significant savings in

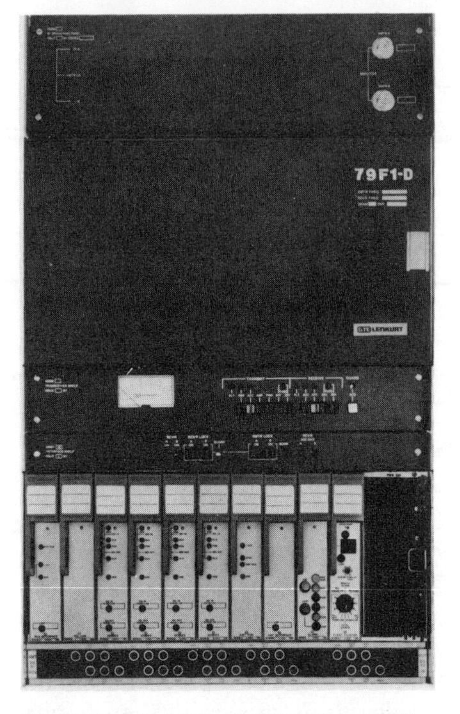


**Fig. 7.27.** 79 FI-D, 2 GHz digital radio system. (Courtesy of GTE Lenkurt, Incorporated)

cost for a multi-hop system are provided. Since order wire is completely independent of the digital modem, it is easily dropped and inserted at repeaters, regardless of the repeater arrangement.

## PROBLEMS

**7.1** For the input sequence $A_t$ of Example 7.1 (duobinary), show sequences $B_t$ and $C_t$ for the modified duobinary signal, using equations (7.8).

**7.2** Suppose the initial digit in sequence $B_t$ is 2 rather than 0 (Section 7.4). Write sequences $B_t$ and $C_t$ for this case. Verify that $C_t$ assumes seven possible levels and that $C_t \bmod 4 = A_t$.

**7.3** The input binary data stream is such that $p(1) = p(0) = \frac{1}{2}$. For a duobinary correlative system with $Q = 4$, what is the probability distribution of the seven levels? What is it for the 7-level modified duobinary?

**7.4** Show that, in the 7-level duobinary or modified duobinary correlative system for $Q = 4$, the extreme levels are formed in a unique way and that the intermediate levels may be formed in more than one way.

**7.5** Derive the probability distribution of the nine signal states shown in Fig. 7.25.

## REFERENCES


[7.1] Lender, A., "The Duobinary Technique for High Speed Data Transmission," IEEE Trans. Communication and Electronics, Vol. 82, pp. 214–218, May, 1963.

[7.2] Lender, A., "Correlative Digital Communication Techniques," IEEE Trans. Communication Technology, pp. 128–135, December, 1964.

[7.3] Kretzmer, E. R., "Binary Data Communication by Partial Response Transmission," Conference Record 1965 IEEE Ann. Communications Conference, pp. 451–455.

[7.4] Nyquist, H., "Certain Factors Affecting Telegraph Speed," B.S.T.J., Vol. 3, pp. 324–326, April, 1924.

[7.5] Bennett, W. R., J. R. Davey, *Data Transmission*, McGraw-Hill Book Company, New York, 1965.

[7.6] Lender, A., "Correlative Level Coding for Binary Data Transmission," IEEE Spectrum, pp. 104–115, February, 1966.

[7.7] Pasupathy, S., "Correlative Coding—A Bandwidth-Efficient Signaling Scheme," IEEE Communications Society Magazine, July, 1977, pp. 4–11.

[7.8] Bennett, W. R., "Statistics of Regenerative Digital Transmission," B.S.T.J., Vol. 37, November, 1958, pp. 1501–1543.

[7.9] Lender, A., "Nonbinary Correlative Techniques for High Speed Data Transmission," NEREM Record, Boston, November, 1968.

[7.10] Gray, F., "Pulse Code Communication," U.S. Patent No. 2,632,058, March 17, 1953.

[7.11] Lender, A., "Correlative Data Transmission with Coherent Recovery Using Absolute Reference," IEEE Tran. Communications Technology, February, 1968.

[7.12] Lender, A., "Correlative Signal Processing," Technical Report No. 7001-5, Stanford University, May, 1972.

[7.13] Kurematsu, H., et al., "The QAM2G-10R Digital Radio Equipment Using a Partial Response System," Fujitsu Scientific and Technical Journal, June, 1977, pp. 27–48.

[7.14] Anderson, C. W., S. G. Barber, "Modulation Considerations for a 91 Mbit/s Digital Radio," IEEE Trans. Communications, May, 1978, pp. 523–528.

[7.15] Godier, I., "DRS-8 A Digital Radio for Long-Haul Transmission," Proc. IEEE International Conference on Communications, Chicago, June, 1977, paper 5.4.

[7.16] Lender, A., "Seven-Level Correlative Digital Transmission Over Radio," ICC 1976 Chicago Conference Record, June, 1976.

[7.17] Costas, J. P., "Synchronous Communications," Proc. IRE, December, 1956, pp. 1713–1718.

[7.18] Austin, M. E., "Decision Feedback Equalization for Digital Communication Over Dispersive Channels," Technical Report 461, Research Laboratory of Electronics, MIT, August 11, 1967.

[7.19] Godfrey, B., et al., "Practical Considerations in the Design of the DRS-8 System," ICC 1977 Chicago Conference Record, June, 1977, paper 515.

[7.20] Seaver, T., "An Efficient 96 PCM Channel Modem for 2 GHz FM Radio," NTC 1978 Birmingham Conference Record, December, 1978, paper 38.4.

[7.21] Elspas, B., "The Theory of Autonomous Linear Sequential Networks," IRE Trans. Circuit Theory, March, 1959, pp. 45–60.

# 8

# DIGITAL AND HYBRID SYSTEM POTPOURRI

In the previous chapters digital modulation techniques which have been used in digital microwave systems are described. Typical performance characteristics of planned and operational $M$-ary PSK, QAM, and quadrature partial response (QPRS) digital microwave systems are examined. In this chapter, some digital and hybrid microwave systems which do not use these modulation techniques are presented. Among the techniques used are amplitude phase keying (APK), pulse-amplitude modulation-FM (PAM-FM), mininum shift keying (MSK), and PAM vestigial sideband (PAM-VSB). In addition to these dedicated digital radio systems, a number of analog FDM-FM microwave systems have been "converted" and carry a mixture of analog FDM and digital TDM traffic. These hybrid FM systems, such as the data under voice (DUV), data in voice (DIV), data above voice (DAV), and data above video (DAVID) systems are also described in this chapter.

In Section 8.4 we describe a novel subscriber radio system configuration that uses digital modulation techniques. This system is conceptually similar to single-channel-per-carrier (SCPC) satellite systems and is expected to find applications predominantly in sparsely populated rural areas.

Now, having read this introduction, we hope that it has become clear to you why the word *potpourri* was chosen for the title of this chapter. A number of microwave systems utilizing a variety of modulation techniques, a wide range of bit rates (64 kb/s to 400 Mb/s), and different system configurations are presented. Due to space limitations, only a short description of these systems is given here. For an in-depth study of these digital and hybrid systems, the references at the end of this chapter provide ample reading material.

## 8.1 PRINCIPLES AND DESCRIPTION OF THE 400 Mb/s NTT AMPLITUDE PHASE KEYED (APK) DIGITAL SYSTEM

In Chapter 3 it is shown that for, a bandwidth efficiency of 4 b/s/Hz, a 16-ary system is required, and that the 16-ary PSK system requires a 3.5 dB higher $C/N$ ratio than the 16-ary amplitude phase keyed (APK) (quadrature AM) system. It is also shown in [8.1] that the $C/N$ degradation caused by intersymbol interference, resulting from imperfect Nyquist filtering, is less severe in an $M = 16$-ary APK system than in 16-ary PSK systems. The $C/N$ degradation, from the theoretical curves, is shown in Fig. 8.1. In this figure it has been assumed that the ISI of the gaussian band-limiting filters is the only cause of degradation. It should be noted that the illustrated degradation applies for the worst-case eye pattern (peak eye-diagram closure) and thus can be interpreted as a somewhat pessimistic upper bound for the $P(e)$ degradation.

The better performance of 16-ary APK relative to PSK led the Yokosuka Laboratories of the Nippon Telephone and Telegraph Company (NTT) to employ this technique in the development of a 400 Mb/s (approximately 6000 PCM telephone channel) digital modem [8.1]. This modem, having a 1.7 GHz IF frequency, is expected to find application in high-speed digital transmission systems such as line-of-sight microwave, guided millimeter waves, satellite, and optical fiber links.

The block diagram of the 16-ary APK modulator and its corresponding signal state-space diagrams are shown in Figs. 8.2 and 8.3. The modulator uses the superposed modulation principle in which two conventional QPSK modulated signals are linearly added. The digital input data streams 1, 2, 3, and 4, as well as the carrier frequencies of the two modulators, can be different. In this case, a non-synchronous multi-level signal-state space diagram is obtained, such as shown in Fig. 8.3(d).

The advantage of a *non-synchronous modulator* is that it does not require data multiplexing equipment. The $I$ and $Q$ quadrature modulators (multipliers) are fed by asynchronous data streams. The phase quadrature of the modulated $I$ and $Q$ carriers assures that the linearly added transmit signals can be unambiguously demodulated at the receiving end of the system. The performance degradation intro-

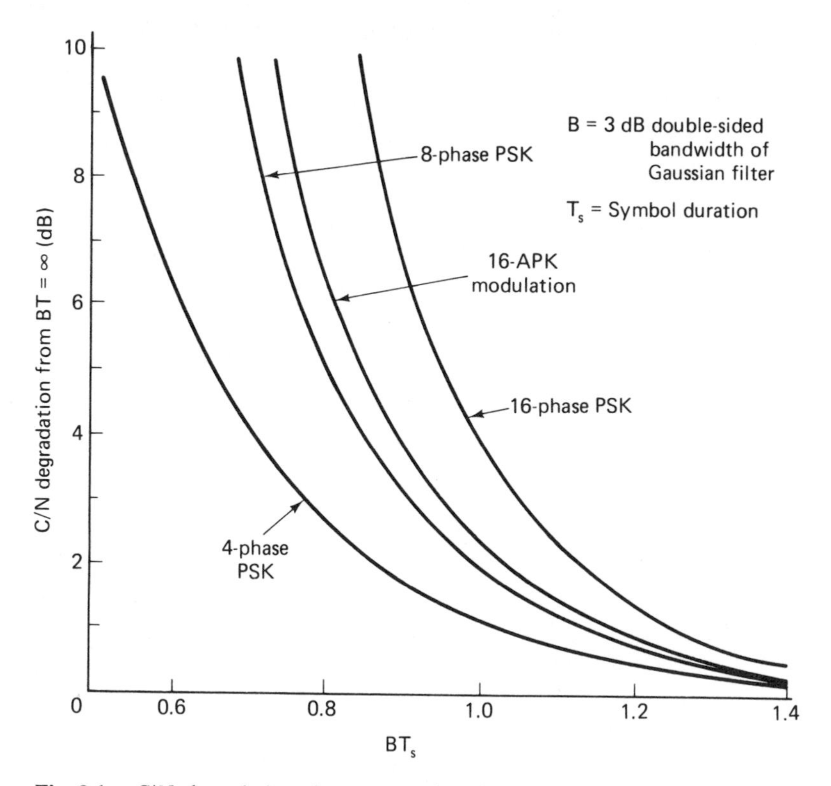


**Fig. 8.1.** $C/N$ degradation due to gaussian filter band-limitation. (Redrawn by permission from Reference [8.1])

**Fig. 8.2.** $M = 16$-ary APK modulator diagram using the superposed modulation principle. (Redrawn by permission from Reference [8.1])

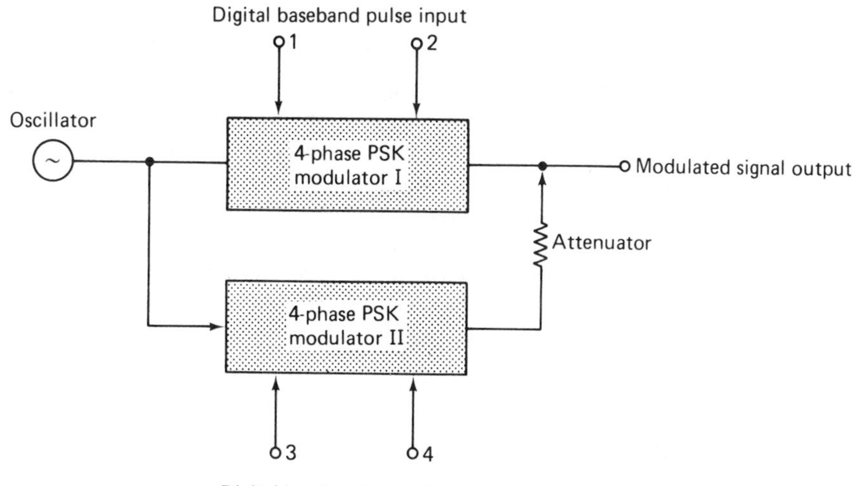

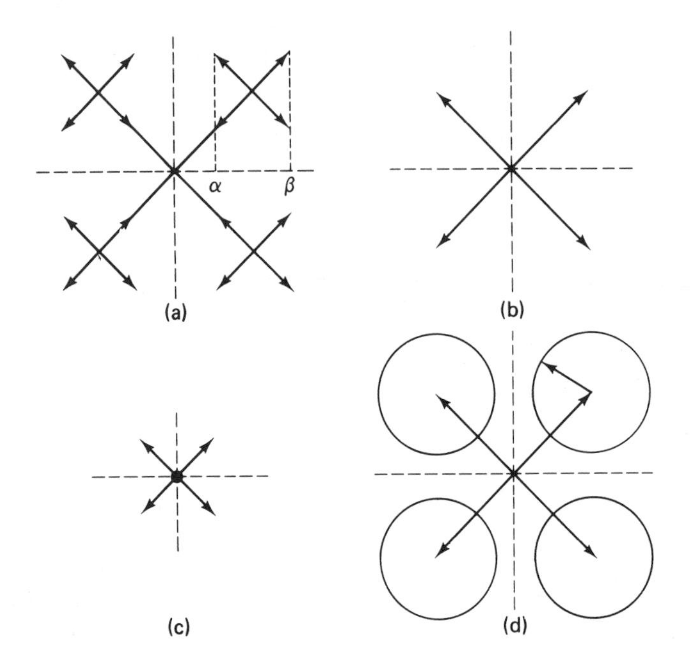


**Fig. 8.3.** Signal space diagram of the $M = 16$-ary APK modulator of Fig. 8.2: (a) 16-state multi-level modulation signal, (b) first path signal, (c) second path signal, (d) non-synchronous multi-level modulation signal. (Redrawn by permission from Reference [8.1])

duced by AM/PM conversion in non-linear amplifiers can be avoided by applying this modulation principle after the non-linear amplifier stage, that is, by combining the two 4-phase PSK signals after amplification. The theory of operation of the demodulator is considerably more complex. The interested reader is advised to consult references [8.1 and 8.13].

The theoretical $P(e) = f(C/N)$ curves have been given in Chapter 3 [8.2 and 8.4] The NTT 16-APK modem requires a $C/N = 25$ dB for a $P(e) = 10^{-10}$. The noise bandwidth of this 400 Mb/s system is 120 MHz, or 20% wider than the minimum theoretical double-sided Nyquist bandwidth. For a 16-ary, 400 Mb/s system this ideal Nyquist bandwidth is 100 MHz (4 b/s/Hz). Thus, the NTT modem performance is more than 2 dB worse than the theoretical $C/N = 23$ dB requirement. This example illustrates that it is feasible to implement 16-ary APK, 400 Mb/s modems which have a bandwidth efficiency of over 3 b/s/Hz (to be exact 400: 120 = 3.33 b/s/Hz) and perform within 2 dB of the theoretical limit. **(Solve Problem 8.1.)**

In the past, APK modulation techniques were not used in digital microwave systems primarily because of their hardware complexity and their significant performance degradation when transmitted through non-linear subsystems.

However, as described, NTT has shown that a relatively simple modem can be constructed and that excellent performance can be obtained. Thus, we can expect to see, in the coming decade, a number of digital microwave systems which employ APK modulation techniques. **(Solve Problem 8.2.)**

## 8.2 EXISTING PAM-FM AND MINIMUM SHIFT KEYING (MSK) SYSTEMS

### PAM-FM

Continuing our examination of digital microwave systems it is in order to mention, at least briefly, existing pulse-amplitude modulated (PAM)-FM systems. Most of these systems were developed during early 1970's and will have continued application for years to come. A block diagram of a non-coherent PAM-FM transmitter is shown in Fig. 8.4. This transmission system, developed by Bell Laboratories, is used for the transmission of three time-division multiplexed, 6.312 Mb/s data streams. In this system, *pulse stuffing* is used to multiplex the *asynchronous data streams.* After pulse stuffing, a 20.2 Mb/s binary stream is obtained. This NRZ data stream is converted by the 2-to-4-level baseband modulator into a 10.1 M Baud 4-level signal, such as shown in Chapter 3. This 4-level signal is filtered and fed to a conventional analog FM modulator. The receiver performs the inverse functions of that of the transmitter. The 20.2 Mb/s, 4-level PAM system has been used in the TD-2 FM microwave system for selected sections of the Bell U.S. transcontinental network. This technique is a digital retrofit of a 25-year-old analog radio system. A more detailed description of this system is found in [8.14]. **(Solve Problem 8.3.)**

Another well-known PAM-FM microwave system used for the transmission of five time-division multiplexed T-1 rate streams (approximately 8 Mb/s) has been manufactured by the Canadian Marconi Company. The most important performance characteristics of this 8-level PAM-FM system are summarized in [8.4] and [8.15]. The primary advantage of this non-coherent PAM-FM system is its hardware simplicity and the ease with which analog FDM-FM systems may be converted into digital PAM-FM systems. However, its major drawback is that, for bandwidth-efficient operation, it requires a relatively high $C/N$ ratio [8.4].

### MSK

Minimum shift keying (MSK) is a coherent FM modulation technique which has a good theoretical $P(e) = f(\mathrm{C/N})$ performance, comparable to that of the QPSK system. An experimental MSK microwave system was reported in 1972 in [8.11]. However, due to its wider main lobe, MSK does not appear to be as bandwidth-efficient as the QPSK technique [8.10, 8.17]. For this reason MSK has not found application in recently developed digital terrestrial microwave systems.

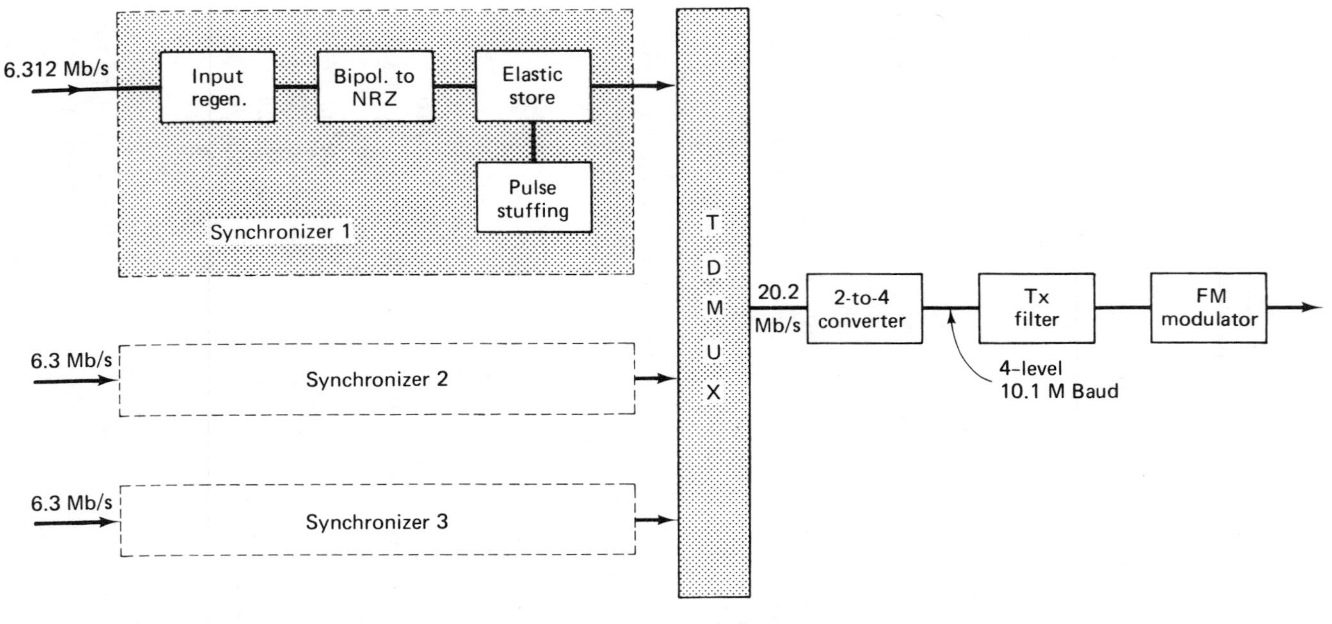


**Fig. 8.4.** Simplified block diagram of the 20.2 Mb/s (3 asynchronously multiplexed 6.3 Mb/s stream) transmitter used for sections of the TD-2 transcontinental radio system.

## 8.3 HYBRID DATA UNDER FDM VOICE (DUV), DATA IN VOICE (DIV), DATA ABOVE VOICE (DAV), AND DATA ABOVE VIDEO (DAVID) SYSTEMS

In this section the principles and applications of several hybrid microwave systems are presented. These systems are used for the *simultaneous* transmission of time-division multiplexed (TDM) data and of frequency multiplexed (FDM) voice signals. These digital and analog signals share the baseband of a microwave system which was originally designed to carry only FDM signals. For a number of applications, if it is required to carry data at a rate between 1.544 and 6.312 Mb/s, it is more economical to modify the existing FDM system into a hybrid system than to install a completely new, dedicated, digital link. For this reason, we foresee that hybrid systems are going to be required as long as analog FDM microwave systems carry the bulk of voice traffic. (While writing this manuscript we have a large crystal ball in front of us, and we are courageous enough to *predict* that hybrid systems will stay with us for at least another decade).

In Fig. 8.5, the baseband spectrum and the transmitter block diagram of the ATT 1.544 Mb/s data under FDM voice (DUV) system is illustrated. In this system, developed by the Bell Telephone Laboratories [8.7, 8.8], the data spectrum is

**Fig. 8.5.** Baseband spectrum and simplified transmitting portion of the 1.544 Mb/s, data under voice (DUV) system.

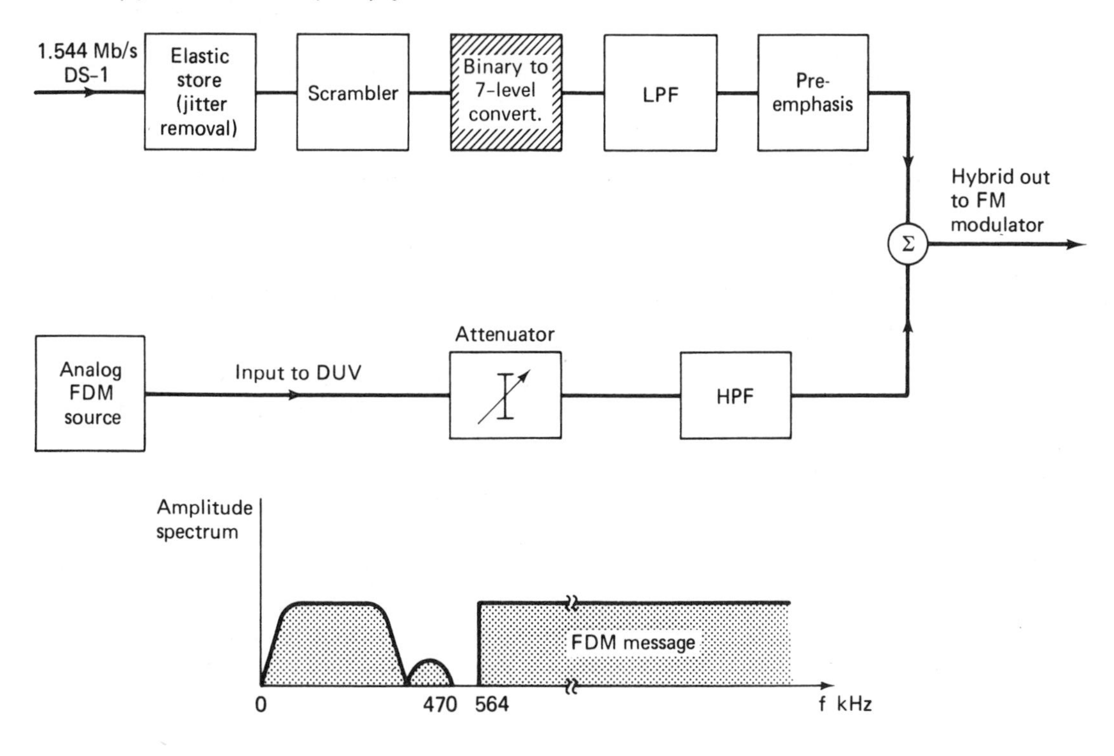

confined to the 0 to 470 kHz bandwidth. The lowest FDM channel is at 564 kHz. The elastic store serves as a timing jitter-removal circuit. The jitter-free data signal is scrambled to suppress the high-power discrete spectral components. An inherent advantage of scrambling is that the scrambled output data spectrum is continuous and has a predictable effect on the FDM radio system, in a manner similar to that of additional FDM load in the 0–470 kHz bandwidth. The serial to 7-level partial response encoder (correlative coder) compresses the data bandwidth. The theory of operation and properties of this binary to multi-level conversion are explained in Chapter 7. The low-pass filter is used to perform the final spectrum shaping of the digital information and to suppress the spectral power above 386 kHz that might impair the pilot control tone transmission or the quality of the FDM channels. The high-pass filter in the FDM path gives assurance that, in the bandwidth allocated for data transmission, there is no analog signal present. A number of circuits such as a DS-1 input power monitor, a DS-1 substitution signal, stage-by-stage monitoring and status indicators, and a 386 kHz pilot monitor are provided for system performance monitoring, control, and maintenance.

The block diagram of the 1.544 Mb/s DUV receiver is shown in Fig. 8.6. The

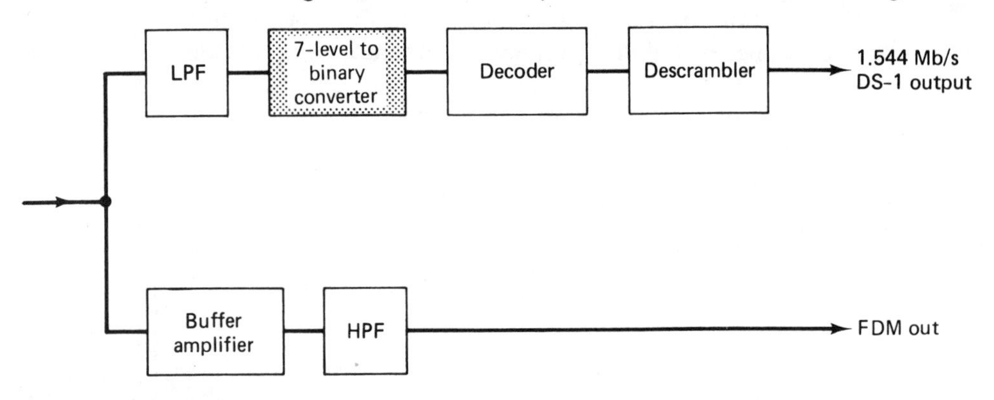


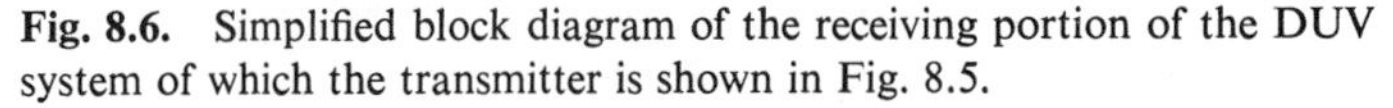

**Fig. 8.6.** Simplified block diagram of the receiving portion of the DUV system of which the transmitter is shown in Fig. 8.5.

digital 7-level information is low-pass filtered and passed on to a 7-level to binary converter circuitry. The binary output of the descrambler is converted into a 3-level bipolar signal, which is used for twisted-wire line transmission in the Bell network [8.8 and 8.4].

DUV systems have been installed in FDM microwave systems and are operating between several large cities in the United States. An improved (high-performance) DUV system, known as *parallel DUV*, has been developed in Canada [8.7]. In the parallel DUV system the digital information is transmitted on two separate RF carriers. The received digital streams are stored in a temporary register. The data stream which has a better performance is read out to the customer. This system is in service from Halifax to Vancouver in the Trans-Canada system. **(Solve Problem 8.4.)**

Alternative approaches to the DUV system were introduced by the author. These systems, known as the *data above FDM voice* (DAV) and the *data above video* (DAVID) systems, provide a cost-effective means of transmitting up to 3.152 Mb/s data above the top baseband of the FDM message or video signal on existing FDM-FM analog systems [8.3, 8.6, 8.16]. **(Solve Problem 8.5.)**

An advantage of the DAV approach is that the low end of the baseband spectrum does not have to be vacated for data transmission, leaving the FDM channels undisturbed. The data spectrum being translated above the top FDM frequency occupies a band which is normally unusable for FDM transmission. The transmitted baseband spectrum and the block diagram of a DAV/DAVID system is shown in Fig. 8.7. A number of 1.544 Mb/s-above-960 FDM-capacity DAV systems and 1.544 Mb/s-above-1260 FDM-plus-vestigial sideband video DAVID systems are operational in Canada. A DAV system carrying 1.544 Mb/s-above-960 FDM channels is operational between Montreal and Toronto in the Canadian National/Canadian Pacific 6 GHz FDM-FM microwave system. The DAV system development was directed by Dr. K. Feher and was designed by the engineers of Spar Aerospace Limited (previously RCA Ltd.).

In the data insert unit, the bipolar data is converted into a binary stream, scrambled, and then frequency-translated (modulated) to the desired frequency in a QPSK modulator. The band-pass filter assures that the QPSK data does not interfere with the analog information. The LPF removes out of band spurious frequencies which have been generated in the FDM equipment or are normally present in a video baseband. The analog and digital signals are added in a linear combiner circuit. The resultant hybrid signal feeds the FM modulator of the radio transmitter. At the receiver, the reverse signal processing is performed. An important system performance monitor and control unit is the DAV pseudo-error detector, which is described in detail in Chapter 11.

A detailed system analysis of DAV/DAVID systems is presented in references [8.3, 8.16, 8.18]. To illustrate the typical performance of hybrid DAV systems, the measured performance of an 8-hop system, having a length of 340 km, is summarized in Table 8.1 [8.3].

For a thorough understanding of the entries in Table 8.1 a basic knowledge of FDM-FM microwave engineering is required. Due to space limitations and the intended scope of this book (being digital), the fundamentals, terminology, and standard abbreviations of FDM-FM microwave engineering are not presented here. Thus, if you are not familiar with these terms, you are advised to consult [8.8] or other suitable references; alternatively, depending on your interest, you could omit reading the following paragraph without loss of continuity.

In Table 8.1 the $C/N$ ratio in a 30-MHz-wide double-sided RF bandwidth has been stated. The received RF wave (column 2) has a power equal to $C$ (dBm) and is a variable, depending on the nominal received carrier level and on the system fade depth. In column 3 the $P(e)$ of the hybrid system is shown. In order to evaluate the degrading effect of the FDM loading on the data, the $P(e)$ of data without FDM loading is shown in column 4. In columns 5 through 8 the measured noise power

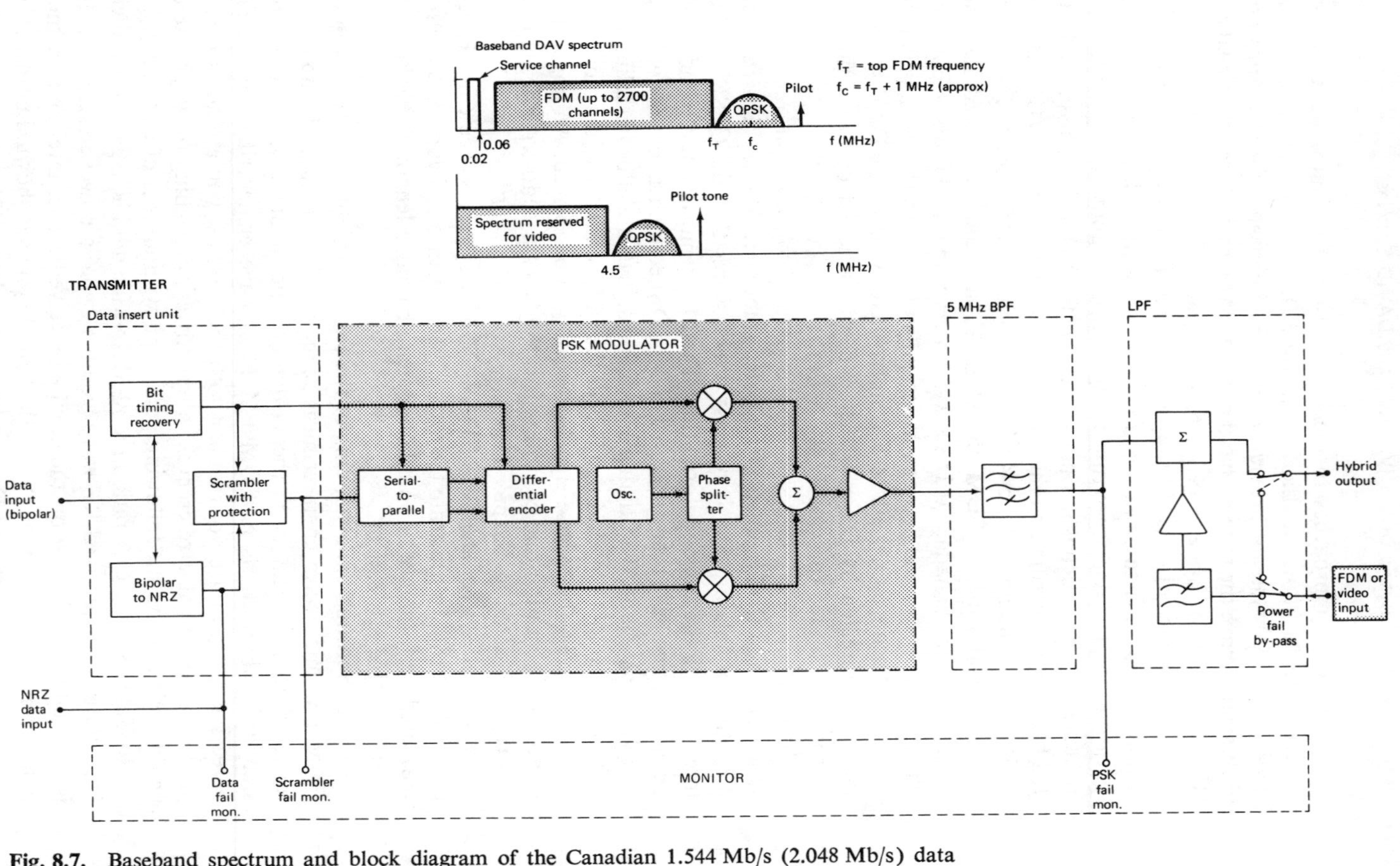


**Fig. 8.7.** Baseband spectrum and block diagram of the Canadian 1.544 Mb/s (2.048 Mb/s) data above FDM voice (DAV) and data above video (DAVID) systems.

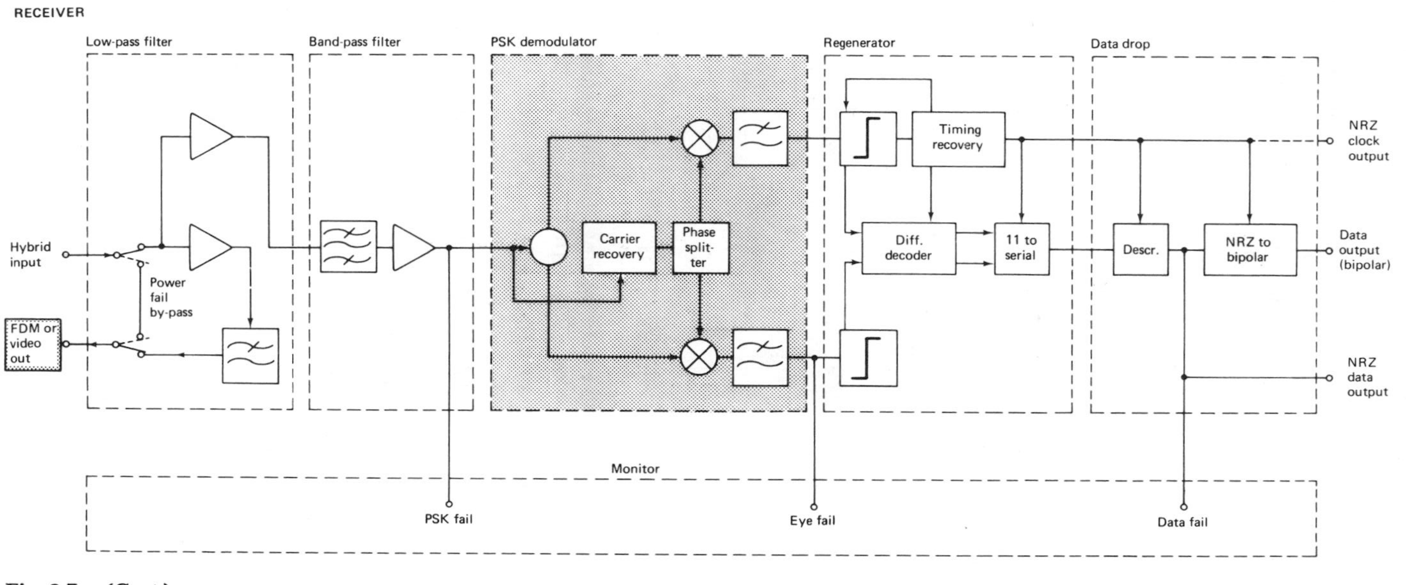
RECEIVER
Low-pass filter
Band-pass filter
PSK demodulator
Regenerator
Data drop
Hybrid input
FDM or video out
Power fail by-pass
Carrier recovery
Phase split-ter
Timing recovery
Diff. decoder
11 to serial
Descr.
NRZ to bipolar
NRZ clock output
Data output (bipolar)
NRZ data output
Monitor
PSK fail
Eye fail
Data fail

Fig. 8.7. (Cont.)

**TABLE 8.1 Measured Performance of the Spar Aerospace Limited 1.544-Mb/s-above-960 FDM Voice Channel DAV System in the Canadian National/Canadian Pacific 6 GHz FDM System**

| 1 | 2 | 3 | 4 | 5 | 6 | 7 | 8 |
|---|---|---|---|---|---|---|---|
| $C/N$ dB 30 MHz | $C$ dBm | HYB $P(e)$ | DATA $P(e)$ | NPR 70 kHz HYB FDM | NPR 1248 kHz HYB FDM | NPR 2438 kHz HYB FDM | NPR 3886 kHz HYB FDM |
| 56 | −33 | $< 10^{-10}$ | $< 10^{-10}$ | 53<br>53 | 48<br>48.5 | 45<br>45.5 | 43<br>44 |
| 24.5 | −64.5 | $3.10^{-8}$ | $10^{-8}$ | | | | |
| 22.5 | −66.5 | $5.10^{-6}$ | $5.10^{-6}$ | | | | |
| 20 | −69 | $10^{-4}$ | $10^{-4}$ | 47.5<br>48 | 27<br>27.5 | 23<br>23 | 20.5<br>20.5 |

ratio (NPR) of the operational hybrid (HYB) system and of the solely 960-channel-loaded FDM system are shown. From this table it is seen that the NPR is degraded less than 1 dB by the data loading, and the system has a $P(e) = 5 \cdot 10^{-6}$ threshold performance at a $C/N = 22.5$ dB. This $C/N$ corresponds to a fade margin of 33.5 dB. By means of an automatic increase of the transmitted QPSK carrier power during fading condition, the fade margin can be increased to about 38 dB [8.6]. For increased reliability, DAV systems are often used in a diversity configuration. Pseudo-error monitor-controlled diversity DAV systems have been achieving the reliability objectives which are described in Chapter 5.

In addition to the DUV, DAV, and DAVID transmission techniques, a method known as *data in voice* (DIV) has been developed by Japanese manufacturers. The DIV system, developed by Fujitsu [8.5], uses an 8-level PAM-VSB modulation technique with very steep filtering ($\alpha = 0.15$). It has a high bandwidth efficiency of nearly 5 b/s/Hz (1.544 Mb/s data is transmitted in a 344 kHz baseband bandwidth). This highly bandwidth-efficient system has, however, the drawback that, for a low $P(e)$, a high $S/N$ ratio is required. For example, from the 8-level PAM curve given in Chapter 3 we conclude that, theoretically, in an additive white gaussian noise channel, an $S/N = 28$ dB is required for a $P(e) = 10^{-8}$. For a practical gaussian noise-controlled system, this $S/N$ requirement might be more than 31 dB. In addition, a number of FDM systems are intermodulation-controlled, so that the probability density of the noise is not gaussian, and wideband $S/N$ ratios higher than 40 dB might be required [8.19].

In conclusion, the hybrid systems described provide efficient means to transmit data at a 1.544 Mb/s rate, in addition to the FDM or to the video message, on conventional, analog, FM microwave, cable, optical fiber, and satellite systems. All of these systems are in use and could be modified to transmit even higher data rates.

## 8.4 SUBSCRIBER DIGITAL RADIO SYSTEMS

In our studies thus far we have been concentrating on digital *point-to-point* microwave systems, that is, on systems in which the information is transmitted from one point in space to another point in space or to a number of points in space, e.g., from San Francisco to Los Angeles and Seattle. In addition to point-to-point digital radio transmission systems, requirements also exist for distributed radio systems. In this section a distributed radio configuration is introduced and references are provided if you are interested in their application.

A *distributed radio* system, also known as *subscriber radio*, is defined as carrying information from one point to many points in space. This system has a network which consists of a central station and spatially distributed secondary stations. As shown in Fig. 8.8, all information is routed through the central station, which may be linked to an external network. Secondary stations are defined as carrying some generally smaller fraction of the system capacity. A distributed system configuration similar to that of Fig. 8.8 has been used successfully in the Intelsat and many other domestic single-channel-per-carrier satellite systems [8.4, 8.17]. Analog and digital

Fig. 8.8. Distributed radio network model. (Redrawn by permission from Reference [8.20])

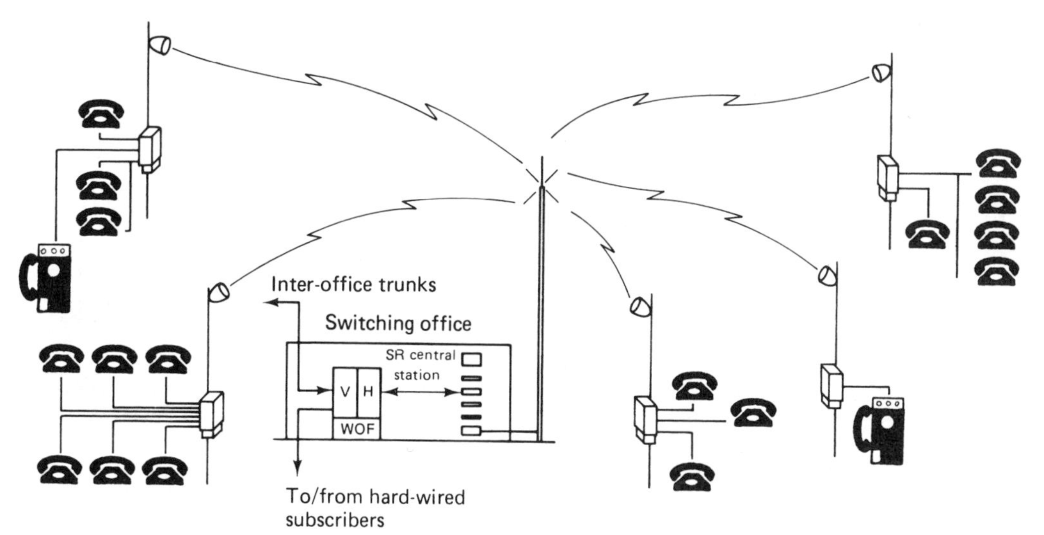

terrestial distributed microwave system configurations and equipment are described in [8.9]; operating aspects of a distributed system, manufactured by the Farinon Company, have been reported by Bell Canada [8.20].

## PROBLEMS

**8.1** Suppose you are a product-planning manager who is responsible for the development program of a new generation of 90 Mb/s radio equipment. You have just received a note from your boss that the company vice-president requires, within one hour, a brief, one-page, comparative, technical performance summary of 8-PSK, 16-PSK, and 16-APK systems. Even though you feel that such short notice is ridiculous, you know that you have to report on time. Good luck: Go ahead and prepare your report, *within one hour*!

**8.2** State the reason for the significant performance degradation exhibited by a band-limited 16-APK signal when it passes through a TWT operating near saturation. If the 16-APK signal is not band-limited (practically infinite bandwidth), then will its performance still be degraded by the TWT? Explain why.

**8.3** What is the minimum RF bandwidth of a 4-level PAM-FM system if it is used for the transmission of a 20 Mb/s data rate?

**8.4** In the DUV system operated by ATT, the 1.544 Mb/s information is transmitted by means of a 7-level partial response code. What is the minimum theoretical baseband bandwidth requirement for this code? What would be the minimum bandwidth required if a 4-level PAM baseband signal were used? What are the reasons for using a 7-level partial response code and not 4-level PAM? Compare the theoretical bandwidth requirement to the practical requirement.

**8.5** Sketch the 2.048 Mb/s, minimum bandwidth, data above video (DAVID) spectrum. Assume that, for high-quality video transmission, a 4.5 MHz video bandwidth is required. A QPSK data modulator should be used.

## REFERENCES

[8.1] Ishio, H., M. Washio, M. Inokuchi, S. Seki, et al., "A New Multilevel Modulation and Demodulation System for Carrier Digital Transmission," Proc. IEEE International Conference on Communications, ICC-76, Philadelphia, June, 1976.

[8.2] Thomas, C. M., M. Y. Weidner, S. H. Durrani, "Digital Amplitude Phase Keying with M-ary Alphabets," IEEE Trans. Communications, February, 1974.

[8.3] Feher, K., R. Goulet, S. Morissette, "1.544 Mb/s Data Above FDM Voice (DAV) and Data Under FDM Voice (DUV) Microwave Transmission," IEEE Trans. Communications, November, 1975.

[8.4] Feher, K., *Digital Modulation Techniques in an Interference Environment, Multi-Volume EMC Encyclopedia*, Vol. 9, Don White Consultants, Inc., Gainesville, VA, 1977.

[8.5] Hagiwara, S., N. Sata, A. Tokimasa, "1.544 Mb/s PCM-FDM Converters Over Coaxial and Microwave Systems," Fujitsu Scientific and Technical Journal, September, 1976.

[8.6] Feher, K., M. Morris, "Developments in Canadian and International Data Above Voice-Video Telecommunications," Proc. IEEE Canadian Communication Conference, Montreal, October, 1978.

[8.7] Glave, F., L. B. Dunn, "Dataroute Transmission: System Growth and Extensions," Proc. IEEE International Conference on Communications, ICC-74, Minneapolis, June, 1974.

[8.8] Technical Staff, American Telephone and Telegraph Company, Bell Telephone Companies and Bell Telephone Laboratories, *Telecommunications Transmission Engineering*, Bell System For Technical Education, Winston-Salem, N.C., 1977.

[8.9] Krzyckowski, M., K. Feher, "Interference Suppression in a Distributed Radio System," Proc. IEEE International Conference on Communications, Vol. 1, ICC-78, Toronto, June, 1978.

[8.10] Morais, D. H., K. Feher, "MSK and Offset QPSK Modulation in Line-of-Sight Digital Radio Systems," Proc. IEEE International Conference on Communications, ICC-77, Chicago, June, 1977.

[8.11] Sullivan, W. A., "High-Capacity Microwave System for Digital Data Transmission," IEEE Trans. Communications, June, 1972.

[8.12] Lender, A., A. Rogers, H. Olszanski, "4 Bits/Hertz Correlative Single-Sideband Digital Radio at 2 GHz," Proc. IEEE International Conference on Communications, Boston, June, 1979.

[8.13] Miyauchi, K., S. Seki, H. Ishio, "New Technique for Generating and Detecting Multi-Level Signal Formats," IEEE Trans. Communications, February, 1976.

[8.14] Broderick, C. W., "A Digital Transmission System for TD-2 Radio," B.S.T.J., February, 1971.

[8.15] Morais, D., K. Feher, "A Survey of North American 2 GHz Digital Radio Systems," Proc. Intelcom-77, Horizon House, Atlanta, October, 1977.

[8.16] Feher, K., M. Morris, "Simultaneous Transmission of Digital Phase-Shift Keying and of Analog Television Signals," IEEE Trans. Communications, December, 1975.

[8.17] Spilker, J. J., *Digital Communications by Satellite*, Prentice-Hall, Inc., Englewood Cliffs, N.J., 1977.

[8.18] Feher, K., R. Y. Goulet, S. Morissette, "Baseband Diversity for Hybrid Microwave Systems," IEEE Trans. Communications, May, 1974.

[8.19] Keelty, J. M., K. Feher, "On-Line Pseudo-Error Monitors for Digital Transmission Systems," IEEE Trans. Communications, August, 1978.

[8.20] Scott, J. D., G. K. Sawinsky, "A New Way to Provide Telephone Services with Subscriber Radio," Proc. IEEE International Conference on Communications, Vol. 1, ICC-78, Toronto, June, 1978.

# 9

# DIGITAL MICROWAVE SYSTEMS DESIGN

The most important regulations of the U.S. Federal Communications Commission (FCC) and the recommendations of the International Radio Consultative Committee (*Comité Consultatif International de Radio*—CCIR), related to digital microwave systems, are presented in Section 9.1.

The FCC regulations are probably the most stringent regulations in existence today. Significant parts of these regulations have been used as a model for the development of the Canadian regulations issued by the Department of Communications (DOC—Canada). They have also been used as a model for the Japanese regulations, and the regulations for many countries in Europe as well as throughout the world. Even though, internationally, the CCIR does not have regulatory power, its recommendations are highly respected and implemented by most nations.

Each systems designer has the responsibility to ensure that the regulations prevailing in his country are adhered to and, if possible, also comply with the CCIR recommendations. In addition to satisfying regulations, the designer has to ensure that the overall system performs satisfactorily, that is, that the accumulated error rate at the far end of the system is sufficiently low. Error and jitter accumulation problems in regenerative repeaters are described in Section 9.2. Service-channel transmission methods, required for the maintenance of digital microwaves, are discussed in Section 9.3. Finally, in Section 9.4 transmission performance objectives are reviewed.

## 9.1 FCC REGULATIONS AND CCIR RECOMMENDATIONS RELATED TO DIGITAL RADIO SYSTEMS DESIGN

To minimize interference between *adjacent* digital and analog microwave channels, the FCC has issued detailed regulations for out-of-band emission limits and the limits and requirements for certain signal characteristics of the digitally modulated carrier wave. Because of frequent simultaneous use of digital and analog systems in the frequency bands below 15 GHz, and greater anticipated impact on analog performance, the regulations are more stringent for bands below 15 GHz. Detailed FCC regulations related to digital microwave systems are contained in FCC Dockets No. 19311 and No. 18920. The most important of these regulations and the CCIR recommendations are described in this chapter [9.2, 9.3, 9.5, 9.12, 9.14, 9.15].

The intent of the FCC regulations is to establish standards which encourage further orderly development of digital microwave systems, while *not degrading* the performance of adjacent radio systems using *analog* or *digital* transmission methods. In setting the regulations the FCC had to assure that the available radio spectrum is efficiently used (specifying the b/s/Hz efficiency requirement) and that the radio equipment meeting these requirements can be cost-competitive with the analog systems. Prior to the establishment of the final regulations the filed comments of major telecommunication carrier companies, equipment manufacturers, and trade associations were studied. Comments were filed by numerous parties, including (reprinted by permission from FCC Docket No. 18920, reference [9.15]): Microband Corporation of America, Southern Pacific Communications Corporation, GTE Service Corporation, CML Satellite Corporation, Western Union Telegraph Company, Data Transmission Company (Datran), American Telephone and Telegraph Company (AT&T), United Video, Inc., and associated companies, Western Telecommunications, Inc. (WTCI), Nebraska Consolidated Communications Corporation (NCCC), Communications Satellite Corp. (Comsat), and Microwave Communications, Inc. (MCI). Four equipment manufacturers: Norden Division of United Aircraft Corporation (Norden), Vicom Division of Vidar Corporation (Vicom), Avantek, Inc., and Varian Division of Micro-Link Products (Varian). Five trade associations: Electronics Industries Association (EIA), United States Independent Telephone Association (USITA), Utilities Telecommunications Council (UTC), American Petroleum Institute (API), and Multipoint Microwave Common-Carriers Association (MMCCA). One private radio user: Aeronautical Radio, Inc. (Arinc). Reply comments were filed by GTE, CML Satellite, Datran, AT&T, NCCC, Comsat, MCI, UTC, and API.

Frequency bands below 12 GHz that are authorized for digital microwave transmission in the United States, allowable bandwidths of individual radio carriers, and minimum capacity of encoded 4 kHz voice channels are listed in Table 9.1. To satisfy the allowable bandwidth specifications, the mean output power in any 4 kHz band of emission must be attenuated below the mean total-wideband output power of the transmitter, in accordance with the following attenuation mask [9.2; 9.5; 9.18]:

$$A(f) = \begin{cases} 0 & \text{for} \quad 0\% < P < 50\% \\ 35 + 0.8(P - 50\%) + 10(\log_{10} B) & \text{for } 50\% < P \\ 80 & \text{for} \quad \text{large } P \end{cases} \tag{9.1}$$

where $A$ = attenuation (dB) below the mean wideband output-power level
$B$ = allowable bandwidth (MHz)
$f_c$ = center frequency (unmodulated carrier)
$f$ = frequency of interest, that is, frequency at which the attenuation specification is being evaluated

$$P = \frac{|f - f_c|}{\text{allowable bandwidth}} \times 100\%.$$

**TABLE 9.1 FCC-Authorized Frequency Bands (U.S.), Below 12 GHz, for Digital Microwave Systems [9.2, 9.5, 9.7, 9.15]**

| Frequency Band | Allowable Bandwidth (B) | Minimum Capacity of Encoded Voice Channels |
|---|---|---|
| 2,110– 2,130 MHz | 3.5 MHz | 96 |
| 2,160– 2,180 | 3.5 | 96 |
| 3,700– 4,200 | 20.0 | 1152 |
| 5,925– 6,425 | 30.0 | 1152 |
| 10,700–11,700 | 40.0 | 1152 |

**EXAMPLE 9.1.** Draw the FCC mask in reference to the $B = 30$ MHz allowable bandwidth, and draw the spectrum of scrambled 90 Mb/s data if the 6 GHz microwave system employs an 8-PSK modulation technique. Does the unfiltered spectrum satisfy the FCC emission limits?

*STOP! Do not* proceed with reading the solution. *Try* to solve the problem yourself. You *are* able to do it. Do it! Once you have solved the problem, compare your results with the following solution.

***SOLUTION:*** The resulting FCC mask, obtained from equation (9.1), is shown in Fig. 9.1. In this case, the allowable bandwidth is 30 MHz; thus, $P = 50\%$ corresponds to $|f - f_c| = 15$ MHz. The mask reaches the 80 dB attenuation point at $|f - f_c| = 26$ MHz; that is, $P = \frac{26}{30} = 86.7\%$. (Here you *should verify* a number of points on this mask).

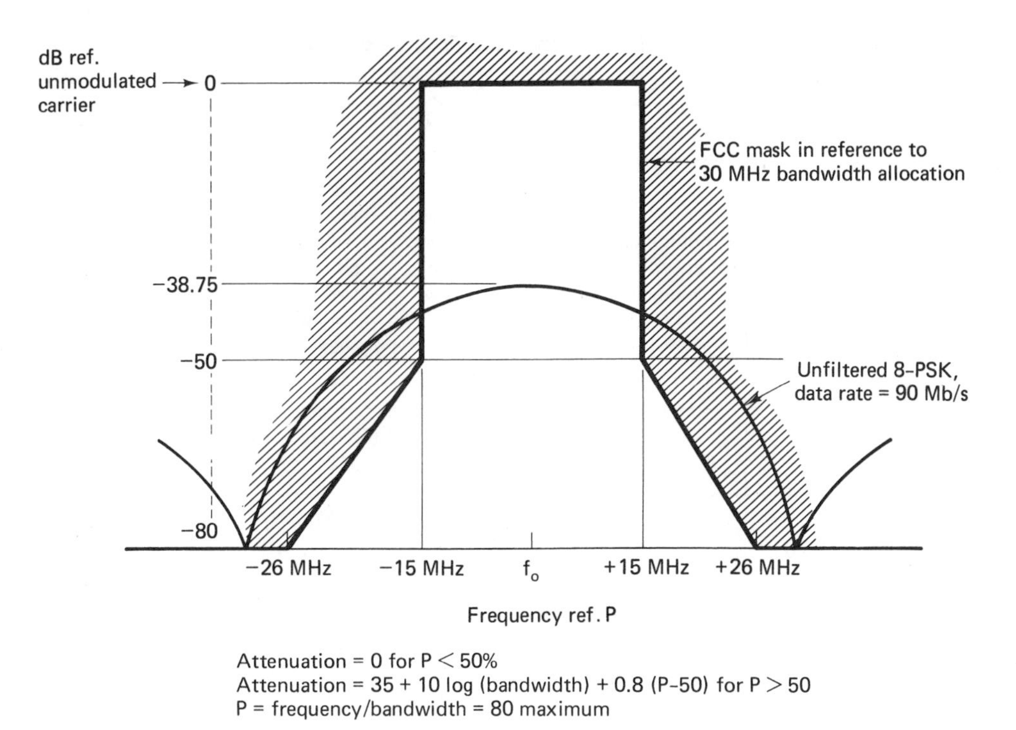


**Fig. 9.1.** FCC mask in reference to 30 MHz bandwidth allocation and unfiltered 8-PSK spectrum of a 90 Mb/s signal.

The power spectral density of the 8-PSK 90 Mb/s data, measured at the center frequency in a 4 kHz band, is 10 log (4 kHz/30 MHz) $= -38.75$ dB below the unmodulated carrier power. The spectral shape of the modulated signal follows the familiar $(\sin x/x)^2$ pattern which was studied in Chapters 2, 3, and 6. From the unfiltered spectrum and the FCC mask, we conclude that severe filtering is required to meet the regulatory requirements. **(Solve Problem 9.1).** ■

In the extreme right column of Table 9.1, the minimum capacity of encoded voice channels is specified. In addition, FCC Docket No. 19311 requires that the *bandwidth efficiency must exceed* 1 b/s/Hz per transmitter. Traditionally, a standard PCM data rate of 64 kb/s has been assumed for encoded 4 kHz telephony-voice transmission. With this rate for 96 voice-frequency (VF) channels, an information rate of 6.144 Mb/s would be required. To this information rate, housekeeping bits for synchronization, monitoring, and asynchronous to synchronous multiplexing (bit stuffing) have to be added. The standard rate used in the digital hierarchy is 6.312 Mb/s (DS-2 interface level, Chapter 1).

Table 9.2 lists, in addition to FCC requirements, the North American standard bit rates and the corresponding VF capacities. To satisfy, simultaneously, the FCC

**TABLE 9.2 FCC-Authorized Frequency Bands and the North American Digital Hierarchy**

| FCC Regulations | | | | Digital Hierarchy | | |
|---|---|---|---|---|---|---|
| Authorized frequency band (GHz) | Allowable bandwidth (MHz) | Minimum capacity of encoded voice channels ($n$) | Corresponding PCM bit rate, $n \times 64$ kb/s (in Mb/s) | Closest hierarchy level and bit rate (Mb/s) | Number of PCM channels in hierarchy | Efficiency (b/s/Hz) |
| 2.110– 2.130 | 3.5 | 96 | 6.144 | (DS-2) 6.312 | 96 | 1.80 |
| 2.160– 2.180 | 3.5 | 96 | 6.144 | (DS-2) 6.312 | 96 | 1.80 |
| 3.700– 4.200 | 20.0 | 1152 | 73.728 | $2 \times$ (DS-2) approx. 90 | 1344 | 4.5 |
| 5.925– 6.425 | 30.0 | 1152 | 73.728 | $2 \times$ (DS-2) approx. 90 | 1344 | 3 |
| 10.700–11.700 | 40.0 | 1152 | 73.728 | $2 \times$ (DS-2) approx. 90 | 1344 | 2.25 |

requirements and those imposed by the digital hierarchy, radio systems having *bandwidth efficiencies* of 3 b/s/Hz have been designed. With the exception of the 3.700 to 4.200 GHz frequency band, in which a 4.5 b/s/Hz efficiency would be required, systems already exist which satisfy all of the other previously stated simultaneous requirements. Considering the present fast pace in research and development, it is expected that within a few years systems will be built which can attain the 4.5 b/s/Hz efficiency. **(Solve Problem 9.2.)**

The FCC also has specifications concerning *minimum permissible path distance.* For example, in the 6 GHz band this distance is 17 km, whereas in the 11 GHz band it is 5 km. The equipment must prevent the transmission of discrete spectral lines, which can be ensured by the use of scramblers [9.8, 9.25]. The FCC permits the use of cross-polarization operation to achieve the minimum-capacity requirement.

Frequency allocations recommended by the CCIR for analog FDM and digital microwave systems are summarized in Table 9.3 (for 2, 4, and 6 GHz) and Table 9.4 (for 7, 8, 11 and 13 GHz) [9.12, 9.14, 9.5]. The recommended RF frequencies and channel spacings are not the same as those specified by the FCC. This is a somewhat unfortunate situation for which no short-term solution is in sight.

**TABLE 9.3 CCIR Frequency Allocations**

| | | | FDM | | Digital | | |
|---|---|---|---|---|---|---|---|
| Frequency band (GHz) | Frequency range (MHz) | Channel spacing (MHz) | Channel capacity | Band capacity* | Channel capacity | Band capacity* | CCIR rec. |
| 2 | 1700–1900<br>1900–2100<br>2100–2300<br>2500–2700 | 14 | 60, 120, 300 | 6 | — | — | 283–2 |
| | 1700–2100 or 1900–2300 | 29 | 600–1800 | 6 | — | — | 382–2 |
| 4 | 3700–4200 | 29 | 600–1800 | 6 | — | — | 382–2 |
| | | 40 | 1260 | 6 | — | — | 382–2 |
| 6 | 5925–6425 | 29.65 | 1800 | 8 | — | — | 383–1 |
| | 6430–7110 | 40 | 2700 | 8 | — | — | 384–2 |
| | | 20 | 1260 | 16 | — | — | 384–2 |

*Go and return channels.

**TABLE 9.4 CCIR Frequency Allocations**

| | | | FDM | | Digital | | |
|---|---|---|---|---|---|---|---|
| Frequency band (GHz) | Frequency range (MHz) | Channel spacing (MHz) | Channel capacity | Band capacity* | Channel capacity | Band capacity* | CCIR rec. |
| 7 | 7,425– 7,725 | 7/14 | 60, 120/300 | 20 | — | — | 385 |
| 8 | 8,200– 8,500 | 11.662 | 960 | 6 | — | — | 386–1 |
| | 7,725– 8,275 | 29.65 | 1800 | 8 | — | — | 386–1 |
| 11 | 10,700–11,700 | 40 | 1800 | 12 | Medium (480–960) | 11 | 387–1 |
| 13 | 12,750–13,250 | 28 | 960 | 8 | 960† | 8 | 497 |
| | | 14 | 300 | Additional | 240 | Additional | 497 |
| | | 35 | — | — | 720 | | 497 |

*Go and return channels.
†Using 480 channels on both polarizations.

## 9.2 JITTER AND ERROR ACCUMULATION

The systems designer has to ensure that a digital microwave system satisfies regulatory requirements, is compatible with the digital hierarchy, and that the system performs well. In this section, the performance of multi-hop regenerative digital systems is considered.

In Chapter 1 we state that, in digital systems, transmission performance is *almost independent* of the number of repeaters and of the system's length and topology. Now, we clarify the subject as to why transmission quality is almost, but not completely, independent of a system's length.

In Fig. 9.2 a three-section digital microwave system is illustrated. All three sections, $AB$, $BC$, and $CD$, have the same length, $l = 50$ km. The total one-way

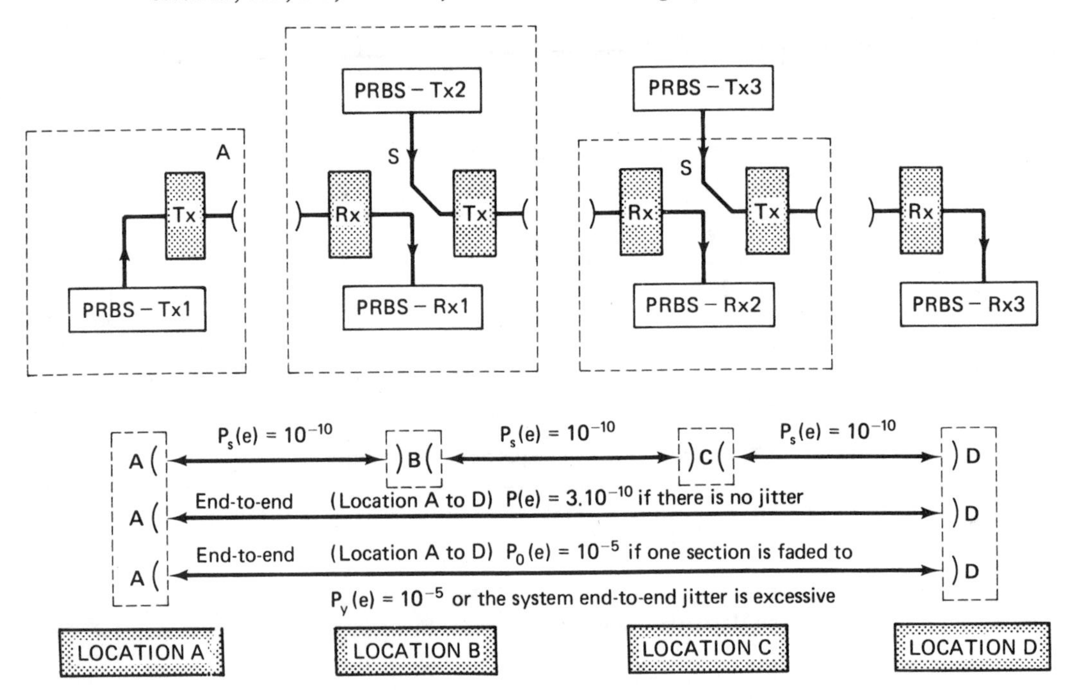


**Fig. 9.2.** $P(e)$ evaluation of a three-section digital radio system.

system length $L$ equals $3 \times l = 150$ km. Let us assume that the error probabilities of individual sections are evaluated with pseudo-random-binary sequence (PRBS) generators and error detectors. In this case, the test switches at locations $B$ and $C$ are in the $S$ positions, indicating that the probability of error, $P(e)$, measurements are performed on a section-to-section basis. If the error probabilities of individual sections, $P_s(e)$, are equal and are very small, then the overall probability of error $P_o(e)$ in an $n$-section system is, theoretically, very nearly equal to

$$P_o(e) = nP_s(e) \tag{9.2}$$

Equation (9.2) holds if $n$ is not too large [9.4]. In our three-section system, $n = 3$, $P_s(e) = 10^{-10}$; thus, $P_o(e) = 3 \cdot 10^{-10}$.

**EXAMPLE 9.2.** The overall (end-to-end) probability of error performance $P_o(e)$ of a multi-section digital microwave system is estimated by using equation (9.2). Is the estimated result a good estimate of the true $P(e)$?

***SOLUTION:*** Most of the time (say 99%) there is no fading on the system; thus, each well-designed section is virtually error-free, that is, $P_s(e) = 10^{-10}$. In this case, equation (9.2) is a good estimate of the overall $P_o(e)$. In Chapter 5 we state that deep fades are the most important cause of performance degradation. It is highly unlikely that very deep equal-depth fades would occur simultaneously on two or more sections of a system, even though the system may be long. Most frequently, overall performance is controlled by the section which has the deepest fade. Let us assume that a long-haul system has $n = 100$ regenerative sections and that, at a given time, two geographically distant sections are deeply faded. During the simultaneous occurrence of these deep fades, one of the faded sections, $x$, has a degraded probability of error performance $P_x(e) = 10^{-7}$, while the other faded section, $y$, has an even worse performance, $P_y(e) = 10^{-5}$. It is realistic to assume that all other sections are unfaded or that the fade on those sections is not sufficiently large to cause performance degradation. The probability of error of the unfaded sections remains unchanged at $P_s(e) = 10^{-10}$. In this case, the overall (end-to-end) $P_o(e)$ is

$$P_o(e) = 98 \times P_s(e) + P_x(e) + P_y(e)$$

$$= 98 \times 10^{-10} + 10^{-7} + 10^{-5} \approx P_x(e) + P_y(e) \approx P_y(e)$$

From this illustrative example it is evident that, during deep fades, equation (9.2) must not be used to estimate $P(e)$. During fading intervals, the overall system performance is dominated by the $P_y(e)$ performance of the deepest faded section. ■

From the solution of Example 9.2 we conclude that the end-to-end $P_o(e)$ of an *unfaded* $n$-section transmission system is $nP_s(e)$, where $P_s(e)$ is the performance of each individual unfaded section. During deep fades, the end-to-end $P_o(e)$ performance of the system is the same as the performance of the section which has the deepest fade, $P_y(e)$. The presented end-to-end $P(e)$ performance calculation is correct if the *clock-jitter* accumulation is negligible. In some operational systems this is not the case; thus, a clarification of the clock-jitter accumulation problem is in order, as described below.

At the receiving end, the symbol-timing recovery (STR) circuitry (see Chapters 3 and 6) extracts the clock information from the modulated carrier wave or from the demodulated baseband signal. In either case, the symbol-timing clock signal is obtained by means of non-linear signal processing from the band-limited random-data signal. Non-linear processing is required because the random-data pattern does not contain discrete spectral lines at the symbol rate [9.4, 9.8, 9.19]. The power spectral density of an infinite bandwidth and of a band-limited random-data signal is shown in Fig. 9.3(a). At the symbol rate $1/T_s$, or at its integer multiple $m/T_s$, it is necessary to have a discrete spectral line, such as shown in Fig. 9.3(b).

This discrete spectral line is necessary in order that the phase-lock-loop, located in the following stage of the STR circuitry, can lock-on and filter out undesired interference. The filtered sinusoid is then converted into a periodic square wave and used as the symbol clock.

In the time-domain representation (Fig. 9.4), it is shown that the jitter-free symbol clock is set to sample the eye diagram at its maximum opening. The traces

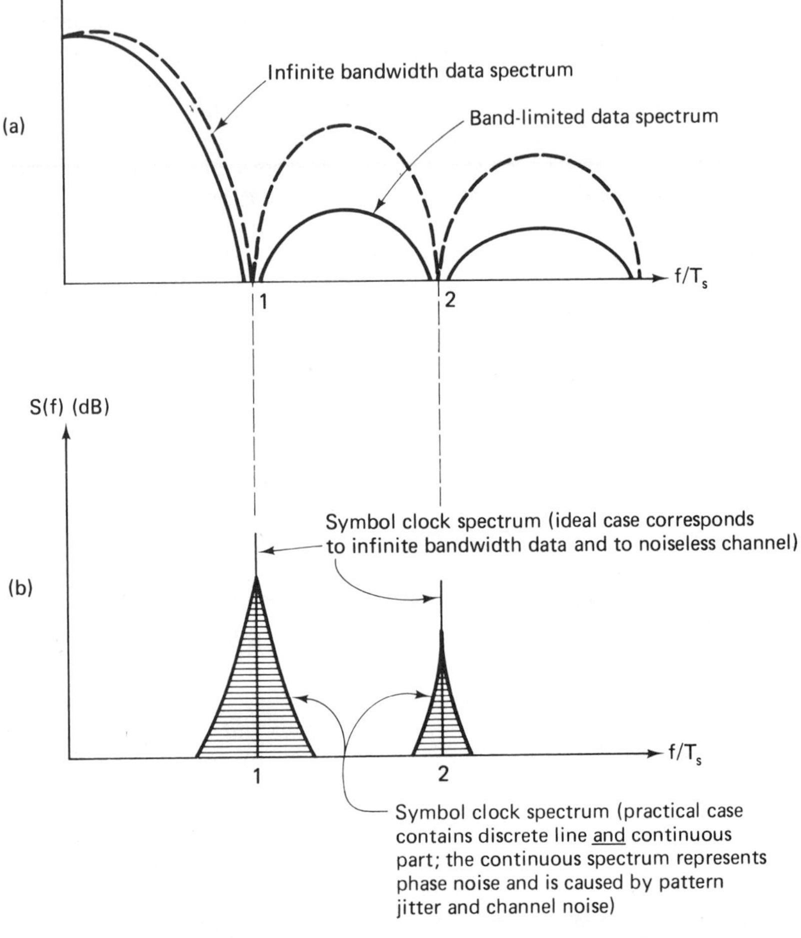

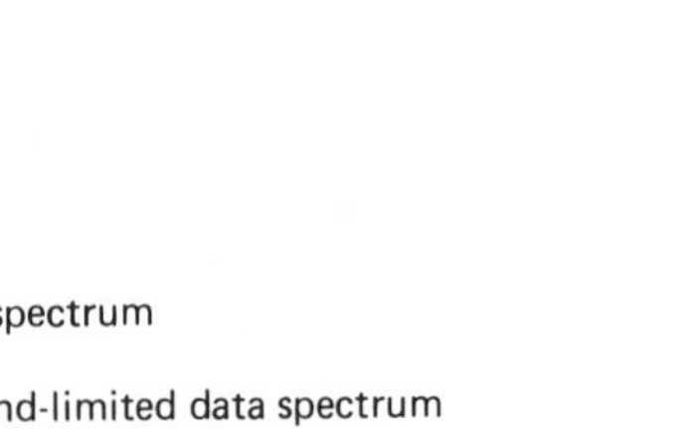

**Fig. 9.3.** Power spectrum of demodulated data and the spectrum of the recovered symbol clock.

of the eye diagram cross the threshold level at various time instants. The data transition peak jitter $J_{D_p}$ is defined as the largest possible shift of the data threshold crossing point from the nominal crossing point $T_s/2$. In Chapter 3 it is shown that even ideally phase-equalized Nyquist filters introduce data transition jitter. **(Solve Problem 9.3.)**

When a band-limited signal is passed through, such as shown in Fig. 9.4 in the time domain and in Fig. 9.3(a) in the spectral domain, a non-linear processor and a phase-lock-loop, a spectrum, such as shown in Figure 9.3(b), is obtained. This non-linearly processed signal exhibits a timing-peak clock jitter $J_{cp}$, as

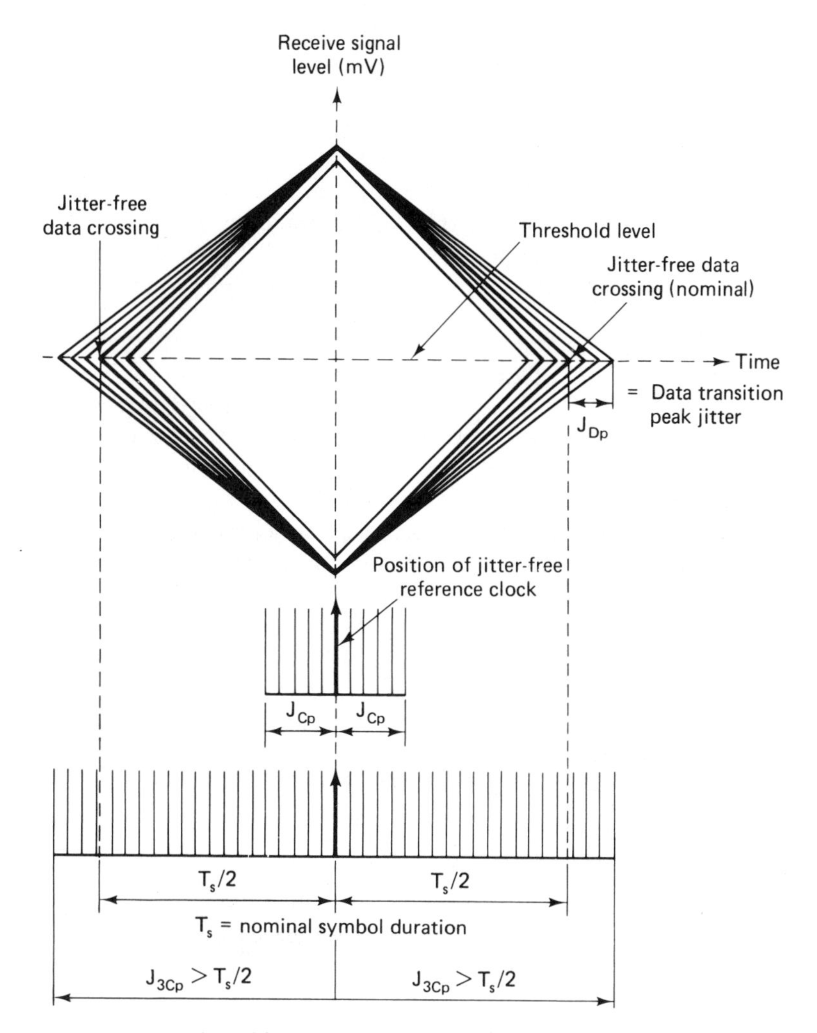


**Fig. 9.4.** Sampling with a jittery reference clock.

shown in Fig. 9.4. In the illustrated example, even though $J_{cp}$ is not excessive, it introduces a performance degradation.

Now, we return to the *multi-section system* of Fig. 9.2. If the $P(e)$ of the unfaded system is evaluated on a section-by-section basis, then the switches are set to the $S$ positions. In this case, the clock-data jitter $J_{cp}$ introduced in the first section does not enter into the second section. In the sectional evaluation, the second section is fed by a jitter-free reference clock which is provided by the PRBS data transmitter Tx2. The situation between the following sections is similar to that of the first and second sections; that is, there is no jitter accumulation effect. For example, if the unfaded $P_s(e) = 10^{-10}$ then, as already stated, the $P_o(e) = nP_s(e) = 3 \cdot 10^{-10}$. The end-to-end probability of error $P_o(e)$ is $nP_s(e)$ if the overall peak-to-peak and

RMS clock jitter is negligible. In the three-section system example shown in Figs. 9.2 and 9.4, the *accumulated* peak-to-peak clock jitter $J_{3cp}$ is larger than one-half of the symbol duration ($J_{3cp} > T_s/2$). This excessive clock jitter degrades the $P(e)$ performance of the sampled bits and is the cause of occasional bit *skipping*. Careful equipment and system designers ensure that a system's worst-case overall peak-to-peak clock jitter is less than 10% of the symbol duration. The excessive clock jitter might cause burst errors and degrade the $P_o(e) = 3 \cdot 10^{-10}$ to $P_o(e) = 10^{-5}$ or even cause a complete system outage. In Chapter 11 original methods for simple off-line (out-of-service) and on-line (in-service) jitter measurements are described.

## 9.3 SERVICE CHANNEL TRANSMISSION METHODS

Control, supervisory, and order-wire signal transmission, that is, service channel transmission is required for the efficient maintenance, performance monitoring, and control of digital microwave systems. In order to have telephone conversations between maintenance personnal at geographically separated locations, it is necessary to have a system in which it is easy to combine the main customer traffic $c(t)$ with the service channel signal $s(t)$.

A one-way multi-section digital transmission system, in which the main customer traffic is transmitted from transmitter $A$ to the final receiver $M$ and in which service channel information can be inserted and extracted (dropped) or cross-connected, is shown in Fig. 9.5. In transmitter $A$, the service channel signal $s_a(t)$ is "combined" with the digital customer traffic $c(t)$. This combined information is transmitted to location $B$. The signal $c(t)$ is cross-connected from receiver $B$ to transmitter $B$; the service channel information $s_a(t)$ is cross-connected or dropped.

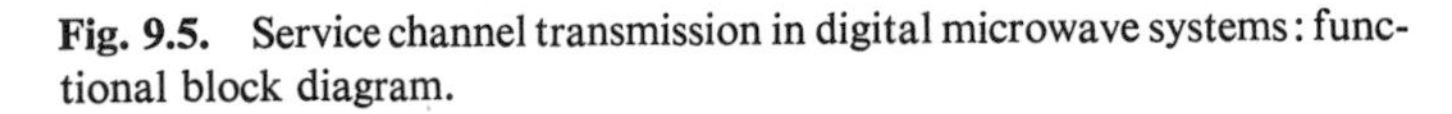


**Fig. 9.5.** Service channel transmission in digital microwave systems: functional block diagram.

The signal $s_a(t)$ may also be replaced by new service channel information $s_b(t)$, which has its origin at location $B$.

At some other locations, such as location $K$, the service channel information might be cross-connected. In order to meet flexible maintenance requirements, it is essential to have a system design in which it is easy to drop and insert or cross-connect the $c(t)$ and $s(t)$ signals.

Several techniques used to "combine" the service channel signal $s(t)$ and the customer traffic signal $c(t)$ are employed. In one frequently used method, service channel information is analog-to-digital converted into a binary synchronous bit stream and then time-division multiplexed (TDM) with the customer data stream $c(t)$. This TDM method is illustrated in Fig. 9.6(a). The operation essentials of this method are illustrated in the following example.

**EXAMPLE 9.3.** One of your customers has a need to transmit 96 PCM voice channels. For flexible system maintenance it is necessary to provide an additional telephony-grade service channel. This channel is intended for use by maintenance personnel. What is the combined transmission bit rate for this system?

***SOLUTION:*** We assume that the customer will use standard North American rate time-division multiplex equipment; thus, the customer bit rate will be $f_c = 6.312$ Mb/s (see Chapter 1). To provide an additional telephony-grade service channel, the analog voice signal is band-limited to 3.4 kHz and then analog-to-digital (A/D) converted. The parallel binary data provided by the A/D converter is parallel-to-serial (P/S) converted, as shown in Fig. 9.6(a). The combined A/D and P/S conversion is accomplished by conventional PCM or by delta modulation (DMOD) converters. If PCM is used, then the service channel bit rate if $f_s = 64$ kb/s, while if DMOD is employed then an $f_s = 32$ kb/s rate is sufficient for good service channel performance.

In order to TDM the non-synchronous $f_c$ and $f_s$ rate signals, it is necessary to "bit stuff" $\Delta f_s = 3$ kb/s. The combined transmitted bit rate is $f_c + f_s + \Delta f_s = 6.312$ Mb/s + 64 kb/s + 3 kb/s = 6.379 Mb/s in the case of a PCM service channel, whereas it is 6.355 Mb/s in the case of a 40 kb/s DMOD service channel. ■

The service channel transmission methods illustrated in Figs. 9.6(b) and 9.6(c) are also used frequently [9.7]. The analog service channel signal $s(t)$ FM modulates a voltage-controlled oscillator (VCO). The FM modulated carrier is used as the local oscillator signal of the $M$-ary data modulator. In Fig. 9.6(b) an $M$-ary PSK modulator is shown, albeit this double modulation method is not restricted to PSK data modulators. In Fig. 9.6(c) the PSK modulated customer traffic $c(t)$ (data signal) is AM modulated by the analog service channel. By using this method a double-modulated data signal is obtained. In Fig. 9.6(d) the analog service channel signal is inserted into the frequency band, below the digital signal band. For PAM signaling it is essential to have a high-pass filter in the $c(t)$ signal path to prevent excessive interference from the digital customer traffic $c(t)$ into the service channel signal $s(t)$. The low-pass filter prevents undue interference from $s(t)$ into $c(t)$. An in-depth analysis and design details of this method have been reported in reference [9.6]. If correlative coding is used (see Chapter 7), then the filtering requirements are

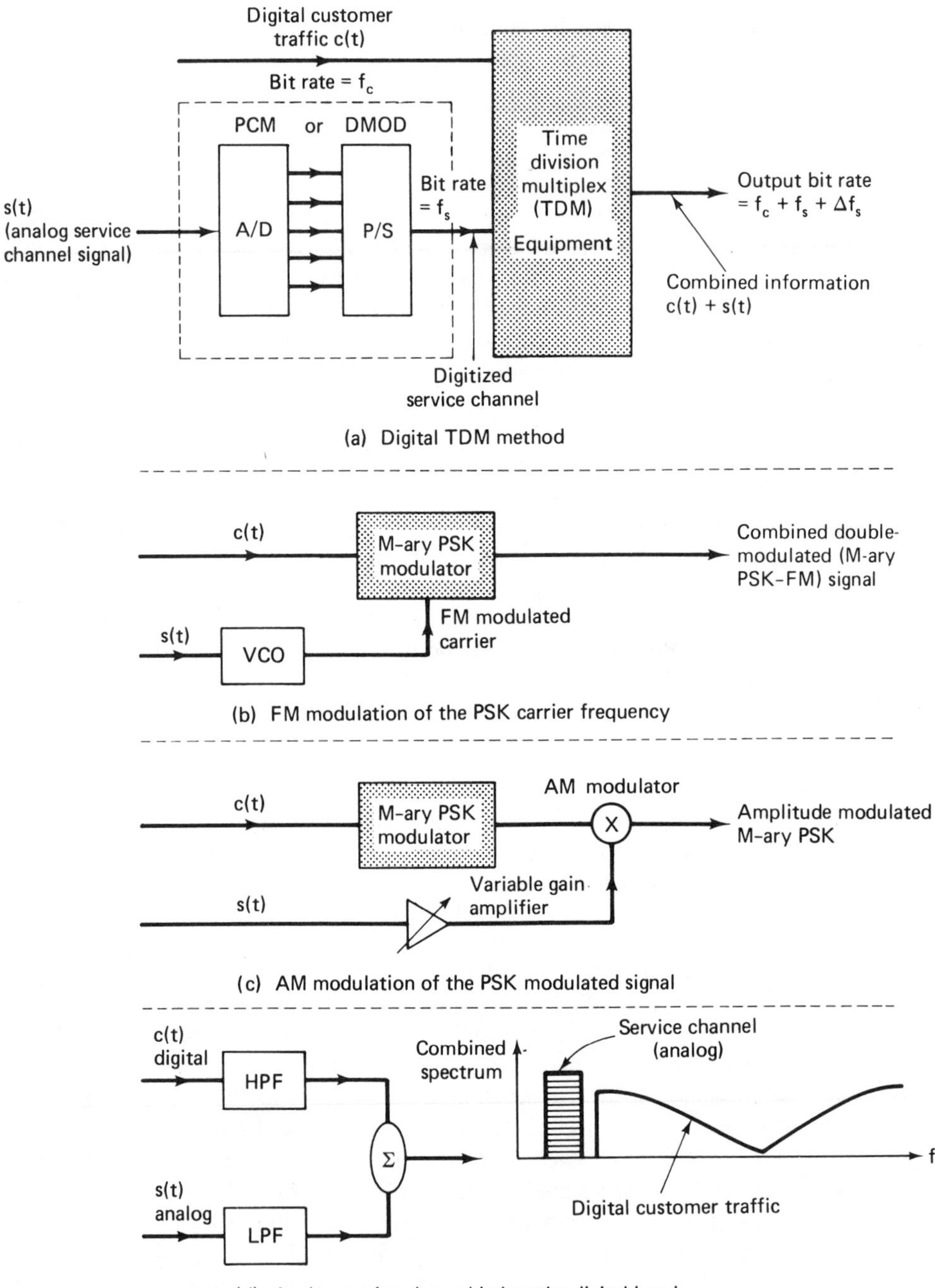


**Fig. 9.6.** Service channel insertion methods.

less stringent than in the PAM case. *Why*? (*Hint*: Think about the spectral properties of correlative coded signals, and compare them with those of PAM signals).

The service channel extraction circuitry performs functions that are the inverse of insertion circuitry functions. The extraction circuits corresponding to Figs. 9.6(a)–9.6(d) employ time-division demuliplex equipment and PCM or DMOD decoders, FM or AM demodulators, and band-splitting filters. Unfortunately, the literature available is insufficient to present an indepth performance comparison of the various service channel insertion and extraction methods. All of the above-described methods are in use and are known to provide good performance [9.16]. The digital method, Fig. 9.6(a), requires asynchronous TDM equipment, and transmits at a somewhat higher rate than the customer data rate. In the other methods, a careful system optimization is required to minimize the *interference* effects from the analog service channel into the digital customer traffic channel and vice versa.

In summary, signals carried over service channels are frequently employed for the transmission of status and performance data to central computers which perform overall system control. Most digital microwave systems are equipped with service channel facilities.

## 9.4 TRANSMISSION PERFORMANCE OBJECTIVES REVIEWED

The reliability objectives of U.S. and Canadian telephone companies and of electric, oil, and gas utilities are described in Chapter 5. We recall, for example, that the reliability objectives of telephone companies for short-haul operations limit the two-way service-failure time caused by propagation effects to 0.01% annually over a 400 km route. Here, service failure is considered to occur whenever the system $P(e) \geq 10^{-6}$. The probability of error, $P(e)$, term represents a statistical average of the ratio of the average number of bits in error to the average number of transmitted bits in a sufficiently long measurement interval [9.8]. In an unfaded system, the overall $P(e)$ might be, for example, $P(e) = 10^{-10}$. Even though this is an excellent $P(e)$ performance, it does not assure the customer that the average time of the error-free intervals is larger than a predetermined value, nor does this specification provide an insight into the average length of an *error burst*. To obtain additional information on error performance (hence, the transmission quality of a digital system) the following definitions have applied in recently developed systems [9.20, 9.21, 9.22].

*Error Burst:* A sequence of one or more bits, which begins and ends with a bit in error and is separated from neighboring error bursts by a guard space of $M$ or more error-free bits.

*Error-Free Interval* (*EFI*): The time duration, or number of bits, between error bursts.

*Outage:* If an error burst length exceeds a predetermined time, say 300 ms, then that error burst is redefined as an outage.

Unfortunately, there are no simple mathematical expressions which relate the EFI and the $P(e)$ specifications for practical digital microwave systems which operate in complex time-variable interference environments [9.22]. The $P(e)$ specification is widely used in most digital microwave systems as a measure of performance; however, in a number of examples, the end-to-end data users specify the EFI requirement.

## PROBLEMS

**9.1** Draw the FCC frequency mask for an allowable bandwidth $B = 30$ MHz. Assuming that ideal brick-wall Nyquist filters are used, what is the highest possible bit rate for this system if a 4-phase PSK modulation technique is used? How much is this bit rate if a 16-QAM modem is used?

**9.2** Assume you are required to transmit $f_b = 90$ Mb/s data in an authorized bandwidth of $B = 20$ MHz. Which modulation techniques would you consider? Explain why.

**9.3** How much is the peak-to-peak data transition jitter if a Nyquist filter having an $\alpha = 0$ roll-off is used. Assume that equiprobable random binary data is transmitted through this filter. How much is this jitter if $\alpha = 0.3$?

**9.4** Suppose the rate of the customer traffic, shown in Fig. 9.6(c), is $f_c = 90$ Mb/s. Describe the modulated spectrum which corresponds to the baseband $c(t)$ signal if an 8-PSK modulator is used. Assume that the customer provides equiprobable random binary data. Explain the spectrum if the service channel information is not present and, also, if $s(t)$ is present. Assume that $s(t)$ is a single sinusoidal tone having a frequency of 100 kHz. Compare the transmitted spectrum of the 8-PSK signal with that of the 8-PSK AM signal. (*Note:* A qualitative assessment is sufficient.)

## REFERENCES

[9.1] Department of Communications (Canada), "Technical Requirements for Line-of-Sight Radio-Relay Systems Operating in the 7725–8275 MHz Band," SRSP-306, Issue 2, June 1976, Telecommunication Regulatory Service, Ottawa.

[9.2] Federal Communications Commission, "Establishment of Policies and Procedures for the Use of Digital Modulation Techniques in Microwave Radio and Proposed Amendments to Parts 2 and 21," FCC 74-985, Docket No. 19311, Washington, D.C., September, 1974.

[9.3] Mertel, H. K., "International and National Radio Frequency Interference Regulations," *Multi-Volume EMC Encyclopedia*, Vol. 1, Don White Consultants, Inc., Gainesville, VA, 1978.

[9.4] Bennet, W. R., J. R. Davey, *Data Transmission*, McGraw-Hill Book Company, New York, 1965.

[9.5] Brody, G., "Considerations in the Development of a State-of-the-Art 3 b/s/Hz, 90 Mb/s Digital Microwave System." Course notes, presented at the Digital Communications and Signal Processing short course, University of Ottawa, Ottawa, December, 1978.

[9.6] Feher, K., R. Goulet, S. Morissette, "Order Wire Transmission in Digital Micro-Wave Systems," Trans. Communications, May, 1974.

[9.7] Morais, D. H., K. Feher, "A Survey of North American 2 GHz Digital Radio Systems," Proc. Intelcom-77, Horizon House, October, 1977.

[9.8] Feher, K., *Digital Modulation Techniques in an Interference Environment*, *EMC Encyclopedia*, Vol. 9, Don White Consultants, Inc., Gainesville, VA, 1977.

[9.9] El-Torky, M., K. Feher, "Design of Bandlimiting Filters for QPSK Radio Systems in an Interference Environment," Proc. IEEE International Conference on Communications, ICC-78, Toronto, June, 1978.

[9.10] CCITT, "Principles of a Method for the Measurement of Signal Phase Jitter." International Telephone and Telegraph Consultative Committee (CCITT), Com XV-No.: 119-E, Question 11/XV, Contribution No. 119, Geneva, January, 1978.

[9.11] CCIR, "Bit Error Performance Measurements for Digital Radio Relay Systems." Report 613, XIIIth Plenary Assembly, Vol. 9, Geneva, 1974.

[9.12] CCIR, "Radio Relay Systems for Television and Telephony: Radio-Frequency Channel Arrangements for Analogue Systems with a Capacity of 600 to 1800 Telephone Channels, or the Equivalent, or Low- and Medium-Capacity Digital Systems of Equivalent Bandwidth, Operating in the 11 GHz Band." Recommendation 387-2, XIIth Plenary Assembly, Vol. 9, Geneva, 1974.

[9.13] CCIR, "Service Channels for Radio-Relay Systems: Types of Service Channel to be Provided." Recommendation 400-2, XIIth Plenary Assembly, Vol. 9, Geneva, 1974.

[9.14] CCIR, "Digital Radio-Relay Systems: Use of Frequencies Above About 12 GHz. Channel Arrangements for the Band 17.7–19.7 GHz." XIIth Plenary Assembly, Vol. 9, Geneva, 1974.

[9.15] Federal Communications Commission, "Establishment of Policies and Procedures for Consideration of Applications to Provide Specialized Common Carrier Services in the Domestic Point-to-Point Microwave Radio Service and Proposed Amendments of Parts 2 and 21 of the Commission's Rules," FCC 74-657, Docket No. 18920, Washington, D.C., July, 1974.

[9.16] Giusto, P. P., "Level Division Multiplexing of Service Channels in Multilevel Digital Transmissions," IEEE Trans. on Communications, Special Issue on Digital Radio, December, 1979.

[9.17] Mertel, H. K., "International and National Radio Frequency Interference Regulations," *EMC Encyclopedia*, Vol. 1, Don White Consultants, Inc,, Gaithersburg, MD., 1978.

[9.18] Morais, D. H., K. Feher, "MSK and QPSK Modulation in Line-of-Sight Digital Radio Systems," Proc. IEEE International Communications Conference, ICC-77, Chicago, June, 1977.

[9.19] Feher, K., G. S. Takhar, "A New Symbol Timing Recovery Technique for Burst Modem Applications," IEEE Trans. Communications, January, 1978.

[9.20] Glave, F. E., L. B. Dunn, "Dataroute Transmissions Systems Growth and Extensions," Proc. IEEE International Conference on Communications, ICC-74, Minneapolis, June, 1974.

[9.21] Balkovic, M. D., et al.: "1967–70 Connection Survey—High Speed Voiceband Data Transmission Performance on the Switched Telecommunication Network," B.S.T.J., Vol. 50, April, 1971.

[9.22] Mukasa, P., "Synchronization," M.A.Sc. Thesis, Department of Electrical Engineering, University of Ottawa, Ottawa, April, 1978.

[9.23] Spilker, J. J., *Digital Communications by Satellite*, Prentice-Hall, Inc., Englewood Cliffs, N.J., 1977.

[9.24] Taub, H., D. L. Schilling, *Principles of Communications Systems*, McGraw-Hill Book Company, New York, 1971.

[9.25] Technical Staff, American Telephone and Telegraph Company, Bell Telephone Companies and Bell Telephone Laboratories, *Telecommunications Transmission Engineering*, Bell System for Technical Education, Winston-Salem, N.C., 1977.

# 10

# DIVERSITY AND PROTECTION SWITCHING TECHNIQUES

In the previous chapters, we studied the performance of unprotected single-channel radio systems. The reliability objectives of digital microwave systems is presented in Chapter 5, where it is pointed out that multi-path fading might have a major impact on the availability of radio systems.

A practical example of operational availability is presented in the specification of the Trans-Canada Telephone System (TCTS) [10.1 and 10.4]. It is a 6560 km, two-way, backbone microwave network. This network has an availability of 99.98 %.

The *main contributions to the unavailability* of a network are categorized as follows:

1) Those controllable by equipment and route design (fading).
2) Those caused by operational activities (maintenance, system expansion, etc.).
3) Catastrophies (fires, antenna/feeder system failures).

About 20 % of operational unavailability is apportioned to type (1).

For the two-way, 6560 km, TCTS, radio reference system, one-half of its outage is attributed to equipment failures (0.01 %) and the other half to propagation outage (0.01 %). Thus, the design availability objective, then, is 99.98 %.

To meet these stringent availability objectives most digital microwave systems have incorporated into them protection channels and automatic switching systems. In this chapter we describe the principles of operation of the best-known protection switching systems. These systems have been successfully used to provide excellent $P(e)$ performance and also to minimize loss of service resulting from fading or equipment failure. The systems of interest to us here are the frequency diversity, space diversity, and hot-standby systems.

## 10.1 SPACE AND FREQUENCY DIVERSITY SYSTEMS

The effect of fading on operational unavailability can be minimized by space or frequency diversity techniques, as illustrated in Fig. 10.1. Both of these techniques are based on the hypothesis that simultaneous fading on both radio transmission paths is unlikely.

In a frequency diversity configuration the same digital information is fed into two transmitters, Tx1 and Tx2. A wide radio-frequency separation of these transmitters ensures less correlation between the fades of the individual radiowaves; thus, better system performance is realized.

In the space diversity system the same radio frequency band is used for the transmission of the digital information. Diversity results from separating the two receiver antennas vertically. This ensures that the received radio waves travel through different transmission paths; thus, they are not likely to be affected simultaneously by fading.

Frequency diversity systems are used most frequently for the protection and performance improvement of FDM-FM microwave systems [10.7, 10.8, 10.10]. The number of radio channels available for protection purposes has been limited, in the United States, by FCC regulations that were introduced in the early 1970's [10.12].

To conserve RF bandwidth and meet regulatory requirements, space diversity is being used increasingly [10.2]. Space diversity techniques are combined, in some applications, with hot-standby switching to protect against fading and equipment failure. For a number of applications a *combination of space and frequency diversity* systems are employed to improve a system's availability beyond that achieved by only one of these techniques.

Frequency diversity techniques are also used for *M for N* protection switching arrangements, in which *M* protection channels are used to protect *N* information-carrying (working) channels. A typical system availability improvement of a frequency diversity microwave system is shown in Fig. 10.2 [10.13]. In this example of a 6 GHz system, the reduction of system unavailability caused by fading is illustrated. The curve indicating frequency diversity performance has been obtained

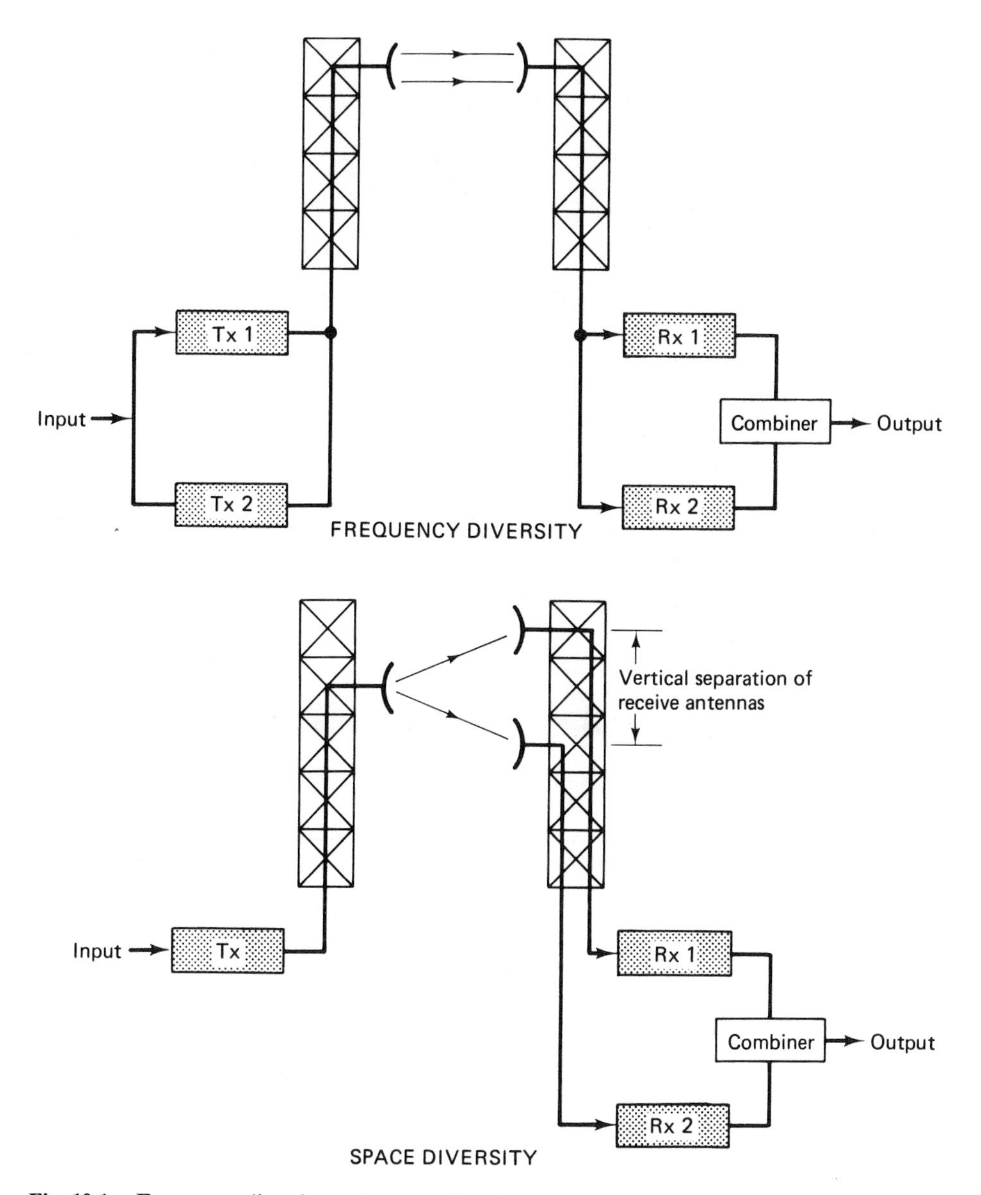


**Fig. 10.1.** Frequency diversity and space diversity accomplish similar ends but use different equipment configurations. (Redrawn by permission from Reference [10.8])

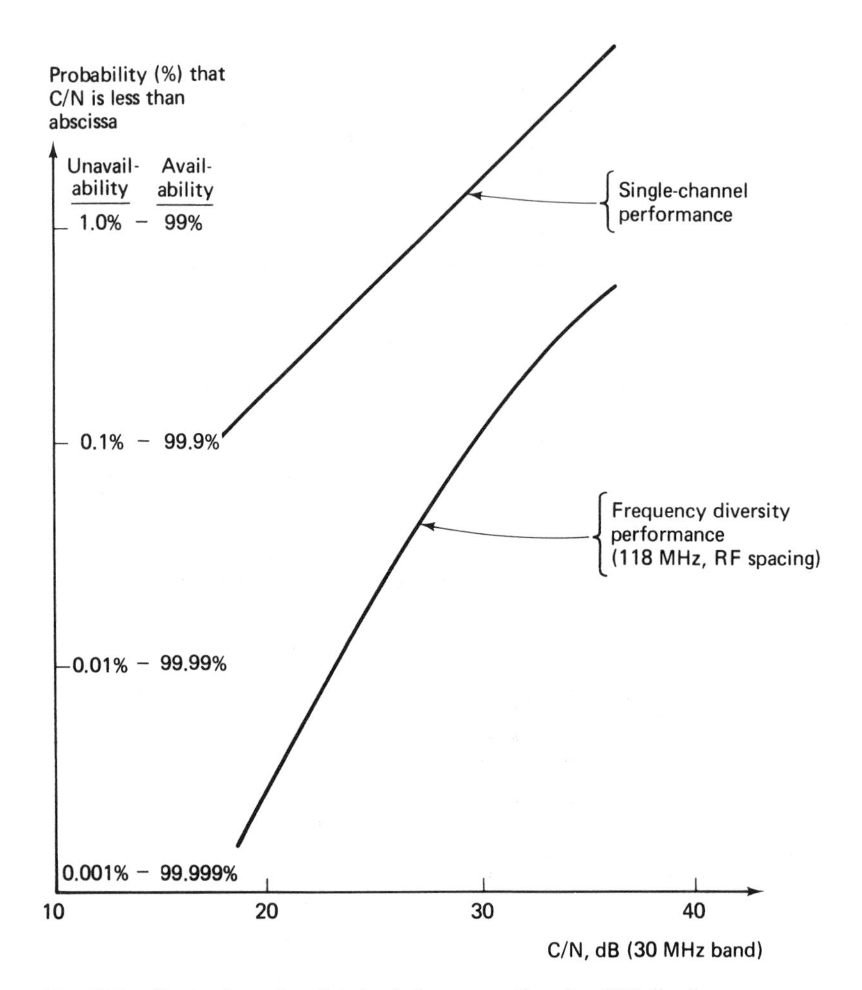


**Fig. 10.2.** Single-channel and 1-for-1 frequency diversity $C/N$ distribution of the Montreal-Toronto, 6 GHz, Canadian National/Canadian Pacific Telecommunications Microwave System.

from the work of Kaylor [10.9], who performed extensive experiments concerning fading statistics on a 4 GHz system. Kaylor's experimental results were extrapolated to the 6 GHz band by assuming that the fading correlation of the 118-MHz-spaced RF frequencies is dependent on the RF channel frequency spacing/RF frequency ratio and not on the absolute value of the difference of the RF frequencies.

Follow carefully the solution of Example 10.1; then **solve Problem 10.1**

**EXAMPLE 10.1.** Assume that for a 6 GHz frequency diversity system, of which the $C/N$ distribution is shown in Fig. 10.2, it is necessary to transmit 90 Mb/s of data. The available 3 dB double-sided RF bandwidth of each of the frequency diversity channels is 30 MHz wide. You wish to decide: (1) which modulation technique should be employed for your radio system; (2) what type of availability would be obtained if you had a single channel system; (3) what is the predicted fading caused unavailability time (in minutes per year) of your single channel system; and (4) what is the unavailability time of your diversity system? *In your calculations assume that the intersymbol interference caused by imperfect channel filters and the effects of selective fading have been canceled by fairly exotic adaptive equalizers in the receiver.* Also assume that the effect of adjacent-channel interference is negligible.

***SOLUTION:*** (1) To transmit 90 Mb/s in the specified 30 MHz bandwidth, a modulation technique having a bandwidth efficiency of at least 3 b/s/Hz is required. Theoretical minimum bandwidth 8-PSK, 8-ary APK, and higher-ary modulation techniques satisfy this requirement (see Chapter 3). In the following, for the 6 GHz radio system example, an 8-PSK coherent-modulation technique is chosen. This modulation scheme has been used successfully in similar radio system designs and is well documented in the literature (see Table 6.3).

(2) The required $C/N$ for a $P(e) = 10^{-6}$ threshold performance is 19 dB. This value is obtained from the 8-PSK curve given in Chapter 3. The $P(e) = 10^{-6}$ threshold performance is specified frequently for time-division multiplexed PCM voice transmission. For single-channel transmission, $C/N = 19$ dB corresponds to a fading-caused unavailability time of 0.1%, that is, the availability time is 99.9%. These values are specified in Fig. 10.2.

(3) The 0.1% unavailability time expressed in *minutes per year* is given by

$$365 \text{ days/year} \times 24 \text{ hr/day} \times 60 \text{ min/hr} \times 0.1\%$$
$$= 525{,}600 \text{ min/year} \times 0.001 = \mathit{525.6\ min/year}$$

(4) For the frequency diversity system, the unavailability time is 0.002%. The value is obtained from Fig. 10.2 for the $C/N = 19$ dB requirement. In minutes per year, the unavailability time is given by:

$$525{,}600 \text{ min/year} \times 0.00002 = \mathit{10.512\ min/year}$$

In this practical example the frequency diversity system has 50 times less fading-caused outage time than the unprotected single-channel system. Also, the outage time due to transmit/receiver bay failures will be reduced several thousand times. ■

Now, do not forget to **solve Problem 10.1.**

The availability improvement offered by space diversity systems is, frequently, equivalent to or better than that of frequency diversity systems. Figure 10.3 shows the required vertical separation of the received space diversity antennas which result in the same improvement as that offered by frequency diversity systems [10.2]. Referring to Example 10.1, if we assume that the carrier separation is 118 MHz (see Fig. 10.2), then the availability for a $C/N = 19$ dB is 99.998%. In a single-channel unprotected system this availability is only 99.9%. The $C/N = 19$ dB requirement was obtained in Example 10.1 for an 8-PSK radio system. (For other system modulation techniques the $C/N$ ratio required to meet the minimum quality objective of $P(e) = 10^{-6}$ should be generated in accordance with the type of modulation used). It is possible to achieve the calculated availability by replacing the frequency diversity system with a space diversity system as follows.

Assuming antennas of equal size in both system configurations, a vertical

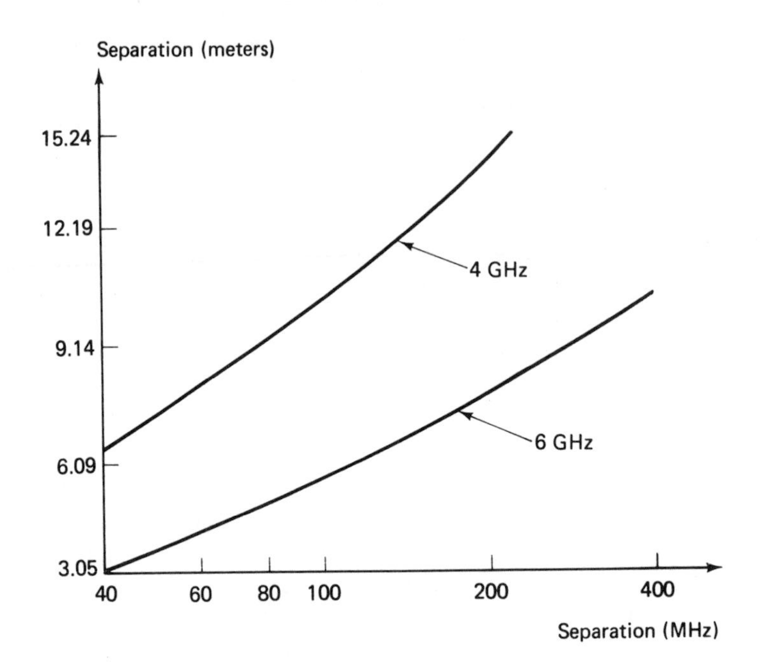


**Fig. 10.3.** Separation in 1-for-1 space and frequency diversity systems providing equal availability time-improvement factors. Equal size antennas have been assumed. (Redrawn with permission from the *Bell System Technical Journal*, copyright 1975, The American Telephone and Telegraph Company)

separation of only 6 m is sufficient (see Fig. 10.3) to produce the aforementioned availability. For most operating systems a larger vertical separation is used. This implies that the corresponding space diversity system has a higher availability. Detailed guidelines, to assist in the calculation of the improvement factor offered by space and frequency diversity systems, can be found in references [10.2 and 10.14]. **Solve Problem 10.2.**

## 10.2 PROTECTION SWITCHING AND HOT-STANDBY ARRANGEMENTS

Analog as well as digital microwave protection switching systems, which are designed to protect against atmospheric fading, may operate within regulatory constraints, as is the case with frequency diversity systems. With the amended FCC rulings, common-carrier operators in the United States may have one protection channel in each of the 4 and 6 GHz bands. This protection channel may be assigned only if there are at least three traffic-carrying, working channels. [10.10 and 10.12].

In Fig. 10.4 the block diagram of a typical 2-for-5 frequency diversity protection switching system is illustrated. Under normal propagation conditions, the five

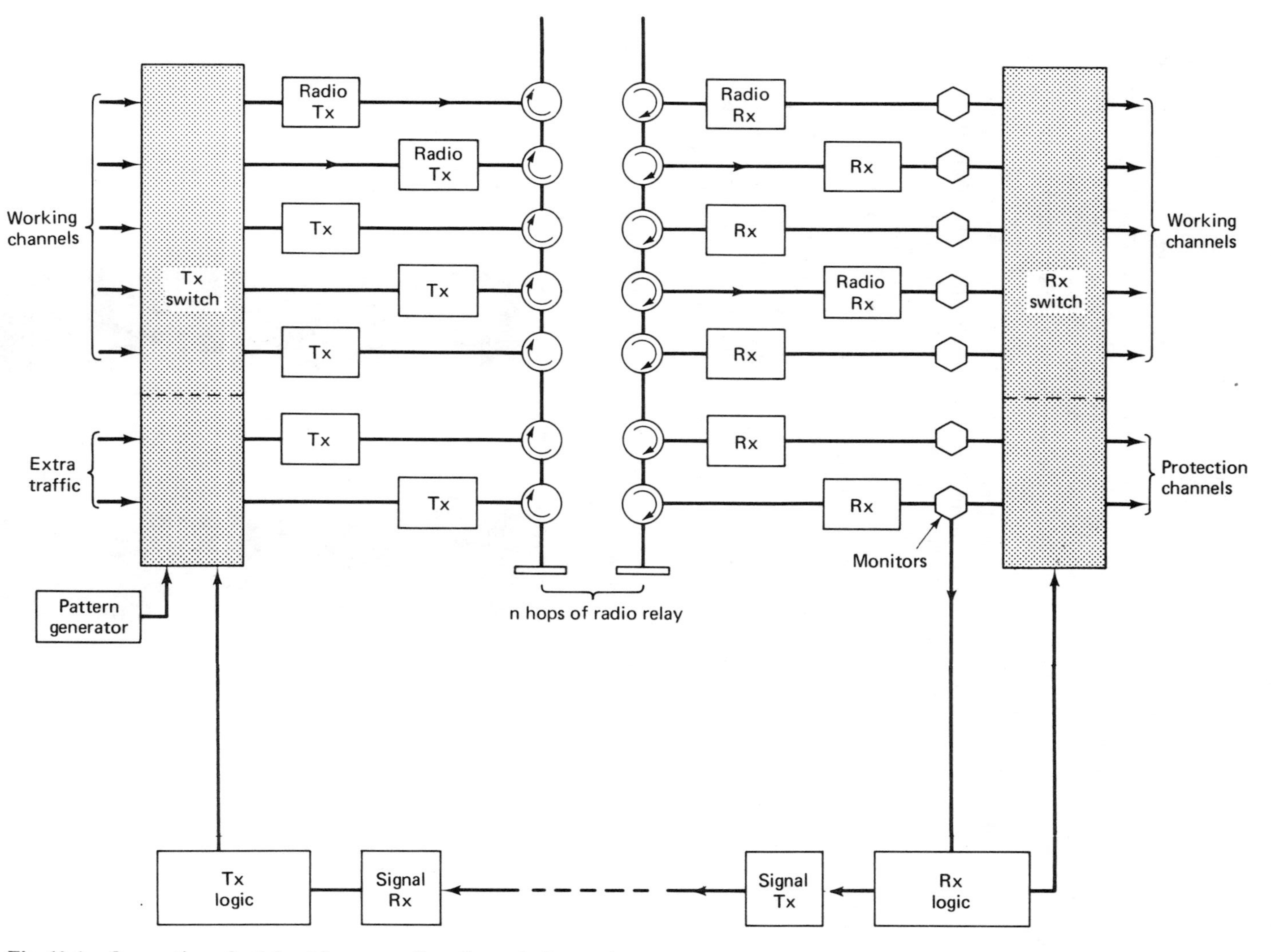


**Fig. 10.4.** One section of a 2-for-5 frequency diversity protection system.

working channels are connected through the switching elements. The two protection channels may carry extra customer traffic or may carry only a digital test pattern. The monitors at the receive end, located prior to the receive switch, monitor the performance of the working channels and of the protection channels. For this purpose, on-line pseudo-error monitors, for which the principle of operation is described in Chapter 11, could be used as they are reliable as well as fast in-service monitors. Once the $P(e)$ of one of the working channels is degraded to a preset threshold performance (e.g., to $P(e) = 10^{-6}$), the pseudo-monitor provides an alarm to the receive logic. This logic sends a signal to the transmit logic which, in turn, switches the traffic to one of the protection channels. This channel operates at a different RF frequency. Traffic is switched back to the working channel, once it recovers. The protection switching operations must be fast, so as to react to multi-path fading and minimize interruption of service when maintenance operations are performed on the system. **(Solve Problem 10.3.)**

Protection switching equipment which provides one spare channel for up to 11 working channels (1-for-11) is illustrated in Fig. 10.5.

Hot-standby systems have a fully redundant systems configuration, both in the transmitter and receiver. The hot-standby system, shown in Fig. 10.6, is often implemented in a space diversity configuration. If an equipment or signal failure

**Fig. 10.5.** 1-for-11 protection switching equipment. (Courtesy of Northern Telecom Canada Limited)

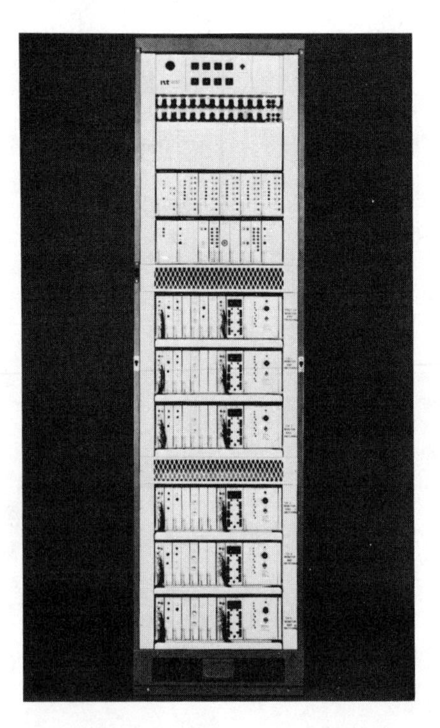

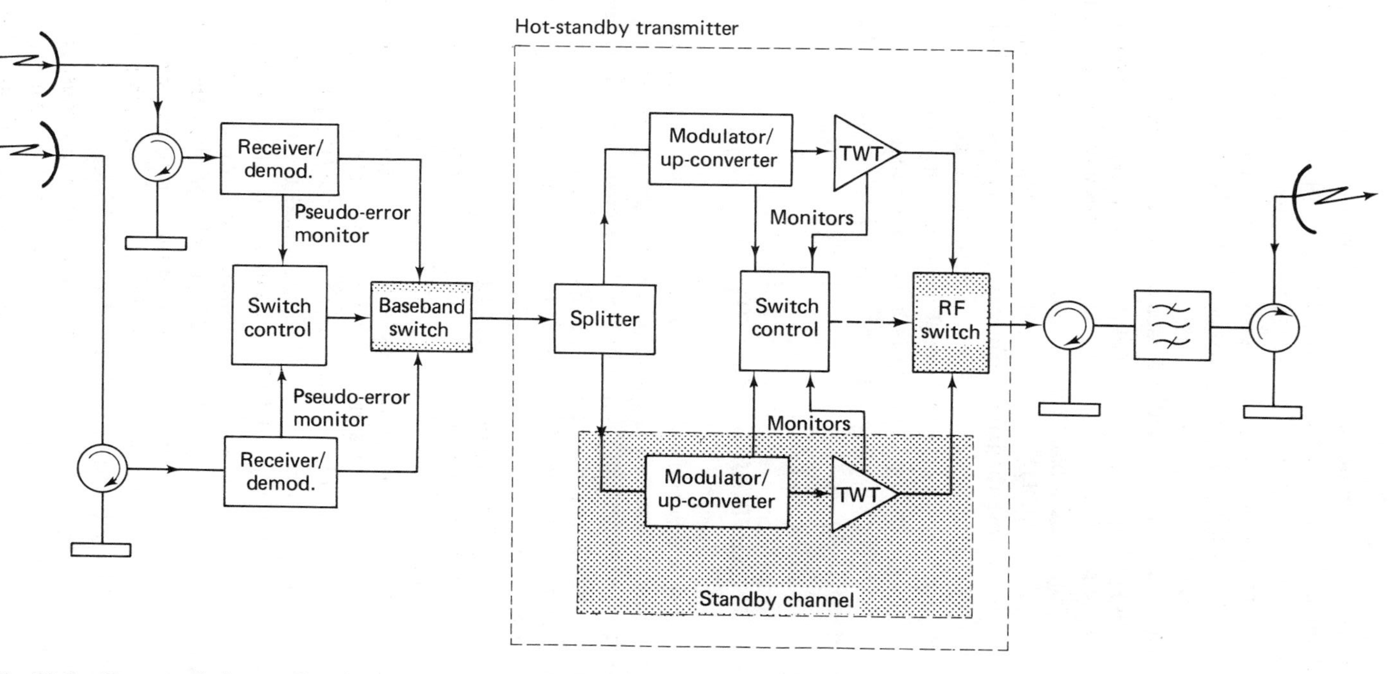


Fig. 10.6. Hot-standby/space diversity (HS/SD) configuration of a digital radio repeater.

is detected in the transmitter, the transmit RF switch connects the standby channel to the antenna. Most frequently, this type of switching introduces an *error burst* into the digital data stream. However, as these types of switchovers are infrequent in most systems applications, the resulting $P(e)$ degradation is tolerable. At the receive end, the switching is performed at baseband on the regenerated binary data streams. This switching is *hitless*.

Thus far, we have observed that space diversity configurations are preferred over frequency diversity systems because of the spectral conservation constraints imposed by the regulatory agencies. In the description of Fig. 10.3, it is pointed out that in the 4 and 6 GHz band (and also in other RF bands) space diversity is the preferred arrangement. Unfortunately, the space diversity hot-standby configuration has a higher cost than the frequency diversity system [10.4]. For example, two RF channels of a hot-standby space diversity configuration require four transceivers per hop, whereas a 1-for-2 frequency diversity system requires only three transceivers per hop. This cost differential becomes even more significant when the protection plans for a larger number of RF channel systems are computed. **(Solve Problem 10.4.)**

## 10.3 SWITCHING AND COMBINING TECHNIQUES

In the 1-for-1 diversity and $M$-for-$N$ protection switching configurations, the signal selection at the receive end is based on the on-line performance of the received signal. The signal selection (switching) or the signal combining functions can be performed at RF, IF, or in baseband. Most digital microwave systems use baseband switching. This is a logical choice, as it is much easier to design a hitless digital baseband switch than a hitless IF or RF switching device.

From an equipment reliability point of view, post-detection switching is preferred. In this case, the receive switch is the last element in the protected radio system. To further improve overall system reliability, redundant switching configurations are used for many applications. A large number of switching and combining techniques (mostly used in analog systems) have been described in considerable detail in the literature and, in particular, in reference [10.7]. **(Solve Problem 10.5.)**

An interesting IF combiner has been reported by Bell-Northern Research in reference [10.15]. (See Fig. 10.7.) This combiner is used for their 91 Mb/s RD-3 radio system. In this system the two IF modulated carriers are dynamically delay equalized prior to signal combining. The combiner adds these IF carriers on a voltage basis to improve the carrier-to-noise ratio. In the case of equal $C/N$ ratios on both channels, the combined $C/N$ ratio could be as much as 3 dB higher than that of the individual channels. **(Solve Problem 10.6.)**

When combining modulated IF carriers, extreme care must be taken to ensure that the IF carriers are phase equalized. A small phase error might cause a large $P(e)$ performance degradation. For example, for a QPSK combiner operating at IF or RF, the $P(e)$ is a function of the available $C/N$ and phase error $\beta$. This $P(e)$

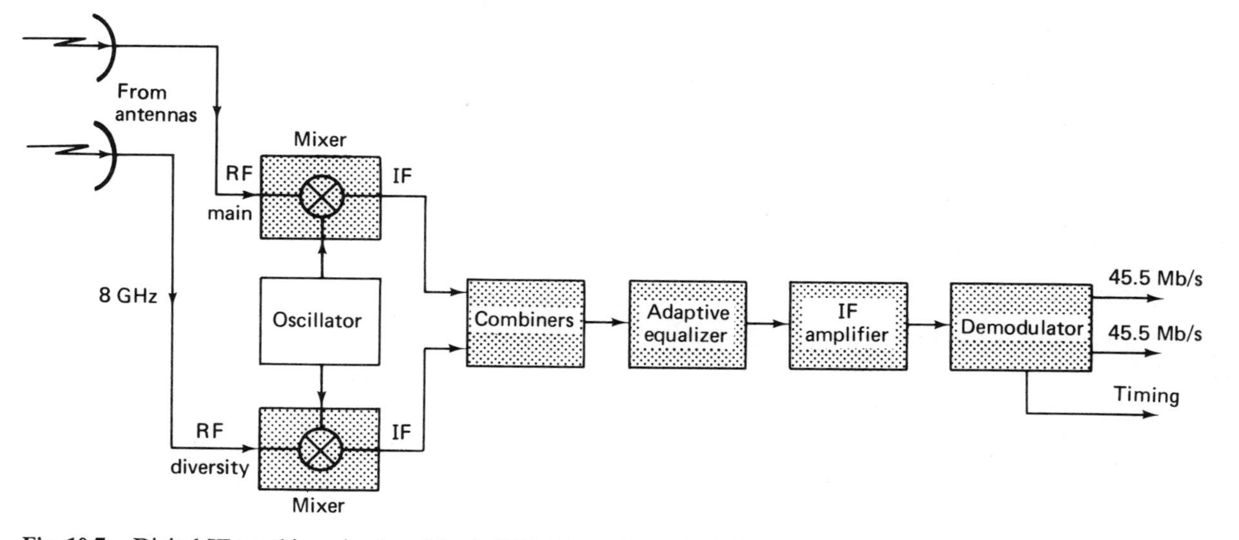


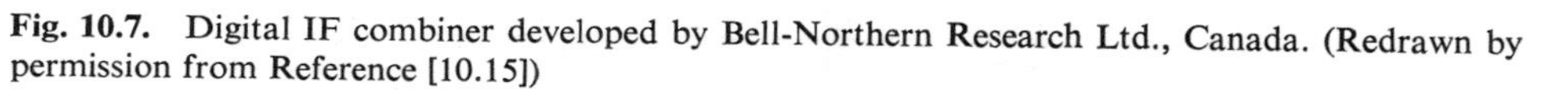
**Fig. 10.7.** Digital IF combiner developed by Bell-Northern Research Ltd., Canada. (Redrawn by permission from Reference [10.15])

is given by:

$$P(e) = \frac{1}{2}\left\{1 - \frac{1}{2}\,\mathrm{erf}\left[A^2T_b\frac{1-\sin 2\beta}{2N_0}\right]^{1/2} - \frac{1}{2}\,\mathrm{erf}\left[A^2T_b\frac{1+\sin 2\beta}{2N_0}\right]^{1/2}\right\} \tag{10.1}$$

where $T_b$ is the unit bit duration, $A$ is the peak amplitude of the carrier wave prior to combining (equal carrier levels have been assumed on both channels), and $N_0$ is the gaussian noise spectral density. In Fig. 10.8 the equivalent $C/N$ degradation, in dB, from the theoretical optimum $P(e) = f(C/N)$ performance is shown for QPSK systems. Higher-ary modulation techniques are even more sensitive to phase errors than the illustrated example of QPSK systems [10.11].

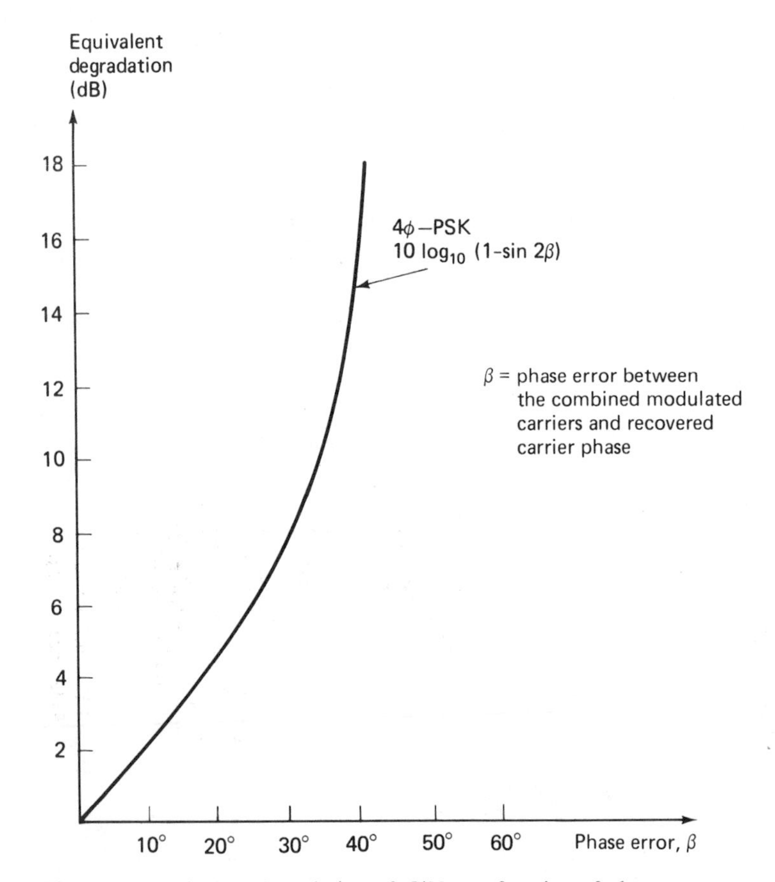


**Fig. 10.8.** Equivalent degradation of $C/N$ as a function of phase error.

**EXAMPLE 10.2.** A 90 Mb/s QPSK system has an IF frequency of $f_c = 140$ MHz. At the receiving end this system employs an IF combiner which linearly adds the received modulated IF carriers. As the in-phase carriers are added on a voltage basis and the rms noise on a power basis (the front-end noise figures of the radio noise sources are independent), the $C/N$ improvement is 3 dB. If, as a result of equipment misalignment, there is a 0.5 ns delay differential between the combined IF paths and the recovered carrier, calculate the degradation caused by this delay differential.

***SOLUTION:*** Assuming perfect alignment, the improvement factor is 3 dB. A 0.5 ns delay corresponds to $360° \times (0.5/7.14) = 25.21°$ phase error of the 140 MHz carrier, having a period of $\frac{1}{140}$ MHz $= 7.14$ ns. From Fig. 10.8, we conclude that this phase error will cause a 5 dB degradation. This example shows that extreme care should be taken in the hardware design in order that the combined modulated carriers are added in phase, and that the carrier recovery introduced phase error is minimized. ■

An interesting *digital baseband combining technique* has been reported in reference [10.5]. The advantage of this combiner is that it does not require as careful a delay equalization as in the case of IF or RF combiner applications. Also, this combiner can be easily modified to perform digital signal combining under equal $C/N$ conditions, and to perform hitless selective switching if the $C/N$ difference on the individual channels exceeds a predetermined threshold level (that is, 5 dB) [10.3]. The block diagram of this baseband combiner is illustrated in Fig. 10.9. Only the in-phase (I) channels of the quadrature demodulators are shown. The combined data output has an improved $P(e)$ performance.

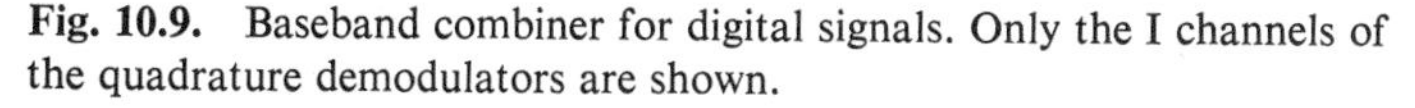
**Fig. 10.9.** Baseband combiner for digital signals. Only the I channels of the quadrature demodulators are shown.

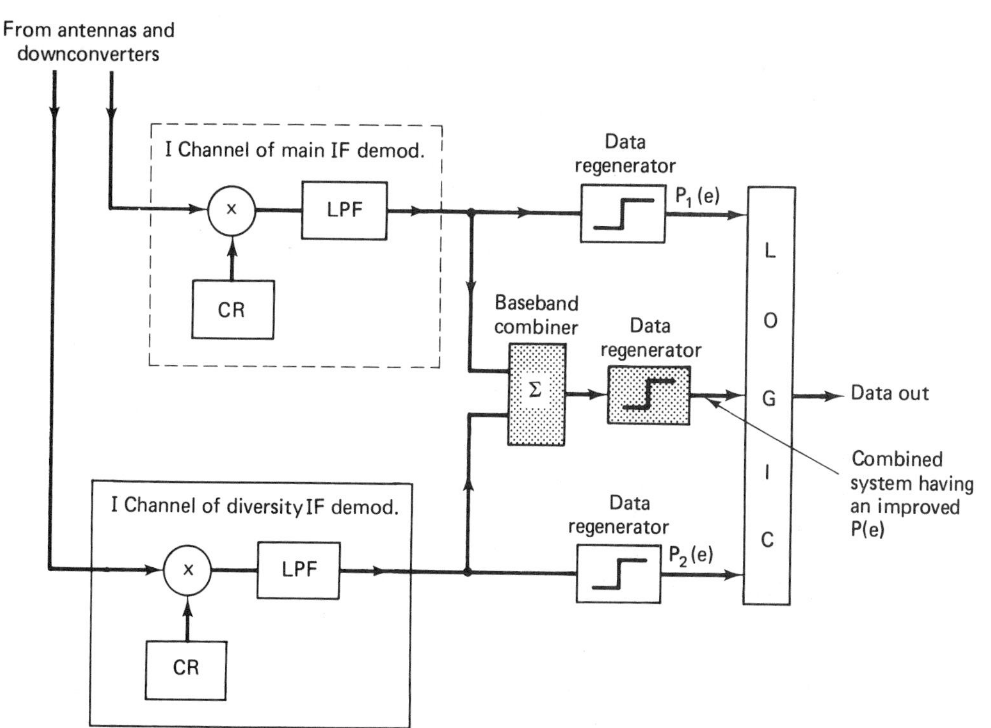

## PROBLEMS

**10.1** A 6 GHz unprotected radio system has 150 min of outage in a year. Assume that this outage is caused by fading. If this system is modified to a 1-for-1 frequency diversity configuration, having a frequency spacing between the RF carriers of 150 MHz, determine the fading-caused outage of this protected system. Assume that the fading curves of Fig. 10.2 are valid for this system calculation.

**10.2** A 4 GHz digital microwave system, using 8-PSK modulation, operates in a 1-for-1 frequency diversity arrangement. The RF carrier separation is 100 MHz. Assume that the same antenna size is used and that it is necessary to modify this system to satisfy regulatory requirements to a 1-for-1 space diversity configuration. Determine the minimal required vertical distance between the antennas operating in a hot-standby configuration. Assume that both configurations offer the same protection against fades. What are the major disadvantages of the space diversity configuration?

**10.3** Draw the block diagram of a 1-for-4 protection switching arrangement. Explain step-by-step the logic functions in one section of this system. Compare a 1-for-4 and a 2-for-5 protection arrangement, and highlight the main differences.

**10.4** Draw the complete block diagram of a one-section hot-standby space diversity system used for the transmission of two RF channels. Compare the equipment required for this system with that of a 1-for-2 frequency diversity system.

**10.5** Assume that a digital baseband switch is used in a protected digital microwave system. To improve the reliability of the overall transmission system, a redundant digital baseband switch is required. Design the block diagram of a redundant baseband switch and describe briefly how you would monitor whether the main or standby switch is functional.

**10.6** On a main channel the carrier-to-noise ratio is assumed to be the same as on the protection channel. This condition prevails for most of the time (99% of the year). Calculate the $C/N$ improvement factor if a linear adder is used as a combiner and if it is assumed that the carriers on individual channels have the same level and are in-phase. Also assume that the additive white gaussian noise sources are independent.

## REFERENCES


[10.1] Roadhouse, R. A., T. G. Fellows, J. L. Spencer, "The Trans-Canada Digital Radio Network," Proc. IEEE International Conference on Communications, ICC-77, Chicago, June, 1977.

[10.2] Vigants, A., "Space-Diversity Engineering," B.S.T.J., January, 1975.

[10.3] Feher, K., R. Y. Goulet, M. Morissette, "Baseband Diversity for Hybrid Microwave Systems," IEEE Trans. Communications, May, 1974.

[10.4] McNicol, J. D., "Diversity and Protection Switching as Applied to Terrestrial Microwave Radio." Report for ELG-7115, Department of Electrical Engineering, University of Ottawa, Ottawa, April, 1978.

[10.5] Feher, K., P. Amlekar, F. Falcao, "Diversity Combiner and Protection Switching Techniques," Proc. Intelcom-79, Dallas, February, 1979.

[10.6] Cowper, R. L., R. Lunnan, "The System Gain Concept Applied to Digital Microwave System Design." Report for EEN-711, Department of Electrical Engineering, Concordia University, Montreal, December, 1977.

[10.7] Schwartz, M., W. R. Bennet, S. Stein, *Communication Systems and Techniques*, McGraw-Hill Book Company, New York, 1966.

[10.8] Lenkurt Demodulator, "Space Diversity," GTE Lenkurt Demodulator, San Carlos, CA, May, 1973.

[10.9] Kaylor, R. L., "A Statistical Study of Selective Fading of Super-High Frequency Radio Signals," B.S.T.J., September, 1953.

[10.10] Technical Staff, American Telephone and Telegraph Company, *Telecommunications Transmission Engineering*, Vol. 2, Bell System Center for Technical Education, Winston-Salem, N.C., 1977.

[10.11] Feher, K., D. Chan, "PSK Combiners for Fading Microwave Channels," IEEE Trans. Communications, May, 1975.

[10.12] Federal Communications Commission, "Rules and Regulations," Part 2, August, 1969, as Amended by Docket 18920, Federal Communications Commission, Washington D.C., 1970.

[10.13] Feher, K., "Digital/Analog Hybrid Microwave Transmission Study," Ph.D. Thesis, Université de Sherbrooke, Sherbrooke, Canada, 1974.

[10.14] CCIR, "Diversity Techniques for Radio-Relay Systems." Report 376-2 (Question 13-1/9), *Green Book*, Vol. 9, International Telecommunications Union, Geneva, 1975.

[10.15] Chow, Q., B. Godfrey, D. Shimozawa, "Implementing the DRS-8 Concept," Telesis/A Bell-Northern Research Ltd. Publication, December, 1977, Ottawa.

# 11

# MEASUREMENT TECHNIQUES

Measurements, whether performed in a research laboratory, on the manufacturing floor of a factory, or on an installed digital radio system are one of the most important tasks of the digital transmission engineer. Measurements are performed on simple building blocks such as prototype breadboards, but they may also be of extreme importance in more sophisticated systems, as in the case of the continuous performance monitoring of complex long-haul traffic-carrying systems. Space limitations does not permit us to describe, in depth, all the measurement methods and techniques which are currently in use. However, we shall describe some of the most important digital performance-measurement techniques. We shall also present *original concepts and techniques* of on-line (in-service) $P(e)$ and jitter-monitor measurements. We assume that the reader of this chapter has some familiarity with the conventional measurement techniques used in analog communications systems [11.5, 11.7].

Unfortunately, many practicing engineers and students in the digital transmission field do not take the time and effort to carefully study the capabilities and limitations of their instrumentation; as a result serious measurement errors occur frequently. (To confess, I lost the equivalent of about two weeks of valuable time on a rush project because I did not pay sufficient attention to constraints imposed by my measurement set-up, so I had to repeat all the measurements. Hopefully, my boss won't get too upset now that I have let the cat out of the bag.)

Off-line (out-of-service) laboratory, factory, and field-acceptance testing methods are described in Section 11.1. The on-line (in-service) measurement techniques which are frequently essential for operational systems are presented in Section 11.2.

## 11.1 LABORATORY MEASUREMENT TECHNIQUES AND MEASUREMENTS FOR FACTORY-ACCEPTANCE TESTING

The main building blocks of three digital radio transmitters and receivers are shown in Fig. 11.1. The measured channel has a center frequency $f_0$, while the center frequencies of the adjacent channels are located at $f_0 + \Delta f$ and $f_0 - \Delta f$. All these radio transmitters are driven by independent pseudo-random-binary sequence (PRBS) generators at the rate $f_b$. If the sequence length of these generators is sufficiently long, then they emulate faithfully the random customer traffic. (In a laboratory environment or for factory testing, the transmit and receive antennas are not part of the test set-up.) Various fading conditions that are characteristic of a radio channel, such as interference and front-end-generated additive white gaussian noise (AWGN), are simulated by an external variable-level AWGN and sinusoidal generator which is added into the measurement channel. The effect of the adjacent channel interference and of the co-channel interference (CCI) on the system performance parameters is evaluated by the insertion of variable attenuators into the adjacent channels. **(Solve Problem 11.1.)**

In order to evaluate the effects of unmodulated and modulated CCI signals on $P(e)$ and system jitter, a sinusoidal carrier-wave oscillator is required in the set-up of Fig. 11.1; also required is a radio transmitter having a center frequency which falls within the receiver bandwidth of the desired (measured) channel. The effects of system phase noise [11.9, 11.10, 11.11], as well as the imperfections in the carrier and symbol timing recovery (CR and STR) subsystems on the overall system performance, are extrapolated from the measured results. To obtain these results an unmodulated reference carrier oscillator and an $f_b$-rate reference clock signal are fed directly to the demodulator circuitry. These *back-to-back* measurements are feasible, if the mentioned jitter and noise-free references are available at the receive end. This might be the case during factory-acceptance testing of radio systems. However, in installed systems in the field, where the transmitter might be separated by 30 km or more from its receiver, it could be difficult to generate noise-free reference signals.

The effect of RF amplifier non-linearities, such as AM-to-AM and AM-to-PM conversion and the effect of spectral spreading, on overall $P(e)$ performance is frequently evaluated in a set-up such as shown in Fig. 11.1. For details on classical AM-to-AM, AM-to-PM, phase-noise, and spectral measurement techniques, you are advised to consult references [11.5, 11.7, and 11.8] and application notes issued by Hewlett-Packard and other instrumentation companies. **(Solve Problem 11.2.)**

The PRBS data source and the $P(e)$ detector, shown in Figs. 11.1 and Fig. 11.2, have the following principle of operation: The binary data stream $D_i$ is modulo-2 added in an EXCLUSIVE-OR gate to the $R_i$ bit stream. This bit stream has been obtained from a predetermined combination of the $n$-bit shift register and a set of coefficients $C_i \dots C_n$. These coefficients take on values of 0 or 1. Thus, we see that when the $R_i$ pseudo-random bit stream is added to the incoming data stream $D_i$, a scrambled data stream $S_i$ is obtained. This stream is fed to the digital radio transmitter. The digital receiver regenerates the data and provides it to the descrambler input. The self-synchronizing descrambler, shown in Fig. 11.2, has the same structure as the scrambler; thus, it provides at its output the descrambled data stream $\hat{D}_i$. This data stream is identical to that of the transmitted data stream; that is, $\hat{D}_i = D_i$, assuming that there are no transmission errors. Thus, if $D_i = 0$ (that is, the input of the scrambler is grounded), then the output is identically zero. If, due to noise, interference, or any other cause, an independent transmission error occurs then, at the descrambler output, up to $k + 1$ errors may be counted. Here, $k$ is the number of feedback taps of the $n$-bit maximum-length shift register [11.2 and 11.9]. The error counter must accumulate the errors over a sufficiently long time interval in order to provide a meaningful estimate of the true $P(e)$ [11.1]. The total number of errors accumulated is then divided by $(k + 1)$ times the total number of transmitted bits, and the result is displayed as the system $P(e)$.

The digital communications laboratory of the Electrical Engineering Department of the University of Ottawa is shown in Fig. 11.3. The PRBS generators and $P(e)$ analyzers are essential parts of this laboratory.

As mentioned in previous chapters, in addition to the $P(e)$ specifications, a customer requires a knowledge of the average error-free seconds and error-free intervals. These parameters are obtained by the addition of an event counter and time register to the set-up of Fig. 11.2.

The $P(e)$ and error-free seconds are final system parameters; that is, they frequently do not give an insight into the system hardware problems or gradual system degradations. However, measurements performed on the received eye diagram might provide an insight into the system problem and are helpful for troubleshooting purposes. A simple eye monitor is shown in Fig. 11.4. This monitor provides better resolution than a conventional oscilloscope display of a received eye diagram. The automatic gain control (AGC) amplifier, the demodulator, receive LPF, data regenerator, and the data converter represent a simplified block diagram of a coherent receiver. The AGC amplifier provides a constant IF input level to the demodulator; thus, the baseband signal level is independent of fading or other carrier variations. The $n$-threshold detectors provide logic 1 output states if, in the sampling instants, the received signal plus noise samples exceed their corresponding preset threshold levels. The logic processor, depending on the adopted logic algorithm, provides the information of the peak or of the rms eye opening.

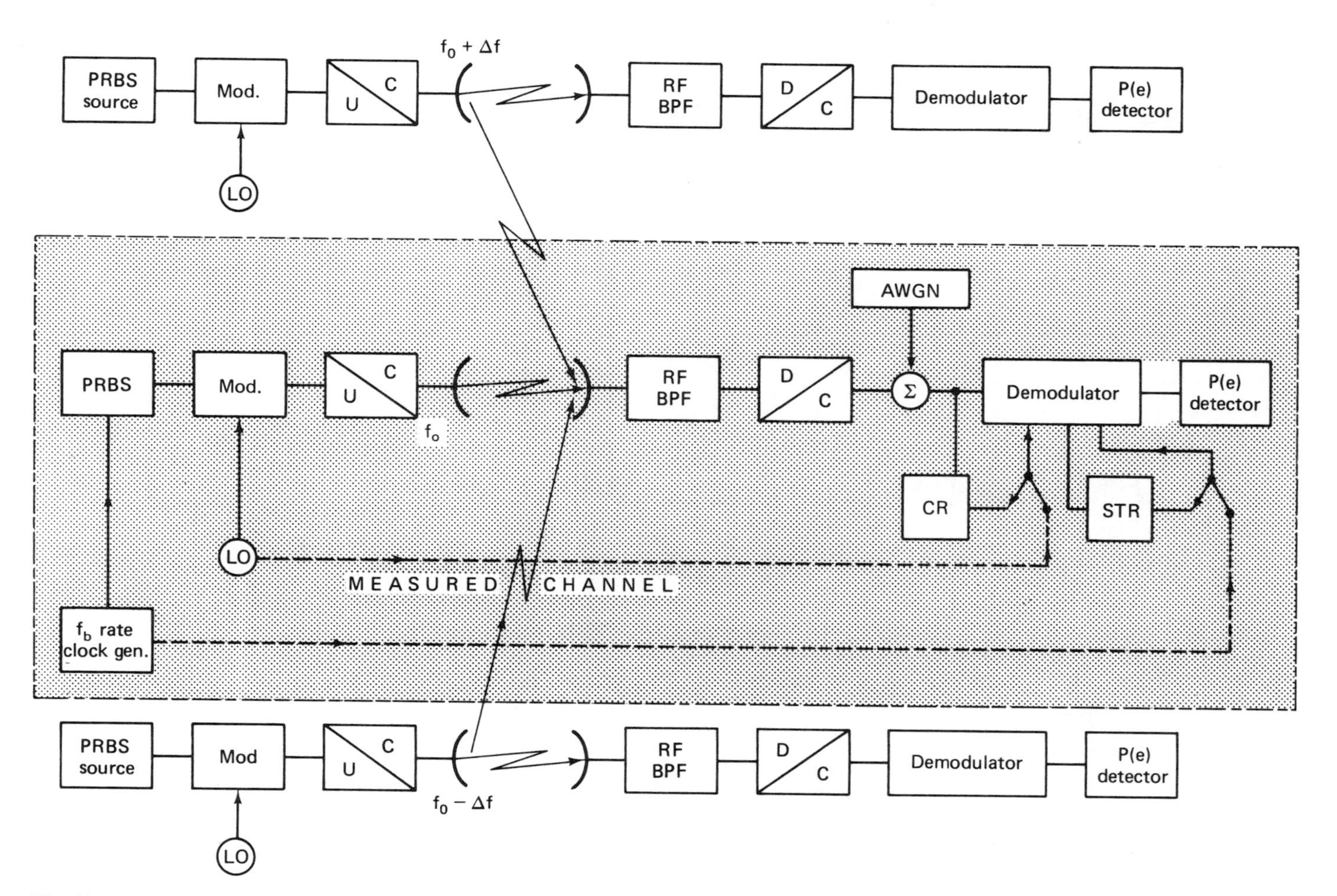


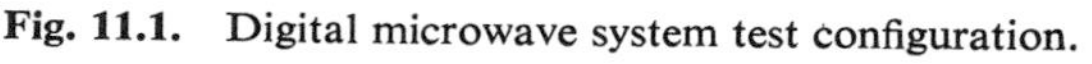

**Fig. 11.1.** Digital microwave system test configuration.

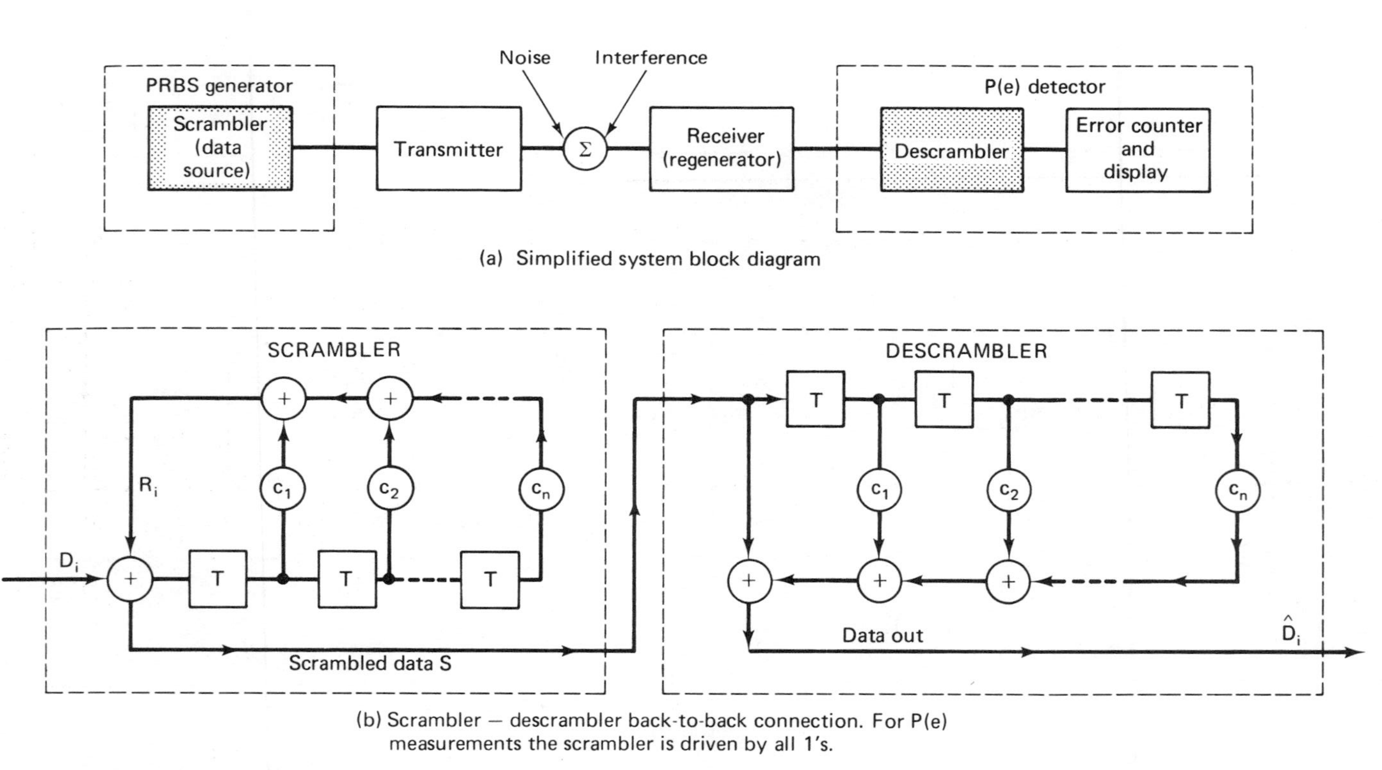


(a) Simplified system block diagram

(b) Scrambler — descrambler back-to-back connection. For P(e) measurements the scrambler is driven by all 1's.

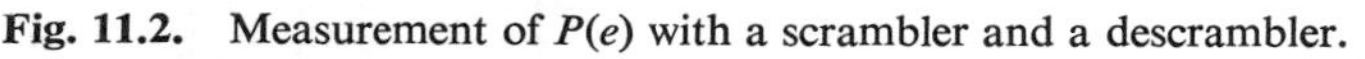

**Fig. 11.2.** Measurement of $P(e)$ with a scrambler and a descrambler.

**Fig. 11.3.** Measurement set-up in the Digital Communications Laboratory of the University of Ottawa. Dr. K. Feher in foreground.

This relatively simple digital eye monitor provides a capability for on line-eye diagram monitoring and automatic display. For diversity or protection switching and system-status monitor purposes, the numerical value contained in the display can be usefully employed. **(Solve Problem 11.4.)**

In most digital radio systems, it is necessary that the radio transmitter be cascaded to the regenerative repeater sections. As is indicated in Chapter 9, the $P(e)$ accumulates from section to section; thus, the overall system $P(e)$ is approximately equal to $nP(e)$, where $n$ is the number of regenerative sections. In a severely band-limited radio system this is true if the total peak-to-peak and rms jitter are within 10 to 20% of the bit duration. A jitter evaluation set-up, for a cascade of digital transmitters and regenerative repeaters, is illustrated in Fig. 11.5. The frequency counter, located at the output of the last receiver, counts the number of zero crossings of the recovered jittery clock. This process is repeated for a number of different positions of the jitter-free clock pulse.

The theory of operation of the jitter measurement set-up, shown in Fig. 11.5, is illustrated in Fig. 11.6. The original description of this set-up was given by Feher, et al. in reference [11.3]. We follow this reference and next describe the test system.

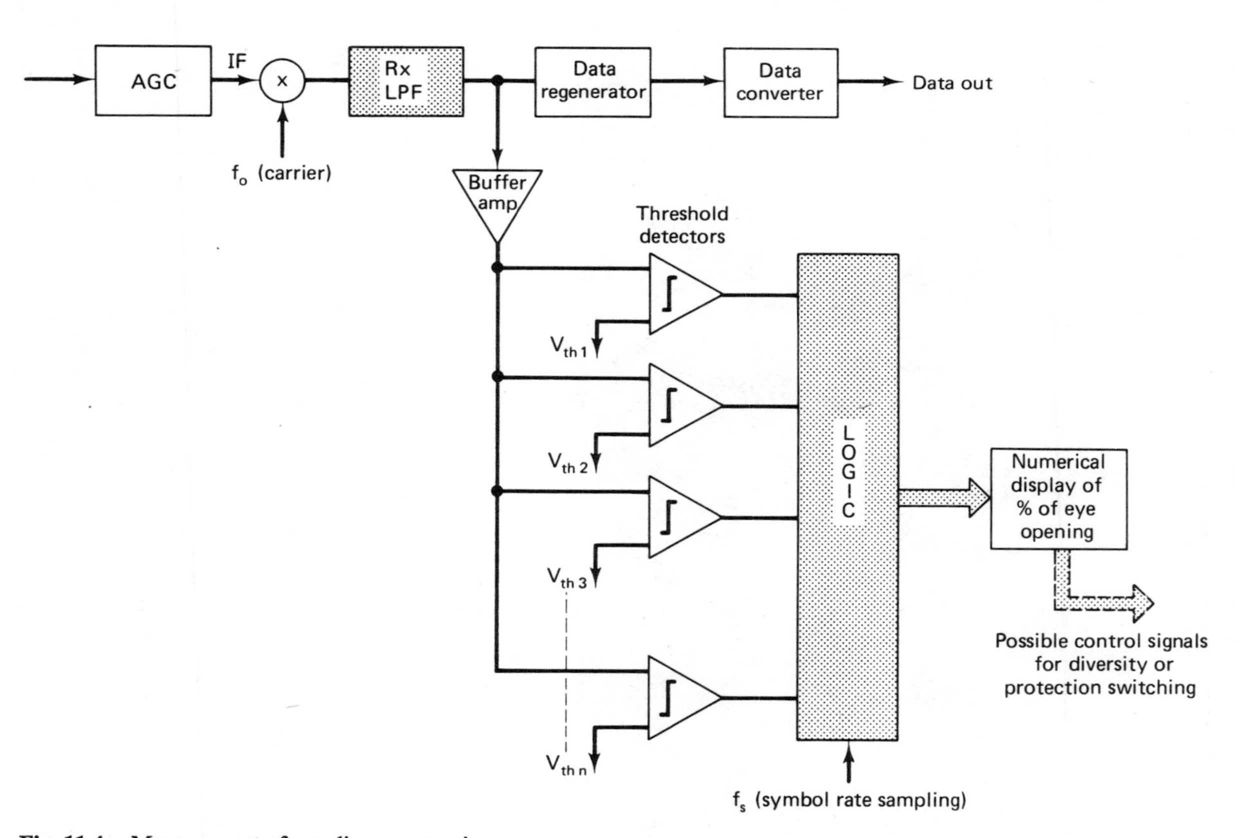


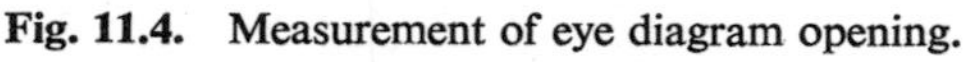

**Fig. 11.4.** Measurement of eye diagram opening.

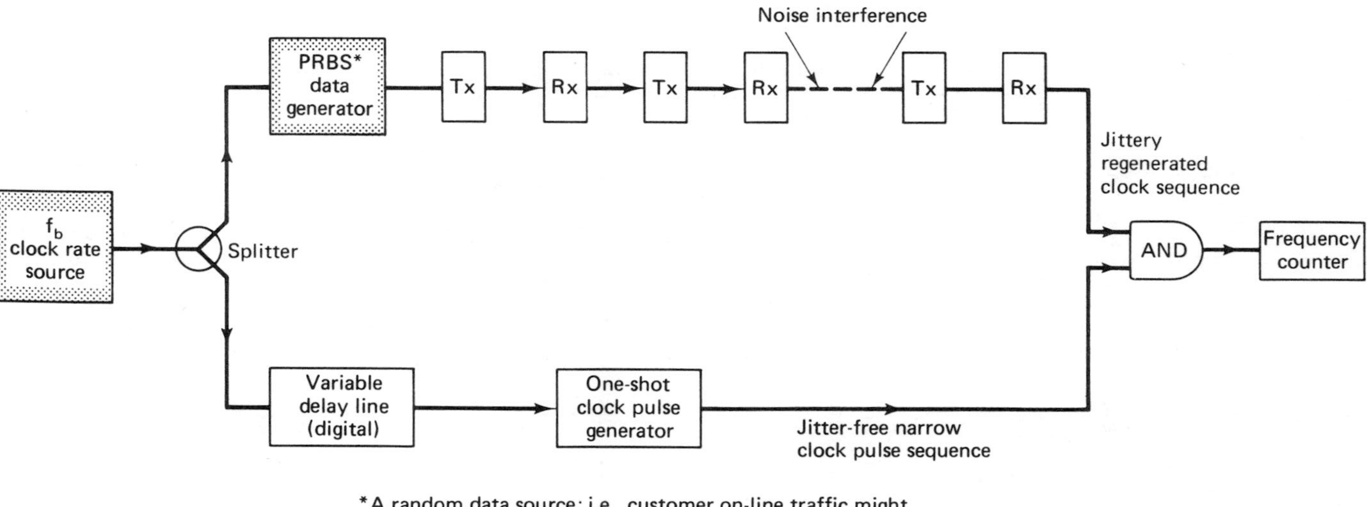


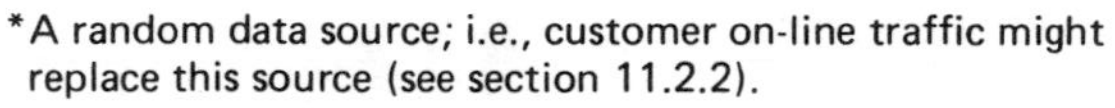
*A random data source; i.e., customer on-line traffic might replace this source (see section 11.2.2).

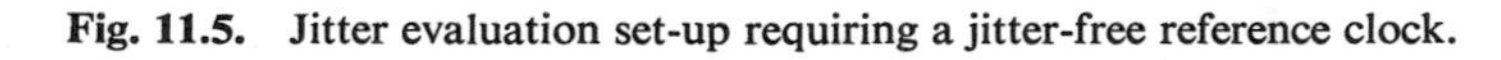
**Fig. 11.5.** Jitter evaluation set-up requiring a jitter-free reference clock.

When the sampling clock pulse is at a position $x_j$, less than $x_0$, then there is no simultaneous high logic input to the AND gate (Fig. 11.5). Thus, for this delay setting there is no response on the frequency counter. On the other hand, when the sampling is set to $x_j$, greater than $x_1$, then the sampling clock and the jittery signal act simultaneously. Thus, for this delay setting the frequency counter counts all clock pulses; that is, it displays the pulse rate.

The peak-to-peak jitter is equal to $(x_1 - x_0)$. This corresponds to the time delay difference of the two time instants in which the frequency counter begins to count, and when it begins to count all clock pulses.

Dividing the accumulated number of zero crossings by the clock rate we obtain $F(x_j)$, the jitter probability distribution function. The jitter probability density function $f(x_j)$ (Fig. 11.6) is obtained from $F(x_j)$ by

$$f(x_j) = \frac{F(x_{j+1}) - F(x_j)}{x_{j+1} - x_j} \tag{11.1}$$

In this equation $x_j$ is the time instant of the corresponding zero crossing. The rms jitter $J_{rms}$ is calculated by

$$J_{rms} = \sqrt{\left[\sum_j (x_j - \bar{x})^2 f(x_j)\right]} \tag{11.2}$$

where $\bar{x}$, in equation (11.2), is given by

$$\bar{x} = \sum_j x_j f(x_j) \tag{11.3}$$

In the method described it was shown how to measure and compute, with the aid of a simple improvised set-up, the peak-to-peak jitter, probability distribution and density functions of the jittery signal, and the rms jitter. This method applies to a large class of randomly varying signals and is particularly useful since, for the commonly used bit rates in digital radio systems, there are no commercially available jitter-measuring test-instruments. **(Solve Problem 11.5.)**

The only drawback of this method is that it requires a jitter-free clock reference at the receiver end. An original way to avoid this difficulty is explained in the next section.

## 11.2 ON-LINE (IN-SERVICE) *P*(*e*) AND JITTER MEASUREMENTS FOR OPERATIONAL SYSTEMS

### *11.2.1 On-Line Pseudo-Error Measurement Techniques*

The characteristics of several on-line (in-service) $P(e)$ measurement techniques, such as test sequence interleaving, parity check coding, code voilation detection, and pseudo-error detection, have been summarized in [11.2]. The most powerful in-service $P(e)$ measurement technique is the pseudo-error monitor technique. We now review the $P(e)$ measurement method for out-of-service systems, and describe the theory of operation for pseudo-error detectors and their applications for in-

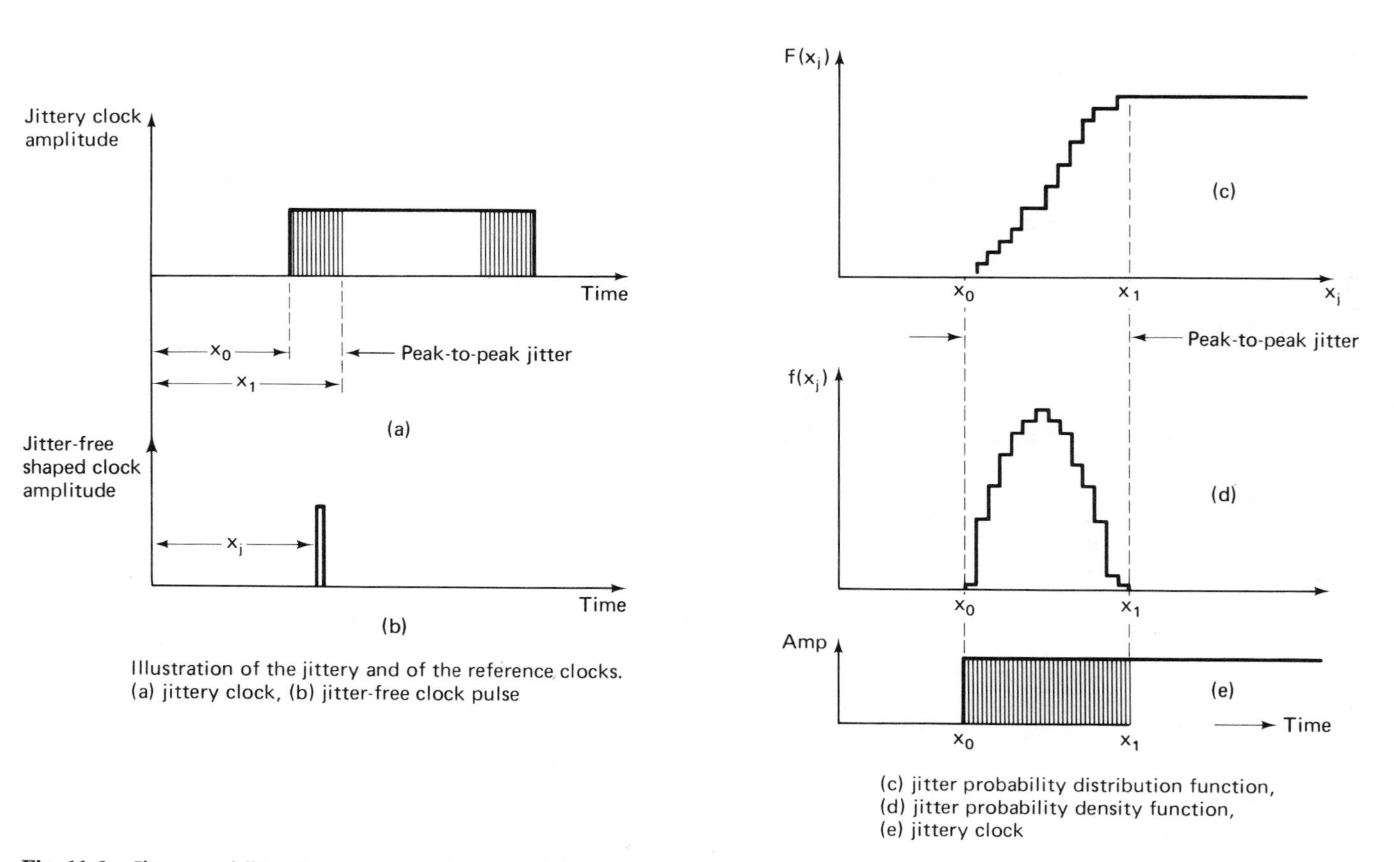


Illustration of the jittery and of the reference clocks.
(a) jittery clock, (b) jitter-free clock pulse

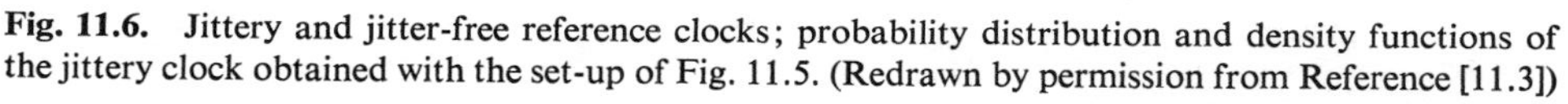
(c) jitter probability distribution function,
(d) jitter probability density function,
(e) jittery clock

**Fig. 11.6.** Jittery and jitter-free reference clocks; probability distribution and density functions of the jittery clock obtained with the set-up of Fig. 11.5. (Redrawn by permission from Reference [11.3])

service performance monitoring of digital radio systems. This description is based on the material provided in reference [11.1].

The $P(e)$ evaluation of a non-operational (out-of-service) digital radio system is done with a predetermined, known, pseudo-random test pattern which is transmitted through a radio channel. The receiver test instrument computes the $P(e)$ by comparing the received bits with a stored replica of the transmitted bit pattern. The main drawback associated with this simple measurement technique is that it is not feasible for evaluating performance of an operating in-service system carrying the *unknown* data stream of the customer. The revenue-carrying traffic has to be interrupted in order to perform system tests. The required measurement duration might also be excessively long. For example, in order to evaluate a $P(e) = 10^{-9}$ for a 10 Mb/s data stream and assuming that, for a meaningful statistical estimate, at least 10 bit errors have to be counted [11.12], the measurement has to last for nearly 20 minutes. This is not practical for time-variable fading radio channels where the on-line measurement result of the $P(e)$ serves as the main control signal of the protection switching equipment.

In order to speed up the evaluation time, pseudo-error detectors use a secondary data path in addition to the main data path. The implementation of a pseudo-error detector in the demodulator circuit of a 40 Mb/s QPSK demodulator, shown in Fig. 11.7, illustrates here the theory of operation of pseudo-error detection circuitry. The in-phase channel ($I$ channel) and the quadrature channel ($Q$ channel) demodulators feed $f_s = 20$ M Baud-rate binary symbols to their corresponding data regenerator outputs. In this example it is assumed that the filtering at the receive end is performed exclusively by means of post-demodulation low-pass filters, such as described in Chapter 3. For the 40 Mb/s (20 M Baud) data rate, the minimum bandwidth $LPF_1$ has a 10 MHz bandwidth. If the $S/N$ ratio at the data regenerator input is 15 dB, then the error rate of the data path is $P(e) = 10^{-8}$. In the secondary data path, a buffer is inserted to avoid any loading of the main data path. This buffer is followed by a low-pass filter, $LPF_P$, which is designed to have a noise bandwidth twice as large as the bandwidth of $LPF_1$. The demodulated signal power at the output of LPF and $LPF_P$ is approximately equal. These signal powers are equal to within 0.6 dB if both filters and the buffer amplifier have the same insertion loss. Assuming that additive white gaussian noise is the only cause of the error-generating mechanism, then the noise power at the output of the $LPF_P$ filter will be 3 dB higher than at the output of $LPF_1$. (This is so because the AWGN has a constant-noise spectral density and the total noise power is directly related to the filter bandwidth.) Thus, in this case the $(S/N)_P$ ratio in the pseudo-error path equals 15 dB $-$ 3 dB $=$ 12 dB. This $S/N_P$ ratio corresponds to a probability of error of approximately $P_{P(e)} = 10^{-5}$ (see Chapter 3).

In an operational system $(S/N)$, $(S/N)_P$, $P(e)$, and the $P_P(e)$ are unknown quantities. However, the *ingenious idea* of the *pseudo-detection* circuitry of using an EXCLUSIVE-OR gate, by means of a simple cancellation "trick," provides a number which is directly proportional to the unknown $P(e)$ of the on-line system. Let us now see what it is all about.

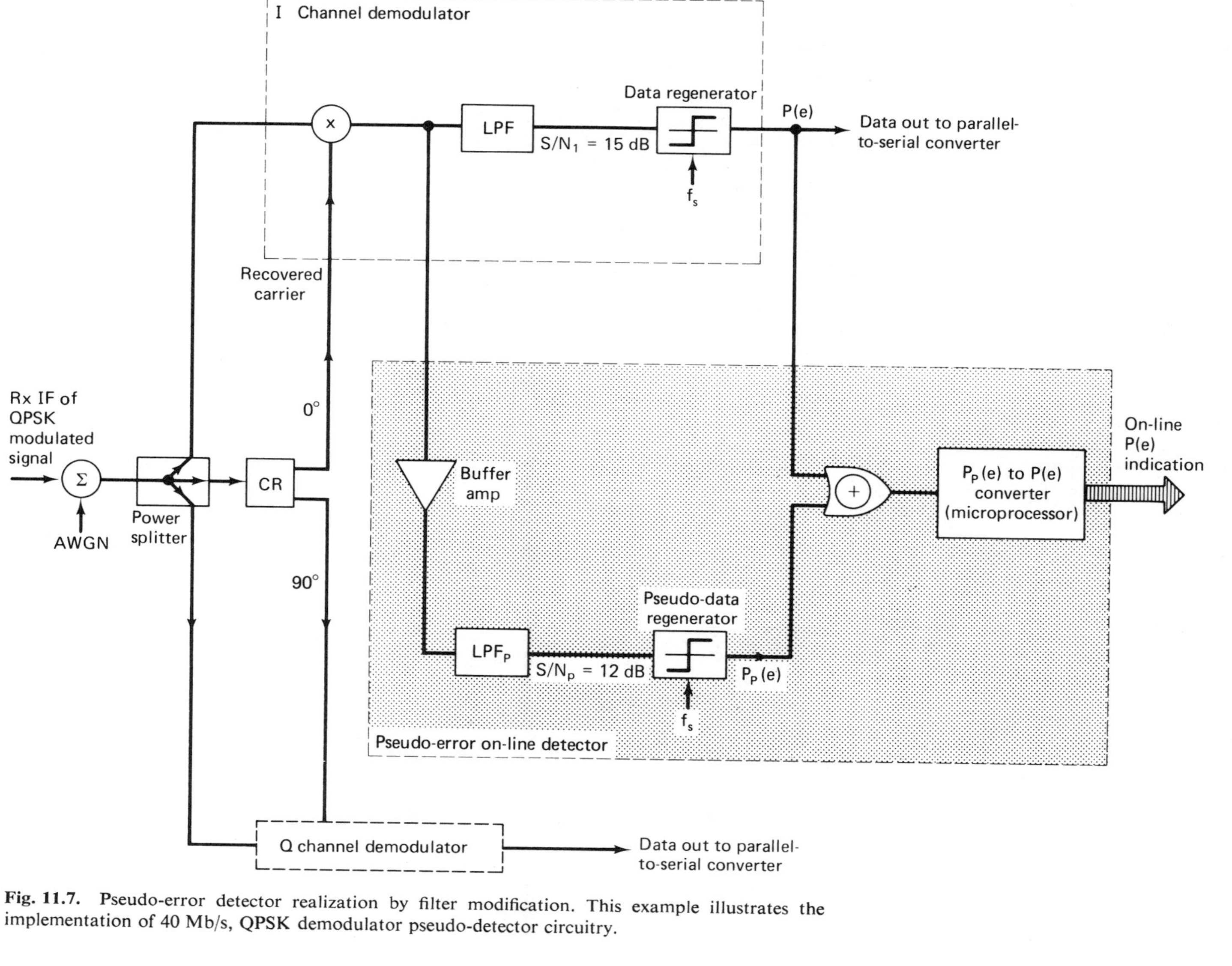


**Fig. 11.7.** Pseudo-error detector realization by filter modification. This example illustrates the implementation of 40 Mb/s, QPSK demodulator pseudo-detector circuitry.

The EXCLUSIVE-OR (Ex-OR) gate has the following truth table.

| Input 1 | Input 2 | Output |
|---|---|---|
| 0 | 0 | 0 |
| 0 | 1 | 1 |
| 1 | 0 | 1 |
| 1 | 1 | 0 |

If the $P(e)$ and the $P_P(e)$ are both zero ($10^{-\infty}$), then the same data is present at both inputs of the Ex-OR gate. Thus, in this case the output of the Ex-OR gate is continually 0. If the errors in the data path do not occur simultaneously with the errors in the pseudo-regenerator path then, at the output of the Ex-OR gate, a 1 state appears whenever there is an error in only one of the two paths. In our example the pseudo-error path, having a $P_P(e) = 10^{-5}$, has an error rate of $10^3$ larger than the $P(e) = 10^{-8}$ of the main data path. Thus, the output of the Ex-OR gate provides logic 1 states at a frequency which is directly proportional to $P_P(e) - P(e) = P_P(e)$. (In our example, $10^{-5} - 10^{-8} \approx 10^{-5}$). The $P_P(e)$ to $P(e)$ converter is an event counter and a divider which provides the $P(e)$ indication. It can be implemented with hard-wired logic circuits or by microprocessors.

Theoretical derivations, various implementation techniques, and extensive applications of pseudo-error detectors are discussed in [11.1, 11.13, and 11.16]. In these references the performance of pseudo-error detectors in an AWGN, in adjacent-sinusoidal interference, and in a burst noise-interference environment is described. In Fig. 11.8 the $P(e)$ performance of a 1.544 Mb/s QPSK digital radio system and its corresponding $P_P(e)$ performance are shown. In this example the $P_P(e)$ is 1000 times larger than the $P(e)$ of the customer traffic. Thus, the on-line performance can be evaluated 1000 times faster than the time that would be required to measure the $P(e)$ with a conventional out-of-service method, described in Section 11.1. **(Solve Problem 11.6.)**

### *11.2.2 On-Line Jitter-Measurement Techniques*

In Section 11.1 a simple jitter evaluation set-up is described. This simple set-up is recommended for laboratory measurements and factory-acceptance testing but might not be appropriate for field measurements where the distance between consecutive sections prohibits the economic realization of a separate carrier for the jitter-free reference clock. In this simple method the PRBS generator, Fig. 11.5, might be replaced with the data source of the on-line customer traffic. Thus, the main problem for on-line jitter measurement is to generate a jitter-free reference clock at the receive end, or to find an alternate method by which we could *estimate the system jitter even though we do not have available a jitter-free clock*. In this section we address this alternative approach, even though it is conceptually more

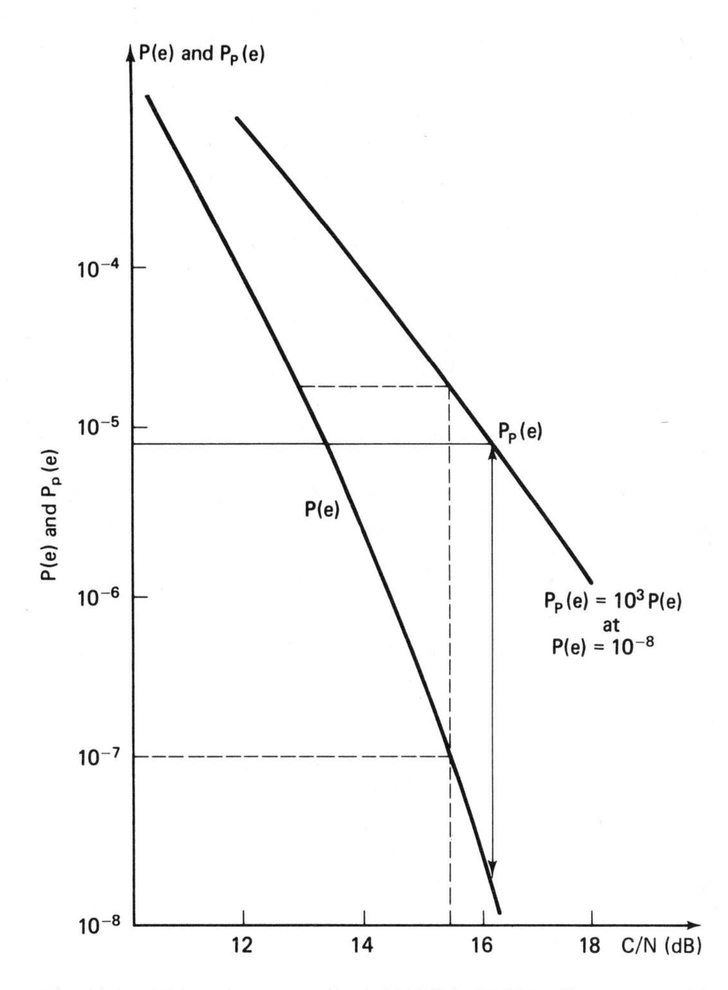


**Fig. 11.8.** $P(e)$ performance of a 1.544 Mb/s QPSK radio system and its corresponding pseudo-error performance $P_P(e)$.

difficult to realize than the method employing a jitter-free reference clock at the receive end.

In the following text a justification might be useful to convince ourselves that the conceptually simpler method might not be the best approach. The importance of on-line jitter in the overall digital transmission system is highlighted in Fig. 9.2. Thus, the designer must not save any effort to ensure that his on-line jitter is within specifications. When a digital radio transmitter and receiver leaves the production floor of any reputable manufacturer it has a jitter within specifications. After installation, it is possible that equipment misalignment, temperature variations, humidity, any type of noise or interference, aging of components, or any of several other causes may be such that the end-to-end system jitter becomes excessive. It may become excessive only during certain times of the day, while at other times the overall system $P(e)$, does not degrade noticeably and thus may not even be noticed. If we assume that even in the best equipment *a time-variable degradation is a real possibility*, then it might be dangerous to assume the availability of a jitter-free reference signal. For example, in a 400 Mb/s digital radio system [11.14] it may be difficult to obtain a jitter-free reference clock for jitter measurement purposes. The bit duration is only 2.5 ns ($2.5 \cdot 10^{-9}$ sec); thus, the *jitter-free* reference would have to have a jitter which is at least 10 times smaller than the bit duration, that is, *0.25 ns*. As pointed out, it would be difficult to have an in-service monitor to ensure that the jitter-free reference did not exceed the specified limits. We note that even for lower bit rates it might be difficult to ensure that the assumed jitter-free reference is jitter-free all the time.

The principle of an in-service jitter measurement set-up which does not require a jitter-free reference is illustrated in Figs. 11.9 and 11.10. [11.15]. The regenerated clock $c_j$ has an unknown on-line jitter. This clock is split into two paths. The upper path is delayed by a fixed amount of delay equaling an integer multiple of the bit clock period. The purpose of this fixed delay line is to provide a jittery clock to the input of the AND gate, such that the delayed jitter has the same peak-to-peak value and probability density as the original regenerated clock $c_j$. However, due to the large amount of delay (typically $n \geq 10$) the correlation of the two jitter paths is

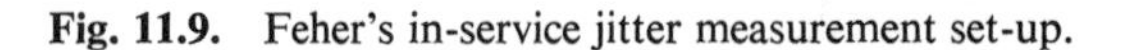
**Fig. 11.9.** Feher's in-service jitter measurement set-up.

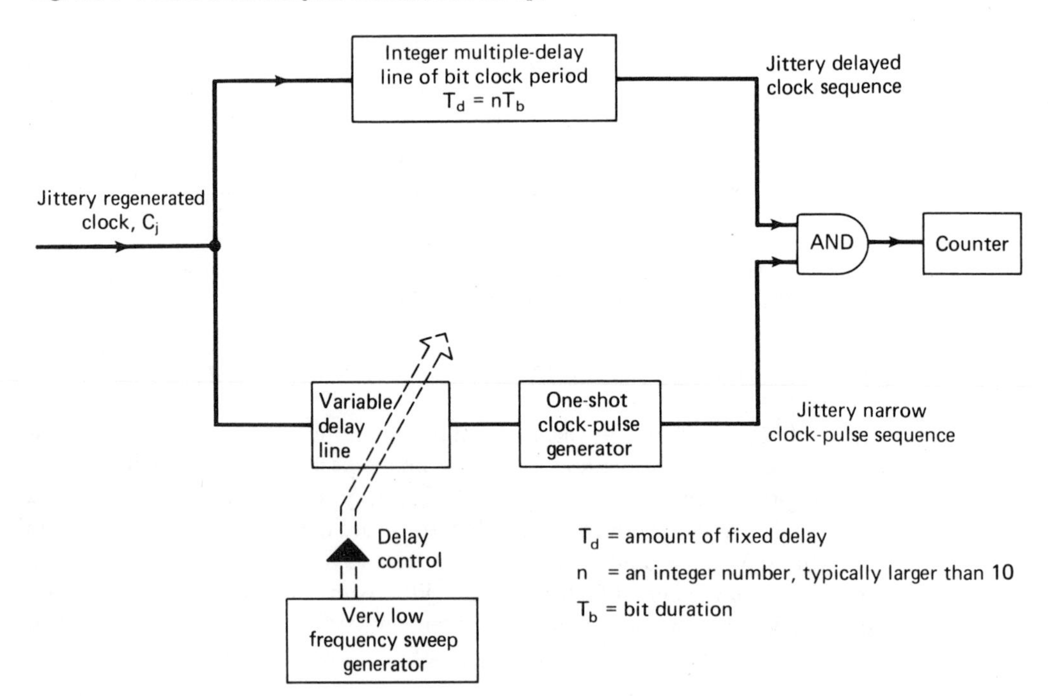

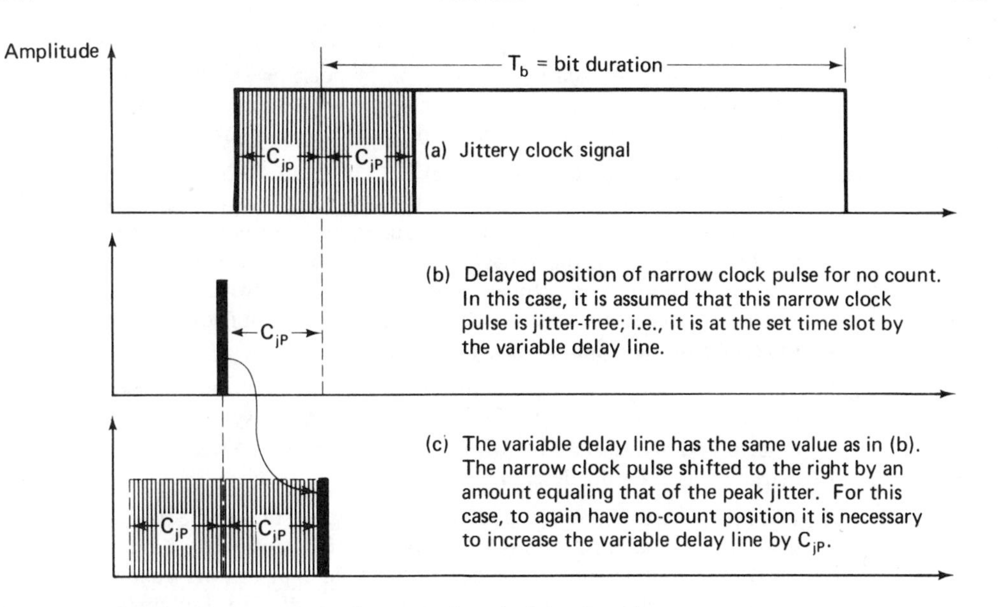


**Fig. 11.10.** Timing diagram of the jittery clock and of the shaped-narrow jittery pulse.

negligibly small. The very low-frequency sweep generator automatically sets the variable delay line to different values. The effect of the variable delay line on the position of the jittery and jitter-free clock is explained in Fig. 11.10. The rest of the on-line measurement set-up and the jitter display has about the same principle of operation as described in Section 11.1 for off-line systems. The only difference is that, in the on-line case of Fig. 11.9, the jitter-free reference is not required. It is replaced by a jittery reference clock which has the same amount of jitter as the unknown jitter of the regenerated clock. Thus, the counter displays a peak-to-peak jitter which is double that of the unknown clock jitter.

In conclusion, the systems engineer should keep in mind that in a multi-section digital radio system, having a large number of regenerative repeaters in cascade, there are two system performance parameters which have acumulative effect and are degraded as the number of sections increases. These are jitter and $P(e)$, respectively. It is desirable for a modern digital radio system to have the facilities built-in, so that these most important system parameters may be continuously monitored. **(Solve Problem 11.7.)**

## PROBLEMS

**11.1** A 90 Mb/s digital radio system, using 8-PSK modulation, is evaluated in a set-up such as shown in Fig. 11.1. The IF center frequency of several manufactured 90 Mb/s systems is 140 MHz. Assume that you are the engineer in charge of production testing for one of these radio systems and that you wish to buy a number of AWGN generators from an external supplier. Specify all pertinent characteristics of the

AWGN generators required for your production testing. Include parameters such as bandwidth, noise density, accuracy of the noise probability density, impedance, total noise power, frequency response of the noise source, and any other pertinent parameters which must be guaranteed by the manufacturer of the AWGN source.

**11.2** The measured mean $C/N$ for a $P(e) = 10^{-8}$ in an 8-PSK digital radio system is 25 dB, while the mean carrier power is $C = -55$ dBm. The source information is an equiprobable, random, 12 Mb/s data stream. Assume that the receiver-noise bandwidth equals the theoretical minimum double-sided Nyquist bandwidth. How much is the noise density (noise power in a 1 Hz bandwidth) of this system? What is the carrier spectral density difference, and how much is the $C/N$ spectral ratio at the center of the band and also at the edge of the receive filter bandwidth?

**11.3** Explain why a descrambler multiplies the $P(e)$. Assume that a typical descrambler multiplies the $P(e)$ by a factor of 3, that the radio system has a 16-state APK modem and a threshold performance of $P(e) = 10^{-6}$. Determine the loss of fade margin caused by the descrambler.

**11.4** It is necessary to monitor the received eye diagram of a QPSK digital radio system operating at the DS-3 rate (44.736 Mb/s). If it is desired to have an accuracy of 5%, establish the required number of threshold comparators $n$ shown in Fig. 11.5. Determine the threshold voltages $V_{\text{th }1}, V_{\text{th }2}, \ldots, V_{\text{th }n}$ for this application. Assume that the peak-to-peak eye diagram opening, without any ISI, equals 100 mV in the sampling instant.

**11.5** Prepare the complete schematic diagram of a digital variable delay line and a one-shot clock-pulse generator required for the jitter measurement set-up of Fig. 11.5. Assuming that the transmission rate equals a standard DS-1 rate, present your component cost estimate for this circuitry. Assume a small production quantity of 10 units. (System designers and senior managers are not required to solve the first part of this problem.) Circuit designers are encouraged to find original cost-effective solutions.

**11.6** Assume that the pseudo-error rate of a system is $P_P(e) = 10^{-5}$ whenever the customer error rate is $P(e) = 10^{-8}$. What is the required measurement interval of the out-of-service PRBS method, and of the pseudo-error method, if a CCITT standard 2.048 Mb/s data rate is transmitted over the radio system and a $P(e) = 10^{-8}$ is estimated?

**11.7** Explain the most important differences between the jitter measurement set-ups of Figs. 11.5 and 11.9. Present a detailed block diagram if an on-line jitter-free reference is available. Which design methods would you consider to generate a jitter-free reference at the receive end?

## REFERENCES

[11.1] Keelty, J. M., K. Feher, "On-Line Pseudo-Error Monitors for Digital Transmission Systems," IEEE Trans. Communications, August, 1978.

[11.2] Feher, K., *Digital Modulation Techniques in an Interference Environment*, *EMC Encyclopedia*, Vol. 9, Don White Consultants, Inc., Gainesville, VA, 1977.

[11.3] Feher, K., M. El-Torky, R. de Cristofaro, M. N. S. Swamy, "Optimum Pulse Shaping Application of Binary Transversal Filters Used in Satellite Communications," The Radio and Electronic Engineer (IRE), June, 1977.

[11.4] CCITT, "Principle of a Method for the Measurement of Signal Phase Jitter," COM XV-No. 119-E; Question 11/xv, France International Telegraph and Telephone Consultative Committee, January, 1978.

[11.5] Oliver, B. M., J. M. Cage, *Electronic Measurements and Instrumentation*, McGraw-Hill Book Company, New York, 1971.

[11.6] CCIR Draft Report No. 613, "Bit Error Performance Measurements of Digital Radio-Relay Systems," *Green Book*, Part I, Interim Meeting, Study Group 9, Geneva, June, 1976.

[11.7] Technical Staff, American Telephone and Telegraph Company, Bell Telephone Companies and Bell Telephone Laboratories, *Telecommunications Transmission Engineering*, Bell System for Technical Education, Winston-Salem, N.C., 1977.

[11.8] Mumford, M. W., E. H. Scheibe, *Noise Performance Factors in Communication Systems*, Horizon House, Dedham, Mass., 1968.

[11.9] Spilker, J. J., *Digital Communications by Satellite*, Prentice-Hall, Inc., Englewood Cliffs, N.J., 1977.

[11.10] Feher, K., G. S. Takhar, "A New Symbol Timing Recovery Technique for Burst Modem Applications," IEEE Trans. Communications, January, 1978.

[11.11] Wolejsza, C. J., "Effects of Oscillator Phase Noise on PSK Demodulation," Comsat Technical Review, Vol. 6, Spring, 1976.

[11.12] Brown, R., "Performance of Pseudo-Error Estimates," IEEE Canadian Communications and Power Conference, Proceedings No. 76-CH-1126, October, 1976.

[11.13] Feher, K., A. Bandari, "Pseudo-Error On-Line Monitoring: Concept Design and Evaluation," Canadian Electrical Engineering Journal, Vol. 2, No. 2, 1977.

[11.14] Ishio, H., et al., "A New Multilevel Modulation and Demodulation System for Carrier Digital Transmission," Proc. IEEE International Conference on Communications, ICC-76, Philadelphia, June, 1976.

[11.15] Feher, K., "On-Line Jitter Monitor: Principle, Design and Evaluation," Canadian Patent Pending, 1979, Ottawa, and U.S. Patent Office, Application No. 089, 585, October 29, 1979.

[11.16] Weinstein, S. B., "Estimation of Small Probabilities by Linearization of the Tail of a Distribution Function," IEEE Trans. Communications, December, 1971.

[11.17] Kantrowitz, P., G. Kousourou, L. Zucker, *Electronic Measurements*, Prentice-Hall, Inc., Englewood Cliffs, N.J., 1979.

# 12

# RESEARCH AND DEVELOPMENT TRENDS AND UNRESOLVED PROBLEMS

In this final chapter, research and development trends, as well as unresolved problems related to digital microwave communications, are summarized.

A number of modulation and signal processing techniques which have been developed and successfully employed in line-of-sight terrestrial digital microwave systems will also find application in *satellite* and *optical fiber* systems. Present digital satellite systems use 4-phase QPSK modulation techniques. The next generation of digital communication satellites will be required to be more bandwidth-efficient than the theoretical limit of QPSK (2b/s/Hz). Previously, digital terrestrial microwave systems used, mostly, QPSK modems; but the trend now is to replace them with QPRS (correlative coded) 8-PSK and 16-QAM modulation techniques. It is expected that the same trend will continue for many new satellite systems applications.

As a result of frequency congestion problems in the lower frequency bands, a number of systems shall be designed to use frequencies in the 15 GHz range. Some of these systems shall be used for high-capacity long-haul systems (5000 or more digitized telephony channels); others will be designed for medium-capacity (100 to 1000 digitized voice channel) short-haul links.

Unfortunately, we do not foresee a short-term solution for the problems created by the different digital hierarchies. As explained in Chapter 1, the European, U.S./ Canadian, and Japanese hierarchies are different. These differences do not pose a major problem for terrestrial microwave and optical fiber systems since these systems are confined for digital transmission within the continent. However, when these systems are interfaced with transcontinental satellite and cable systems, the problem of different hierarchies becomes very serious. The scope of this problem is broadened because it is not strictly a technical problem but also an economic one, on a multi-national scale. This problem has to be resolved by national organizations which are in technological, economic, and also political competition with each other.

The available statistical tools required for the performance analysis of digital transmission systems are very sophisticated. Probably the major problem is that it is just about impossible to be a "top-notch" mathematician who knows all the newest statistical research methods and, at the same time, be a practical digital communications engineer. Sophisticated computer programs are being used increasingly to analyze and predict the performance of digital systems. One of the fields which has not been sufficiently covered in theoretical studies is the mathematical representation of the *impulse noise in interference environment* which prevails in a number of digital microwave systems. Theoretical research reported in the *IEEE Transactions on Communications* [12.2, 12.3] clearly indicates that this problem has been taken seriously by scientists and may be resolved in the near future. Efficient noise and interference cancellation methods to improve the $P(e)$ performance of digitally modulated signals in an impulsive noise interference environment will, hopefully, be discovered [12.4]. Some of the issues of the *IEEE Transactions on Communications* and the *IEEE Transactions on Information Theory* will provide sufficient references for digital communications theorists and engineers. These references are useful, in particular, for those digital transmission problems characteristic of an impulsive noise and time-variable interference environment. An excellent reference for advanced detection and estimation theory, which is required for the theoretical study of this complex interference environment, is the book by Van Trees [12.5].

Research in new bandwidth-efficient digital modulation techniques is actively being pursued by many national and international research and development organizations. Several modern digital modulation techniques have been presented in [12.6]. In the Special Issue on Digital Radio of the *IEEE Transactions on Communications*, December, 1979 [12.13], a number of papers describing 3b/s/Hz, 4b/s/Hz, and even 5b/s/Hz efficient digital radio systems were published. It is not unreasonable to expect that some of the future systems will have bandwidth efficiencies of 6b/s/Hz or more. In addition to the research on bandwidth-efficient transmission methods, modulation techniques which will permit bandwidth-efficient data transmission without significant performance degradation, when transmitted through non-linear RF power amplifiers, will be searched for [12.7 and 12.16]. Transmitter RF power-amplifier and receiver low-signal amplifier trends are described in Chapter 4. If you are interested in the future scenario of amplifiers, other components, and complete communications systems, Martin's book [12.1] is highly recommended. For in-depth reading on this subject the *IEEE Transactions on Microwave Theory and Techniques*, the *Bell System Technical Journal*, and the *Comsat Journal* are recommended. Frequently, good survey papers can be found in trade journals such as the *Microwave Journal* and *Microwaves*.

By increasing bandwidth efficiency (that is, the number of transmitted b/s/Hz) of digital transmission systems, future systems designers will require a higher received carrier-to-noise ratio ($C/N$) than found in currently operational systems. To achieve the low $P(e)$ performance of present systems, future high-speed systems (about 300 Mb/s) will require more transmit power, a lower receiver-noise figure, or closer spacing between the repeaters. The performance objectives and the system gain calculations will be similar, however, as described in Chapter 5. In radio systems transmitting at a 40 Mb/s or higher rate, it has been noticed that the time-variable frequency-selective fading might significantly degrade the system gain and thus the system availability. Research by many organizations indicates clearly that the effect of frequency-selective fades on wideband digital radio systems can be minimized by adaptive equalization techniques [12.8 and 12.15]. For low-speed (below 20 Mb/s), medium-speed (up to 100 Mb/s), and high-speed (above 100 Mb/s) digital radio systems, $M$-ary PSK, QAM, and APK modulation methods have been developed and will be in use for years to come. In addition to these modulation techniques, which are described in Chapter 6, serveral recently developed systems use Dr. A. Lender's correlative coding, that is, quadrature partial response (QPR) modulation techniques [12.14]. These techniques are described in depth in Chapter 7. It is expected that, during the next decade, new and more bandwidth-efficient QPR systems will be developed by manufacturers [12.9, 12.11, 12.12].

Digital microwave systems shall predominate in the late 1990's. During the interim transition period, analog systems will coexist with the digital transmission facilities. Many operating companies will require new bandwidth-efficient hybrid systems to carry, simultaneously, their analog telephony, video, and digital traffic. Hybrid DUV, DIV, DAV, and DAVID Systems are described in Chapter 8. These cost-effective systems shall be in demand during the next decade [12.10].

To improve the performance and the traffic-handling flexibility of digital radio systems, new system configurations will be investigated. Novel protection switching and diversity configurations will be sought; additionally, more on-line measurement techniques shall be introduced.

Before the end of this century, digital microwave systems shall replace almost all analog microwave facilities. These digital systems shall be an integral part of an overall digital network which will include digitized telephone signals, digitized video, digital multiplex equipment, digital switching centers, digital cable, digital fiber, and digital satellite systems [12.13].

*Field-proven digital microwave systems of the 1980's and 1990's will have high operational reliability and excellent performance; they will be bandwidth-efficient and one of the most cost-effective data transmission facilities.*

## REFERENCES


[12.1] Martin, J., *Future Developments in Telecommunications*, Prentice-Hall, Inc., Englewood Cliffs, N.J., 1977.

[12.2] Spaulding, A. D., D. Middleton, "Optimum Reception in an Impulsive Interference Environment," Parts I and II, IEEE Trans. Communications, September, 1977.

[12.3] Koizuwi, T., J. Inoue, M. Ohta, "The Effect of Non-Gaussian Noise on the Performance of a Binary CPSK System," IEEE Trans. Communications, February, 1978.

[12.4] Krzyckowsky, M., K. Feher, "Interference Supression in Distributed Radio Systems," IEEE International Communications Conference, ICC-78, Toronto, June, 1978.

[12.5] Van Trees, H. L., *Detection, Estimation, and Modulation Theory*, John Wiley & Sons, Inc., New York, 1968.

[12.6] Feher, K., *Digital Modulation Techniques in an Interference Environment, EMC Encyclopedia*, Vol. 9, Don White Consultants, Inc., Gainesville, VA, 1977.

[12.7] Yazdani, H., "Constant Envelope Bandlimited M-Ary PSK Systems," M.A.Sc. Thesis, Department of Electrical Engineering, University of Ottawa, Ottawa, 1979.

[12.8] Sewerinson, A., D. Morais, K. Feher, "The Effect of the Amplitude and Delay Slope Components of Frequency Selective Fading on QPSK, Offset QPSK, and 8 PSK Systems," IEEE Trans. Communications, special issue on Digital Radio, December, 1979.

[12.9] Huang, J. C. Y., "On Bandwidth Efficient Pulse Shaping Methods and Modulation Techniques for Digital Communications in Linear and Nonlinear Channels," Ph.D. Thesis, Department of Electrical Engineering, Concordia University, Montreal, April, 1979.

[12.10] Feher, K., M. Morris, "Developments in Canadian and International Data Above Voice/Video Telecommunications," Proc. IEEE Canadian Communications Conference, Montreal, October 1, 1978.

[12.11] Lender, A., R. Rogers, H. Olszanski, "Four Bits Per Hertz Correlative Single-Sideband Digital Radio at 2 GHz," Proc. IEEE International Conference on Communications, ICC-79, Boston, June, 1979.

[12.12] Alexander, J. E., R. P. Cheung, T. W. Kao, "A Four Bits/Hertz QPR Radio at 8 GHz," IEEE International Conference on Communications, ICC-79, Boston, June, 1979.

[12.13] Feher, K., P. Hartman, R. Tetarenko, V. Prabhu (Editors), IEEE Trans. Communications, special issue on Digital Radio, December, 1979.

[12.14] Feher, K., M. Wachira, W. Steenaart, "Noise and Interference Effects in Quadrature Partial Response Radio Systems," Proc. IEEE International Conference on Communications, ICC-79, Boston, June, 1979.

[12.15] Hartman, P., "Adaptive Equalizer for 6 GHz Digital Radio," IEEE International Conference on Communications, ICC-79, Boston, June, 1979.

[12.16] Feher, K., "Jitter and ISI Free Nyquist Filtering of Data Signals by Means of Feher's Processor Filter," Canadian Patent Office, Patent Pending, Ottawa, 1979.

# GLOSSARY

| | | Typical Equation or Section Reference |
|---|---|---|
| $\alpha$ | Received phase | Eq. 3.13 |
| $\alpha$ | Roll-off factor | Sec. 3.1 |
| $\beta$ | Phase error between the combined modulated carriers and recovered carrier phase | Fig. 10.8 |
| $\delta(t)$ | Impulse | Sec. 7.2 |
| $\Delta f_s$ | Bit stuffing rate | Sec. 9.3 |
| $\Delta f$ | Bandwidth of the amplifier in Hertz | Eq. 4.12 |
| $\Delta = e^{-j2\pi fT}$ | One delay unit | Sec. 7.2 |
| $\Delta^2 = e^{-j4\pi fT}$ | Two delay unit | Sec. 7.2 |
| $\eta$ | Sampling instant | Sec. 3.2 |
| $\eta$ | Overall efficiency of an amplifier | Sec. 4.1 |
| $\theta_k$ | Uniformly distributed random phase of the *k*th sine wave | Eq. 2.28 |

| | | Typical Equation or Section Reference |
|---|---|---|
| $\theta_1, \theta_2, \theta_0$ | Angle of emission | Sec. 5.3.2 |
| $\mu$ | Parameter, companding characteristics | Fig. 1.11 |
| $\sigma$ | Rms or root-mean-square value | Eq. 2.14 |
| $\sigma^2$ | Variance | Eq. 2.13 |
| $\tau$ | Average duration of a fade | Eq. 5.7 |
| $\mathfrak{F}$ | Fourier transform | Sec. 7.2 |
| $\phi$ | Clock pulses | Sec. 7.6.2 |

**A**

| | | |
|---|---|---|
| $A$ | Peak amplitude of the carrier wave | Eq. 10.1 |
| $A$ | Roughness factor | Eq. 5.3 |
| A/D | Analog-to-digital converter | Sec. 1.1 |
| AGC | Automatic gain control | Sec. 11.1 |
| AM-AM | AM to AM conversion | Sec. 6.4 |
| AM-PM | AM to PM conversion | Sec. 6.4 |
| APK | Amplitude phase keyed | Sec. 3.4<br>Sec. 8.1 |
| AWGN | Additive white gaussian noise | Sec. 2.5 |
| $A_t$ | Binary input sequence | Sec. 7.2 |
| $a_n$ | Original sequence | Sec. 7.3 |
| $A(f)$ | Attenuation mask | Eq. 9.1 |
| $\overline{a^2}$ | Average ac symbol power | Eq. 3.5 |
| $A^2$ | Constant proportional to PSK power | Eq. 6.1 |

**B**

| | | |
|---|---|---|
| $B$ | Bandwidth of baseband channel | Sec. 3.1 |
| BER | Bit-error-rate | Sec. 2.1 |
| BPF | Band-pass filter | Sec. 2.3 |
| BPSK | Binary phase shift keyed | Sec. 3.3 |
| BW | Bandwidth | Eq. 3.17 |
| BWT | Backward wave tube | Sec. 4.3.1 |
| $B_t$ | Binary encoded sequence | Sec. 7.2 |
| b/s/Hz | Bits per second per Hertz, spectrum efficiency | Sec. 3.1 |
| $b$ | Signaling levels | Sec. 7.3 |

| | | Typical Equation or Section Reference |
|---|---|---|

## C

| | | |
|---|---|---|
| $C$ | Average carrier power | Eq. 3.17 |
| CCI | Co-channel interference | Sec. 11.1 |
| CCIR | Comité Consultatif International de Radio (International Radio Consultative Committee) | Sec. 9.1 |
| CCITT | Comité Consultatif International de Téléphonie et Télégraphie (International Telephony and Telegraphy Committee) | Sec. 1.1 |
| CIR | Carrier to interference ratio | Fig. 6.13 |
| C/N | Mean carrier power to mean noise power ratio | Sec. 6.5<br>Sec. 3.4 |
| CNR | Carrier to noise ratio | Fig. 6.13 |
| CPDF | Cumulative probability distribution function | Sec. 2.1 |
| CR | Carrier recovery | Sec. 6.2 |
| $C_{\min}$ | Received carrier level for a minimum quality objective | Eq. 5.1 |
| $C_t$ | Duobinary sequence | Sec. 7.2 |
| $c(t)$ | Customer traffic | Sec. 9.3 |
| $C_1, C_2, \ldots, C_n$ | Coefficients (0 or 1) | Sec. 11.1 |
| $c_j$ | Regenerated clock | Sec. 11.2.2 |
| $c(t - nT_b)$ | Sampling instants | Sec. 3.1 |
| $C_\phi$ | Phase nonlinearity | Fig. 5.10 |
| $C_1, C_2$ | Digits in a sequence | Sec. 7.5 |

## D

| | | |
|---|---|---|
| DAV | Data above voice system | Sec. 8.3 |
| DAVID | Data above video system | Sec. 8.3 |
| D/C | Down-converter | Sec. 1.3 |
| DIV | Data in voice system | Sec. 8.3 |
| DMOD | Delta modulation | Sec. 9.3 |
| DSB-SC | Double-sideband-suppressed carrier | Sec. 3.3 |
| DUV | Data under voice system | Sec. 8.3 |
| $D_i$ | Binary data stream | Sec. 11.1 |
| dB | Decibels | Sec. 3.1 |

| | | Typical Equation or Section Reference |
|---|---|---|
| $d_n$ | Binary sequence | Sec. 7.3 |
| Dem | Demodulator | Sec. 1.3 |
| $\hat{D}_i$ | Descrambled data stream | Sec. 11.1 |
| $dv$ | Infinitesimal width interval | Sec. 2.1 |
| $d$ | Distance from the "nominal" received level to the nearest decision threshold level | Sec. 3.2 |
| D/A | Digital to analog | Sec. 1.1 |
| $d$ | Path length in km | Eq. 5.2 |
| Duo | Doubling the speed of binary | Sec. 7.0 |

E

| | | |
|---|---|---|
| $E$ | Parameter depending on fading environment | Eq. 5.8 |
| $E_b$ | Average energy of a bit | Eq. 3.17 |
| EF | Error free region | Sec. 3.4 |
| EFI | Error free interval | Sec. 9.4 |
| EX-OR | Exclusive OR gate | Sec. 11.2 |
| $E(V)$ | Expected or mean value | Eq. 2.8 |
| $E(V^2)$ | Mean square value | Eq. 2.12 |
| $\mathrm{erf}(v)$ | Error function | Eq. 2.21 |
| $\mathrm{erfc}(v)$ | Complementary error function | Eq. 2.22 |

F

| | | |
|---|---|---|
| $F$ | Receiver noise figure | Eq. 6.6 |
| FCC | Federal Communications Commission | Sec. 1.1<br>Sec. 9.1 |
| FDM | Frequency division multiplexed | Sec. 1.1 |
| FF | Flip-flop | Sec. 2.1 |
| FM | Frequency Modulation | Sec. 8.3 |
| FM | Maximum allowable fade margin | Eq. 5.3 |
| $F(v)$ | $= P(V \leq v)$, Cumulative probability distribution function | Eq. 2.1 |
| $F(x, y)$ | Joint cumulative probability distribution function | Eq. 2.30 |
| $f_m$ | Highest frequency spectral component | Sec. 1.2 |
| $f_s$ | Rate of instantaneous sampling symbol rate | Sec. 1.2 |
| $f_b$ | Transmission bit rate | Sec. 3.1 |

| | | Typical Equation or Section Reference |
|---|---|---|
| $f_c$ | Unmodulated carrier frequency | Eq. 6.1 |
| $F(\omega)$ | Overall transfer function of a correlative system | Sec. 7.1 |
| $f_o$ | Center frequency of the measured channel | Sec. 11.1 |
| $F(x_j)$ | Jitter probability distribution function | Sec. 11.1 |
| $f(x_j)$ | Jitter probability density function | Eq. 11.1 |
| $f_k$ | Frequency of the $k$th sine wave | Eq. 2.28 |

## G

| | | |
|---|---|---|
| $G$ | Absolute gain of the amplifier | Sec. 4.2 |
| $G_s$ | System gain | Eq. 6.8<br>Sec. 5.2.1<br>Eq. 5.1 |
| $G_t$, $G_r$ | Gain of transmitter and receiver antennas | Eq. 5.1 |
| $g$ | Gain in dB | Eq. 4.9 |
| $g(V)$ | Notation of a function | Eq. 2.11 |
| $g_{\text{min}}$ | Minimum gain | Eq. 4.1 |
| $g_{\text{nom}}$ | Nominal gain | Eq. 4.2 |

## H

| | | |
|---|---|---|
| $H$ | Hybrid element | Sec. 1.3 |
| HYB | Hybrid | Sec. 8.3 |
| $H(f)$ | Transfer function of a filter | Sec. 2.5 |
| $h_1(t)$ | Impulse response of a filter | Sec. 7.2<br>Eq. 7.3 |

## I

| | | |
|---|---|---|
| $I$ | In-phase channel | Sec. 10.3 |
| $I_{AB}$ | Interfering signal from site $A$ | Sec. 5.4 |
| $I_{CB}$ | Interfering signal from site $C$ | Sec. 5.4 |
| IF | Intermediate frequency | Sec. 1.3 |
| ISI | Intersymbol interference | Sec. 3.1 |
| $I_a$ | Interfering carrier from site $A$ (on frequency $f_1$) | Fig. 5.7 |
| $I_c$ | Interfering carrier from site $C$ (on frequency $f_1$) | Fig. 5.7 |

| | | Typical Equation or Section Reference |
|---|---|---|

**J**

| | | |
|---|---|---|
| $J_{cp}$ | Timing peak clock-jitter | Sec. 9.2 |
| $J_{Dp}$ | Data transition peak jitter | Sec. 9.2 |
| $J_{rms}$ | rms jitter | Eq. 11.2 |

**K**

| | | |
|---|---|---|
| $k$ | Boltzmann's constant ($1.38 \times 10^{-23}$ joules/degree Kelvin) ($-228.6$ dBW sec/K°) | Eq. 4.12<br>Eq. 6.6 |
| $k$ | Number of feedback taps | Sec. 11.1 |
| kHz | kilo-Hertz | Sec. 2.3 |
| kb/s | kilobits per second | Sec. 1.2 |
| $k_n$ | Number of sine waves used to generate an approximation to the gaussian noise signal | Eq. 2.28 |

**L**

| | | |
|---|---|---|
| $L$ | Depth of fade | Sec. 5.3.3 |
| $L$ | Number of demodulated baseband levels | Sec. 6.2.2 |
| $L$ | Total one-way system length | Sec. 9.2 |
| LO | Local oscillator | Sec. 1.3 |
| LPF | Low pass filter | Sec. 3.1 |
| $L_B$ | Branching loss | Eq. 5.1 |
| $L_F$ | Feeder loss | Eq. 5.1 |
| $L_p$ | Free space path loss | Eq. 5.1 |
| $L_{up}$ | Upper bound of validity of the straight-line approximation of $P\ (V \leq L)$ | Eq. 5.8 |
| $L = 0, L = 1$ | Logic states | Sec. 2.1 |
| $l$ | Length of each section | Sec. 9.2 |

**M**

| | | |
|---|---|---|
| $M$ | Noise measure | Sec. 4.2<br>Eq. 4.16 |
| MHz | Megahertz | Sec. 1.2 |
| MSK | Minimum shift keying | Sec. 8.2 |

| | | Typical Equation or Section Reference |
|---|---|---|
| $M$-ary | $M$-state signal (modulation) | Sec. 3.1<br>Sec. 6.6 |
| Mb/s | Megabits per second | Sec. 1.1<br>Sec. 1.2 |
| $m = E(V)$ | Expected value of continuous random signals | Eq. 2.10 |
| $m(t)$ | Magnitude-time function | Sec. 1.2 |
| Modem | Modulator and demodulator | Sec. 3.3 |
| $m(t) \cdot s(t)$ | Sampled output signal | Sec. 1.2<br>Fig. 1.9 |
| Mod | Modulator | Sec. 1.3 |
| $m$ | dc component | Eq. 2.15 |

## N

| | | |
|---|---|---|
| $N$ | Number of bits per one Hertz of bandwidth | Eq. 7.19 |
| NF | Noise figure | Sec. 4.2 |
| NPR | Noise power ratio | Sec. 8.3 |
| NRZ | Non return-to-zero | Sec. 3.1 |
| $N_{bw}$ | Noise bandwidth | Eq. 2.29 |
| $N_k$ | Peak value of the amplitude of the $k$th sine wave | Eq. 2.28 |
| $N_o$ | Noise power spectral density (i.e., average noise power in 1 Hz BW) | Eq. 3.17 |
| $N_p$ | Noise on secondary path (or pseudo-error path) | Sec. 11.2.1 |
| $N_T$ | Total noise power at demodulator input | Eq. 6.6 |
| $n$ | Total number of sampled values | Sec. 2.2 |
| $n = \log_2 M$ | Number of information bits per symbol | Sec. 3.1 |
| $n_c(t)$ | In phase gaussian noise component | Eq. 3.11 |
| ns | Nano-second $= 10^{-9}$ second | Sec. 11.2.2 |
| $n_s(t)$ | Quadrature phase gaussian noise component | Eq. 3.11 |

## O

| | | |
|---|---|---|
| O-QPSK | Offset QPSK | Sec. 5.5 |

| | | Typical Equation or Section Reference |
|---|---|---|

**P**

| | | |
|---|---|---|
| PA | Power amplifier | Fig. 4.8 |
| PAM | Pulse amplitude modulation | Sec. 8.2<br>Sec. 3.1 |
| PCM | Pulse code modulation | Sec. 1.1 |
| PF | Peak factor | Fig. 6.13 |
| PRBS | Pseudo-random-binary sequence | Sec. 9.2 |
| PSK | Phase shift keying | Sec. 2.3<br>Sec. 3.3 |
| $P(e)$ | Probability of error | Sec. 3.2 |
| pdf | Probability density function | Sec. 2.1 |
| $p(v)$ | Probability density function | Eq. 2.2 |
| $p(u, v)$ | Joint probability density function | Eq. 2.30 |
| $P_{\mathrm{im3}}$ | Output power of third order intermodulation product | Eq. 4.4 |
| $P_{\mathrm{si}}$ | Available input signal power | Eq. 4.6 |
| $P_{\mathrm{ni}}$ | Available input noise power | Eq. 4.6 |
| $P_{\mathrm{no}}$ | Available output noise power | Eq. 4.6 |
| $P_{\mathrm{so}}$ | Available output signal power | Eq. 4.6 |
| $P_n$ | Thermal noise power | Eq. 4.11 |
| $p_n$ | Polybinary pulse train | Sec. 7.3 |
| $P_t$ | Transmitter output power | Eq. 5.1 |
| $P_o(e)$ | End-to-end probability of error of unfaded $n$-section transmission system | Sec. 9.2 |
| $P_s(e)$ | Probability of error of each individual unfaded section | Sec. 9.2 |
| $P_y(e)$ | Probability of error of the section which has the deepest fade | Sec. 9.2 |
| $P_p(e)$ | Probability of error of pseudo-error path | Sec. 11.2 |
| pel | Picture element | Sec. 1.2 |
| $p(V \leq v)$ | Probability that the value of the random variable $V$ is smaller than or equal to a specified value $v$ | Eq. 2.1 |
| $P_{\mathrm{in}}$ | Input power | Sec. 4.1 |
| $P_1$ | Output power in dBm at frequency $f_1$ | Eq. 4.4 |
| $P_2$ | Output power in dBm at frequency $f_2$ | Eq. 4.4 |
| $P_{3i}$ | Third order intercept level in dBm | Eq. 4.4 |
| $P_{\mathrm{inh}}$ | Inherent amplifier noise | Eq. 4.7 |

| | | Typical Equation or Section Reference |
|---|---|---|

## Q

| | | |
|---|---|---|
| $Q$ | Quadrature channel | Sec. 11.2 |
| QAM | Quadrature amplitude modulation | Sec. 3.4<br>Sec. 6.2.2 |
| QPR | Quadrature partial response | Sec. 3.4 |
| QPSK | Quadrature or quaternary phase shift keying | Sec. 3.3 |
| $Q = 2^n$ | Levels of input pulse train, $n > 1$ | Sec. 7.4 |
| $Q(x)$ | Complement of the normal cumulative distribution function | Eq. 3.9 |

## R

| | | |
|---|---|---|
| $R$ | $= \log_2 (1 + S/N)$ Shannon limit | Eq. 3.10 |
| RF | Radio frequency | Sec. 1.1<br>Sec. 6.5 |
| $R_c$ | Number of levels in correlative systems | Eq. 7.20<br>Sec. 7.4.2 |
| $R_e(t_1, t_2)$ | Autocorrelation function | Eq. 2.31 |
| $R_i$ | Pseudo-random bit stream | Sec. 11.1 |
| $r(t)$ | = Received carrier and noise wave | Eq. 3.11 |
| Reg. | Regenerator | Sec. 1.3 |
| $R(\tau)$ | Time autocorrelation function | Eq. 2.32 |
| Rx | Receiver | Sec. 1.2 |
| $R_z$ | Number of levels for zero-memory systems | Eq. 7.19<br>Sec. 7.4.2 |

## S

| | | |
|---|---|---|
| SCPC | Single channel per carrier | Sec. 8.0 |
| S/N | Signal to noise ratio | Sec. 11.2.1 |
| SSA | Small signal amplifier | Fig. 4.8 |
| STR | Symbol timing recovery | Sec. 3.3<br>Sec. 6.2 |
| $S_A(f)$ | Modulated power spectrum | Sec. 6.4 |
| $S_b$ | Victim carrier at site *B* from site *C* | Fig. 5.7 |
| $S_{CB}$ | Signal transmitted from *C* to *B* | Sec. 5.4 |

| | | Typical Equation or Section Reference |
|---|---|---|
| $S_C(f)$, $S_D(f)$ | Adjacent interfering signals | Sec. 6.4<br>Fig. 6.11 |
| $S_E(f)$ | Transmitted spectrum | Sec. 6.3 |
| $S_i$ | Scrambled data stream | Sec. 11.1 |
| $S(f)$ | Normalized power spectrum density | Sec. 2.6<br>Eq. 3.3 |
| $S(t)$ | Service channel signal | Sec. 9.3 |
| $S_x(\omega)$ | $S(\omega)$, power spectral density | Eq. 2.43 |
| $(S/N)_P$ | S/N in pseudo error path | Sec. 11.2.1 |

**T**

| | | |
|---|---|---|
| $T$ | Absolute temperature in Kelvin degrees | Eq. 6.6 |
| TCTS | Trans-Canada Telephone System | Sec. 10.0 |
| TDM | Time-division multiplexed | Sec. 1.1 |
| TWT | Traveling-wave tube | Sec. 4.3.1 |
| Transceiver | Transmitter and receiver | Sec. 1.3 |
| $T_b$ | Unit pulse (bit) duration | Sec. 2.1 |
| $T_d$ | Amount of fixed delay | Fig. 11.9 |
| $T_n$ | Noise temperature | Sec. 4.2 |
| $T_s$ | Symbol duration | Sec. 3.1 |
| Tx | Transmitter | Sec. 1.2 |
| $t_{\phi_2}$ | Time instants of $\phi_2$ relative to $\phi_1$ | Eq. 7.22 |

**U**

| | | |
|---|---|---|
| $u$ | Dummy variable of integration | Eq. 2.20 |
| U/C | Upconverter | Sec. 1.3 |

**V**

| | | |
|---|---|---|
| $V$ | Peak voltage of the input signal | Sec. 1.2 |
| $V$ | Discrete or continuous random variable | Sec. 2.2 |
| VCO | Voltage controlled oscillator | Sec. 9.3 |
| VF | Voice-frequency | Sec. 1.2 |
| VSB | Vestigial sideband | Sec. 3.4 |
| VSB-SC | Vestigial-sideband-suppressed carrier | Sec. 3.4 |
| $v(x)$ | Output voltage | Sec. 1.2 |
| $v_{\text{th}}$ | Voltage threshold level | Eq. 2.6 |

| | | Typical Equation or Section Reference |
|---|---|---|
| $v(t)$ | Discrete states of the signal in the time domain | Sec. 2.1 |
| $V_i$ | Numerical value of the random variable for $i$th experiment | Eq. 2.8 |
| $v_i(t)$ | Input signal | Sec. 3.1 |
| $v_o(t)$ | Output signal | Sec. 3.1 |
| $\bar{V}^2$ | Normalized power | Sec. 2.2 |

**W**

| | | |
|---|---|---|
| WGN | White gaussian noise | Sec. 2.3 |
| $W_1(f)$ = | $\left\{\frac{1}{T}\lvert G(f)\rvert^2 \cdot pq\right\}$ Continuous component of the spectral density of the sequence consisting of uncorrelated binary signals. | Sec. 7.3 |
| $W_2(f)$ | Spectral density for the $d_n$ sequence | Eq. 7.9 |
| $W_3(f)$ | Spectral density of the $p_n$ sequence | Eq. 7.12 |

**X**

| | | |
|---|---|---|
| $x$ | Input voltage | Sec. 1.2 |
| $x$ | Random quantity | Sec. 2.4 |
| $X$ | Random variable | Sec. 2.6 |
| $x_j$ | Sampling clock | Sec. 11.1 |
| $X(t)$ | Sample function from a random process | Eq. 2.31 |
| $X_1 = X(t_1)$ | Random variables | Eq. 2.31 |
| $X_2 = X(t_2)$ | Random variables | Eq. 2.31 |
| $x_j$ | Time instant of zero crossings | Eq. 11.1 |
| $(x_1 - x_0)$ | Peak-to-peak jitter | Fig. 11.6 |

**Y**

| | | |
|---|---|---|
| $y$ | Random quantity | Sec. 2.4 |
| $Y$ | Random variable | Sec. 2.6 |

**Z**

| | | |
|---|---|---|
| $Z$ | Weighting factor | Sec. 7.3 |

# INDEX